Practical Digital Forensics: A Guide for Windows and Linux Users

Authored by

Akashdeep Bhardwaj

Pradeep Singh

&

Ajay Prasad

School of Computer Science
University of Petroleum and Energy Studies
Dehradun, India

Practical Digital Forensics: A Guide for Windows and Linux Users

Authors: Akashdeep Bhardwaj, Pradeep Singh & Ajay Prasad

ISBN (Online): 978-981-5305-57-9

ISBN (Print): 978-981-5305-58-6

ISBN (Paperback): 978-981-5305-59-3

First published in 2024.

Bentham Science Publishers Pte. Ltd.
80 Robinson Road #02-00
Singapore 068898
Singapore
Email: subscriptions@benthamscience.net

CONTENTS

FOREWORD

In the ever-evolving realm of digital forensics, where evidence resides in the intricate pathways of computers and digital devices, the need for a comprehensive and practical guide has never been greater. "Practical Digital Forensics: A Hands-on Guide for Windows & Linux Users" rises to this challenge, offering an invaluable resource for both seasoned investigators and those embarking on their journey into this critical field. This book transcends theory, providing a hands-on approach that empowers readers with the skills to navigate the complexities of digital investigations. From establishing a secure forensic workstation to meticulously recovering deleted data and analysing intricate file systems, the book delves deep, equipping readers with the tools and techniques needed to uncover the truth hidden within digital landscapes.

"Practical Digital Forensics" is more than just a collection of techniques; it recognizes the legal and ethical considerations paramount in this field. By addressing these crucial aspects, the book ensures that investigators not only gather evidence effectively but also maintain its integrity for use in legal proceedings. This book caters to a diverse audience, from law enforcement professionals to cybersecurity analysts and legal practitioners. Each chapter builds upon the foundation of the previous, ensuring a smooth learning curve for novices while offering valuable insights and advanced techniques for experienced investigators.

With its clear explanations, practical exercises, and real-world case studies, "Practical Digital Forensics: A Hands-on Guide for Windows & Linux Users" is poised to become a trusted companion in the ever-growing field of digital forensics. It empowers readers to navigate the intricate landscape of digital evidence, ensuring that no digital footprint remains hidden from the pursuit of justice.

Dr. Sam Goundar
RMIT University, Australia

PREFACE

Welcome to the ever-expanding world of digital forensics! In our increasingly digital age, evidence often resides not in physical objects but in the intricate pathways of computers and networks. This book, "Practical Digital Forensics: A Hands-on Guide for Windows & Linux Users", aims to equip you with the knowledge and skills necessary to navigate this complex digital landscape.

Whether you are a seasoned investigator, a burgeoning cybersecurity professional, or simply someone with a keen interest in digital forensics, this book provides a comprehensive yet accessible introduction to the field. We will delve into the core principles and methodologies that underpin digital forensics, ensuring you understand the foundation before diving into the practical aspects.

This book is specifically crafted for both Linux and Windows users. We will guide you through setting up a robust forensic lab environment on both operating systems, equipping you with the essential software tools and utilities needed for in-depth analysis. Throughout the journey, you will gain hands-on experience with critical forensic techniques, from acquiring volatile data and analysing file systems to dissecting Windows registries and investigating network traffic.

As technology evolves, so do the challenges faced by digital forensic investigators. We will explore advanced techniques for tackling web browser artifacts and delve into the ever-present threat of anti-forensic measures. This book equips you not only to uncover hidden evidence but also to document your findings and present them effectively in a court of law.

Finally, we will conclude by exploring the exciting advancements and emerging challenges within the field of digital forensics. By understanding the ever-changing landscape, you will be well-positioned to adapt your skills and stay ahead of the curve.

This book is designed to be an interactive learning experience. Each chapter builds upon the previous one, culminating in a well-rounded understanding of the entire digital forensics process. We encourage you to actively engage with the material, practice the presented techniques, and explore further resources to deepen your knowledge.

Get ready to embark on a thrilling journey into the world of digital forensics. With dedication and this book as your guide, you will be well on your way to becoming a skilled digital investigator, ready to uncover the truth hidden within the digital realm.

Akashdeep Bhardwaj

Pradeep Singh

&

Ajay Prasad
School of Computer Science
University of Petroleum and Energy Studies
Dehradun, India

CHAPTER 1

Navigating the Ethical Landscape of Digital Investigations

Abstract: This book aims to provide you with a comprehensive understanding of Digital Forensics, from its relatively new beginnings as a Digital forensics sub-discipline to its rapidly growing importance when combined with the more established digital forensic field of investigations. You should be able to comprehend the function of digital forensic professionals as well as the business and cybercrime contexts in which they are actively looking for proof of criminal and civil offenses after reading this chapter. You can gain an understanding of the difficulties faced by forensic practitioners and the intricacy of many cases by looking through case studies and examples presented in the book chapters.

Keywords: Cybercrime, Case studies, Criminal offenses, Digital forensics, Digital evidence, Forensic disciplines, Investigative techniques.

INTRODUCTION

Interest in Digital Forensics [1] as a subject for higher education and as a possible career path in business and law enforcement investigations has developed over the last ten years or more. To handle the increasing number of cases involving digital evidence, new forensic techniques and technology have emerged. But it is clear that practitioners are having trouble keeping up with the growing complexity, size, and quantity of cases. They also have limited funding and resources, and there is a dearth of qualified, experienced staff. The book aims to help practitioners, both current and prospective, address problems effectively in the future by discussing these challenges while providing some solutions that have helped me in my work and studies.

Due to the widespread use of personal computers in the workplace, inherent security issues with them have created new challenges for law enforcement. For instance, companies conducting internal audits or criminal investigations frequently must spend a lot of time going through computer data to locate digital evidence. New forensic procedures and instruments are desperately needed for these kinds of exams to support practitioners in doing their work more quickly. For practitioners looking to strengthen their crucial role in supporting the legal

Akashdeep Bhardwaj, Pradeep Singh & Ajay Prasad

community, these are exciting times. In terms of developments impacting evidence recovery and management, practitioners are at a crossroads when it comes to new entries into the field.

A category of forensic science called Digital Forensics investigates and analyzes digital devices and data to find evidence of fraud, espionage, cybercrimes, and other illegal activity. In order to collect, maintain, review, and present digital evidence in court, its guiding concepts and procedures are essential. Within this discipline, complacency, banality, and exhaustion are commonplace, and despite the work's intrinsic importance and excitement, the monotony and hefty caseloads can quickly stifle initial enthusiasm. This book presents new and efficient methods for cutting down on boredom and time-wasting, energizing practitioners, and bringing back the thrill of the evidence-gathering process. Courts and judicial procedures use digital forensic evidence, despite the opinions of certain purists who do not see forensics as science. Although the word may be deceptive, it might refer to the technology associated with certain disciplines rather than the sciences themselves.

The judiciary has become more aware of the growing use of digital evidence in court disputes. This places a great deal of pressure on digital forensic experts to strive to present reliable data and careful analyses of their findings, which may also be useful in establishing and evaluating precedents for future court rulings. Information security management must be improved because of the sharp rise in desktop computing and the spread of cybercrime that targets network infrastructure. It also calls for practitioners to sort through the chaos and try to hold the violators accountable. Specializations in digital forensics include the following domains as career options.

• Computer Forensics: This is the traditional area of digital forensics, which focuses on recovering and analyzing data from computers and other electronic devices. Computer forensic specialists are often involved in criminal investigations, but they can also be used in civil litigation and corporate investigations.

• Network Forensics: Network forensics specialists focus on investigating network traffic to identify security breaches and other criminal activity. They use a variety of tools and techniques to track down the source of attacks and to collect evidence.

• Mobile Device Forensics: As mobile devices have become more and more popular, the need for mobile device forensics specialists has grown. These specialists are experts in recovering data from mobile devices, such as smartphones and tablets.

• Cloud Forensics: Cloud forensics is a new and emerging specialization that focuses on investigating crimes that involve cloud-based storage and applications. Cloud forensic specialists need to have a deep understanding of cloud computing technologies and how they can be used to store and transmit evidence.

• Incident Response: Incident response specialists are responsible for responding to security incidents, such as data breaches and malware attacks. They work to contain the damage from the incident and to collect evidence that can be used to identify the attackers and bring them to justice.

The area of digital forensics emerged as more crimes involved the use of computer systems as the object of a crime, a tool for committing a crime, or a source of evidence for a crime. It did not take long to identify crucial tasks the need for looking at and analysing digital evidence while also making sure that the original evidence's integrity is maintained.

DIGITAL FORENSICS PRINCIPLES

The investigation and prosecution of cybercrimes and other digital offenses depend heavily on the concepts and procedures of Digital Forensics. Forensic specialists may efficiently gather, examine, and present digital evidence to support judicial processes and guarantee justice in the digital sphere by abiding by these guidelines and using reliable procedures. This section provides an overview of the concepts and procedures related to Digital Forensics.

• Evidence Preservation [2] is crucial to maintain the integrity of digital evidence. This involves protecting the digital environment, or crime scene, against manipulation. This ensures that the integrity of the evidence is maintained during its collection, preservation, and examination. Forensic specialists, for instance, take a forensic image of the hard disk while confiscating a computer used in a cybercrime investigation so they may work with a duplicate while protecting the original data.

• Chain of Custody [3] creates and preserves the formal chain of custody to ensure the admissibility and dependability of the evidence by documenting how it is handled, moved, and stored. For example, keeping track of who, when, and why someone used a confiscated device aids in preserving the integrity of the evidence.

• Volatility [4] involves if digital evidence is not handled quickly, it may be volatile and vulnerable to change or deletion. Before beginning a comprehensive investigation, forensic specialists give priority to gathering dynamic data first, such as real-time system information or network connections. For instance, transient information from active processes or network connections might offer vital information on current cyberattacks.

• Forensic Acquisition [5] maintains the integrity and authenticity of data, forensic acquisition entails removing it from digital devices in an appropriate and safe manner. Typically, this procedure uses specialized equipment and methods to build a forensic image, of the original stored digital medium. Forensic specialists, for example, employ write-blocking devices to stop modifications being made to the original evidence while it is being acquired.

• Digital Analysis Techniques [6] uses a variety of methods to efficiently review and decipher digital evidence. This includes keyword searching to find pertinent information, file carving to recover lost or fragmented files, and metadata analysis to ascertain the origin and validity of files. An image file's metadata, for instance, can provide information on the equipment that was used to take the picture as well as its creation date and time.

• Steganography detection [7] is the process of finding hidden information in digital files or communications. Experts in Digital Forensics find and retrieve concealed data from pictures, audio files, and other digital media using specific instruments and techniques. For example, locating hidden files or messages within seemingly innocent photos might yield important proof in digital fraud or espionage cases.

• Malware Analysis [8] comprehends the behavior, operation, and impact of harmful software. Forensic professionals perform malware analysis in situations involving cyberattacks or digital intrusions. Reverse engineering malware entails determining its origin, function, and possible exploitable vulnerabilities. For instance, figuring out the encryption methods employed and creating mitigation techniques might be aided by examining the code of a ransomware strain.

• Timeline analysis [9] is the process of reassembling the events that led up to a digital incident using metadata, file system artifacts, and timestamps. This aids in the investigation team's comprehension of the offenders' conduct and the sequence of events that preceded the occurrence. A history of file creation, modification, and access, for instance, might help shed light on a suspect's actions during a data breach.

• Network Forensics [10] focuses on investigating and analyzing network traffic to uncover evidence of unauthorized access, data exfiltration, or other malicious activities. This involves capturing and analyzing network packets, logs, and communication protocols to identify anomalies and intrusions. For instance, examining firewall logs and packet captures can reveal suspicious connections or unauthorized access attempts.

• Report and Presentation [11] include the digital forensic findings being documented in detailed reports that summarize the investigation process, methodologies employed, and the evidence discovered. These reports are presented to stakeholders, including law enforcement, legal teams, or corporate management, to support decision-making and legal proceedings. For example, a forensic report may include a summary of findings, analysis results, and recommendations for strengthening digital security measures.

LEGAL AND ETHICAL CONSIDERATIONS

Concerns about politicians' and lawyers' ignorance of the problems resulting from the increasing use of digital evidence in court cases were raised in the 1980s. The rapid rise in computer use and the introduction of new technologies, including digital mobile phones, were the main causes of this worldwide phenomenon. Consequently, a concerted plan of action was put forth in the United States to assist forensic and legal experts in overcoming obstacles associated with digital evidence tendering. The US and the EU created a research corpus at the beginning of the new millennium to solve forensic cases driven by practitioner needs using scientific techniques. Back then, scientists expressed alarm over a general misperception of what digital evidence is. They were more concerned about the inefficiency and ineffectiveness of the different forensic techniques used in its recovery, analysis, and eventual use in court proceedings.

It was acknowledged that the first steps in conducting digital forensic investigations were to identify potential violators and, most importantly, to create a digital trail connecting the suspect to the binary data. While it was widely believed that having a digital computer would connect a transgressor to all the information on it, questions were being raised about the validity of these presumptions. The defence was represented in Clarkson *versus* Clarkson of the Circuit Court for Roanoke Court [12] in 1999 by Digital Forensics designer Andrew Rosen. In the end, it was determined that the defendant's wife had planted child porn on his computer and tried to use it as leverage to get him to divorce, retain custody of the kids, and marry her new partner. Because of this case, practitioners who were focused on law enforcement and prosecution and who were clearly more interested in winning the case than achieving a just resolution started to call Rosen a traitor. This set a dangerous precedent, as some practitioners assumed that the person who owned and used the computer the most was likely the one who had broken the law.

In my experience, when it comes to addressing defence cases in criminal trials, the sound identification of other individuals who might be suspects has often been given lip service. This implies investigations that are suspect-driven rather than evidence-led, which is hardly a fair and objective method. This runs counter to the notion that the practitioner is the court's servant. The years 1999–2007 were considered the "golden age" of digital forensics because they gave investigators the ability to observe crimes and stop time by retrieving deleted emails, texts, and files that contained insights into the motivations of criminals. Formerly, Digital Forensics was a specialized field of study that mainly assisted in criminal investigations. These days, popular crime programs and books frequently include elements of Digital Forensics.

The web series Crime Scene Investigation (CSI) [13] dramatizes digital forensics and greatly exaggerates the technical proficiency of forensic experts and equipment. By 2005, Digital Forensics was still devoid of standards and technique and was naturally mostly focused on Windows and, to a lesser extent, typical Linux PCs. Even in 2010, there was still considerable debate among academics over the development of a formal digital forensic model, even though the fundamental stages of Digital Forensics tests were well documented. Those onlookers saw it as obviously inferior to other tangible forensic criteria like blood analysis.

There are currently no standards that particularly address the topic, despite the Joint Technical Committee of the International Standard Organization seeking to have a standard governance model on digital forensics. Nonetheless, there is a global understanding of the issues surrounding the disparities in the information sharing of judicial procedures between jurisdictions. Since the field of digital forensics has grown quickly, it requires governance like that of information systems and information technology (IS and IT), even though there are currently very few international standards for methodology, procedures, or administration. Being a highly specialized field, digital forensics has raised concerns recently from several academics about how the highly technical discipline and the commercial approach to governance interact.

Digital forensic investigations and criminal prosecutions are often conducted by government organizations operating under the auspices of criminal law. Under applicable criminal legislation, law enforcement officials are authorized to search and seize property to find and seize equipment that may be used in criminal activity or to aid in criminal activity. Ordinarily, oral evidence is not admissible in court and witness opinions are expressly forbidden. However, if their opinions are limited to the evidence that has been presented, expert witnesses and scientific experts may offer their opinions based on their significant training and study. If it is within their area of expertise, these privileged witnesses may share with the court any conclusions they have drawn from the evidence they have seen. Professionals in the field of forensics not only gather and examine evidence, but they also present it to attorneys, investigators, and juries, explaining its significance to them. Of course, having good analytical skills is essential, but practitioners also need to be able to clearly convey to the public their conclusions and expert opinions. Because evidence is blind and cannot speak for itself, it needs an interpretation to explain what it means or could mean as well as why it is significant to the case.

To make sure that the juries and legal teams fully comprehend the evidence, Digital Forensics experts spend a lot of time on casework presenting technical details to them. Experts in forensics are supposed to offer data that might aid the court in reaching a decision, as well as the expert's personal viewpoint. Based on the presented testimony, the court must still reach its own judgment regarding the defendant's guilt or innocence. When serving as a forensic expert, the forensic practitioner should only offer their scientific opinion about the data to assist the court in making judgment calls. Experts should refrain from offering their own final conclusions since expertise is not always 100% definite. Courts in a variety of legal countries need forensic experts to have a solid grasp of computer technology for their evidence to be taken seriously.

There are several subcategories within Digital Forensics, with each one concentrating on certain kinds of digital evidence and methods of investigation. It is vital to comprehend these classifications to conduct efficient investigations and analyses of digital occurrences. The following lists some of the main subcategories of Digital Forensics.

• Computer Forensics finds evidence of digital crimes, forensics examines and analyses digital equipment including computers, laptops, servers, and storage media. Investigators recover lost files, analyse metadata and system logs, and restore data using specialist tools and methodologies. This type of forensics is frequently used in situations involving fraud, theft of intellectual property, hacking, or illegal access.

• Network Forensics involves finding security lapses, intrusions, or unapproved activity by examining and analysing network traffic, communication protocols, and hardware like switches and routers. To reconstruct events, identify attackers, and assess the scope of a security incident, investigators gather and examine network packets, logs, and metadata. Investigating cyberattacks, data breaches, and network-based crimes requires the use of network forensics.

• Mobile Forensics focuses on the digital evidence from smartphones, tablets, and other mobile devices, which is extracted and analysed in mobile device forensics. To retrieve information from device storage, SIM cards, and cloud backups, including call logs, text messages, emails, photographs, and app usage histories, investigators employ specialized tools and methodologies. In situations involving digital fraud, cyberbullying, child exploitation, or corporate espionage, mobile device forensics is frequently used.

• Forensic data analysis finds patterns, anomalies, and proof of illegal activity by looking through and analysing massive amounts of digital data, including databases, log files, and financial records. To find patterns, connections, and questionable transactions, investigators employ data mining, statistical analysis, and visualization approaches. Investigating financial crimes, insider threats, and sophisticated cyberattacks all need forensic data analysis.

• Memory Forensics retrieves information regarding current network connections, running programs, and system configurations through the study of volatile memory (RAM). Memory dumps are obtained and analysed by investigators using specific tools and procedures to detect harmful behaviours, malware, or rootkits that may not be visible through disk-based forensics alone. When looking at memory-resident malware and advanced persistent threats (APTs), memory forensics is hugely rewarding.

• Database Forensics examines and analyzes databases to find proof of illegal access, data modification, or data breaches is the main goal of database forensics. Forensic techniques are employed by investigators to detect abnormalities in transaction histories and database logs, as well as suspicious searches or unlawful modifications to database entries. Investigating data breaches, insider threats, and cyberattacks that target confidential information kept in databases requires the use of database forensics.

• With cloud computing environments, such as infrastructure-as-a-service (IaaS), platform-as-a-service (PaaS), and software-as-a-service (SaaS), researchers examine cloud user activity, access logs, and cloud service logs to ascertain the origin and extent of security events, data breaches, or unapproved access. Investigating cyber crimes utilizing cloud-based services and data requires the use of cloud forensics.

For each type of Digital Forensics to properly examine and evaluate digital evidence, certain knowledge, abilities, and resources are needed. In the digital age, forensic investigators can find important information and proof to help court cases, law enforcement investigations, and corporate security initiatives by utilizing these categories.

TRAITS OF FORENSIC INVESTIGATORS

Digital Forensic work comprises three distinct roles: that of a lawyer, knowledgeable about court procedures and legislation, a detective experienced in conducting criminal investigations, and an analyst acquainted with the operation of digital devices, OS, Apps, and networks. Self-trained experts confound the judicial process, seldom face opposition and rarely have their evidence's veracity investigated. However, the courts, governments, businesses, and computer and information security organizations all have fundamental requirements for the expertise and experience of practitioners.

When examining digital crime scenes, forensic professionals need to search and analyse all relevant evidence and be in charge of the scenario. This information must be gathered and professionally reported so that the attorneys and the courts can see it. It is crucial that a digital forensic investigation be both compelling in the real world and legally sound to satisfy a court of law. When restoring data from computer storage media, the practitioner must use safe, tried-and-true procedures that verify the data's dependability and correctness.

DIGITAL INVESTIGATIONS USE CASE EXAMPLES

Digital forensics has always played a crucial role in uncovering digital evidence and solving cybercrime and attacks. Few real-world examples are listed below.

Financial Fraud

In 2016, the Bangladesh Bank heist [14] involved hackers infiltrating the bank's systems and transferring millions through fraudulent SWIFT (Society for Worldwide Interbank Financial Telecommunication) messages, which is a global messaging network used by financial institutions to securely transmit instructions for financial transactions. This heist highlighted vulnerabilities in the worldwide financial ecosystems and raised security concerns on SWIFT messaging used by global banks. It also underscored the significance of robust cybersecurity controls and need for collaboration between financial institutions and the law enforcement agencies to prevent and mitigate such attacks in the future. Digital forensic investigations on the bank servers helped track the stolen funds and identify the perpetrators as illustrated in Fig. (**1**).

The steps involved in this breach are listed below.

• Initial Compromise: The attackers accessed the banking system using malware that was designed to infiltrate the bank's network and gain access to the SWIFT messaging system.

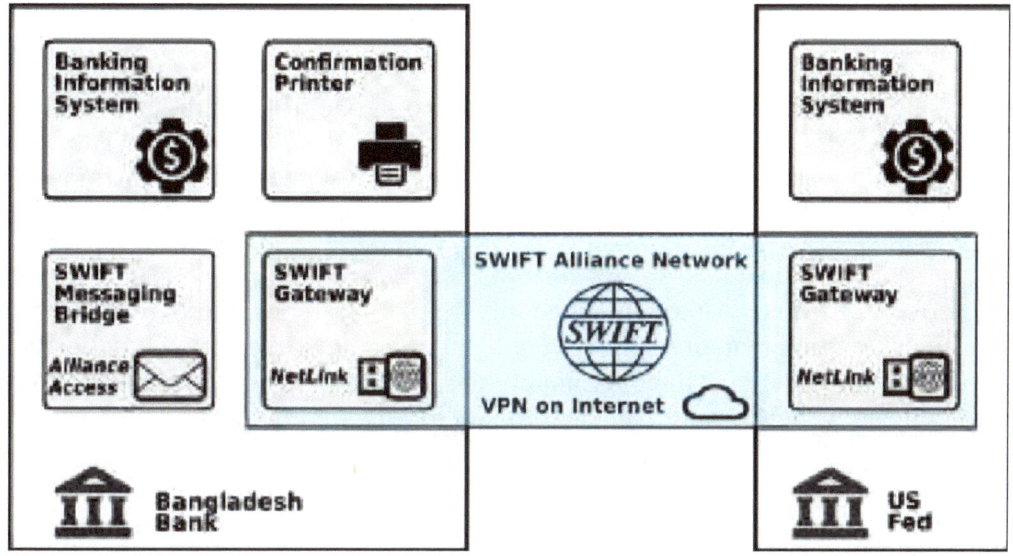

Fig. (1). Bangladesh bank heist [14].

• SWIFT Messages: After breaking into the system, the attackers requested that money be transferred from Bangladesh Bank's New York Fed account to accounts in the Philippines and Sri Lanka *via* fictitious SWIFT messages sent to the Federal Reserve Bank of New York. The messages appeared legitimate, as they were authenticated using valid SWIFT credentials stolen from the bank as illustrated in Fig. (**2**).

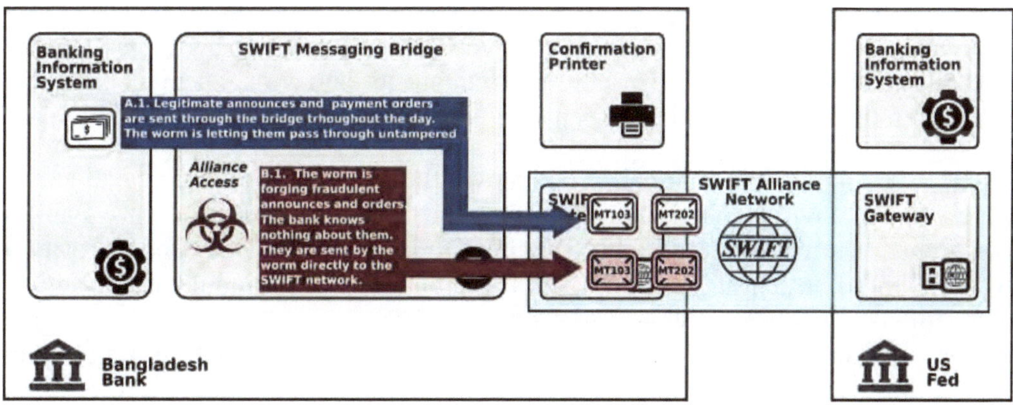

Fig. (2). Swift messaging *via* malware [14].

• Execution of Transfers: The Federal Reserve Bank of New York processed the transfer requests, totalling approximately $81 million, and sent the funds to accounts in the Philippines and Sri Lanka as instructed in the fraudulent SWIFT messages.

• Detection: The heist was detected when a typo in one of the fraudulent transfer requests raised suspicion at the Federal Reserve Bank of New York. The word "foundation" was misspelled as 'fandation' in one of the transfer instructions, leading bank officials to seek clarification from Bangladesh Bank. This prompted an investigation, revealing the fraudulent transactions.

• Recovery Efforts: Although some of the stolen funds were recovered, a significant portion remains unrecovered. Investigations by various authorities, including the Bangladesh government, the FBI, and other international law enforcement agencies, were launched to identify the perpetrators and recover the stolen funds.

• Attribution: While the exact identity of the hackers remains unclear, cybersecurity experts and investigators have linked the heist to a sophisticated cybercrime group, possibly based in North Korea. However, no definitive attribution has been made.

The timeline of this attack is as follows: Enrico Teodoro Vasquez, Alfred Santos Vergara, Michael Francisco Cruz, and Jessie Christopher Lagrosas established three US$ bank accounts in the Jupiter, Makati branch of the Rizal Commercial Banking Corporation (RCBC) on May 15, 2015, each with a 500 US$ initial deposit. These accounts were inactive until February 4, 2016, when it was discovered that they were fraudulent. Shortly before they started the fraudulent money transfers on February 4, the hackers planted the virus on the bank's system in January 2016. This was also quite clever because if it had been installed too late, they might not have been able to evaluate its behavior, and if it had been installed too soon, it might have been discovered prior to the theft.

By February 4, 2016, the virus had taken over the hackers' account and had gained access to Bangladesh Bank's VOSTRO account with the Federal Reserve Bank of New York. The hackers ordered 35 payments of 951 million USD, the majority of which were to be sent to the RCBC Jupiter branch. Thirty fraudulent transactions were found and stopped by the Fed; however, five transfers one hundred and one million dollars were not stopped. The feds attempted to get in touch with Bangladesh Bank on February 5, 2016, to obtain an explanation regarding these payments, including the five that were not banned. However, February 5th was a bank holiday in Bangladesh, so no one could respond. The five transfers are carried out by the routing banks and correspondent banks between February 5 and February 8, 2016. Twenty million USD worth of transactions have been recovered. This came after Deutsche Bank, one of the routing banks, suspended an instruction to a fictitious Sri Lankan organization due to an error. However, the remaining 81 million USD in pilfered money ended up in four RCBC fictitious bank accounts. Bangladesh Bank issued a 'stop payment' directive to RCBC on February 8, 2016. The request indicates that the central bank wanted the monies that were stolen to be returned or, if they had not been transferred yet, frozen.

In the Philippines, February 8 was a non-working holiday observed in honour of the Chinese New Year. Bangladesh Bank sent RCBC their SWIFT code on February 9, asking for a return, to freeze the funds until further investigation could be conducted, or to put them on hold if they had already been transferred. The RCBC Jupiter branch continued to permit withdrawals from the accounts in defiance of the 'stop payment' order. The funds were then combined and placed into William So Go's dollar account, which was opened that same day by DBA Centurytex Trading. The money was laundered in the casinos for the next few days. The time was ideal. An exceptional weekend that was perfectly timed to coincide with Bangladesh's business holiday and the Philippines' Chinese New Year holiday. The Fed failed to attempt to retrieve the five orders that passed right away since they were unable to obtain the necessary clarity from Bangladesh Bank the next day. Because Monday being a Philippine banking holiday, the RCBC was unable to process the stop orders that the Bangladesh bank had submitted to freeze the funds. In addition, the money was easily laundered due to the Chinese New Year and the volume of transactions that occur in casinos during this time, as well as the Philippines' lax AML regulations and procedures.

Data Breaches

Equifax, a credit bureau, suffered a massive data breach in 2017 [15] that compromised the personal information of approximately 147 million people in the United States. Digital forensics helped determine the attackers' point of entry, the data accessed, and the timeline of the breach, aiding future security measures.

Technical details of the breach are:

• Exploiting Vulnerability: By taking advantage of a flaw in the Apache Struts web application framework, the breach was started. To enable consumers to contest errors in their credit reports, Equifax included Apache Struts into its online dispute portal. The attackers took use of CVE-2017-5638, a known vulnerability in Apache Struts that permitted remote code execution.

• Infiltration and Persistence: The attackers were able to obtain unauthorized access to Equifax's network after taking advantage of the vulnerability and established persistence within the network by deploying various tools and malware to maintain access and escalate privileges. This likely involved lateral movement across the network to locate valuable data repositories.

• Exfiltration of Data: After entering the network, the attackers went after sensitive databases holding personally identifiable information (PII), such as names, birth dates, addresses, Social Security numbers, and, in certain situations, driver's license numbers. They exfiltrated this data over an extended period, potentially going undetected for months.

• Obfuscation and Cover-up Attempts: During the breach, the attackers took steps to obfuscate their activities and cover their tracks. This included deleting log files and using encryption to mask data exfiltration, making it more challenging for Equifax's security team to detect the intrusion.

• Detection and Response: Equifax detected suspicious network activity in late July 2017 and subsequently launched an investigation. However, it wasn't until August 2017 that Equifax discovered the full extent of the breach. The bank contacted law police right away and hired cybersecurity companies to help with the investigation and clean-up procedures.

• Public Disclosure and Fallout: The extent of the issue and the sensitive nature of the exposed data led to significant worry and indignation, which Equifax publicly reported on September 7, 2017. The breach led to congressional hearings, regulatory scrutiny, lawsuits, and significant reputational damage for Equifax.

• Post-Breach Remediation: In the aftermath of the breach, Equifax implemented various measures to improve its cybersecurity posture and enhance data protection practices. This included patching the Apache Struts vulnerability, enhancing network monitoring and intrusion detection capabilities, and implementing stronger access controls and encryption measures.

Child Exploitation

In investigations involving child pornography or online solicitation, digital forensics on seized devices helps identify victims, trace the source of abuse material, and build a strong case against perpetrators.

Digital forensics has been utilized for such work in recent times as follows.

• Image and Video Analysis: Digital forensics experts use specialized software tools to analyse digital images and videos for signs of child pornography. These tools can identify, and flag explicit content based on predefined criteria such as nudity, age of individuals depicted, and context. Forensic examiners meticulously examine file metadata, including timestamps and geolocation data, to establish the origin and authenticity of illicit content.

• Keyword and File Hash Analysis: Investigators utilize keyword searches and file hash analysis to identify known child pornography images and videos. Law enforcement agencies maintain databases of known illicit files and their unique cryptographic hashes. Digital forensics tools can quickly compare file hashes found on suspect devices against these databases to identify matches and prioritize evidence collection.

• Internet History and Chat Logs Examination: Digital forensics experts analyse internet browsing history and chat logs from computers and mobile devices to uncover evidence of online solicitation and communication with minors. They examine chat transcripts, emails, and social media messages for inappropriate language, grooming behavior, and explicit content exchanged between suspects and victims.

• Metadata Examination: Digital file metadata, such as the EXIF data found in photos and movies, can offer important hints regarding the production, alteration, and distribution of illegal content. Digital forensics specialists analyse metadata to establish timelines, identify devices used in the production and distribution of child pornography, and track the online activities of suspects.

• Network Traffic Analysis: Law enforcement agencies monitor network traffic to identify and track individuals engaging in the distribution and sharing of child pornography through peer-to-peer networks, file-sharing platforms, and online forums. Digital forensics tools can capture and analyse network traffic to identify IP addresses, file transfers, and communication patterns associated with illegal activities.

• Steganography Detection: Perpetrators of child pornography often use steganography techniques to conceal illicit images and videos within seemingly innocent files, such as digital photographs or documents. Digital forensics experts employ specialized software tools to detect and extract hidden content from files, revealing hidden layers of illicit imagery and aiding in the identification of perpetrators.

• Cloud Forensics: With the increasing use of cloud storage and online platforms for sharing illicit content, digital forensics has expanded to include cloud forensics techniques. Investigators analyse data stored on cloud servers, including file metadata, access logs, and user account activity, to identify individuals involved in the production, distribution, and consumption of child pornography.

Cyber Espionage

Detecting cyber espionage involves a combination of advanced digital forensics techniques and tools to uncover evidence of unauthorized access, data exfiltration, and covert surveillance activities. In 2014, the Sony Pictures hack [16] involved a group stealing confidential data and releasing it online. Digital forensics on Sony's network helped identify the attackers' methods and trace their origin.

Examples of how digital forensics has been utilized for detecting cyber espionage in recent times are as follows:

• Malware Analysis: Cyber espionage often involves the use of sophisticated malware designed to infiltrate target systems, steal sensitive information, and maintain persistent access. Digital forensics experts conduct malware analysis to dissect malicious code, identify its capabilities, and trace its origins. They examine indicators of compromise (IOCs), such as file signatures, command-an--control (C2) infrastructure, and behavioural patterns, to attribute the malware to specific threat actors or campaigns.

• Intrusion Detection and Analysis: Digital forensics teams deploy intrusion detection systems (IDS) and security information and event management (SIEM) platforms to monitor network traffic and identify suspicious activities indicative of cyber espionage. They analyse log data, network packets, and system alerts to uncover unauthorized access attempts, lateral movement within the network, and data exfiltration activities. Advanced threat hunting techniques, such as anomaly detection and behavior analysis, are used to proactively identify stealthy intrusions.

• Memory Forensics: Memory forensics involves the analysis of volatile memory (RAM) to uncover evidence of malicious activity that may not be present on disk. Digital forensics experts use specialized tools to capture and analyse memory dumps from compromised systems, allowing them to identify running processes, loaded modules, and artifacts indicative of malware or unauthorized access. Memory forensics can reveal stealthy malware implants, backdoors, and rootkits used by cyber espionage actors to evade traditional detection methods.

• Endpoint Forensics: Endpoint forensics involves the analysis of digital evidence collected from compromised endpoints, such as desktops, laptops, and mobile devices. Digital forensics experts use forensic imaging tools to create forensic copies of disk drives and conduct in-depth analysis of file systems, registry hives, and user activity logs. They identify suspicious files, registry modifications, and system artifacts associated with cyber espionage activities, such as unauthorized software installations, privilege escalation, and data exfiltration.

• Network Forensics: Network forensics focuses on the analysis of network traffic to reconstruct cyber espionage operations and uncover evidence of malicious activity. Digital forensics teams capture and analyse packet-level data using network forensics tools, intrusion detection sensors, and network traffic analysers. They identify communication patterns, command-and-control channels, and data exfiltration pathways used by threat actors to infiltrate target networks, compromise sensitive assets, and exfiltrate stolen information.

• Attribution and Intelligence Analysis: Digital forensics plays a crucial role in attributing cyber espionage activities to specific threat actors, nation-state actors, or criminal organizations. Forensic analysts correlate technical indicators, malware signatures, and tactics, techniques, and procedures (TTPs) observed in cyberattacks with known threat actor profiles and intelligence reports. This attribution analysis helps law enforcement agencies, intelligence agencies, and cybersecurity researchers identify the motives, objectives, and capabilities of cyber espionage actors and develop effective countermeasures and mitigation strategies.

Email Fraud (Phishing)

Digital forensics plays a crucial role in detecting and investigating phishing emails to identify spoofed sender addresses, malicious links, and track down the source of the attack, helping dismantle phishing operations.

Examples of how digital forensics has been utilized for this purpose are as follows:

• Email Header Analysis: Digital forensics experts analyse email headers to trace the origin of phishing emails and identify indicators of fraudulent activity. They examine metadata, such as sender IP addresses, mail transfer agents (MTAs), and message routing information to determine if emails have been spoofed or sent from malicious sources. This analysis helps investigators identify patterns and signatures associated with phishing campaigns and track down perpetrators.

• Link and Attachment Analysis: Phishing emails frequently include harmful attachments or links that are meant to fool recipients into downloading malware or disclosing personal information. Digital forensics teams analyse embedded URLs and file attachments to assess their legitimacy and potential threat level. They use sandboxing and malware analysis techniques to detonate suspicious files in a controlled environment and identify malicious behavior, such as code execution or data exfiltration attempts.

• Email Content Analysis: Digital forensics experts examine the content of phishing emails to identify common phishing tactics and social engineering techniques used by attackers. They analyse language, formatting, and visual elements to detect signs of impersonation, urgency, or deception. Text analysis tools and natural language processing (NLP) algorithms help identify phishing patterns and keywords indicative of fraudulent intent.

• Endpoint Forensics: Endpoint forensics involves the analysis of email-related artifacts on individual devices, such as computers and mobile devices, to uncover evidence of phishing attacks and email frauds. Digital forensics specialists examine email client logs, browser history, and temporary files to reconstruct the timeline of email interactions and identify any suspicious activities, such as clicking on phishing links or downloading malicious attachments.

• User Behavior Analysis: Digital forensics teams analyse user behavior and email activity logs to detect anomalous patterns indicative of phishing attacks. They spot anomalies in email usage, like abrupt increases in volume, strange login locations, or unwanted access attempts. Behavior analysis techniques, such as user profiling and anomaly detection, help identify compromised accounts and alert security teams to potential phishing threats.

• Email Header Forensics: In-depth analysis of email headers is conducted to uncover hidden information and detect email spoofing and manipulation. Digital forensics experts examine header fields such as Return-Path, Message-ID, and Received to trace the path of emails through the internet and identify inconsistencies or anomalies. Advanced techniques, like Domain keys identified mail and Sender policy framework validation, help verify the authenticity of email sources and prevent domain spoofing attacks.

• Phishing Simulation and Incident Response: Digital forensics teams conduct phishing simulation exercises to assess the susceptibility of users to phishing attacks and evaluate the effectiveness of security controls and during the phishing incidents, perform incident response to contain the threat, mitigate the impact, and collect digital evidence for further investigation and legal action.

Identity Theft

Digital forensics is essential for detecting and investigating identity theft, where someone's personal information is used without their consent for fraudulent purposes.

Examples of how digital forensics is utilized in such cases are as follows:

• Data Breach Analysis: Digital forensics experts analyse data breaches to identify compromised personal information, such as Debit & Credit cards, Social Security numbers, and Account passwords. They examine breached databases, logs, and network traffic to determine how attackers gained access to sensitive data and track the movement of stolen information. Forensic tools and techniques are used to reconstruct the timeline of the breach and identify potential vulnerabilities in the victim organization's security controls.

• Stolen Device Analysis: If a device containing sensitive personal information is stolen, digital forensics can be used to track the device's location, identify unauthorized access attempts, and recover deleted data. Forensic analysis of stolen devices, such as laptops, smartphones, and tablets, involves imaging the device's storage media and examining file systems, logs, and application data for evidence of identity theft. Mobile device forensics tools are used to extract data from smartphones and analyse communication logs, GPS coordinates, and installed applications.

• Phishing Investigation: Digital forensics teams investigate phishing attacks targeting individuals or organizations to uncover evidence of identity theft. They analyse phishing emails, websites, and malicious attachments to identify phishing campaigns and track down perpetrators. Forensic analysis of phishing emails involves examining email headers, content, and attachments for indicators of fraudulent activity. Digital footprints left by phishing actors, such as IP addresses, domain registrations, and hosting providers, are traced using network forensics techniques.

• Fraudulent Account Activity Analysis: Digital forensics experts analyse financial records, transaction logs, and account statements to detect signs of identity theft-related fraud. They examine suspicious account activity, such as unauthorized transactions, account takeovers, and changes to account settings, to identify patterns indicative of fraudulent behavior. Forensic analysis of digital payment systems, such as credit card transactions and online banking transfers, helps trace the flow of stolen funds and identify potential money laundering activities.

• Social media and Online Profile Analysis: Digital forensics teams analyse social media accounts, online profiles, and digital footprints to identify signs of identity theft and impersonation. They examine user-generated content, friend lists, and communication history to detect unauthorized account access and fraudulent activity. Forensic analysis of social media accounts involves collecting digital evidence, such as screenshots, chat logs, and metadata, to support identity theft investigations and legal proceedings.

• Digital Identity Verification: Digital forensics plays a role in verifying digital identities and detecting identity theft through biometric authentication, digital signatures, and cryptographic techniques. Forensic experts analyse digital certificates, cryptographic keys, and authentication tokens to validate the authenticity of digital identities and detect unauthorized access attempts. Advanced authentication methods, such as multi-factor authentication and biometric recognition, are used to enhance security and prevent identity theft.

Cryptocurrency Theft

Digital forensics plays a vital role in detecting and investigating cryptocurrency thefts, which involve the unauthorized access and transfer of digital assets from cryptocurrency wallets or exchanges.

Examples of how digital forensics is utilized in such cases are as follows:

• Blockchain Analysis: Digital forensics experts analyse blockchain transactions to trace the flow of stolen cryptocurrency funds. They use blockchain explorers and specialized tools to examine transaction histories, wallet addresses, and transaction amounts associated with the theft. By tracking the movement of stolen funds across the blockchain, forensic analysts can identify suspicious transactions and potential recipients of stolen assets.

• Wallet Forensics: Forensic examination of cryptocurrency wallets involves analysing wallet software, private keys, and transaction records to identify evidence of unauthorized access or tampering. Digital forensics experts use wallet recovery tools and forensic imaging techniques to extract data from compromised wallets and analyse transaction logs, address book entries, and wallet.dat files for signs of theft or manipulation.

• Exchange Analysis: If cryptocurrency theft occurs on a cryptocurrency exchange platform, digital forensics teams investigate the exchange's systems and databases to identify security vulnerabilities and unauthorized access attempts. They analyse exchange logs, user accounts, and transaction histories to reconstruct the sequence of events leading up to the theft. Forensic analysis of exchange platforms involves identifying security breaches, insider threats, and compliance violations that may have facilitated the theft.

• Phishing and Social Engineering Investigation: Digital forensics experts investigate phishing attacks and social engineering scams targeting cryptocurrency users to uncover evidence of theft and fraud. They analyse phishing emails, malicious websites, and communication logs to identify perpetrators and trace the flow of stolen funds. Forensic analysis of phishing campaigns involves examining email headers, URL redirects, and malicious payloads to identify tactics, techniques, and procedures (TTPs) used by attackers.

• Network Forensics: Forensic analysis of network traffic helps identify unauthorized access attempts, data exfiltration, and communication channels used in cryptocurrency thefts. Digital forensics teams capture and analyse network packets, DNS requests, and IP traffic to identify malicious actors and command-and-control (C2) infrastructure associated with cryptocurrency thefts. Network forensics tools and intrusion detection systems (IDS) are used to detect anomalous behavior and alert security teams to potential threats.

• Forensic Accounting: Digital forensics experts perform forensic accounting and financial analysis to trace the movement of stolen cryptocurrency funds across multiple wallets and exchanges. They examine cryptocurrency transaction records, account balances, and blockchain data to identify patterns indicative of money laundering and illicit activity. Forensic accounting techniques, such as transaction analysis and source-of-funds tracing, help uncover the identities of individuals involved in cryptocurrency thefts and facilitate asset recovery efforts.

Social Media Crimes

Digital forensics is increasingly utilized in detecting and investigating social media crimes, which encompass a wide range of illicit activities conducted through social media platforms.

Examples of how digital forensics is applied in such cases are as follows:

• Evidence Collection: Digital forensics experts collect digital evidence from social media platforms, including posts, messages, images, videos, and user profiles, relevant to the investigation. They use forensic tools to capture and preserve digital artifacts, ensuring the integrity and admissibility of evidence in legal proceedings. Metadata associated with social media content, such as timestamps, geolocation data, and user identifiers, is analysed to establish the context and authenticity of digital evidence.

• User Identification: Digital forensics teams analyse social media profiles, friend lists, and communication logs to identify individuals involved in criminal activities, such as cyberbullying, harassment, and online fraud. They use open-source intelligence (OSINT) techniques and social media analytics tools to map social networks, track user interactions, and uncover hidden connections between suspects and victims. User attribution analysis involves correlating digital footprints, IP addresses, and device identifiers to link social media accounts to specific individuals.

• Content Analysis: Digital forensics experts analyse social media content for evidence of criminal behavior, including threats, hate speech, and illegal activities. They use text analysis tools and natural language processing (NLP) algorithms to detect patterns, keywords, and sentiments indicative of criminal intent. Image and video analysis techniques, such as image recognition and deep learning algorithms, are used to identify and classify multimedia content associated with social media crimes.

• Geo-Location Tracking: Digital forensics teams leverage geo-location data embedded in social media posts and digital images to track the movements and activities of suspects. They use geospatial analysis techniques and mapping tools to visualize the spatial distribution of social media content and identify hotspots of criminal activity. Geo-location tracking helps law enforcement agencies establish timelines, reconstruct crime scenes, and identify witnesses or accomplices involved in social media crimes.

• Network Analysis: Digital forensics experts conduct network analysis to identify coordinated efforts and organized crime networks operating on social media platforms. They analyse communication patterns, user interactions, and group memberships to identify key actors and hierarchical structures within criminal organizations. Network analysis tools, such as social network analysis (SNA) software and graph databases, help uncover hidden relationships and communication channels used in social media crimes.

• Metadata Examination: Metadata associated with social media content, such as EXIF data in digital images and GPS coordinates in check-in posts, provides valuable insights into the context and authenticity of digital evidence. Digital forensics specialists analyze metadata to establish timelines, verify alibis, and corroborate witness statements in social media crime investigations. Metadata examination helps validate the credibility of digital evidence and support prosecution efforts in court.

• Deep Web Investigation: Digital forensics teams investigate criminal activities conducted on the deep web and dark web, including illicit marketplaces, forums, and communication channels. They use specialized tools and techniques to access hidden services, monitor underground communities, and gather intelligence on cybercriminals operating in anonymity. Deep web investigation involves analyzing cryptocurrency transactions, encrypted communications, and digital artifacts to identify perpetrators and disrupt criminal networks involved in social media-related crimes.

Insider Threats

Detecting and investigating insider threats, where individuals with authorized access to an organization's systems and data misuse their privileges for malicious purposes, relies heavily on digital forensics. If a company suspects an employee of stealing intellectual property or leaking confidential data, digital forensics on their work devices can uncover the extent of the crime.

Examples of how digital forensics is utilized in such cases are as follows:

• Log Analysis: Digital forensics experts analyse system logs, network traffic logs, and application logs to identify suspicious activities indicative of insider threats. They examine log entries for anomalies, such as unauthorized access attempts, unusual file transfers, and privilege escalation events. Log analysis helps forensic investigators reconstruct timelines of insider activity, identify compromised accounts, and attribute malicious actions to specific individuals.

• User Behavior Analysis: Digital forensics teams analyse user behavior and access patterns to detect anomalies and deviations from normal activity. They use behavioural analytics tools and machine learning algorithms to profile user behavior, establish baselines, and identify threats indicative of insider threats. User behavior analysis involves monitoring login times, access frequencies, and data access patterns to identify unauthorized or unusual behavior by insiders.

• Endpoint Forensics: Forensic examination of endpoint devices, such as computers, servers, and mobile devices, helps identify evidence of insider threats. Digital forensics experts use forensic imaging tools to capture disk images and analyse file systems, registry hives, and memory dumps for signs of malicious activity. Endpoint forensics involves identifying unauthorized software installations, data exfiltration attempts, and evidence of insider collusion or sabotage.

• Email and Communication Analysis: Digital forensics teams analyse email communications, chat logs, and other digital communications to uncover evidence of insider threats. They examine email headers, content, and attachments for signs of data leakage, intellectual property theft, or collusion with external adversaries. Communication analysis involves identifying insider conversations, sharing of sensitive information, and coordination of malicious activities through digital channels.

• Data Exfiltration Detection: Digital forensics experts use data loss prevention (DLP) tools and network monitoring solutions to detect and prevent data exfiltration by insiders. They analyse network traffic, file transfers, and data access patterns to identify unauthorized attempts to copy or transfer sensitive data outside the organization. Data exfiltration detection involves monitoring outbound network traffic, inspecting encrypted communications, and implementing data access controls to prevent insider misuse of corporate resources.

• Forensic Accounting: Forensic accounting techniques are used to trace financial transactions and identify evidence of insider fraud or embezzlement. Digital forensics teams analyse financial records, transaction logs, and account statements to identify discrepancies, fraudulent activities, and unauthorized transfers of funds. Forensic accounting involves reconstructing financial transactions, following money trails, and quantifying the financial impact of insider threats on the organization.

• Employee Monitoring: Digital forensics plays a role in monitoring employee activities and detecting insider threats through employee monitoring solutions. Digital forensics experts deploy monitoring tools to capture user keystrokes, screen captures, and application usage data to identify suspicious behavior by insiders. Employee monitoring involves analysing user activity logs, web browsing history, and productivity metrics to detect policy violations, data breaches, and insider misconduct.

Denial-of-Service (DoS) Attacks

Detecting and investigating denial of service (DoS) attacks involves digital forensics techniques to identify the source of the attack, gather evidence, and mitigate its impact.

Examples of how digital forensics is utilized in such cases are as follows:

• Traffic Analysis: Digital forensics experts analyse network traffic to identify patterns and anomalies indicative of a DoS attack. They examine packet headers, traffic volumes, and communication patterns to detect excessive traffic originating from single or multiple sources. Traffic analysis helps forensic investigators identify the type of DoS attack (*e.g.*, volumetric, protocol, application layer) and determine its impact on network performance.

• Packet Capture and Analysis: Forensic analysts capture network packets using packet sniffing tools or intrusion detection systems (IDS) to capture evidence of a DoS attack in real time. They analyse packet headers and payloads to identify attack signatures, such as SYN floods, UDP floods, and HTTP GET floods. Packet analysis involves reconstructing attack packets, identifying attack vectors, and tracing the origin of malicious traffic.

• IP Address Attribution: Digital forensics teams trace the source of the DoS attack by analysing IP addresses associated with malicious traffic. They use IP geolocation databases, WHOIS records, and Internet routing tables to identify the geographical location and ownership of attacking IP addresses. IP address attribution helps forensic investigators identify the responsible parties and take appropriate legal or administrative actions.

• Forensic Logging: Digital forensics experts enable detailed logging on network devices, servers, and firewalls to capture forensic evidence of DoS attacks. They analyse log entries for anomalies, such as failed login attempts, connection timeouts, and resource exhaustion events. Forensic logging helps reconstruct the timeline of the attack, identify compromised systems, and correlate attack patterns across multiple devices.

• Botnet Analysis: In cases where DoS attacks are launched by botnets, digital forensics teams conduct botnet analysis to identify infected devices and disrupt botnet operations. They analyse command-and-control (C2) communications, malware payloads, and botnet infrastructure to identify botnet controllers and compromised endpoints. Botnet analysis involves reverse engineering malware, sink-holing botnet domains, and collaborating with internet service providers (ISPs) to block malicious traffic.

• Cloud Forensics: With the increasing use of cloud-based services for launching DoS attacks, digital forensics extends to cloud environments. Forensic experts analyse cloud logs, virtual machine instances, and network traffic within cloud platforms to identify evidence of DoS attacks. Cloud forensics involves collecting digital evidence from cloud service providers, preserving data integrity, and coordinating with law enforcement agencies to investigate cross-border attacks.

• Incident Response: Digital forensics plays a critical role in incident response efforts during and after a DoS attack. Forensic analysts triage affected systems, isolate compromised devices, and restore services to mitigate the impact of the attack. Incident response involves preserving digital evidence, documenting the attack timeline, and conducting post-incident analysis to identify vulnerabilities and enhance cyber defences.

As technology evolves, so do the methods used by criminals. Digital forensics will continue to be a vital tool in solving these crimes and ensuring a safer digital space.

CONCLUSION

This chapter defined Digital Forensics' goal in relation to other well-established forensic disciplines, gave a brief history of the field's evolution, and described the nature of forensics. To emphasize the issue, use cases of digital forensic crime are presented describing the role of digital forensic investigators, the knowledge and expertise needed, and the difficulties they encounter. The chapter included a succinct overview of the difficulties the field faces as well as some suggestions for how to better handle them with the help of improved forensic procedures and recently developed technologies. In the end, the chapter tried to provide some fundamental concepts that you may find helpful and enlightening if you are thinking about becoming a practitioner.

REFERENCES

[1] Interpol, "Digital forensics," www.interpol.int, 2022. Available from: https://www.interpol.int/en/How-we-work/Innovation/Digital-forensics (accessed January 16, 2024).

[2] "Module 03: Preserving Evidence," projects.nfstc.org. Available from: https://projects.nfstc.org/property_crimes/module03/pro_m03_t18.htm (accessed February 16, 2024).

[3] A. Badiye, N. Kapoor, and R. G. Menezes, "Chain of Custody (Chain of Evidence)," PubMed, Feb. 13, 2023. Available from: https://www.ncbi.nlm.nih.gov/books/NBK551677/ (accessed February 25, 2024).

[4] "The Importance of Volatile Data Capture in Digital Forensics," www.linkedin.com. Available from: https://www.linkedin.com/pulse/importance-volatile-data-capture-digital-forensics-jeffcoat-cissp (accessed February 07, 2024).

[5] EC-Council, "How to Handle Data Acquisition in Digital Forensics," Cybersecurity Exchange, Mar. 11, 2022. Available from: https://www.eccouncil.org/cybersecurity-exchange/computer-forensics/da-a-acquisition-digital-forensics/ (accessed January 16, 2024).

[6] Bluevoyant, "Understanding Digital Forensics: Process, Techniques & Tools," BlueVoyant, 2023. Available from: https://www.bluevoyant.com/knowledge-center/understanding-digital-forens-cs-process-techniques-and-tools (accessed February 07, 2024).

[7] "Forensics - Detecting steganography in images," Information Security Stack Exchange. Available from: https://security.stackexchange.com/questions/2144/detecting-steganography-in-images (accessed January 07, 2024).

[8] "What is Malware Analysis? Types and Stages of Malware Analysis," Fortinet. Available from: https://www.fortinet.com/resources/cyberglossary/malware-analysis (accessed February 25, 2024).

[9] MailXaminer, "Timeline Analysis In Digital Forensics Investigation & Link Analysis Feature," Official Blog of E-mail Examiner Software, May 03, 2020. Available from: https://www.mailxaminer.com/blog/link-analysis-timeline-analysis-in-digital-forensic/ (accessed January 07, 2024).

[10] KMBH, "What is Network Forensics?" GeeksforGeeks, 2022. Available from: https://www.geeksforgeeks.org/what-is-network-forensics/ (accessed February 25, 2024).

[11] "Computer Forensic Report Writing and Presentation | Infosec," www.infosecinstitute.com. Available from: https://www.infosecinstitute.com/resources/digital-forensics/computer-forensic-report-wri-ing-presentation/ (accessed February 16, 2024).

[12] "Court Cases | Roanoke County, VA - Official Website," www.roanokecountyva.gov. Available from:

https://www.roanokecountyva.gov/447/Search-Court-Cases-Online (accessed February 25, 2024).

[13] "Prime Video: CSI: Crime Scene Investigation Season 1," www.primevideo.com. Available from: https://www.primevideo.com/detail/0J7D33P8FP460FO9511OC5CYOY/ref=atv_dp_season_select_s1 (accessed February 07, 2024).

[14] "Nation State Hackers Case Study: Bangladesh Bank Heist – cyber.uk," cyber.uk. Available from: https://cyber.uk/areas-of-cyber-security/cyber-security-threat-groups-2/nation-state-hackers-case-study-bangladesh-bank-heist/

[15] I. Miyashiro, "Case study: Equifax Data Breach," Seven Pillars Institute, Apr. 30, 2021. Available from: https://sevenpillarsinstitute.org/case-study-equifax-data-breach/

[16] K. Young, "Cyber Case Study: Sony Pictures Entertainment Hack," CoverLink Insurance - Ohio Insurance Agency, Nov. 08, 2021. Available from: https://coverlink.com/case-study/sony-pictures-entertainment-hack/

CHAPTER 2

Constructing A Robust Digital Forensics Environment

Abstract: Establishing a Digital Forensic laboratory is paramount in modern investigative practices. This chapter delineates the essential components and procedures necessary for setting up an effective Digital Forensic lab. It covers various aspects, including infrastructure requirements, hardware, and software provisioning, as well as the implementation of standardized procedures and protocols. Additionally, it discusses the significance of maintaining the integrity and security of Digital evidence throughout the Forensic process. By offering practical insights and recommendations, this chapter aims to empower Forensic practitioners with the knowledge and resources required to establish a robust Forensic laboratory capable of addressing the complex challenges of Digital investigations in today's Digital landscape.

Keywords: Digital forensic laboratory, Digital evidence integrity, Forensic investigation, Forensic environment, Infrastructure requirements, Standardized procedures, Technological advancements.

INTRODUCTION

The need for computer forensics labs [1] to gather and analyse digital evidence accurately is growing due to the rise in cybercrime assaults that affect both the public and private sectors. You might believe that only law enforcement organizations have access to digital forensics labs. This is untrue, though, as Fig. (**1**) shows that numerous American corporations keep state-of-the-art Digital Forensics labs equipped with cutting-edge investigative tools. Although digital forensics labs were first established by law enforcement and security services, most common crimes nowadays are linked to some form of digital evidence due to advancements in computing technology [2] and the increasing usage of smartphones and wearables.

This puts a strain on police labs by creating lengthy waiting lists for digital evidence from several court cases that need to be investigated. These waiting lists can occasionally go on for months or even years. This has prompted big and even medium-sized businesses to establish internal labs to investigate cybercrime concerns pertaining to their assets and work. These days, to expedite the investi-

Akashdeep Bhardwaj, Pradeep Singh & Ajay Prasad

gation process [4] and lower the numerous expenses related to digital investigations, banks, IT corporations, merchants (like Amazon and Walmart), and energy providers use their own Digital Forensics labs. Private companies have greater leeway when it comes to obtaining the newest hardware and software including upgrades necessary to outfit their labs than do police departments.

Fig. (1). Digital forensics lab [3].

However, due to financial constraints and a shortage of qualified personnel, some police laboratories can still be using outdated software versions. To resolve matters pertaining to their companies, in-house digital forensics experts typically collaborate closely with law enforcement organizations. For example, if someone witnesses or finds evidence of illegal activity (such as breaking company policy, industrial sabotage, leaking secrets, or other related crimes), the e-discovery team or the Digital Forensic investigators of the reporting company will get in touch with law enforcement and collaborate with them to gather and evaluate the evidence, as well as to take the case to court.

Any business that values its data assets should invest in an internal Digital Forensics lab [5], but this has costs associated with it. For example, even the smallest lab will require an annual budget of at least $150,000 if only one forensic analyst is recruited, and one forensic workstation is equipped with the primary tools required to perform the job (both hardware and software). If there are not many incidences, small businesses might not be willing to pay for this additional expense. To cut expenses, a lot of small and medium-sized businesses contract out their Digital Forensics work to a recognized third-party lab.

Whether you intend to construct an in-house lab for your company or think about outsourcing your Digital Forensics work to a third-party supplier, accreditation of the Digital Forensics lab is an important consideration. A Forensic laboratory's accreditation guarantees that it adheres to the authoritative body's specified requirements for the use of dependable procedures, suitable hardware and software, and qualified staff in carrying out its responsibilities. Digital forensics labs can vary widely in size. While funding is undoubtedly important, the anticipated duties (or work scope) for this lab will serve as the primary guide in identifying the hardware and software tools required. Big businesses are spending, for example, in setting up state-of-the-art labs that can handle any kind of computer device and cases, including malware, network, GPS, and mobile forensics.

These labs are staffed by highly skilled individuals and equipped with a variety of specialized hardware tools as well as the most recent versions of forensic software. The bare minimum of equipment is required to gather, store, process, and display digital evidence in a forensically sound manner, regardless of the size of your forensics lab. The most common type is a small digital forensics lab because it can start up fast and just requires a little budget. These labs are often managed by one to five individuals and concentrate on managing a specific kind of device (e.g., Windows OS Forensic, or mobile Forensic). It does not require the expensive equipment that large labs require for networking and security, but it still needs the right digital forensic software to analyse evidence, along with necessary hardware like cables, a hardware write blocker (some of which are built into the forensic workstation itself), other electrical devices like digital cameras and UPS, and a dedicated forensic computer to perform the analysis.

LAB FACILITY

It is crucial to talk about the physical space requirements of the Digital Forensics lab before enumerating the hardware and software equipment required for the Forensic lab. Ensuring the safety and soundness of digital evidence, along with the technology in the lab, should be of utmost importance. This is because hackers may attack these labs to halt or disrupt investigations. When examining digital evidence, forensic examiners will spend hours at their workstations; therefore, to stay productive, they need to be comfortable in their seats. For forensic workstations, employ ergonomic seats that can be adjusted to the user's demands. Computer screens should also be of high quality because examiners will be staring at them for extended periods of time. To prevent potential health impacts on the examiner, such as neck and head pain, excessive weariness, and eye strain, as shown in Fig. (**2**), the computer monitor must be positioned so that it faces the examiner's head at least 20 inches away and the top line of the screen is at or below eye level.

Fig. (2). Digital forensics lab setup [6].

The basic lab requirements are listed below.

Physical Requirements

- Must be secure and have one entrance door with a physical lock.
- The lab should ideally be windowless.
- It needs to be soundproof so that no one can listen in on talks taking place within. • Soundproofing materials for the walls, ceiling, and floor as well as carpeting the floor can help achieve this.
- A biometric system and alarm system at the entry are required for lab access control. Every visit to the lab must be recorded by the access biometric system, and for auditing purposes, this log needs to be kept in backup form for several years.
- All areas of the lab, particularly the digital evidence room and main entrance, should be covered by surveillance cameras including the evidence storage area.

Environment Control

Strict controls must be implemented in the lab to prevent damage to digital devices that have been confiscated and forensic equipment. The following requirements for environmental controls must be met:

- System of air cooling to absorb the heat produced by workstations. This is crucial because, especially in cramped areas, forensic workstations might run continuously for several days while analysing evidence (such as by cracking a password), which generates heat.
- The lab needs to be spotless and well-organized. It needs to have a temperature that is pleasant, low humidity, and clean air.
- Good illumination in every room of the lab, including the forensic workstations.
- Equipment for organizing electricity to prevent unexpected power outages, as well as UPS units for the entire lab, with a focus on the forensic workstations, storage server, and security cameras.

LAB EQUIPMENT

The following lab equipment is required as illustrated in Fig. (**3**), these are grouped into three categories as related to systems, tools, electrical, and networking.

Fig. (3). Hardware equipment lab setup.

System Equipment

- Licensing server for software apps and suites.
- Storage server set up to accept standard detachable hard drives, which are used to store digital evidence photographs along with data that has been processed and retrieved from them. This server is not allowed to be connected to the Internet at all.
- Portable laptop for forensics, which is utilized for gathering evidence and conducting analysis outside of a lab.
- Dedicated computer or computers for intranet and/or internet connectivity.
- Administrative PC for handling logs and other matters.
- Throughout the acquisition procedure, there was a hardware write blocker to the data on the evidence drive.
- Other equipment: Compact disc/DVD drive, USB reader, USB 3.0 interfaced container for SSD and HDD, Reader for SD cards, USB thumb drives (USB 2.0 and USB 3.0), external hard drives in various capacities, and Tape drives for the long-term preservation of data.

Electrical - Tools Equipment

- Uninterruptible power supply (UPS) for every networking device and workstation/server.
- Projector (in the meeting space).
- Printer, Scanner, Copier, and Paper Shredder.
- Digital and Video cameras
- Phone, ideally wireless.
- WiFi hotspot.
- Screwdrivers, multi-meter
- Flashlight

Network Devices

- Internet access should be kept apart from the lab's internal network.
- Router and switch link the forensic workstations to the lab's storage server.
- Networking cables.

Forensic Workstation

For the forensic workstations, the most recent 64-bit version of Windows OS is advised. Because Windows 10 Pro and Enterprise editions handle high-end hardware and demanding computing activities, they are recommended. Although those two editions are part of the Windows desktop product line, they are less expensive in terms of licensing when compared to more recent Windows Server editions (Windows Server 2016 Standard edition enables 24 TB of RAM memory). Both editions support up to 6 TB of RAM and four processors.

A powerful computer is required to process and search image files when working with digital evidence. In addition to having a lot of RAM memory and processing power, forensic computers also need a lot of storage and expansion slots to connect many kinds of devices. Although creating a forensic workstation from scratch is more expensive than buying a pre-built computer forensic workstation, building one is still thought to be a more cost-effective option for small businesses. Table **1** lists the suggested hardware requirements for constructing a fundamental forensic workstation from the ground up.

Table 1. Basic forensic workstation specifications.

CPU	Two Intel i9 8th-Generation processor, IO-cores and 20-threads)
Memory	At least 24 GB (DDR4)
Motherboard	Accommodate required processors and RAM, and video controller card.
Hard drives	Combination ofSSD and HDD, at least 512 GB ofSSD and 4 TB ofHDD
Video controller	Nvidia Geforce, latest version is recommended with at least 8 GB of GDDR5X memory
Triple burner	Blu-ray, DVD, CD
External drive	Disk enclosure with USB 3.0 interface
Cooling system	Prefer to use liquid CPU cooling system with dual fans
Display	LCD panel with high resolution (full HD IPS display), at least 22 inches for better display
Ports	USB 3.0 ports, Thunderbolt 3, Microphone, and headphone jack. Integrated LAN controller to access the lab's LAN network

In addition to furniture, the Digital Forensic lab needs the following general office supplies for administrative work: The items include pencils paper, pens, envelope sealers, staplers, labels, folders, suspension files, sheet protectors, binders, punches, clipboards and files, plastic static bags, and notice boards accessories, non-electronic whiteboards, and packaging materials like cardboard boxes. These are some of the recommended hardware components for constructing a forensic workstation; however, bear in mind that, to gather and analyse data outside of the lab, your lab must have at least one portable digital forensic laptop workstation. For example, it is better to get a single Forensic laptop from a supplier that specializes in providing such pre-made systems.

COMMERCIAL WORKSTATIONS

Several vendors specialize in creating pre-built forensic workstations; these workstations typically feature integrated hardware for digital forensics, such as a hard drive duplicator and a hardware write blocker, and are strong in terms of computing power and storage. The companies that sell pre-built workstations include the ones listed below.

Momentum T1000 Digital Forensic Workstation

With the forensics investigator in mind, the Momentum T1000 Digital Forensics Workstation [7] boasts top-tier desktop CPUs and motherboards that have won awards. The high-performance Momentum Digital Forensics Workstations are constructed with specifically developed casings that lower noise levels and maintain system cooling. They are geared to suit the demanding digital forensics situations of today.

Tableau T35689iu or WiebeTECH LabDock Forensics Bridges are fitted into Momentum T1000 Digital Forensics Workstations. The investigator can anticipate shorter data processing times and higher system uptime with this arrangement. The Momentum T1000 has built-in 12 TB of RAID 5 long-term storage, unlike other workstations [8]. The industry standard forensics write-blocking bridge is Tableau T35689iu. IDE, SATA, SAS, USB 3.0, and FireWire 400/800 are supported. All requirements [9] for write-blocking bridges are satisfied by WiebeTECH Forensics LabDock. FireWire, eSATA, USB, and IDE are all supported.

FRED Forensic Workstation

The FRED (Forensic Recovery of Evidence Device) [10] was developed specifically for use in eDiscovery and digital forensics. FREDs are extremely versatile and integrated devices that come equipped with the processing and storage capacity required to execute contemporary industry-standard software programs as displayed in Fig. (**4**).

FRED workstation has integrated design and cutting-edge technology to meet modern software demands with ease. Some of the main features include:

- Exclusive Advantages: FRED systems boast unique features like the Digital Intelligence UltraBay 4d Write Blocker and Ventilated Imaging Shelf, enhancing their capabilities beyond the ordinary.
- Essential Tools: FRED systems come with vital tools bootable Blu-ray restore media, Symantec Ghost software, Tableau Imager (TIM), and diverse drive adapters for efficient forensic operations.
- PCIe SSD Adaptability: FRED's PCIe SSD drive adapters cater to various SSD types, increasing system versatility.

- Practical Accessories: Wireless keyboard, mouse combo, and a security screwdriver set with assorted bits simplify operations.
- FRED purchases include a Digital Forensics with FRED class for optimal usage.

Fig. (4). Momentum T1000 & FRED forensics workstations.

CONCLUSION

Setting up a Digital Forensic lab requires careful planning, close attention to detail, and following industry best practices. This chapter has given a thorough review of all the important elements and factors to consider when establishing an effective Forensic environment. Every element, from software deployment and procedural standardization to hardware purchase and infrastructure design, adds to the effectiveness and dependability of Digital Forensic investigations. Furthermore, preserving the validity and admissibility of Forensic results in legal processes depends critically on the integrity and security of Digital evidence.

Forensic experts can create a robust Digital Forensic laboratory that can handle a wide variety of Digital evidence and investigative scenarios by adhering to the standards provided in this chapter. Furthermore, in the field of Digital Forensics, continuing education and development are crucial for keeping up with growing dangers and technical developments. In the end, having a strong Forensic laboratory not only makes it easier to pursue justice but also emphasizes how crucial it is to maintain the accuracy and dependability of Digital evidence in the legal system.

REFERENCES

[1] "Atlantic Council's Digital Forensic Research Lab," Atlantic Council. Available from: https://www.atlanticcouncil.org/programs/digital-forensic-research-lab/

[2] A. Bhardwaj, F. Al-Turjman, M. Kumar, T. Stephan, and L. Mostarda, "Capturing-the-Invisible (CTI): Behavior-Based Attacks Recognition in IoT-Oriented Industrial Control Systems", *IEEE Access,* vol. 8, pp. 104956-104966, 2020. [http://dx.doi.org/10.1109/ACCESS.2020.2998983]

[3] "Digital Forensic Lab | Computer Forensics Lab | SalvationDATA." Available from: https://www.salvationdata.com/business-list-page/digital-forensic-lab/

[4] A. Bhardwaj, F. Al-Turjman, V. Sapra, M. Kumar, and T. Stephan, "Privacy-aware detection framework to mitigate new-age phishing attacks", *Comput. Electr. Eng.,* vol. 96, p. 107546, 2021. [http://dx.doi.org/10.1016/j.compeleceng.2021.107546]

[5] A. Bhardwaj, V. Avasthi, and S. Goundar, "Cyber security attacks on robotic platforms", *Netw. Secur.,* vol. 2019, no. 10, pp. 13-19, 2019. [http://dx.doi.org/10.1016/S1353-4858(19)30122-9]

[6] "Momentum T1000 Digital Forensic Workstation," Tri Tech Forensics. Available from: https://tritechforensics.com/df-t1000-t-Momentum-t1000-digital-forensic-workstation

[7] "Secure, Save and Analyse data with the FRED Workstation - DataExpert EN," www.dataexpert.eu. Available from: https://www.dataexpert.eu/products/forensic-hardware-digital-intelligence/f-ed-workstation/

[8] A. Bhardwaj, S. Bharany, A. Almogren, A. Ur Rehman, and H. Hamam, "Proactive threat hunting to detect persistent behaviour-based advanced adversaries", *Egyptian Informatics Journal,* vol. 27, p. 100510, 2024. [http://dx.doi.org/10.1016/j.eij.2024.100510]

[9] K. Kaushik, A. Bhardwaj, M. Kumar, S. K. Gupta, and A. Gupta, "A novel machine learning□based framework for detecting fake Instagram profiles", *Concurrency and Computation: Practice and Experience,* vol. 34, no. 28, p. e7349, 2022. [http://dx.doi.org/10.1002/cpe.7349]

[10] Digital Intelligence," digitalintelligence.com. Available from: https://digitalintelligence.com/products/fred

CHAPTER 3

Acquisition of Live Analysis and Volatile Data

Abstract: The process of conducting a proactive Forensic investigation begins with data acquisition. The process of obtaining Forensic data involves more than just moving files from one device to another. To generate a Forensic duplicate of the data, investigators use Forensic data acquisition to try and retrieve every bit of information from the victim system's memory and storage. Furthermore, the creation of this Forensic duplicate needs to ensure that the data's verifiable integrity is maintained and that it can potentially be used as evidence in court. The basic ideas of data acquisition are covered in this chapter, along with the several processes that make up the data acquisition methodology.

Keywords: Acquisition methodology, Data acquisition, Evidence integrity, Live analysis, Volatile data.

INTRODUCTION

Basics of Data Acquisition

The first stage in conducting the Forensic investigation on a potential evidence source is to duplicate the data from any digital storage device, such as a Solid-State Drive (SSD), Hard Disk Drive (HDD), Flash Drive, or SD Card that is discovered at the crime scene. It is up to Forensic investigators to decide whether to move the device to a secure location beforehand or complete the data-acquiring procedure on the spot. This chapter elaborates on live and dead acquisition and covers basic principles in data acquisition. The chapter objectives include:

- Understanding the basics of data acquisition
- Understanding various types of data acquisition
- Understanding the format of data acquisition
- Understanding the data acquisition methodology
- Perform the data acquisition on volatile data using FTK imager
- Perform analysis on live data acquisition using volatility framework
- Perform the static data acquisition using FTK imager.

Akashdeep Bhardwaj, Pradeep Singh & Ajay Prasad

The process of collecting and recovering sensitive data from a suspect computer and developing procedures to retrieve electronically stored information to obtain information about a crime or incident is known as data acquisition. The methods involved in acquiring data and presenting it to the law are the two most crucial aspects of Forensic work, and when these processes are completed, we will be able to comprehend the full chain of custody involved in this procedure. We will either work with a live system or an image of the system when doing Forensics. It is advised practice to image the system or create a copy of the necessary data and run Forensics on it to ensure accuracy. The entire procedure should be auditable and admissible in court, and the investigator must be able to confirm the accuracy of the data they have obtained. Finding the likely source of the evidence is the first and most important stage.

Time is an essential component to consider when gathering Forensic data. While information in certain sources, such as hard drives, remains intact and retrievable long after the system is shut down, data in some sources such as RAM are highly volatile and very rapidly changing and must therefore be collected in real-time. In accordance with this perspective, there are two types of data acquisition: live data acquisition and dead data acquisition.

Extraction of digital evidence from a computer system that is powered on is the technique known as live data acquisition. In Digital Forensics and incident response, it is an essential approach that lets investigators take a picture of a system in action. This makes it possible to get erratic data that is brittle and disappears when the system is turned off or loses power. These kinds of data are kept in RAM, caches, and registries. Volatile data is transient and vanishes when the system is terminated. Investigators can examine this data using live acquisition to look for indications of ongoing illicit activity, malware infestations, or hidden activities. Furthermore, real-time gathering of information is necessary because volatile data, like that in RAM, is dynamic and changes frequently. Nonvolatile data that stays in the system even after shutdown is gathered in dead or static data acquisition. In Digital Forensics, dead acquisition, often referred to as offline acquisition, is the recommended technique for gathering data from storage devices. Data collection is done from a device that is not powered on or from a storage device that is disconnected from the main system. Investigators can recover such data from Hard Disk Drive (HDD) as well as from slack space, swap files, and unallocated drive space. Additional non-volatile data sources are Solid State Drives (SSDs), Optical Discs (CDs, DVDs, Blu-ray Discs), Non-volatile Memory (NVM), PDAs, CD-ROMs, USB thumb drives, and cellphones.

ORDER OF VOLATILITY

The method by which Digital data is gathered for a Forensic investigation is known as the order of volatility. Since this kind of data vanishes the moment, the system is turned off, it gives priority to capturing the most volatile data first. Investigators must consider both the impact of data collection on the suspect system and the data's possible volatility when gathering live data. Since not all data are equally volatile, investigators must gather the most volatile data first before moving on to the least volatile data. An investigator must assess the data volatility order based on the circumstances and the suspected machine when gathering evidence. The order of volatility for a typical system is illustrated in Fig. (**1**).

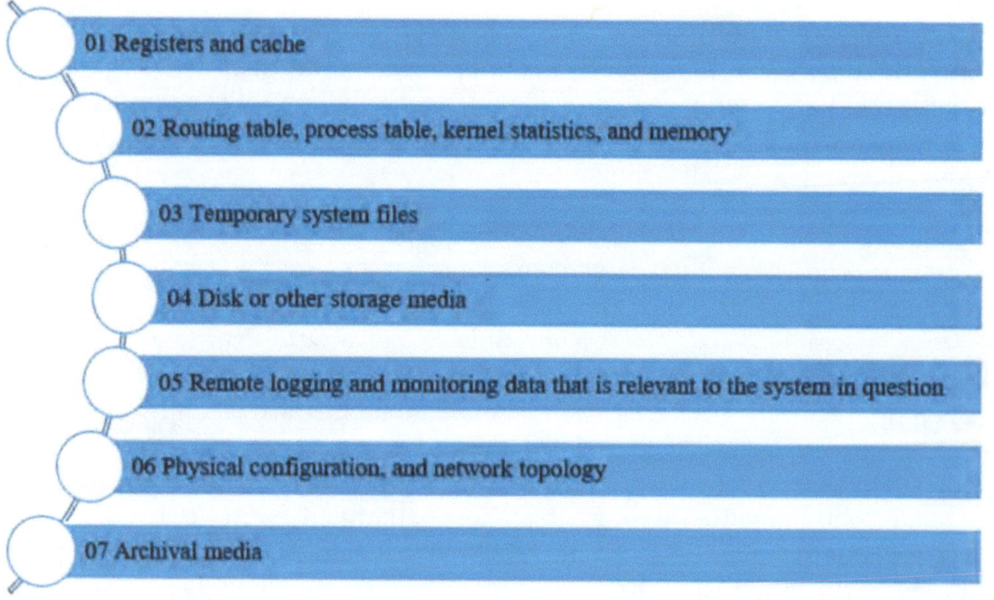

01 Registers and cache
02 Routing table, process table, kernel statistics, and memory
03 Temporary system files
04 Disk or other storage media
05 Remote logging and monitoring data that is relevant to the system in question
06 Physical configuration, and network topology
07 Archival media

Fig. (1). Order of volatility.

According to RFC 3227 [1] Guidelines for Evidence Collection and Archiving, the sequence of volatility for a typical computing system is as follows:

- **Registers, processor cache:** These are areas of the central processing unit (CPU) where data that is presently being processed is temporarily stored. When the system loses power, this data vanishes. The computer's registers and processor cache hold information that is only there for a limited amount of time. It is categorized as the most volatile data since it is ever-changing.

- **Routing table, process table, kernel statistics, and memory:** The computer's conventional memory houses the kernel statistics, ARP cache, and routing table. With a lifespan of roughly ten nanoseconds, these are marginally less volatile than the data in the registers. While the ARP cache keeps track of associations between IP addresses and MAC addresses (physical addresses) of networked devices, the routing table contains information about network paths for data transmission. The contents of these two temporary caches are erased when the system restarts. Programs and data are loaded into here, the computer's primary working memory, for immediate use. When the machine is turned off, all the data stored in RAM is lost.
- **Temporary system files:** Compared to routing tables and ARP caches, temporary system files typically remain on the computer for a longer period. These systems are eventually modified or overwritten, often within minutes or even seconds. Applications create temporary files while they are running, which can include configuration settings or transient data. When RAM fills up, swap files—hidden system files—are used as virtual memory. Even though these data are not immediately recorded during live acquisition, Forensic investigations may find that examining these files after acquisition is essential.
- **Disk or other storage media:** Everything kept on a disk remains there for a time. However, these data can sometimes be overwritten or deleted as a result of unanticipated circumstances. As a result, disk data, which has a few minutes lifespan, may likewise be regarded as fairly volatile. The physical storage device (hard disk, SSD) where data is kept permanently is referred to here. Deleted data, however, might not be completely erased and might still be retrievable from unallocated disk space.
- **Remote logging and monitoring data related to the target system:** Logs are produced by a router or switch when data flows across it. These logs may be kept elsewhere by the system. In an hour, a day, or a week, these logs might overwrite themselves. Still, these are typically fewer erratic statistics.
- **Physical configuration and network topology:** Provides details regarding the network configuration and the physical arrangement of the hardware components. Compared to certain other logs, the physical configuration and network topology exhibit lower volatility and a longer lifespan.
- **Archival media:** Data backups or archives kept on other media, such as external drives or cassettes. The least volatile data is found on a DVD-ROM, CD-ROM, or tape since Digital data in these types of data sources does not automatically alter until it is physically damaged.

Rules of Thumb for Data Acquisition

A rule of thumb is a best practice that, when followed, helps ensure a positive result. In Digital Forensics investigations, higher evidence quality often provides better analytical results and increases the possibility of solving the crime. Maintaining the authenticity and integrity of the evidence is essential to the data collecting process in Digital Forensics. The device's state or its data should never be altered by any actions taken during acquisition. This ensures that the data gathered accurately represents the evidence now of the seizure. Just as you would not tamper with tangible evidence at a crime scene, Digital Forensics follows the same rules. The original evidence or source of the evidence should never be the subject of a Forensic investigation or other procedure by investigators since this could change the data and make the evidence inadmissible in court. Alternatively, to view and examine the static data, investigators can make a duplicate bit-stream image of a device or file that appears suspect. This procedure not only protects the original evidence but also gives room for error-free replication in the event of a problem as illustrated in Fig. (**2**). Before beginning the investigative procedure, two copies of the original media must be generated - first copy serves as the analysis's working copy and if the working copy is corrupted, the second copy the library/control copy is kept for disclosure reasons.

Don't work with the original Digital evidence. ToA begin working on a dubious disk or file, create a bit stream or logical image.

Make two or more copies of the source material.

- **First is the draft copy that will be examined further.**
- **In the case that the working copy becomes corrupt, the other copies serve as the library/control copies that are kept for disclosure purposes.**

Store the duplicates on clean media.

Check the integrity of copies made after creating original media with the original.

Fig. (2). Rules for gathering and analyzing data.

TYPES OF DATA ACQUISITION

The goal of data acquisition in Digital Forensics is to obtain Digital evidence from devices while maintaining its integrity for future legal challenges. Even while it would seem optimal, obtaining a bit-by-bit copy of all the evidence in a system could take a long time for big drives. Based on the condition of the devices under investigation, there are two types of acquisition - Logical and Sparse.

- **Logical Acquisition**

Logical acquisition could be the best option if there are time limits, and the investigator knows which files must be obtained. Only the files necessary for the case investigation are gathered through logical acquisition. In Forensics, especially mobile Forensics, logical acquisition is a specialized method for obtaining data from a device. The goal of logical acquisition is to obtain data that is easily obtainable, such as files and directories that are visible to the user. It makes a copy of these "logical" items from the storage space on the device. Logical acquisition uses the file system and operating system of the device, as compared to physical acquisition, which generates an entire image of the storage. To access and duplicate the data, this typically entails connecting the device to a computer and utilizing software. When accessibility and speed are critical, logical acquisition is the way to go. User data like message histories, call logs, contacts, surfing histories, and documents can be retrieved with its help. Examples include retrieving specific records from a massive RAID server and gathering Outlook.pst or.ost files for email queries.

- **Sparse Acquisition**

Sparse acquisition is a method used in Digital Forensics to gather only particular parts of Digital media, as opposed to making an entire duplicate. The primary objective is to obtain pertinent information with the least amount of time spent on gathering and storage. Logical acquisition and sparse acquisition are similar. Investigators can gather pieces of unallocated (deleted) data using this technique. When a complete drive inspection is not required, this procedure can be helpful. It snatches targeted information. Sparse acquisition targets particular files or directories according to the demands of the investigation, as compared to a full image where everything is copied. While gathering erroneous data fragments additionally, it might be able to recover deleted data pieces that might be hiding in the storage device's unallocated space. This can be very important for finding evidence that was previously believed to be lost. Strategic use of sparse acquisition can be a useful tool in digital forensics. Investigators can use it to efficiently gather pertinent evidence while maximizing time and storage resources by being aware of its advantages and disadvantages.

We next explore the types of data acquisition including the data sources used. The categories of data acquisition are:

LIVE ACQUISITION

The depths of live data acquisition are beyond the ordinary copying of your personal data. It is a Forensics method for retrieving evidence from a computer system that is powered on. Collecting erratic data from an active system is known as live data acquisition. Volatile data helps identify potential suspects and the logical sequence of events leading up to the security incident. It involves collecting information from a powered-on system. The versatility of live acquisition to capture erratic data is its primary benefit. This data is only present in the system's memory when it is operating. Volatile data is dynamic and likely lost if the device under investigation is turned off. It can be found in RAM, cache, DLLs, running programs and applications, open network connections, logged-in user information and system memory contents.

After completing the live acquisition, the investigator can proceed to the static or dead acquisition, in which they turn off the suspect computer, take out the hard drive, and take a Forensic image of it. To reduce the possibility of changing evidence on the live system, live acquisition uses specialist software tools. Usually, these tools use one of two basic strategies.

- **Memory acquisition** is the process of recording what is stored in the system's random-access memory. While the system is operating, the utility makes a Forensic copy of the memory, protecting the volatile data for further examination.
- **Logical Acquisition.** This technique gathers data from the live system's installed storage devices. It can be helpful in getting copies of files, system configurations, and other evidence that may be relevant to the inquiry, even though it would not capture volatile data.

Investigators are still able to collect information through live data capture even if the material that holds evidentiary value is kept on the cloud with services like Dropbox or Google Drive. Additionally, data from open, unencrypted drives or containers on the system that are automatically encrypted upon system shutdown can be obtained by investigators. Investigators may be able to discover evidence of attempted data overwriting if the suspect tried to hide information by erasing portions of the actual hard drive by looking through the contents of the RAM. For incident response and Digital Forensics, live data acquisition is an invaluable tool. On the other hand, it calls for specific knowledge, equipment, and awareness of the hazards that could be present. According to where it comes from, volatile data falls into two primary categories: system data and network data. These are some instances and a thorough description of each category. Volatile data can be divided as follows.

- **System Data**

Information that is generated and used dynamically by the operating system and programs that are running is referred to as system data. While essential to the system's current functioning, this RAM-based data is lost upon computer shutdown. The data pertaining to a system that can be used as proof in a security event is called system information. The running state and current configuration of the suspect computer are included in this data. System profile (configuration details), login history, the date and time of the system, command history, the amount of uptime the system is now experiencing, running processes, open files, startup files, clipboard data, users that are logged in, DLLs, and shared libraries are examples of volatile system information. Additionally, vital data kept in the hard drive's slack spaces is included in the system information. Typical system data types and their functions are presented in Table **1**.

Table 1. System data type and functions.

System Data Type	Functions
Running processes	Every program in use has a corresponding process that runs in memory. This data contains details such as Process ID (PID), process name, memory usage, open files, and priority.
System Configuration	RAM holds temporary configurations and settings that the operating system uses. This data includes Kernel data structures, device drivers, and environment variables.
Data from User Sessions	RAM holds data on the user who is currently logged in and their activity. Example - Details of the user account, open applications, and contents of the clipboard.
Cache	Caches are used by the operating system and many programs to store frequently requested data for quicker retrieval. Caches contain details such as system file cache, application cache, and web browser cache.
Current system uptime	You may find out how long the computer system has been operating since its last reboot by looking up the current system uptime element in system data. Measurement Unit: Days, hours, minutes, and seconds are the most frequent time units to indicate uptime.
Date and Time	The date and time acquired from system data during live data gathering for Forensics provide various important elements that help with the investigation. Details such as timestamps for system events, system boot time, and time synchronization are crucial for the investigation.

• Network Data

Network information is the data associated with the network that is kept on linked network devices and the suspect system. Open connections and ports, routing configuration and data, shared files, ARP cache, and services accessed are examples of volatile network data. Network data includes transitory information on the computer's network connections and activity. While necessary for continuous network connectivity, this data is lost when the system is shut down. The data gathered from the network is presented in Table **2**.

Table 2. Network Data and Functions.

Network Data type	Functions
Connection Information	Information regarding active network connections, such as IP addresses, port numbers, and protocol information.
Routing Tables	Temporary data that the operating system uses to choose the optimal route for forwarding network packets.
ARP Cache	A temporary database containing the mapping between network device MAC (physical addresses) and IP addresses.
DNS Cache	A temporary database that contains recently converted domain names to IP addresses to expedite further DNS lookups.
Network Buffers	Temporary repositories where network traffic is kept pending processing or transmission before it is sent out again.

DEAD ACQUISITION

Nonvolatile data, or 'static data', is information that remains unchanged long after the system has been shut down. Static acquisition, another name for dead acquisition, is a Digital Forensics technique that gathers data from a storage device while the computer system is off. Its primary objective is to record non-volatile data that endures beyond system shutdown. It entails gathering information from a system that is powered off. Data from storage devices including hard drives, DVD-ROMs, USB drives, flashcards, and smartphones are frequently acquired through dead acquisition. One useful weapon in the toolbox of a Digital Forensics investigator is dead acquisition. Although it is unable to capture volatile data, it provides a dependable method for obtaining non-volatile evidence from storage devices in a way that adheres to Forensic best practices. Dead acquisition is the process of taking these data out of a storage medium and gathering them in an unaffected way. Nonvolatile data sources include external hard drives, flashcards, smartphones, USB drives, DVD-ROMs, and hard drives. Slack space, swap files, unallocated drive space, word processing documents, spreadsheets, emails, and other deleted items are examples of this kind of data. On properly kept disk evidence, investigators can replicate the dead acquisition process. By being aware of its advantages and disadvantages, investigators can select the best data collection method for any given circumstance. The static data which can be recovered from a hard drive is presented in Table 3.

Table 3. Static Acquisition Data.

Static Acquisition Data type	Functions
OS & System Files	The operating system encompasses essential system files, drivers, and configuration parameters. Installation of application software and related program files.
Temporary files	Although there are limits to data recovery from temporary (temp) files during static data gathering, this technique can nevertheless reveal important Forensic information. Details that can be obtained from temp files, such as traces of user activity, details that were partially removed, artifacts of malware and application data that is hidden.
System registries	During the collection of static data, system registries can provide a wealth of useful information. Even though it may not be possible to recover the complete registry, Forensic tools can retrieve important information from certain registry hives that provide insights into the configuration of the system and historical activity. Examples of possible recoverable in static data gathering from system registries are software installations and configuration, hardware configuration, user activity, and system startup and shutdown.
Event System Logs	Creating a timeline, spotting suspicious activity, deciphering application behavior, and troubleshooting system issues are all advantages of recovering event/system logs that can provide investigators with vital information. Event logs and system logs provide a distinct viewpoint when gathering static data. They serve as a record of system activity and events rather than directly containing user files or application data. Investigators can retrieve data from event/system logs such as events of system startup and shutdown, hardware events, software installation and updates, security events, application logs and system configuration changes.
Boot Sectors	Finding boot sector data during static acquisition provides some insight into possible manipulation attempts and the boot configuration of the system. Despite its limitations, this data can be an important component of the Forensic inquiry jigsaw. During a static hard drive acquisition, boot sectors can provide restricted and specialized data. Boot sectors, which contain vital code that tells the computer where to find and load the operating system, are fundamental to the booting process. Information can usually be retrieved from boot sectors such as bootloader code, identifying the operating system, partition table information, and Master Boot Record (MBR) or GUID Partition Table (GPT).
Web Browser Cache	Data retrieved from the web browser cache can provide important information about browsing behavior during a static hard drive acquisition. In a Forensic investigation, information retrieved from the web browser cache during static acquisition can be a crucial piece of the puzzle. Through the analysis of this data in conjunction with other available evidence, investigators can obtain valuable insights into user behavior and perhaps unearth critical case-related information. Investigators can potentially recover information from browsing history, cached web objects, form data and cookies.

(Table 3) cont.....

Static Acquisition Data type	Functions
Cookies and hidden files	During the process of gathering static data, cookies, and hidden files might contain a wealth of information. Investigators can obtain from here partially recovered login credentials (less likely with modern practices), browsing history, session data, site preferences, system configuration settings (hidden OS files), application settings and data (hidden application files), and personal documents and information (user-hidden files).

IMAGING USING BIT STREAMS

An exact replica of any storage medium, comprising cloned copies of all sectors and clusters, is called a bit-stream image. All the latent data needed for investigators to recover deleted files and folders is present on this cloned duplicate of the storage medium. To keep the original material clean, investigators frequently utilize bit-stream photos of dubious media. To make things even easier, most computer Forensic tools, such as EnCase and FTK Imager, can read bit-stream images. Bit-stream imaging processes can be classified as either bit-stream disk-to-disk or bit-stream disk-to-image-file.

- **Bit-stream disk-to-image-file**

A bit-stream disk-to-image file in Digital Forensics is a Forensic duplicate of a whole storage device, such as a hard drive or SSD. In essence, it is an exact duplicate of the original disk, down to the last bit. This technique for gathering data is frequently used by Forensic investigators. It is an adaptable technique that permits the creation of one or more clones of the drive under investigation. Image files can be created using tools like EnCase, FTK, The Sleuth Kit, *etc.*

- **Bit-streaming from disk to disk**

Bit-streaming from disk to disk describes the process of generating a bit-stream image of a storage device, such as a hard drive or SSD, in Digital Forensics. Basically, it involves copying every bit (0 or 1) from the source disk to the destination disk flawlessly and soundly from a Forensic perspective. Investigators are unable to generate a bit-stream disk-to-image file from the suspect drive if it is extremely old and not compatible with the imaging program or if the recovering login passwords for websites and user accounts are missing. In these situations, the original disk or drive can be copied bit-stream disk-to-disk. The geometry of the target disk, including its head, cylinder, and track arrangement, can be changed to align with the suspicious drive while doing a disk-to-disk copy. As a result, the process of acquiring data runs smoothly. EnCase, and Tableau Forensic

Imager are a few tools that can assist in making a disk-to-disk bit-stream duplicate of the suspicious drive.

DATA ACQUISITION FORMAT

The kind of data being gathered, and the application will determine the format of the data acquisition.

• Raw Format

Within the framework of acquiring data, the raw format typically denotes unprocessed or minimally treated data. It shows the rawest, most fundamental form of the data that was gathered. A bit-by-bit clone of the suspicious drive is made using raw format. Typically, the dd command is used to obtain images in this format. Table **4** presents the advantages and disadvantages of the raw data format.

Table 4. Raw format advantages and disadvantages.

Advantages	Disadvantage
Preserves Details: An examination that is more thorough is made possible by the fact that raw data includes all information from the source. You may find intricate details or hidden patterns that were overlooked during processing.	Large File Size: Compared to processed forms, raw data files can be much larger, requiring additional storage space and sometimes slowing down transfer times. Considering this carefully can be important, depending on how much data you are gathering.
Flexibility: Unprocessed data provides more control over analysis because of its lack of processing. We can adjust settings and apply various processing techniques to retrieve the precise information you require.	Processing needs: To analyze and extract relevant information from raw data analysis, it is frequently necessary to have technical competence and specialized tools. Not everyone possesses the knowledge or resources necessary to deal directly with raw data.
One of the main benefits of acquiring data in raw format is that little data read errors on the source drive are ignored.	Not user-friendly: Most programs cannot examine raw data files directly. For sharing or viewing by others, they must be transformed into a more widely used format. This additional processing step may cause inconvenience.
One major benefit of using a raw format for acquisition is the ability to ignore small read errors throughout the process of gathering Forensic data. Even if it means correcting some mistakes later in the process, gathering all relevant evidence for analysis later is given first priority.	One significant drawback is the requirement for an equivalent or greater quantity of storage space for the raw format copy compared to the original medium.
One of the primary benefits of utilizing raw files in Digital Forensics is their broad interoperability with Forensic tools.	Tools that are primarily open source may not be able to identify or gather marginal or problematic sectors from the suspicious drive.

• Proprietary Format

In Digital Forensics, proprietary formats are one kind of a format that is used to get data from Digital devices. They may not be generally usable by other Forensic tools, in contrast to raw formats, which are exclusive to the software used for acquisition. Commercial Forensics tools take images in their formats and extract data from the drive under investigation. Table **5** presents the advantages and disadvantages of the proprietary format in Digital Forensics.

Table 5. Advantages and disadvantages of proprietary format.

Advantages	Disadvantages
Efficiency and Speed: Often, proprietary formats have been optimized for the specific software that they are intended to work with. When working with vast storage devices, this can result in faster acquisition times and possibly lesser file sizes than with raw formats.	Restricted Compatibility: The main issue with proprietary formats is that they are not universally compatible. Only the program used to create the data can easily examine data that has been obtained in a proprietary format. This could be an issue if you need to share the evidence with other investigators who might not have the same software or use other techniques for analysis.
Usability: Certain proprietary formats could have features that make the user's acquisition process easier. For less technical investigators or in circumstances when efficiency and quickness are critical, this can be helpful.	Vendor lock-in: If you rely too much on proprietary formats, you may be forced to use a certain software provider. This reduces your freedom to select the best tool for each analysis work and may put you at risk of becoming reliant on the format's ongoing maintenance from the vendor.
Embedded Metadata: Some proprietary formats can incorporate metadata, or details about the data, right into the captured image. Since the evidence's specifics are easily accessible, this may save analysis time.	Future Proofing: Compared to open standards like raw formats, proprietary formats are more likely to become outdated. In the future, it can be challenging to retrieve the obtained data if the vendor closes or ceases to support the format.

• Advanced Forensics Format (AFF)

AFF is an open-source data acquisition format used for storing metadata associated with disk pictures. The format was developed with the intention of giving users an open disk imaging format as an alternative to being forced to use a proprietary format. The AFF file extensions are .afd for segmented image files and .afm for the AFF metadata. Since AFF is an open-source format, there are no implementation limitations placed on Forensic investigators. AFF is compatible with many operating systems and computing platforms and has a straightforward design. It offers the ability to compress image files and sets aside space for segmentation or image file metadata to be recorded. Internal consistency checks are offered for self-authentication. AFF offers a standardized method for storing a disk image, which is a bit-stream copy of a storage device, in one or more files together with the metadata that describes the image. This method strikes a compromise between the advantages of proprietary formats (lower file sizes, possibly faster processing) and raw formats (universally readable, retains all data).

- **Advanced Forensic Framework 4**

Advanced Forensic Framework 4 (AFF4) is a rebuilt and revamped version of the AFF format, developed by Bradly Schatz, Simson Garfinkel, and Michael Cohen. It is intended to handle large-capacity storage devices. Because the format is made up of generic objects having externally accessible functionality, such as volumes, streams, and graphs, its designers called it object-oriented design. In the AFF4 universe, you can address these things by name. They have a distinct URL that allows for worldwide reference. Disk-image data can be saved in one or more locations using this abstract information model, while the data's associated metadata is kept in another location. It keeps more types of structured data in the evidence file. It provides a uniform naming convention and data model.

In addition to supporting many images, the format provides basic directories and a variety of container formats, including Zip and Zip64 for binary data. Additionally, it allows network storage and the usage of WebDAV, an HTTP protocol extension that allows imaging to be sent straight to a central HTTP server. Maps, which are zero-copy data transformations, are also supported by this format. Zero-copy transformations increase the efficiency of the CPU by removing the need for it to copy data between memory locations. AFF4 is a strong and adaptable format with several benefits for Digital Forensics. It is a useful tool for contemporary investigations because of its capacity to manage intricate evidence structures, hold extensive documentation, and foster interoperability.

DATA ACQUISITION METHODOLOGY

An essential first step in any Digital Forensics inquiry is gathering information. It entails gathering and storing Digital evidence from electronic devices in a manner that preserves its integrity and allows further examination as displayed in Fig. (**3**).

When gathering information from suspicious media, Forensic investigators need to follow a methodical and sound Forensic procedure. By doing this, the likelihood that the evidence will be admitted into the court of law will be increased. The several procedures that investigators need to adhere to when gathering information with evidential value are covered in detail in this section.

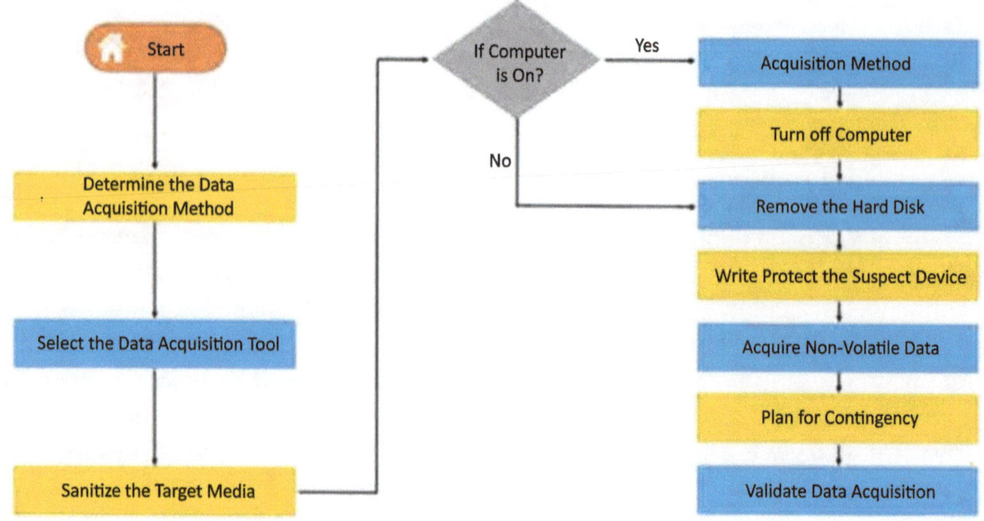

Fig. (3). Data acquisition methodology [2].

HANDS-ON: LIVE DATA ACQUISITION TOOLS

Tool: FTK Imager

With the help of FTK imager, we will discover how to obtain live or volatile data from a suspect's computer system. For this goal, we will utilize a suspect's Windows OS computer as an example.

FTK Imager offers two choices. To obtain evidence from the hard drive, all you must do is create a disk image. However, if you want to capture all the evidence that could be kept in RAM, that is all the live data, or volatile data, since volatile data is any information that could be lost temporarily after your computer is shut down. This method, known as a "ram dump," requires us to keep the computer capped on the whole time until we have collected all the evidence from the RAM. We are doing this ram dump using Acccss Data's FTK imager.

The steps taken are listed below.

Step 1: Navigate to FTK imager, select the File tab, and then select the Capture Memory option as illustrated in Fig. (**4**).

Step 2: We will now select the path to be used to store this RAM dump and select the option to capture memory as shown in Fig. (**5**).

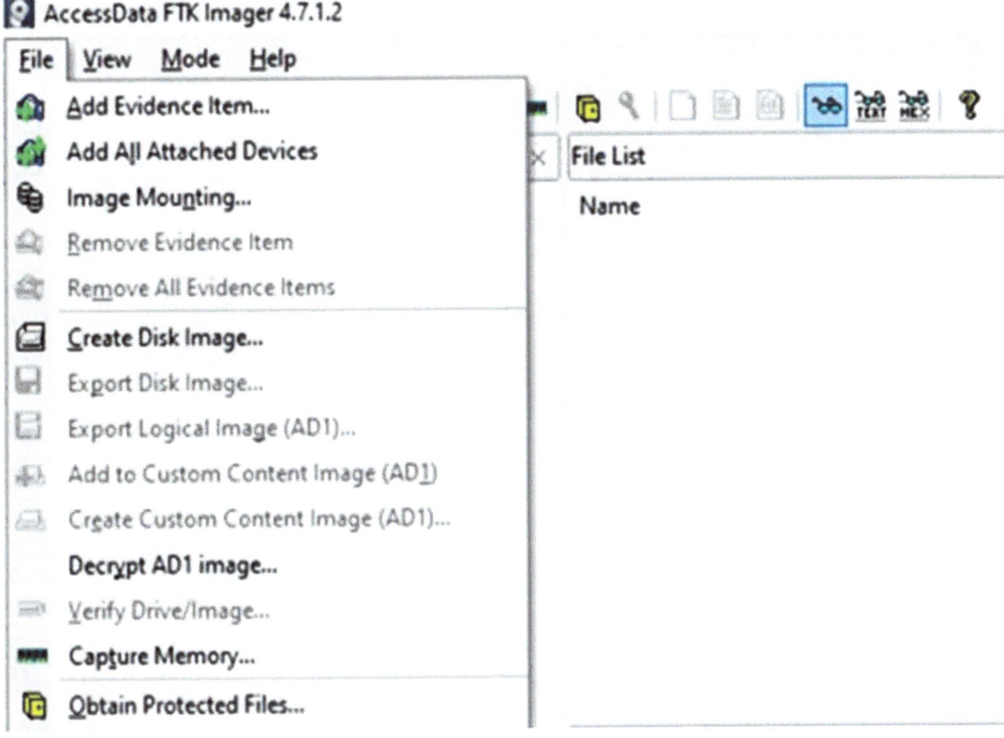

Fig. (4). Access data FTK imager.

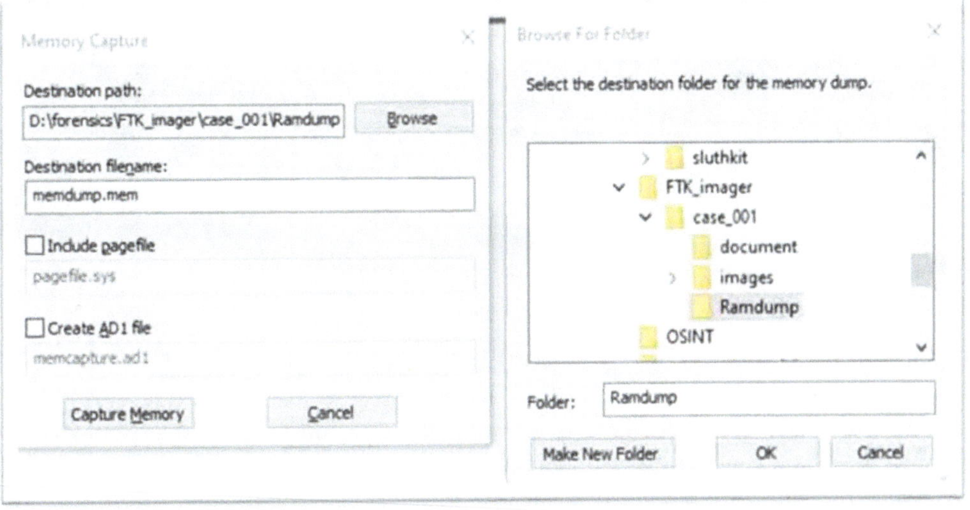

Fig. (5). Destination path for the RAM dump.

Step 3: Do not alter the extension in the destination file name, which is. Give the file name; do not modify the extension as shown in Fig. (**6**).

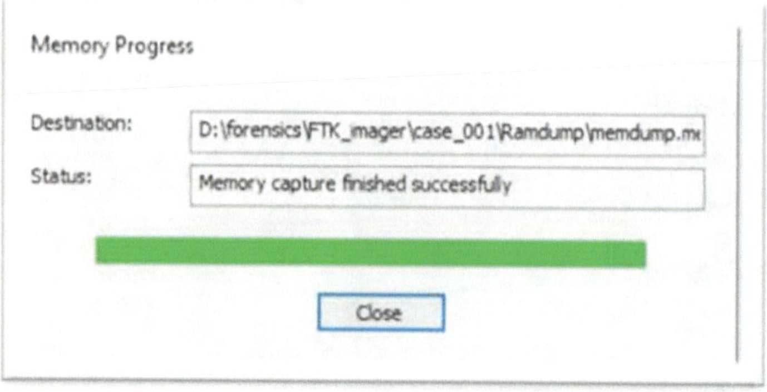

Memory Progress

Destination: D:\forensics\FTK_imager\case_001\Ramdump\memdump.me

Status: Memory capture finished successfully

Close

Fig. (6). Memory captured.

Step 4: We will now proceed to the actual path or identify where we have kept our proof, which is located along this path. D:\FTK_imager\case_001\ForensicsRamdump, we now additionally need to obtain its hash value as shown in Fig. (7).

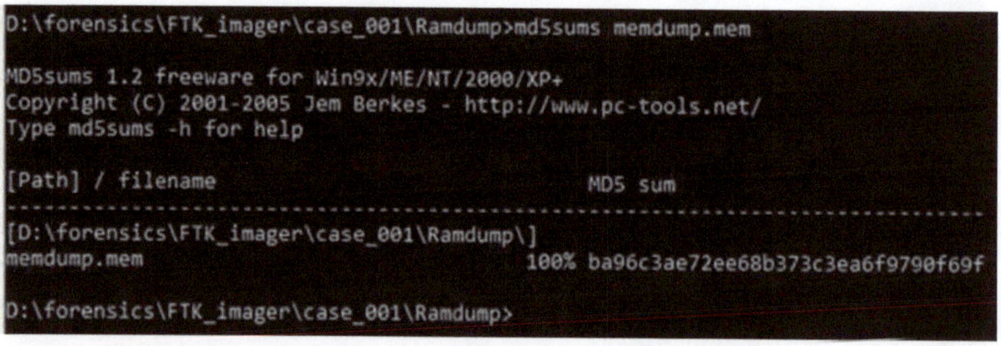

```
D:\forensics\FTK_imager\case_001\Ramdump>md5sums memdump.mem

MD5sums 1.2 freeware for Win9x/ME/NT/2000/XP+
Copyright (C) 2001-2005 Jem Berkes - http://www.pc-tools.net/
Type md5sums -h for help

[Path] / filename                                   MD5 sum
-------------------------------------------------------------------------------
[D:\forensics\FTK_imager\case_001\Ramdump\]
memdump.mem                               100% ba96c3ae72ee68b373c3ea6f9790f69f

D:\forensics\FTK_imager\case_001\Ramdump>
```

Fig. (7). Hash value for Memdump.mem.

We must ensure that no data has been tampered with in between whenever we share this information with Forensic investigators. The hash value will remain the same whether we take it now or years from now as long as there is no change in the data. Even a small change in the data will result in a significant variation in the hash output or value. That is what the term "avalanche effect" refers to. There are three aims of security, confidentiality, integrity, and availability, which is why hashing is done for integrity checks. Hashing is done to ensure that the data is accurate and unaltered, as much as feasible. It can be used to verify if the data is accurate.

Step 5: We should send the recipient this md5 sum in addition to the memdum.mem file so he can confirm whether this file has been altered during transit. Thus, this is the method by which we extract the dynamic or living evidence from the target system as shown in Fig. (**8**).

This PC › New Volume (D:) › forensics › FTK_imager › case_001 › Ramdump

Name	Date modified	Type	Size
hashvalue	4/2/2024 9:22 AM	Text Document	1 KB
md5sums	1/31/2005 12:50 PM	Application	28 KB
memdump.mem	4/2/2024 8:48 AM	MEM File	18,472,960 ...

Fig. (8). Ramdump file with hash value.

Tool: Volatility Framework (Live Data)

The volatile or live evidence that we collected throughout the data collection stage will now be evaluated. Previously we used FTK imager to record all the live evidence that is displayed with a hash value. As such, we want to utilize the application to examine these recorded live ramdump acquisitions. The goal of the independent 501(c) (3) non-profit Volatility Foundation's founding was to advance and preserve open-source memory Forensics [3]. Volatility is the most widely used framework globally for removing Digital remnants from volatile memory (RAM) samples. The extraction techniques are completely independent of the system being investigated, even though they offer insight into its runtime state. The framework is aimed at introducing people to the techniques and difficulties involved in eliminating Digital artifacts from volatile memory samples, as well as to provide a platform for future research in this exciting area of study.

Step 1: To use Volatility 3, we must have Python 3.7.0 or later. Install as few dependencies as possible using software such as this one (some plugins won't work). The most recent stable build of Volatility may always be found in its GitHub stable branch. The most recent version of the code can be obtained as shown in Fig. (**9**).

Step 2: We will now access the volatility folder as shown in Fig. (**10**).

Step 3: To enable every function in Volatility 3, install PIP as shown in Fig. (**11**). For partial functionality, comment out any unnecessary packages in requirements.txt before running the application.

```
PS D:\forensics\volatility> git clone https://github.com/volatilityfoundation/volatility
3.git
Cloning into 'volatility3'...
remote: Enumerating objects: 33032, done.
remote: Counting objects: 100% (4009/4009), done.
remote: Compressing objects: 100% (990/990), done.
remote: Total 33032 (delta 3559), reused 3216 (delta 3017), pack-reused 29023
Receiving objects: 100% (33032/33032), 6.48 MiB | 17.84 MiB/s, done.
Resolving deltas: 100% (25198/25198), done.
PS D:\forensics\volatility>
```

Fig. (9). Download & install volatility.

```
D:\forensics\volatility\volatility3


     LastWriteTime           Length Name
     -------------           ------ ----
3/6/2024    8:30 AM                 .github
3/6/2024    8:30 AM                 development
3/6/2024    8:30 AM                 doc
3/7/2024   10:56 AM                 dump_07
3/6/2024    8:30 AM                 test
3/6/2024    8:44 AM                 volatility3
3/6/2024    8:30 AM             558 .gitignore
3/6/2024    8:30 AM             564 .readthedocs.yml
3/6/2024    8:30 AM            8200 .style.yapf
3/7/2024    9:05 AM            1324 20240305.mem.info.txt
3/6/2024    8:30 AM            1502 API_CHANGES.md
3/6/2024    8:30 AM            1315 CITATION.cff
3/6/2024    8:30 AM            3956 LICENSE.txt
3/6/2024    8:30 AM             207 MANIFEST.in
3/6/2024    8:30 AM              83 mypy.ini
3/6/2024    8:30 AM            6094 README.md
3/6/2024    8:30 AM             781 requirements-dev.txt
3/6/2024    8:30 AM              76 requirements-minimal.txt
3/6/2024    8:30 AM             765 requirements.txt
3/6/2024    8:30 AM            1907 setup.py
3/6/2024    8:30 AM             300 vol.py
3/6/2024    8:30 AM            5560 vol.spec
3/6/2024    8:30 AM             307 volshell.py
3/6/2024    8:30 AM            3029 volshell.spec
```

Fig. (10). Volatility3 folder.

```
PS D:\forensics\volatility\volatility3> pip install -r .\requirements.txt
Collecting pefile>=2023.2.7 (from -r .\requirements.txt (line 2))
  Downloading pefile-2023.2.7-py3-none-any.whl.metadata (1.4 kB)
Collecting yara-python>=3.8.0 (from -r .\requirements.txt (line 8))
  Downloading yara_python-4.5.0-cp310-cp310-win_amd64.whl.metadata (2.9 kB)
Collecting capstone>=3.0.5 (from -r .\requirements.txt (line 12))
  Downloading capstone-5.0.1-py3-none-win_amd64.whl.metadata (3.5 kB)
Collecting pycryptodome (from -r .\requirements.txt (line 15))
  Downloading pycryptodome-3.20.0-cp35-abi3-win_amd64.whl.metadata (3.4 kB)
Collecting leechcorepyc>=2.4.0 (from -r .\requirements.txt (line 18))
  Downloading leechcorepyc-2.17.2-cp36-abi3-win_amd64.whl.metadata (535 bytes)
Collecting gcsfs>=2023.1.0 (from -r .\requirements.txt (line 21))
  Downloading gcsfs-2024.2.0-py2.py3-none-any.whl.metadata (1.6 kB)
Collecting s3fs>=2023.1.0 (from -r .\requirements.txt (line 22))
  Downloading s3fs-2024.2.0-py3-none-any.whl.metadata (1.6 kB)
```

Fig. (11). Install requirements.

Step 4: To determine the Volatility version, use **python vol.py -v** as displayed in Fig. (**12**).

```
PS D:\forensics\volatility\volatility3> python vol.py -v
Volatility 3 Framework 2.7.0
INFO     volatility3.cli: Volatility plugins path: ['D:\\forensi
\forensics\\volatility\\volatility3\\volatility3\\framework\\plu
INFO     volatility3.cli: Volatility symbols path: ['D:\\forensi
\forensics\\volatility\\volatility3\\volatility3\\framework\\sym
usage: volatility [-h] [-c CONFIG] [--parallelism [{processes,th
                  [-s SYMBOL_DIRS] [-v] [-l LOG] [-o OUTPUT_DIR]
                  [--save-config SAVE_CONFIG] [--clear-cache] [-
                  [--filters FILTERS] [--single-location SINGLE_
                  [--single-swap-locations [SINGLE_SWAP_LOCATION
                  plugin ...
```

Fig. (12). Volatility framework version.

Step 5: After installing the volatility framework, the memory image that was created during live data acquisition needs to be analyzed as shown in Fig. (**13**). The basic system information that is read from memory is included in this output. For instance, the number of processes, system time, system root, major operating system version, and time data stamp are all included. These details may be important for the remaining portions of the investigation.

```
PS D:\forensics\volatility\volatility3> python vo
Volatility 3 Framework 2.7.0
Progress:  100.00               PDB scanning fini
Variable        Value

Kernel Base     0xf80111200000
DTB     0x1ad000
Symbols file:///D:/forensics/volatility/volatilit
Is64Bit True
IsPAE   False
layer_name      0 WindowsIntel32e
memory_layer    1 FileLayer
KdVersionBlock  0xf80111e0f2e0
Major/Minor     15.19041
MachineType     34404
KeNumberProcessors      12
SystemTime      2024-04-02 03:15:25
NtSystemRoot    C:\WINDOWS
NtProductType   NtProductWinNt
NtMajorVersion  10
NtMinorVersion  0
PE MajorOperatingSystemVersion  10
PE MinorOperatingSystemVersion  0
PE Machine      34404
PE TimeDateStamp        Wed Nov 22 15:44:41 2056
```

Fig. (13). Analysis of memory file.

Step 6: This information can be saved into a text file for our investigation's documentation as shown in Fig. (**14**).

Volatility 3 Framework 2.7.0

Variable	Value
Kernel Base	**0xf80111200000**
DTB	**0x1ad000**
Symbols	**file:///D:/forensics/volatility/volatility3/v**
Is64Bit	**True**
IsPAE	**False**
layer_name	**0 WindowsIntel32e**
memory_layer	**1 FileLayer**
KdVersionBlock	**0xf80111e0f2e0**
Major/Minor	**15.19041**
MachineType	**34404**
KeNumberProcessors	**12**
SystemTime	**2024-04-02 03:15:25**
NtSystemRoot	**C:\WINDOWS**
NtProductType	**NtProductWinNt**
NtMajorVersion	**10**
NtMinorVersion	**0**
PE MajorOperatingSystemVersion	**10**
PE MinorOperatingSystemVersion	**0**
PE Machine	**34404**

Fig. (14). Memory file details.

Step 7: When examining the memory ramdump, it is best to first view the process list, which is found in the windows.pslist module. Next, we pipe the list into more to print out every process that was running in Windows during the imaging process as shown in Fig. (**15**).

```
Volatility 3 Framework 2.7.0
PID     PPID    ImageFileName   Offset(V)       Threads Handles SessionId       Wow64   CreateTime      ExitTime        File output
4       0       System  0xcc0fa0a5b040  241     -       N/A     False   2024-04-01 03:26:25.000000      N/A     Disabled
148     4       Registry        0xcc0fa0cef040  4       -       N/A     False   2024-04-01 03:26:19.000000      N/A     Disabled
564     4       smss.exe        0xcc0fa2e92080  2       -       N/A     False   2024-04-01 03:26:26.000000      N/A     Disabled
904     880     csrss.exe       0xcc0fa7e4b300  14      -       0       False   2024-04-01 03:26:49.000000      N/A     Disabled
812     880     wininit.exe     0xcc0fa7f9d0c0  1       -       0       False   2024-04-01 03:26:51.000000      N/A     Disabled
```

Fig. (15). Output of the Windows.pslist.

Step 8: We now have the process ID (PID) which is 4 like the parent process ID (PPID) 0, image file name system, offset (V) being 0xcc0fa0a5b040, Threads and create time and exit time. From all these fields, what we are mostly interested in is the image file name since that way, we can filter and focus on programs that we are interested in their process ID and parent process ID as well as sometimes how many threads are there . So investigators tend to focus on things like what files is this process are being accessed at that time when we take the system process. We have the process ID of 4, and the parent process ID is 0 because the system is effectively one of the first processes that are started and everything else is started by the system so you can see that we have 0, meaning that it's one of the first processes. Its process ID is 4 and here we have the registry opened by process 4 and the registry process ID is 148 smss.exe also opened by process 4 and its process ID is 564.

By using this we can reconstruct how applications were opened and who were the parents like where they are coming from; this is very interesting for the investigation process. We will now utilize the built-in string search function of PowerShell, called select-string. This function does not belong to volatility; rather, it helps us filter data. For instance, investigators may want to examine any activity or processes that occur within the Chrome browser as illustrated in Fig. (**16**).

```
PS D:\forensics\volatility\volatility3> python vol.py
Progress:  100.00                PDB scanning finished
14196   8412    chrome.exe       0xcc0fb24ec080  57
10628   14196   chrome.exe       0xcc0fb54b0080  7
13828   14196   chrome.exe       0xcc0fb3490080  33
9264    14196   chrome.exe       0xcc0fb2bf1080  17
13680   14196   chrome.exe       0xcc0fab85c080  10
10752   14196   chrome.exe       0xcc0fb304e080  10
3308    14196   chrome.exe       0xcc0fb548f080  29
9096    14196   chrome.exe       0xcc0fb30ec080  24
10764   14196   chrome.exe       0xcc0fb30bf080  22
11588   14196   chrome.exe       0xcc0fb06c50c0  25
9388    14196   chrome.exe       0xcc0fb56c60c0  0
2772    14196   chrome.exe       0xcc0fafaa4340  8
9012    14196   chrome.exe       0xcc0faf8f3080  24
7400    14196   chrome.exe       0xcc0faf7f3300  20
```

Fig. (16). Process related to Chrome in Memdump.mem.

Step 9: Now that we know the process ID for the chrome activities running, we can investigate the chrome.exe processes and concentrate on process ID 14196. Since the parent process ID of every other process is also 14196, this can be an interesting investigation process and provide us with important results as shown in Fig. (**17**).

```
PID     Process Offset  HandleValue     Type    GrantedAccess   Name

14196   chrome.exe      0xcc0fb68eaae0  0x4     Event   0x1f0003
14196   chrome.exe      0xcc0fb68ea1e0  0x8     Event   0x1f0003
14196   chrome.exe      0xcc0fb5343840  0xc     WaitCompletionPacket    0x1
14196   chrome.exe      0xcc0fb31064c0  0x10    IoCompletion    0x1f0003
14196   chrome.exe      0xcc0fb3053a30  0x14    TpWorkerFactory 0xf00ff
14196   chrome.exe      0xcc0fb666dc50  0x18    IRTimer 0x100002
14196   chrome.exe      0xcc0fb5349ea0  0x1c    WaitCompletionPacket    0x1
14196   chrome.exe      0xcc0fb666cb50  0x20    IRTimer 0x100002
14196   chrome.exe      0xcc0fb5349820  0x24    WaitCompletionPacket    0x1
14196   chrome.exe      0xcc0fb3106af0  0x28    EtwRegistration 0x804
14196   chrome.exe      0xcc0fb3107650  0x2c    EtwRegistration 0x804
14196   chrome.exe      0xcc0fb31078f0  0x30    EtwRegistration 0x804
```

Fig. (17). Result for process ID 14196.

Step 10: We want the event type that is a file in this process ID, thus we will use Select-String to filter the file once again so that only the file type will print in our shell as shown in Fig. (**18**).

```
14196   chrome.exe      0xcc0fb0257550  0x58    File    0x100020
14196   chrome.exe      0xcc0faf2df3d0  0x6c    File    0x100001
14196   chrome.exe      0xe30d66bc7f10  0x84    Key     0x9      M/
14196   chrome.exe      0xcc0faf2e5640  0x250   File    0x120089
14196   chrome.exe      0xcc0fb3a627d0  0x2e4   File    0x12019f
Data\BrowserMetrics\BrowserMetrics-660B6C09-3774.pma
14196   chrome.exe      0xcc0faefc98b0  0x358   File    0x130196
14196   chrome.exe      0xcc0faf253090  0x374   File    0x120089
14196   chrome.exe      0xcc0fb024e590  0x384   File    0x120089
```

Fig. (18). Process ID 14196 event type.

TOOL: FTK IMAGER (DEAD DATA ACQUISITION)

We are going to learn about the full chain of custody as, as part of this book on Digital Forensics, we'll now see the entire procedure involved between the two most crucial things: acquiring data and presenting it in court. The first and most important phase is determining the most likely sources of evidence. After we have narrowed down the potential sources, our first responsibility is to gather the evidence, which is also known as data acquisition. Therefore, gathering data comes first, followed by duplicating data. The distinction between data duplication and data gathering is extremely thin. Data duplication is nothing but the process by which we have already determined that x, y, and z are our data evidence, and we need to safeguard them by duplicating. This statement simply means that it is always recommended to keep a duplicate of that evidence stored somewhere else in a secure location to prevent unnecessary or accidental damage to evidence. Thus, gathering data is the initial step, which is then followed, if necessary, by data duplication, and last, forensic analysis.

When we are certain that this is the evidence we need to gather and examine, we begin using Forensics tools. We will be learning how to use the FTK imager for static acquisition. To shorten our examination, we can presume that all the evidence is contained in the suspect's pen drive. We can then use the suspect's pen drive as a source of evidence and continue our investigation. We will learn how to obtain data from a static device, which could be a hard disk, pen drive, *etc*. For both live and dead data capture circumstances, FTK Imager is an excellent tool for extracting Digital evidence from storage media [4].

Step 1: To acquire data from storage devices that are either powered off or suspected of malfunctioning, FTK Imager can be utilized in the following ways for dead data acquisition as shown in Fig. (**19**).

Fig. (19). FTK imager interface.

Step 2: For a static collection of evidence, we are going to select this option disk image, and for live data acquisition which is collecting data from the RAM we are going to select the option capture memory. Now will see create disk image once you click this you will get options such as physical drive, logical drive, image file, the content of a folder, and multiple devices like CDs/DVDs. We now work on gathering static evidence, and using the options listed in Fig. (**20**).

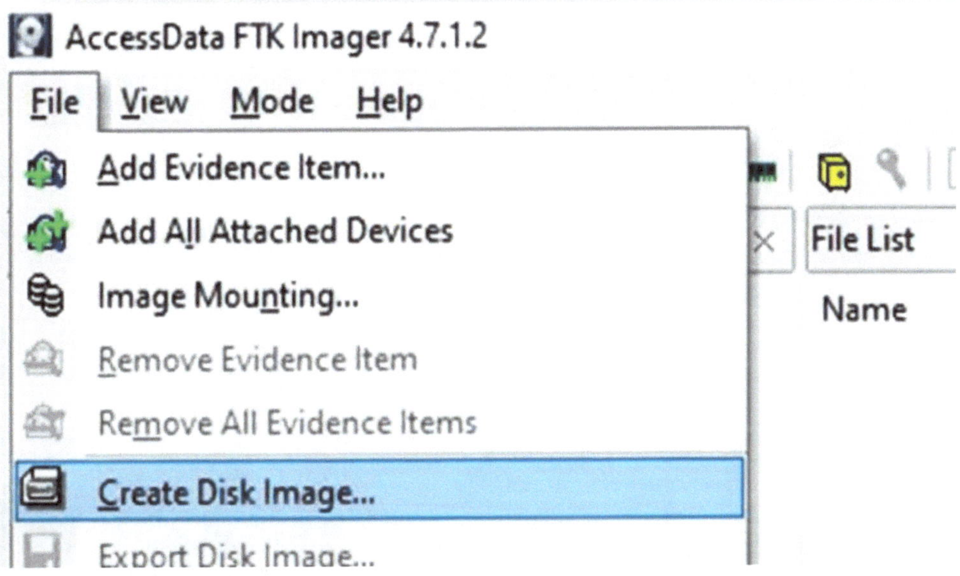

Fig. (20). Options for live & static acquisition.

Step 3: The evidence is contained in a 16 GB pen drive; thus, this 16 GB pen drive serves as our actual evidence drive. In real-world settings, the evidence drive may take the form of a pen drive or a genuine hard disk as displayed in Fig. (**21**).

Step 4: After choosing the physical drive, a window will appear allowing us to choose the evidence drive. In our case, the evidence is stored on a 1 TB hard drive, and the second drive is where we are storing the evidence. (15 GB) Pen Drive contains the evidence, so this specific 15 GB pen drive serves as our actual evidence drive. This evidence drive might just be a pen drive, or it might be a real hard drive as displayed in Fig. (**22**).

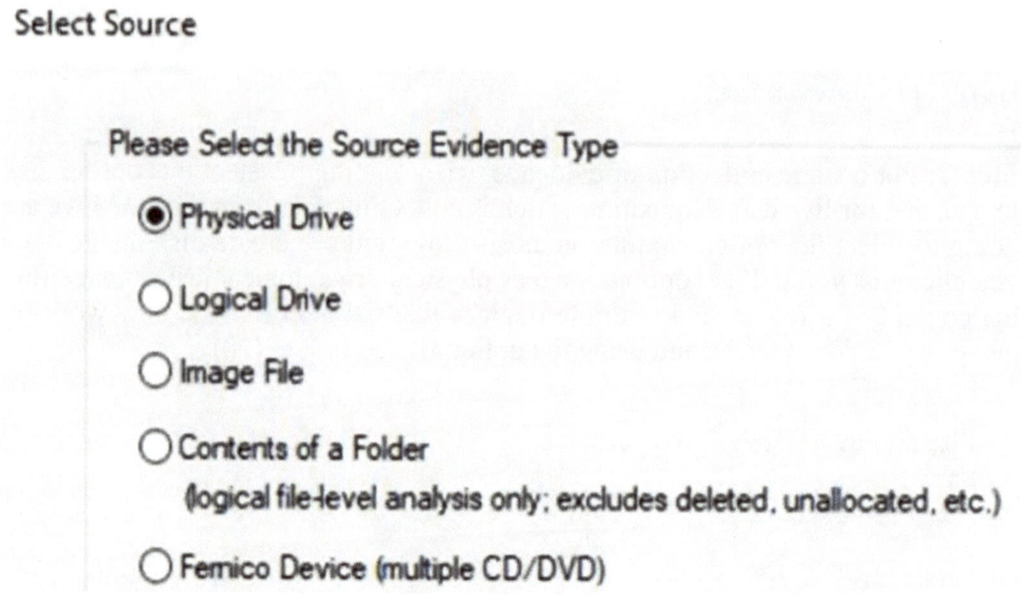

Select Source

Please Select the Source Evidence Type

◉ Physical Drive

○ Logical Drive

○ Image File

○ Contents of a Folder
(logical file-level analysis only; excludes deleted, unallocated, etc.)

○ Femico Device (multiple CD/DVD)

Fig. (21). Selection of source evidence.

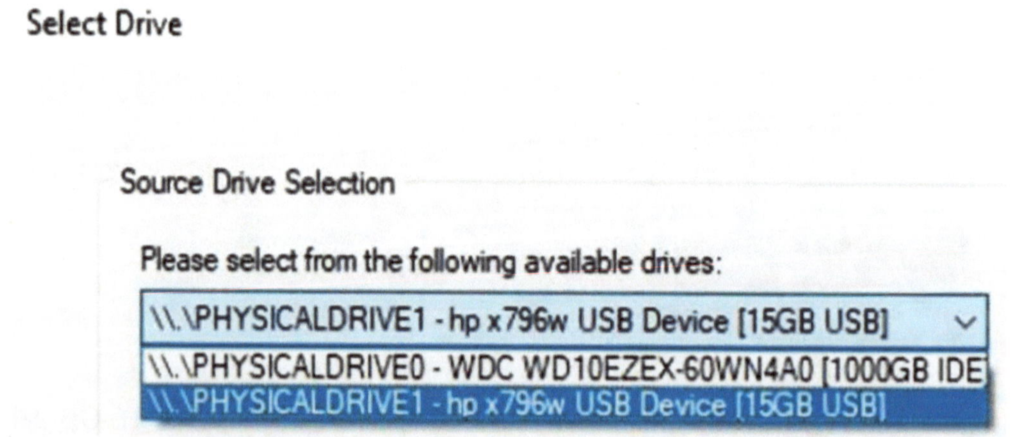

Select Drive

Source Drive Selection

Please select from the following available drives:

\\.\PHYSICALDRIVE1 - hp x796w USB Device [15GB USB]

\\.\PHYSICALDRIVE0 - WDC WD10EZEX-60WN4A0 [1000GB IDE]

\\.\PHYSICALDRIVE1 - hp x796w USB Device [15GB USB]

Fig. (22). Options for evidence drive.

The reason we are utilizing this FTK imager to make a copy is that, although we could just copy the pen drive and paste it onto our target drive, copying anything from one place to another always carries some level of risk. The problem is that we cannot be completely certain that, even if we copy an evidence drive or folder from one place to another, we would not accidentally erase or change the files' original information. On the other hand, we can be certain that any evidence we gather from that source will be posted in a way that complies with Forensic standards if we use this specific tool or any other imaging tools.

Step 5: We therefore chose this 15 GB drive, which our case study indicates is our evidence file or evidence source. After selecting it, we hit the finish button as shown in Fig. (**23**).

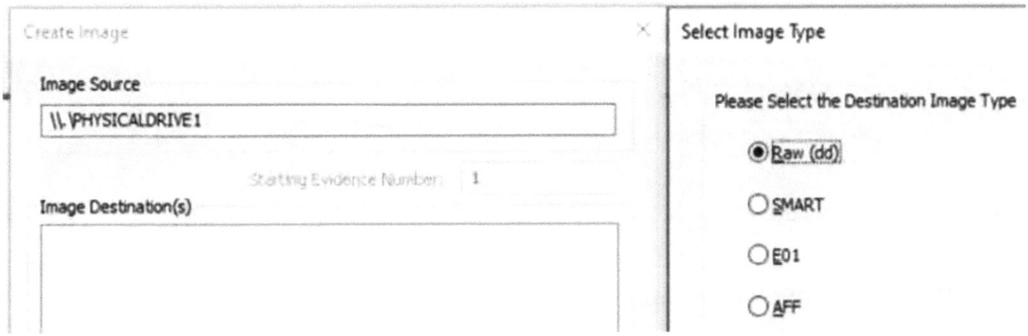

Fig. (23). Create & select image type and format.

Therefore, let us choose this specific image location in this window where we will select the target disk where the actual proof image will be kept. We can save our image in either of these formats; most common Forensics images are stored in the DD format by default; therefore, we will choose to save our image in raw alone as displayed in Fig. (**24**). As we are working on the initial case, we can assign a number, such as 001, because a single case may contain multiple pieces of evidence. We can also assign distinct numbers to the evidence, along with a unique description, the examiner's name, and a note.

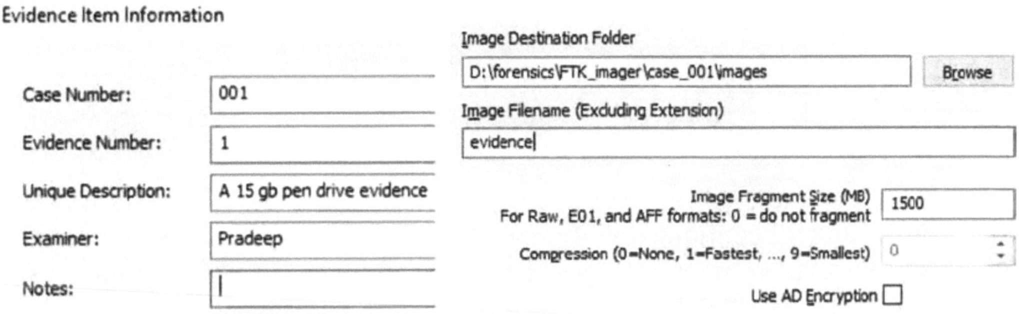

Fig. (24). Evidence information & selection.

Step 6: Now specify the image and documents to select the evidence as displayed in Fig. (**25**).

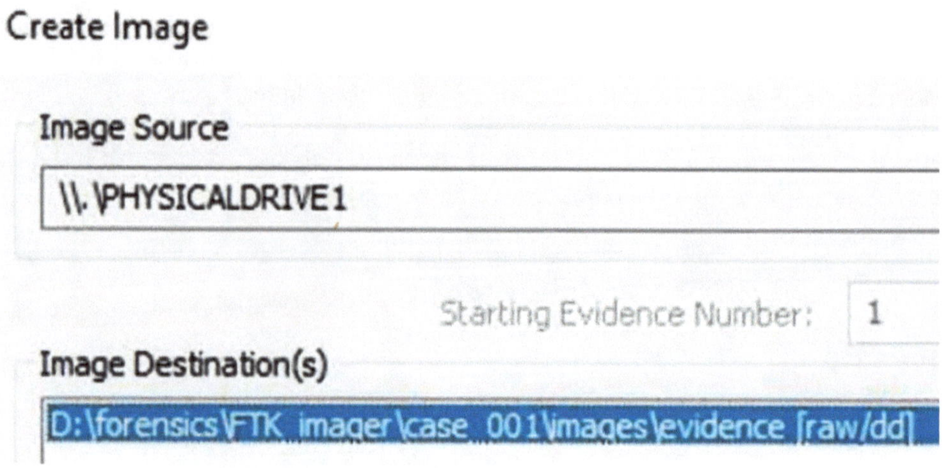

Fig. (25). Specify final evidence path.

Step 7: We can choose an appropriate format if you would prefer, for instance, this image to be in SMART, E01, or AFF. However, in this instance, we were forced to choose the raw format, which is compatible with practically all Forensic investigation tools as shown in Fig. (**26**).

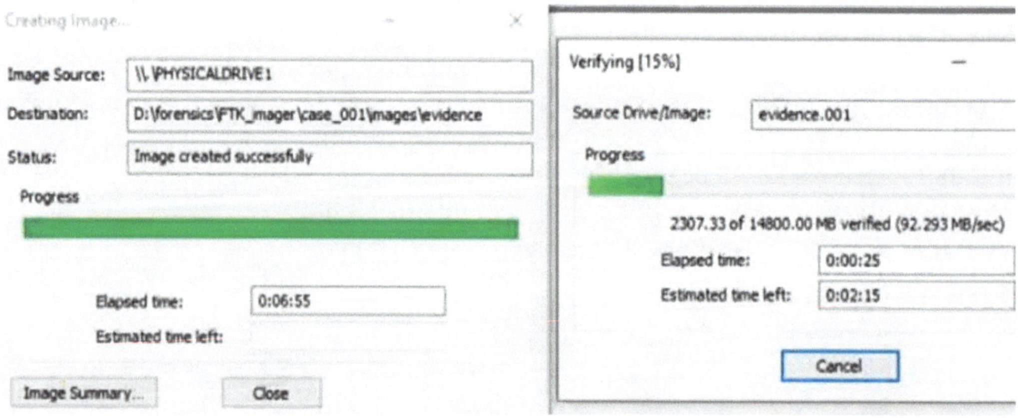

Fig. (26). Image creating process.

As a result, we will continue with the raw format and can choose the options that by default select to verify the images after they are created. It will take some time, but in addition to creating the evidence file itself, it will also generate an MD5 or SHA1 hash for the corresponding image hashes. Therefore, we can easily use these hash files or hash values to validate the contents of the evidence file in the future if required. Next, precalculated progress statistics (this is optional; if we choose to do so, the time required will be added again). Furthermore, construct a directory listing of all the files in the image once they have been created (again, this is optional; we can leave them as is and hit Start). This can take some time to complete, depending on the volume of source evidence.

Step 8: Fig. (**27**) shows a comprehensive overview of our process generated by the AccessData FTK imager, along with the version number. The examiner's name, the unique description we provided in the previous phase, the case number, and so forth. The drive geometry of our source material is visible toward the end, and this is information that an investigator presenting in court may find extremely important.

Step 9: As we navigate through the image summary in Fig. (**28**), we can see that the hash for our evidence has been computed. It will be very helpful to have the hash value in the MD5 and SHA1 formats to confirm whether the evidence file has been modified both before and after the procedure. So that we can monitor whether accidental modifications have been made there. The avalanche effect refers to the possibility that even a single bit change could have a significant impact on computed checksums or hash values. The segment list, the location of which is provided, and the image verification result are all extremely important pieces of information for our investigation.

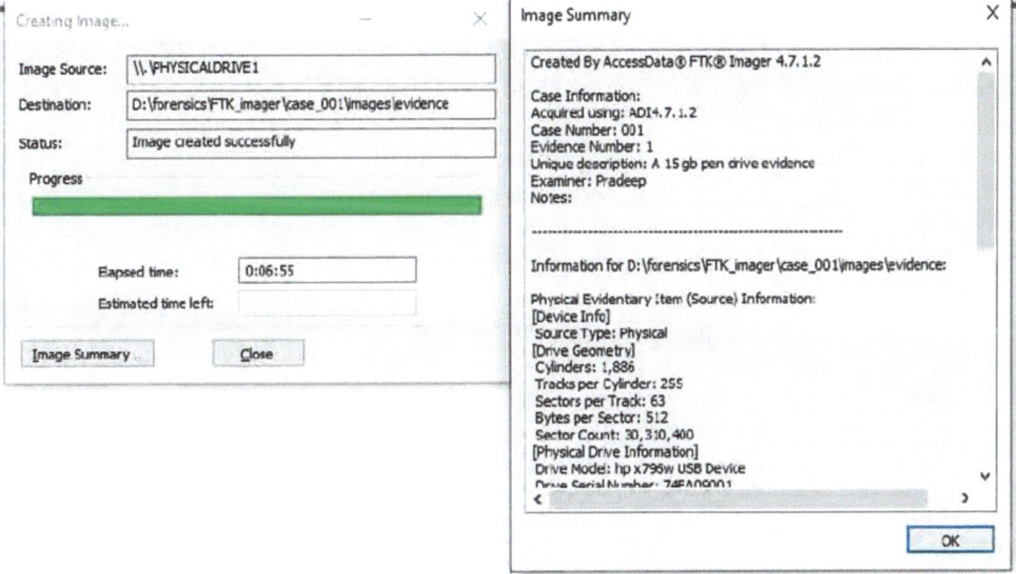

Fig. (27). Image summary by access data FTK imager.

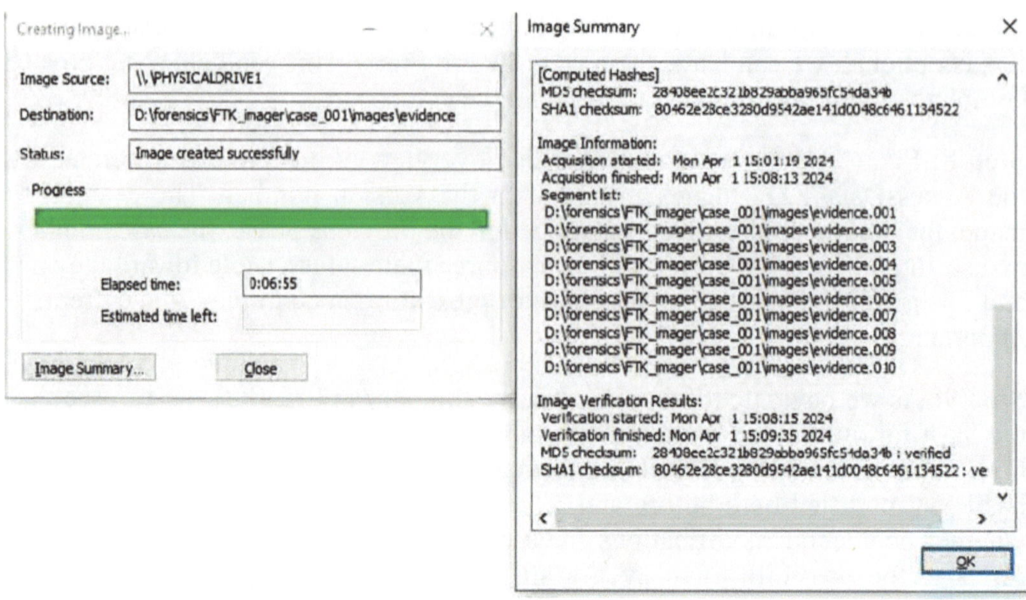

Fig. (28). Image summary with computed hash.

CONCLUSION

This chapter successfully covered the fundamentals of data acquisition, giving you the information and abilities you need to manage various kinds of data gathering scenarios. We started by building a solid foundation in the fundamental ideas of data acquisition, including its various types, formats, and finally gave a thorough explanation of the data acquisition methodologies. After gaining this theoretical foundation, we used industry-standard techniques to accomplish data acquisition tasks as we delved into practical applications. We obtained practical experience with the Volatility Framework for live data acquisition and analysis and FTK Imager for static data acquisition. We will go into more detail regarding File System Analysis in the upcoming chapter.

REFERENCES

[1] Brezinski, Dominique, and Tom Killalea. "Guidelines for Evidence Collection and Archiving". *Request for Comments, RFC 3227, Internet Engineering Task Force*, Feb. 2002. IETF. https://datatracker.ietf.org/doc/rfc3227/ [http://dx.doi.org/10.17487/rfc3227]

[2] "EC-Council Learning," codered.eccouncil.org. https://codered.eccouncil.org/courseVideo/Digital-Forensics-essentials?lessonId=83bf05df-971b-441e-a814-f5e8735bb378&finalAssessment=false (accessed Apr. 05, 2024).

[3] volatilityfoundation, "volatilityfoundation/volatility," GitHub, Oct. 08, 2019. https://github.com/volatilityfoundation/volatility

[4] "Loading...," https://onlinecourses.swayam2.ac.in/nou22_cs09/course

CHAPTER 4

File System Forensics

Abstract: Hard Disk Drives (HDDs) and Solid-State Drives (SSDs) are two types of storage devices that are crucial information sources for forensic investigations. The information gathered from storage devices should be located and safeguarded by the investigator as evidence. As a result, the investigator must be familiar with the design and operation of storage devices. Additionally, the file system is crucial since it determines how data is distributed and stored on a device.

Keywords: Digital evidence, Data acquisition, Disk imaging, Data recovery, File system, HDD, Storage devices, SSD, System analysis.

INTRODUCTION - UNDERSTANDING STORAGE DRIVES

A computer's memory, or storage device, is a crucial part that stores data and information. There is a necessity to store even the operating system. A computer without storage is like a car without wheels. Computers store digital data on HDDs and SSDs. Because HDDs have moving elements and record data magnetically on a spinning platter, they are vulnerable to physical harm. SSDs do not have any moving parts and store data on NAND flash memory chips. Classification of computer storage is illustrated in Fig. (**1**).

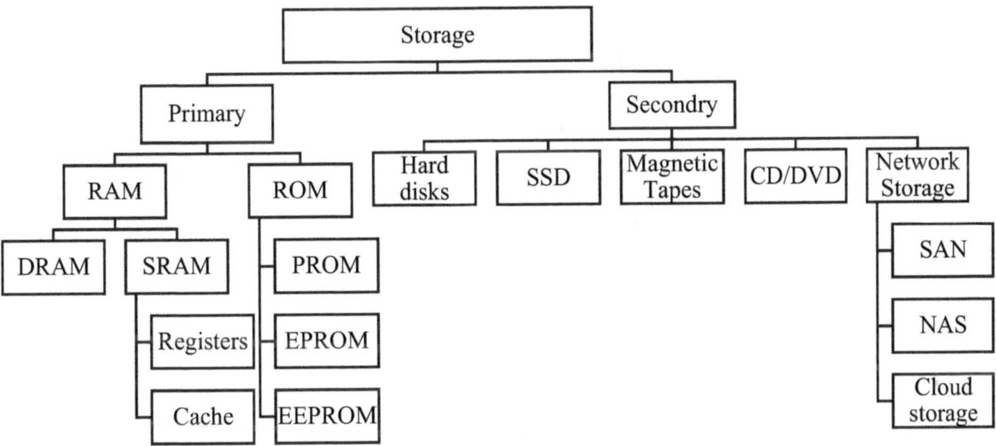

Fig. (1). Classification of computer storage.

Akashdeep Bhardwaj, Pradeep Singh & Ajay Prasad

The hardware and technologies used to store digital information are referred to as computer storage. It functions similarly to the memory on your computer, but unlike temporary memory (RAM), it can hold onto data even when the power is off. There are two main types of computer storage; Primary Storage and Secondary Storage

PRIMARY STORAGE

This is a quick internal memory that stores data that the CPU is currently using. Because it is volatile, data is lost when a computer shuts down. Primary memory, which is situated close to the CPU to facilitate speedy access, is made up of RAM and ROM. Primary memory can be accessed directly by the CPU.

RAM (Random Access Memory)

Consider it to be like a workstation you would use for a project. It contains the data that your computer requires to function at that precise instant, such as the open files, open programs, and any data you are working with right now. RAM is unique due to its speed, random access, and volatility. Any random location can be used to get data from a RAM, which is a volatile memory, meaning that if the power is interrupted, the data is lost. This is utilized for temporary storage and is incredibly quick, there are two kinds of RAM:

DRAM (Dynamic Random Access Memory)

DRAM uses discrete memory cells, each of which normally consists of a transistor and a capacitor, to store data. The real data, which is represented by an electrical charge in the capacitor and is a 0 or 1, is stored there as the fundamental unit of digital information. When it comes to limiting access to the capacitor so that data can be read or written, the transistor functions as a gatekeeper. Programs and data that the CPU requires instantly are stored in DRAMs. Cells used in Dynamic RAM (DRAM) construction store data as the charge on capacitors. Dynamic RAMs require periodic charge refreshing to preserve data storage because capacitors naturally have a tendency to discharge. Most systems use DRAM as their primary RAM option because of its speed and low cost. It offers the necessary temporary memory for your computer to perform programs and operations effectively, even though it is not for permanent storage.

SRAM (Static Random Access Memory)

SRAM is faster than DRAM because it uses latches, which are permanent data storage devices. This makes SRAM perfect for CPU caches and registers that require extremely quick access. However, there is a price for this speed: SRAM is used sparingly for some jobs where speed is crucial because it is more costly, larger due to complicated circuitry, and power-hungry. SRAM is different from DRAM in that it does not require data refreshes, instead, it may store data for as long as power is on. In addition to being more costly, SRAMs are faster than DRAMs. SRAM is therefore only occasionally used. The main categories of SRAM available are Registers and Cache:

- **Registers:** A tiny amount of storage found inside the CPU is called a register. A few hundred are found in most contemporary CPUs. They are used to hold data, locations, or instructions that the CPU must access immediately. The CPU's lightning-fast partners for data manipulation are registers. They are the fastest memory devices in the hierarchy due to their small size and on-chip placement, but their capacity limitation forces them to handle just the data that is necessary for the CPU to perform its current functions.
- **Cache:** Cache is essential for improving computer performance because it keeps frequently used data easily accessible to the CPU. It is a clever method of bridging the processor and slower storage device speed difference. In computers, cache refers to the layer of transient data storage situated between the central processing unit (CPU) and random-access memory (RAM), or between RAM and slower storage devices such as solid-state drives (SSDs) and hard drives (HDDs). By keeping frequently requested information or instructions closer to the processor, it functions as a speed booster by enabling speedier retrieval than contacting the original data source.

ROM (Read Only Memory)

Read-only memory (ROM) on computers allows you to read data but not alter it, as the name implies. It is like one of those library books you can check out but cannot write in. During regular operation, data written on ROM cannot be removed or altered because it is permanent. Usually, a particular procedure or manufacturing process is used to program this information. Important instructions that your computer needs to correctly boot up are stored in the RAM. Firmware is the term for these instructions. Hardware components are powered on and the operating system is loaded from a storage medium by the basic input/output system (BIOS), an example of a firmware. Other necessary software applications or data that are rarely modified can also be stored in ROM. Calculators and a few embedded devices, for instance, store their operating programs in RAM. Different types of ROM are available namely PROM, EPROM, and EEPROM.

PROM

The term PROM refers to Programmable Read-Only Memory. It cannot be reprogrammed; once manufactured, it is programmed using a burner or PROM programmer. An irreversible fuse switch blow is caused by the PROM programmer. PROM enables the programming of the data after it is built, whereas conventional ROM has data fixed permanently during manufacturing. Consider it as an empty form that you can only fill out once. When programming a PROM, high-voltage pulses are used to burn the data into the memory using a specialized electronic device. Information that has been programmed is unchangeable and cannot be removed. When data or software required to be permanent but was not fixed during manufacturing, PROMs were previously frequently used. For instance, PROMs were occasionally employed by early arcade games and personal computers to store their operating systems or game code.

EPROM

The term EPROM stands for Erasable Programmable Read-Only Memory. When exposed to UV light, EPROM can be reprogrammed by burning it, just like PROM. A more reusable form of PROM that lets you erase and rewrite data several times is called EPROM. Although EEPROMs and flash memory have since surpassed them, EPROMs were a crucial development in the field of writable read-only memory.

EEPROM

EEPROM and EPORM are not the same things; EEPROM cannot be removed from a device to be wiped and reprogrammed. It has a 100k reprogramming limit. EEPROM combines the non-volatile storage properties of ROM with the reusability of writable memory. It has better endurance for in-system reprogramming than EPROMs, which makes it a flexible option for a range of applications requiring sporadic data updates.

SECONDARY STORAGE

This is where long-term data storage is done. There are trade-offs between speed, size, and cost in its different internal and external forms. Flash drives, solid-state drives (SSDs), and hard drives (HDDs) are a few types. The CPU cannot directly access secondary storage. Data is permanently stored in non-volatile secondary memory. They are larger because they are more affordable than primary storage. Typically, secondary storage is optical or magnetic. Secondary storage comes in a variety of forms.

HDD (Hard Disk Drives)

A hard disk is among the most widely used types of secondary storage. It is made up of moving read and write heads and revolving platters covered in magnetic material. Each sector is further subdivided into a track, which are the concentric circles that make up the platter. The platter must be turned to the appropriate sector and the head must travel to the appropriate track to read or write to a sector. When it comes to large-scale data storage, HDDs are a reliable and affordable option. For regular computer purposes, they are a popular choice due to their vast capacities and affordability, even though they may not be the quickest as illustrated in Fig. (**2**).

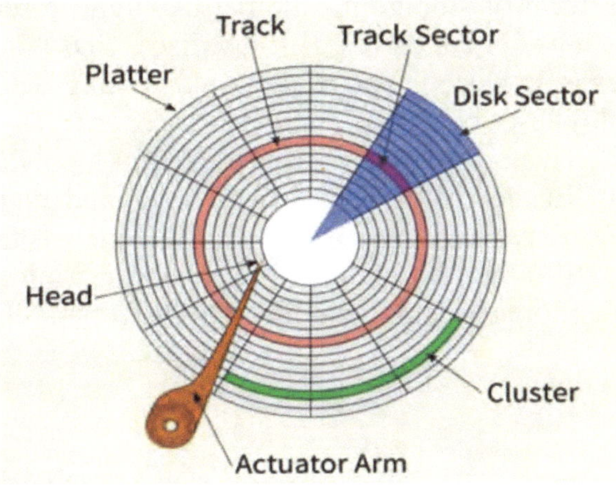

Fig. (2). Working of HDD [1].

SSD (Solid State Drives)

Solid-state drives, a modern form of storage technology, are gradually taking the place of hard drives. NAND gates are used in the construction of electrically programmable NAND flash memory, which is used for storing in SSDs. SSDs read and write data to and from linked flash memory chips. In addition, a flash controller governs the reading and writing of data. SSDs are less likely to fail than hard drives because they do not have any moving parts. In addition, they consume relatively little energy and are far faster than hard disks. Depending on the connecting interface, SSDs come in a variety of types. The more modern NVMe, which uses the PCIe bus, and SATA are two significant instances. SSDs are the way of the future for storage since they operate silently, perform incredibly quickly, and have better endurance. Their speed and other advantages make them an attractive option for current computers, even though they may not be able to match HDDs in terms of raw storage space for the same price.

Magnetic Tapes

A thin plastic film that has been magnetically treated is used to make magnetic tapes. You have to access the data in a sequential manner because it is a sequential data access medium. Their primary purpose is to store audio and video files. Long-term storage is not recommended for magnetic tape due to its deterioration. Magnetic tape is a dependable and affordable option for storing large amounts of data, but because of its slower access speeds, it is not as useful for routine computer operations where quick data retrieval is essential.

Optical Drives (CD/DVD)

Optical discs are a form of storage media that use light to read and write data. They are also known as optical drives, Blu-ray discs, CDs (Compact Discs), and DVDs (Digital Versatile Discs). For reading and writing data on optical disks, optical drives employ laser beams. A compact disc's, or CD's, maximum storage capacity is 700 MB. To store the data, it is made out of a polycarbonate disk with pits pressed into it. In the era of digital downloads and high-capacity storage devices, optical discs have lost some of their prominence as the primary storage medium. They are still a helpful choice, though, for sharing media, backing up data for long-term storage, and guaranteeing interoperability with outdated hardware.

Network Storage

Secondary storage also includes network storage. It is made up of storage devices that are networked together. This system comprises cloud storage, network attached storage (NAS), and storage area networks (SAN). A scalable and adaptable method of managing and sharing data amongst several devices on a network is provided by network storage. Network storage solutions may simplify data access and collaboration, whether you require a high-performance SAN for your company or an easy-to-use NAS for your home network.

DISK LOGICAL STRUCTURE

Data is physically stored on the rotating platters of a physical hard disk drive (HDD) in a certain way. We refer to this as a physical structure. However, the operating system's file system imposes a logical structure on how we interact with and manage that data. The hard drive's tree structure governs how the data kept in a computer are arranged as files and directories. An OS loaded on a hard drive is compatible with its logical structure. For the hard drive to comprehend itself and fix any disk-related issues, it needs a logical structure. The boot loaders and partition tables that the operating system reads are contained in the MBR, which is the first sector of the hard drive. The software, such as the operating system, and the file systems that are employed determine a hard disk's logical structure. These elements define and regulate the hard drive's data access procedure. Operating systems use different file systems, and these file systems use a range of extra techniques to manage and access data that is stored on hard drives. The same hard disk is arranged differently by different operating systems. The hard disk's storage subsystems' consistency, effectiveness, dependability, and versatility are directly impacted by its logical structure.

Clusters

We have looked at files, directories, and partitions inside the logical structure of a disk. However, how precisely is the data saved in these files? This is when clusters, the unsung heroes of file management, come into play. Consider a file system like a library. Files are individual books, directories are bookshelves, and partitions are sections of the library. On shelves, books are not kept in their entirety, though. They are separated into further pages. For files on a disk, clusters operate in a similar way. A cluster is the smallest unit of data allocation that a file system can manage on a disk. Clusters make sense logically, in contrast to sectors, which are the actual unit sizes. The file system's approach to balancing access speed and storage economy determines their size, which usually ranges from 512 bytes to 64 KB. The file system divides a file that you save into cluster-sized chunks. Then, though not always consecutively, these chunks are written to disk clusters that are available. These random bits might lead to fragmentation as you add, remove, and edit files.

Think about a book that has several missing pages across the library, because the read/write head must jump around to gather all the fragments, fragmentation can cause disk access to delay. Certain file systems include methods for defragmenting data to combat fragmentation. Data access is accelerated by these technologies, which combine dispersed clusters that are part of the same file. The smallest reachable storage units on a hard drive are called clusters. File systems split the volume of data on the disk into distinct information chunks for optimal and economical disk utilization. Sectors are combined to form clusters, which makes file handling easier. Clusters, which are collections of tracks and sectors that range from cluster number 2 to 32 or higher, depending on the formatting system, are also known as allocation units. To assign the necessary sectors to files, file allocation systems need to be adaptable. Each cluster may receive an allocation as large as one sector. A cluster's worth of space is required for every read or write operation. The file system must allot enough clusters to a file in order to store it. From 4 to 64 sectors, the cluster size varies and is solely dependent on the disk volume. There are instances where the cluster size can reach 128 sectors. A cluster's sectors run continuously from one another. Consequently, each cluster on the hard disk is a continuous section of space. The extra space in a cluster that is squandered when a file smaller than the cluster size is stored on the file system is called slack space.

Size of Cluster

Disk consumption and OS performance are severely affected by cluster sizing. Disk partitioning determines cluster sizes; larger volumes necessitate larger cluster sizes. The system may alter an existing partition's cluster size to increase speed. If a file has 5000 bytes, the file system allocates a complete cluster to store it, provided that the cluster size is 8192 bytes. If the file size is 10,000 bytes, the file system allocates storage space into two clusters totaling 16,384 bytes. For the disk to be used as efficiently as possible, cluster size is crucial. While using a big cluster size reduces the fragmentation issue, there is a significant rise in the likelihood of unused space.

Lost Clusters

File Allocation Table (FAT) mistake known as a "lost cluster" is what happens when the operating system marks clusters as utilized, nevertheless, it gives them no file allocation. The FAT file system's method for allocating spaces and combining files is where the issue comes from. The primary flaw is in the logical structure, not the physical disk error. When an application is closed before a computer is shut down or when files are not closed correctly, lost clusters can happen. Additional causes of these issues include resource conflicts and faulty drives on the disk. Even though these clusters are empty of files, OSs nonetheless identify them as in use. Programs for disk inspection can search an entire disk volume for lost clusters. A program that can clean or store lost clusters as a file can be used to find them. The latter creates fictitious files and connects them to these clusters. The newly created file will be damaged because of this procedure, although the orphaned data are visible and can be partially recovered.

A built-in Windows tool called Chkdsk.exe, often known as Check Disk, aids in the detection of disc media and file system problems. Use the Check Disk program if you are experiencing problems like blue screens and trouble opening or saving files or folders. Additionally, this program looks for lost clusters and problematic sectors. Use the Run utility to type cmd to open the Command Prompt. To open the Check Disk utility in read-only mode, type chkdsk into the Command Prompt. The Check Disk program will show the current drive's state after completing a scan as shown in Fig. (**3**).

```
D:\>chkdsk
The type of the file system is NTFS.
Volume label is New Volume.

WARNING!  /F parameter not specified.
Running CHKDSK in read-only mode.

Stage 1: Examining basic file system structure ...
  14336 file records processed.
File verification completed.
 Phase duration (File record verification): 1.40 seconds.
  36 large file records processed.
 Phase duration (Orphan file record recovery): 0.00 milliseconds.
  0 bad file records processed.
 Phase duration (Bad file record checking): 0.22 milliseconds.

Stage 2: Examining file name linkage ...
  102 reparse records processed.
  21626 index entries processed.
Index verification completed.
 Phase duration (Index verification): 7.79 seconds.
  0 unindexed files scanned.
 Phase duration (Orphan reconnection): 6.73 milliseconds.
  0 unindexed files recovered to lost and found.
 Phase duration (Orphan recovery to lost and found): 0.16 milliseconds.
  102 reparse records processed.
 Phase duration (Reparse point and Object ID verification): 2.13 milliseconds.

Stage 3: Examining security descriptors ...
Security descriptor verification completed.
 Phase duration (Security descriptor verification): 84.60 milliseconds.
  3645 data files processed.
 Phase duration (Data attribute verification): 0.80 milliseconds.

Windows has scanned the file system and found no problems.
No further action is required.

 163837951 KB total disk space.
 131252988 KB in 10385 files.
      2688 KB in 3647 indexes.
         0 KB in bad sectors.
     85327 KB in use by the system.
     65536 KB occupied by the log file.
  32496948 KB available on disk.

      4096 bytes in each allocation unit.
  40959487 total allocation units on disk.
   8124237 allocation units available on disk.
Total duration: 9.28 seconds (9287 ms).
```

Fig. (3). Checking disk utility.

Slack Space

Consider a parking lot. Every vehicle (your file) has a specific parking spot (cluster). But clusters are fixed in size, unlike individual car parking spaces that are just the right size. This implies that a tiny file, such as a grocery list, could wind up parked in a cluster the size of an SUV (imagine a 4KB cluster for a 1KB file). The slack space is the remaining unoccupied area in that cluster, which is the vacant space next to the miniature automobile. File systems' storage allocation process results in slack space. It is not always possible to find a perfect fit for every file size because the actual storage units are bundled into larger clusters for efficiency. This involves a trade-off. Because heads would move more frequently in smaller clusters, there would be less slack space but more access time. Now standard, larger clusters provide faster access but always create slack space.

When a file that is less than the cluster size receives a whole cluster from the file system, slack space is created. The empty area that lies between a file's end and the cluster's end in a disk cluster is referred to as slack space. Slack space causes wasted disk space when there are a lot of files and a large cluster size. The file systems for Windows and DOS both use fixed-size clusters. Even if the file system reserves all the space inside a cluster for a file, the size that a file uses within a cluster is independent of the data storage. Big partitions need a big cluster size due to the 16-bit allocation table utilized by earlier DOS and Windows versions. For instance, the system will allocate an entire 32 KB cluster, leaving 22 K of slack space, if each partition has a size of 4 GB, each cluster has a size of 32 KB, and a file needs just 10 KB as Fig. (**4**) illustrates the slack space.

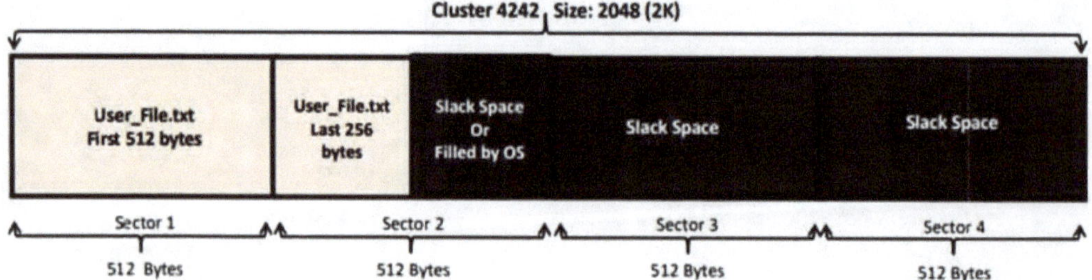

Fig. (4). Slack space.

Partitioning is used by the system to get rid of this inefficiency. Using the New Technology File System (NTFS), which permits considerably smaller clusters on huge partitions than FAT does, is another method to reduce the idle space. Compression of seldom used files can also be utilized to minimize slack when archiving them. The problem of slack space is becoming more significant as disk sizes increase. Following are the types of file slacks:

- **RAM slack:** RAM slack is the data storage space that exists between a file's finish and its last sector.
- **Drive slack:** From the end of a file's last sector until the end of the file's final cluster, there is data storage space.

Slack space is a crucial type of evidence in the realm of forensic investigation. Slack space frequently contains pertinent suspect information that a prosecutor must provide as proof in court. For instance, half of a hard drive cluster might not be empty if the suspect erased all its contents, then saved new ones, filling the other half of the cluster. It can include the information from the erased files. Computer forensic tools can be used by forensic examiners to gather this data.

Master Boot Record (MBR)

The first sector, or sector zero, of a hard drive contains the MBR, which notifies an operating system where to load into the primary storage. Because the MBR contains a table that tracks partitioned disk data, it is commonly referred to as the partition sector or master partition table. The rest of the operating system is loaded into RAM by a program in the record. An MBR file has details about the different files that are on the disk, including their sizes, locations, and contents. The 512-byte disk boot or partition sector is almost universally referred to as the MBR in real-world usage. In Windows and DOS, the fdisk/MBR commands enable the creation of MBR. The BIOS connects to this first sector for information on loading the operating system and boot-process instructions when the computer first boots up. A partition table, which lists a hard disk's partitions, is stored in the MBR. Launching an operating system from scratch. Distinctly identifying each hard drive using a 32-bit disk signature.

The following structures constitute the MBR:

- **Partition Table:** A 64-byte data structure called a partition table carries details about the various kinds and locations of partitions on a hard drive. The typical layout of this table is independent of the operating system. It can only describe primary, or physical, divisions, which number four. Logically, each additional partition is connected to at least one major partition.
- **Master Boot Code:** To initiate the boot process, the system loads the master boot code—a short section of computer code—into the BIOS and executes it. The system gives the boot software on the active partition control to load the operating system after it has been executed. The partition table is examined by the master boot code to determine which partition is currently active. Finds the active partition's initial sector. Loads a copy of the boot sector from the active partition into memory. Instructs the executable code located in the boot sector. Fig. (**5**) illustrates the structure of MBR [2].

Address			Description		Size in bytes
Hex	Oct	Dec			
0000	0000	0	Code Area		440 (max. 446)
01B8	0670	440	Disk Signature (Optional)		4
01BC	0674	444	Usually Nulls; 0x0000		2
01BE	0676	446	Table of Primary Partitions (Four 16-byte entries, IBM partition table scheme)		64
01FE	0776	510	55h	MBR Signature; 0xAA55	2
01FF	0777	511	AAh		
MBR, Total Size: 446 + 64 = 2 =					512

Fig. (5). Structure of MBR.

Partitions of Disks

The process of dividing a storage device (HDD or SSD) logically so that the user can apply logical formatting unique to their operating system is known as disk partitioning. With SSDs and HDDs, the disk-partitioning procedure is the same. A partition is a logical drive used to store data, and partitioning is the process of creating logical drives for efficient memory management. Data can be hidden on a drive by creating hidden partitions. The distance between the primary and secondary partitions is known as the inter-partition gap. If there is hidden data on the inter-partition drive, it can be modified using disk-editor software such as Disk Editor. Any references to the hidden partition that the operating system has kept hidden will be removed by doing this. Placing material—which could include digital evidence—at the end of the disk and declaring less bytes than the drive's actual capacity is another way to hide data.

An investigator can access these unoccupied or hidden disk regions by using Disk Editor. There are two sorts of partitions:

- **Primary partition:** This disk holds information on the operating system, system space, and additional information required for booting. The first partition (C:) on MS-DOS and older Microsoft Windows systems needs to be a primary partition.
- **Extended partition:** Information about the files and data on the disk is kept on the logical drive. There are several tools available to examine disk partitions. Hex Workshop, WinHex, and Disk Edit are a few disk-editing tools. Users can inspect file headers and other pertinent file metadata with these tools. Both

functions need an analysis of the hexadecimal codes that an OS recognizes and uses to manage the file system.

BIOS Parameter Block (BPB)

The first sector of a storage volume contains the data structure known as the volume boot record (VBR), also referred to as the BIOS Parameter Block (BPB). It functions as a map, outlining the essential characteristics and physical arrangement of the disk or partition it is located on. For the operating system or bootloader to comprehend how to access and handle data on the storage volume, essential information must be stored in the BPB. The volume boot record (VBR) of a hard drive contains the BPB, a data structure that describes the physical layout of a disk volume. Sector 1 is where you can locate it. It encompasses both the complete medium and the volume partition on partitioned media, like hard disks. The fundamental file-system architecture is described in BPB, which can be used with any partition that contains floppy drives. The length of the BPB varies among the listed file systems (*i.e.,* FAT16, FAT32, and NTFS) since different file systems store and maintain different kinds of fields in the BPB and hold varying volumes of data. BPB helps investigators find the hard drive's file table.

While the BPB was essential for older operating systems like MS-DOS, more recent file systems like Linux's EXT4 and Windows' NTFS have made it less significant. By maintaining internal structures for controlling disk space, these file systems lessen their dependency on the BPB. The BPB, however, can still be a useful source of information for forensic analysis or data recovery since it offers details about the original structure and format of a storage volume.

Globally Unique Identifier (GUID)

A 128-bit integer called a GUID or Universally Unique Identifier (UUID) determines an object's unique identity in computer systems. GUIDs are often shown as 32 hexadecimal digits with hyphens separating the groups of numbers. For instance, a GUID is created and assigned to the browser when a user browses a website; this aids in monitoring and documenting the user's browsing session. To identify user accounts by username (domain), dynamic-link libraries (DLLs) for the Component Object Model (COM), and user accounts themselves, the Windows operating system gives the registry a GUID. To identify DLLs (dynamic-link libraries) and COMs (component object model), GUIDs are commonly utilized in the Windows Registry. GUIDs are primary key values in database tables. A GUID may occasionally be assigned by a website to a user's browser to log and monitor the session. Windows uses a GUID to identify user accounts based on a username. Windows Registry GUIDs are shown in Fig. (**6**).

Choose Start > Run, type regedit, and open Registry Editor by going to Computer\HKEY_LOCAL_MACHINE\.

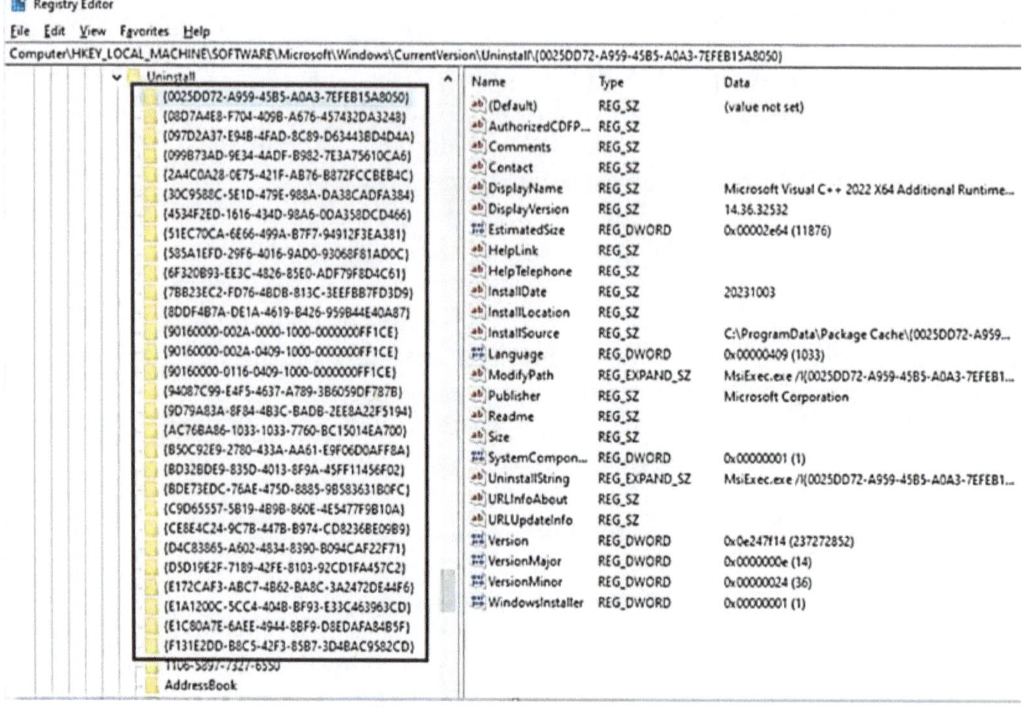

Fig. (6). GUIDs in windows registry editor.

GUIDs are equivalent to unique digital fingerprints. They offer a dependable and effective means of differentiating between various elements within a computer system.

GUID Partition Table (GPT)

The industry standard for disk partitioning is the GUID Partition Table (GPT). It offers multiple benefits over the MBR, which was its predecessor, especially for larger storage devices. A disk's partitioning information is stored in a specified layout called a GPT. GPT provides a number of advantages over MBR, which is restricted to 4 primary partitions and uses 32-bit addressing: Partitions with Unique IDs: GPT uses globally unique identifiers, or GUIDs, to give each disk partition a unique ID. This lowers the possibility of inadvertently overwriting partitions and improves organization. Scalability for Big Disks: Because of its 32-bit addressing constraint, MBR has trouble handling disks larger than 2.2 TB. By using 64-bit addressing, GPT gets over this obstacle and supports substantially bigger storage capacities. GPT includes two copies of the partition table at various locations on the disk to provide redundancy for reliability. Even if one copy becomes corrupted, data integrity is guaranteed by this redundancy.

Flexibility with More Partitions: GPT offers you a large increase, usually up to 128 or more partitions, whereas MBR only permits you to have four primary partitions. This gives you more options when it comes to disk space management. 32 bits are used by the MBR partition scheme to store the size information on 512-byte sectors as well as Logical Block Addresses (LBAs). GPTs employ logical block addressing (LBA) as opposed to cylinder-head-sector (CHS) addressing, just like contemporary MBRs. Each logical block in the GUID partition table (GPT) has 512 bytes, and each partition entry has 128 bytes. Logical block negative addressing addresses the final addressable block with a value of -1, beginning at the end of the volume. The protected MBR is stored in LBA 0, the GPT header is stored in LBA 1, and the partition table, also known as the Partition Entry Array, is stored in LBA 2 and is referred to in the GPT header. Among the benefits of the GPT disk configuration are partition sizes of up to two Tebibytes (TiB) and eight Zebibytes (ZiB).

With the GPT partition pattern, it enables users to have 128 partitions in Windows. Because GPT stores data in several locations across a disk, it is more secure than MBR for both the boot data and the partition, offering redundancy through primary and backup partition tables. To guarantee data integrity, cyclic redundancy checks, or CRCs, are used. Use CRC32 checksums to identify anomalies in the partition table and header. The GUID partition table architecture is shown in Fig. (7).

BOOT PROCESS OF WINDOWS AND LINUX

This section covers both the BIOS-MBR and UEFI-GPT Windows boot methods, as well as how to determine whether a disk has an MBR or GPT partitioning scheme. The fundamental concepts of booting up the system, initializing the hardware, and loading necessary services to get you into a functional environment are shared by both Windows and Linux. The specific tools and techniques that each operating system uses account for the minor changes.

Boot Process

The essential step that powers your computer is called booting. It ensures that everything is in harmony before you see the recognizable login screen. This process is initializing the hardware and software. Two different types of booting processes are possible:

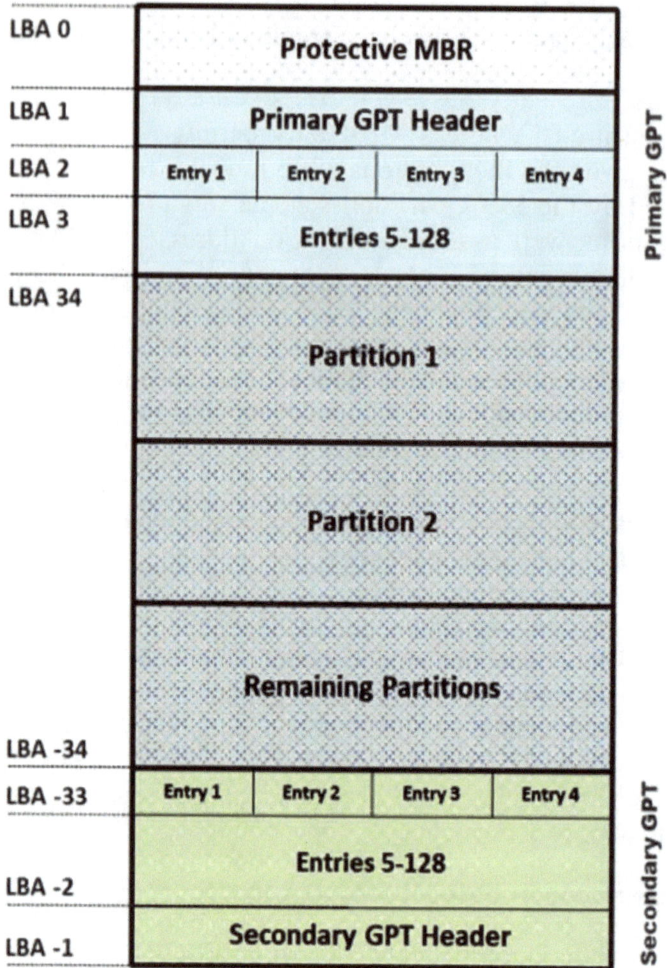

Fig. (7). GUID partition table architecture.

- When a user turns on their computer for the first time, a procedure known as "cold boot" (hard boot) takes place. Hard booting, as it is also known, is necessary when the user fully disconnects the system's power source.
- Restarting a computer that has already been turned on is known as "warm boot" or "soft boot." If a program problem occurs, or a restart is necessary after installing a program, among other scenarios, the system may experience a warm boot.

The computer loads the operating system (OS) into RAM and gets ready for usage during the boot process. During system initialization, the BIOS is activated and loaded into RAM. The BIOS contains the initial instruction to perform the power-on self-test (POST). The BIOS chip and complementary metal-oxid--semiconductor (CMOS) RAM are checked by the system during POST. Following is the process of the general booting procedure that works with Linux and Windows systems as shown in Table **1**.

Table 1. Booting process of operating system.

Process	Description
1	**Switching on and UEFI/BIOS activation:** The motherboard, the beating heart of your computer, receives electricity when you push the power button. The motherboard's built-in firmware turns on and is known as BIOS or UEFI. This firmware uses a POST to determine whether all your crucial hardware parts, including your CPU, RAM, and storage devices, are functioning properly.
2	**Selecting the Boot Device:** Following POST completion, your system's attached devices are searched for bootable devices by the BIOS/UEFI. Your hard drive, a solid-state drive (SSD), or even a bootable USB device could be this. The BIOS/UEFI settings define the boot order, which dictates which device is searched for bootable files first.
3	**Loading the Boot Loader:** After determining the boot device, the BIOS locates and loads a little program known as the boot loader. The task of the bootloader is to locate the kernel, which is the operating system's core component.
4	**Kernel Loading:** Once the boot device has been loaded, the boot loader loads the kernel—a crucial component of the operating system—into the main memory (RAM) of the machine.
5	**Initialization of the kernel:** The kernel begins initializing to establish communication with the hardware and get the system ready for additional processes.
6	**Device Drivers Loading:** Like interpreters, device drivers enable the OS to interact with hardware devices. The kernel loads the required device drivers during booting in order for your keyboard, mouse, network card, and other peripherals to function.
7	**Setup of the System and Initial Programs:** After that, the kernel loads system configuration files and launches startup apps in accordance with OS directives. This could entail loading background programs or essential system services that launch automatically.

Essential Windows System Files

The setup program creates the necessary files and directories on the system disk after an OS installation. Traces of user activity and system activities may be present in these files. A chronology of events, for instance, can be generated by timestamps on the creation or alteration of files inside system files. Programs utilized and maybe when they were used can be found by looking *via* registry entries in pertinent system files (such as the running apps record of user32.dll). Malware can intentionally alter our target system files to conceal its presence or ensure its persistence. Forensic investigators may want to take notice of anomalies in these files, such as unforeseen modifications or attempts at illicit access. Investigators may be able to piece together a history of events on the digital device by examining timestamps, access logs, and other information included in system files.

Knowing what transpired during a possible crime or incident can be aided by this. What software was installed on the system can be deduced from traces found in specific system files. Investigators may find this helpful in understanding the possible programs or technologies that were utilized maliciously. Table **2** provides an overview of the essential Windows system files.

Table 2. Description of the essential Windows system files.

File Name	Description
Ntoskrnl.exe	One essential Windows file is ntoskrnl.exe, which is the kernel executable for the Windows NT operating system. It serves as the beating heart of the operating system. To maintain the smooth operation of your Windows system, ntoskrnl.exe is an essential system process that operates in the background. Located in the C:\Windows\System32.
Ntkrnlpa.exe	A crucial system file for Windows systems that employ Physical Address Extension (PAE) is ntkrnlpa.exe. 32-bit Windows has a memory management mechanism called PAE that lets it access more RAM than the 4GB limit. located within the C:\Windows\System32 directory
Hal.dll	An additional crucial Windows system file is called Hardware Abstraction Layer Dynamic Link Library, or Hal.dll for short. It is essential to the seamless running of the hardware and software on your computer. Typically, the C:\Windows\system32 folder contains hal.dll.
Win32k.sys	A vital Windows system file that directly affects what you see on your screen is called Win32k.sys. The Windows experience would not be complete without Win32k.sys, which keeps the graphical user interface seamless and functioning. It is a valid system file, so you should not try to edit or uninstall it. The directory C:\Windows\System32\drivers contains the Win32k.sys file.
Ntdll.dll	A crucial part of Windows, ntdll.dll serves as the basis for important system functions and allows programs to communicate with the kernel. The standard location for Ntdll.dll is C:\Windows\SYSTEM32.
Kernel32.dll	One of Windows' essential DLLs (Dynamic Link Libraries) is kernel32.dll, which serves as a link between your apps and the system's primary features. Usually, the directory C:\Windows\System32 contains kernel32.dll.
Advapi32.dll	A number of tools and functions linked to advanced Windows functionality are provided by Advapi32.dll. These features enable applications to carry out tasks. You can find Advapi32.dll in the C:\Windows\System32 directory. Numerous crucial system files, such as DLLs and core executables required for Windows functionality, are kept under this folder.
User32.dll	A crucial DLL (Dynamic Link Library) in Windows, User32.dll is essential to your graphical user interface (GUI) experience. User32.dll is normally located in the C:\Windows\System32 directory.
Gdi32.dll	Applications can use the functions and utilities provided by Gdi32.dll to generate simple visual elements and carry out graphical actions. Gdi32.dll located in the C:\Windows\System32 directory.

Bios-mbr Methods

BIOS and MBR are the traditional methods utilized to boot up older machines. The steps involved are broken down as follows:

- Turn on and activate the BIOS: The BIOS is a firmware program that is pre-installed on a chip on your motherboard, and it is what the computer starts when you push the power button. To confirm that all of your hardware, including the CPU, RAM, and storage devices, is operating correctly, the BIOS does a POST.
- Selecting the Boot Device: The BIOS must identify the operating system (OS) that will be loaded following POST. It looks for a bootable device, usually your hard drive, but depending on how your boot settings are set up in the BIOS, it might also look for an external drive, USB stick, or network drive.
- Loading the MBR: After deciding which device to boot from—typically the hard drive—the BIOS finds and reads the drive's first 512 bytes. The first and most significant sector is the MBR.
- Bootloader loading: The bootloader code included in the MBR is now executed by the BIOS. The main job of this code is to find the kernel, or the central component of your operating system, which is probably kept on your hard drive's primary partition, as indicated by the partition table.
- Kernel Loading: After reading the partition table, the bootloader code determines which partition is active (typically the one designated for booting). The operating system's kernel, which is then loaded into the machine's main memory (RAM), is the result of that partition.
- Initialization of the kernel: The kernel begins initializing in order to establish communication with the hardware and get the system ready for additional processes.
- Loading Device Drivers: Device drivers enable the OS to connect with certain hardware devices by functioning as interpreters. The kernel loads the required device drivers during booting for your keyboard, mouse, network card, and other peripherals to function.
- System Configuration and Startup Programs: Next, the kernel loads the OS-specified startup programs and loads system configuration files. This could entail loading background programs or essential system services that launch automatically.

There are several reasons why the Windows Boot Process which uses the BIOS and MBR (Master Boot Record) might be significant in a digital forensics' investigation.

- Understanding System State: By looking at the boot process, one can learn about the system's basic configuration at the time of its last boot. This can help identify any changes made to the boot configuration or sequence, which may indicate malware presence or tampering.
- Recognizing Possible Boot Manipulation: To stay persistent on a system, malicious actors occasionally try to alter the boot process. This could entail altering the MBR to load a secret operating system or swapping out the default bootloader for a malicious one. Investigators can spot indications of this kind of modification by looking through the MBR contents and boot process configuration.
- Evidence of Hidden Partitions: To hide dangerous software or store stolen data, robbers have been known to make hidden partitions on drives. Only primary partition data is stored in the MBR partition table. On the other hand, abnormalities or unused space that can point to the existence of hidden partitions can be found using forensic techniques.
- Boot Sector Analysis: The MBR is in the first sector of a hard drive, which may retain remnants of previous boot configurations or even erased bootloader files. This industry can be examined by forensic tools to look for these kinds of traces, which could provide historical details about the system or proof of previous manipulation attempts.

Digital forensics investigations benefit from the Windows Boot Process, which uses BIOS and MBR. Investigators can learn important details about the state of the system, spot evidence of tampering, and provide the groundwork for additional forensic examination of the storage device by examining the boot configuration, MBR contents, and possible manipulation efforts. Fig. (**8**) illustrates how to identify the MBR partition.

UEFI-GPT Windows Boot Process

The EFI boot manager is responsible for managing the UEFI boot process. In order to initialize platform functionalities, the boot manager loads UEFI software and drivers, including UEFI OS boot loaders, during the first stage of platform firmware startup. The final stage involves the system loading the OS loader, which triggers the OS to boot up. The OS stops the UEFI boot service when it gets the controls. As shown in Fig. (**9**).

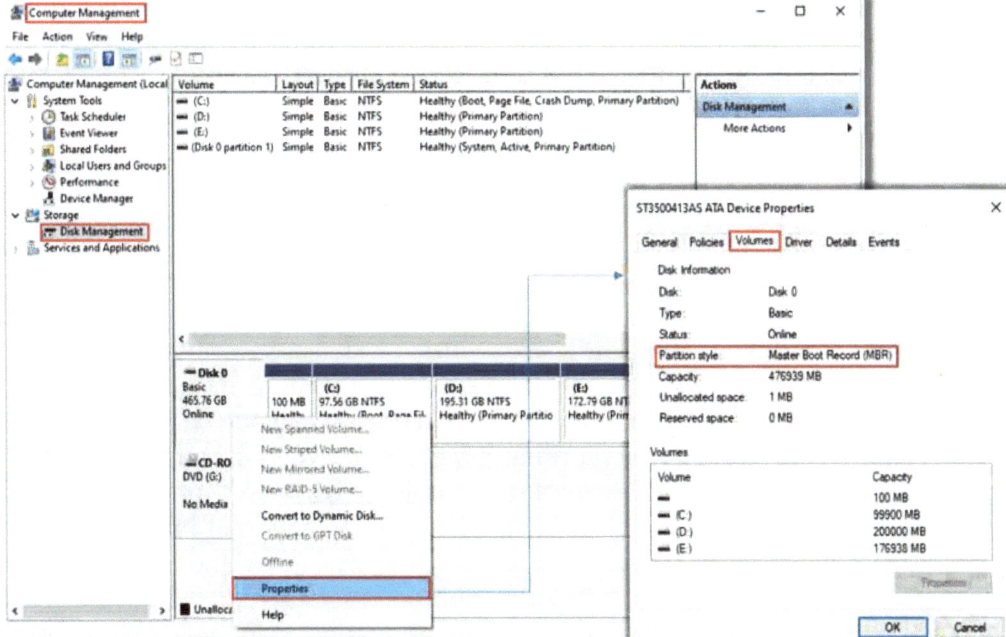

Fig. (8). Identifying the MBR partition.

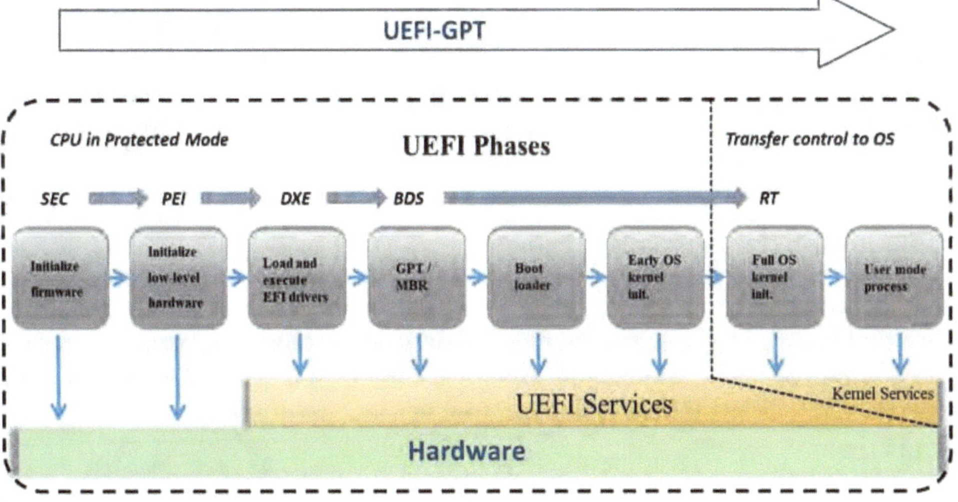

Fig. (9). UEFI-GPT method for Windows boot process.

Guid Partition Table (GPT)

An investigator can examine the disk layout with the use of a GUID partition table (GPT) header, which contains information on the partition table and its backup copies, as well as the locations of the partition areas. The Windows

PowerShell cmdlets listed below can be used by investigators to determine whether GPT is present as shown in Fig. (**10**). Digital forensics investigations can benefit from determining whether a disk drive has a GUID Partition Table (GPT). The GPT partition table is stored in several copies throughout the disk, in contrast to the MBR (Master Boot Record) seen in previous systems. If the primary partition table is corrupted or damaged, this redundancy increases the likelihood of data recovery. On a GPT disk, each partition has a GUID assigned to it. This helps forensic investigators recognize partitions and their contents even when the partition label, often known as the name, is altered, or deleted.

Secure Boot is frequently used in UEFI (Unified Extensible Firmware Interface) systems that make use of GPT. By preventing the system from booting from unapproved or unsigned bootloaders, this security feature may lower the possibility that malware may compromise the system by using boot manipulation techniques. Comparing GPT drives to classic MBR disks provides digital forensics investigators with a more comprehensive collection of information and possible paths for evidence extraction. It facilitates more thorough timeline development, enhanced partition identification, and more successful data recovery attempts all of which contribute to a more thorough digital forensic investigation as shown in Fig. (**10**).

```
PS C:\Windows\System32> Get-Disk

Number Frie Serial Number                 HealthStatus       OperationalStatus       Total Size Partition
       ndly                                                                                     Style

       Name
------ ---- -------------                 ------------       -----------------       ---------- ---------
0      W...      WD-WCC6Y4ZSRXY1          Healthy            Online                   931.51 GB GPT
```

Fig. (10). Get-GPT command.

Examining GPT Entries and Headers

Most operating systems that allow GPT disk access contain a simple partitioning utility that shows information about GPT partition tables. Linux users utilize the GNU Parted program, while Mac users use the OS X Disk utility and Windows users use applications like the DiskPart tool to view partition details as depicted in Fig. (**11**).

By adopting adaptable and extendable disk partitioning algorithms, hackers may be able to conceal data on GPT disks in a manner comparable to that of traditional MBR disks. Data may be concealed on GPT drives in the following places: inter-partition gaps, partitioned space at the end of the disk, reserved spaces, and the GPT header. Additional artifacts could be reserved tag sections, misplaced starting and terminating LBAs, or altered GPT headers that create places for data hiding. The forensic techniques and instruments available today are inadequate for doing GPT analysis. Analyzing header data and GPT entries is a useful method in computer forensics investigations. It gives investigators a plethora of knowledge regarding the arrangement of the disk, any alterations, and the chronology of events. Understanding possible security breaches, finding buried evidence, and assisting with data recovery can all benefit from this information.

```
DISKPART> list disk

  Disk ###  Status         Size     Free     Dyn  Gpt
  --------  -------------  -------  -------  ---  ---
  Disk 0    Online          931 GB      0 B        *
  Disk 1    Online           57 GB      0 B

DISKPART> select disk 0

Disk 0 is now the selected disk.

DISKPART> detail disk

WDC WD10EZEX-60WN4A0
Disk ID: {5CE6D770-4C3C-4ADF-A001-DDAC8DE28265}
Type   : SATA
Status : Online
Path   : 0
Target : 0
LUN ID : 0
Location Path : PCIROOT(0)#PCI(1700)#ATA(C00T00L00)
Current Read-only State : No
Read-only  : No
Boot Disk  : Yes
Pagefile Disk  : Yes
Hibernation File Disk  : No
Crashdump Disk  : Yes
Clustered Disk  : No

  Volume ###  Ltr  Label        Fs     Type        Size     Status     Info
  ----------  ---  -----------  -----  ----------  -------  ---------  --------
  Volume 0         Recovery     NTFS   Partition    529 MB  Healthy
  Volume 1     C                NTFS   Partition    344 GB  Healthy    Boot
  Volume 2     D   New Volume   NTFS   Partition    156 GB  Healthy
  Volume 3     E   New Volume   NTFS   Partition    146 GB  Healthy
  Volume 4                      FAT32  Partition    100 MB  Healthy    System
```

Fig. (11). View disk partitions with the diskpart utility.

FORENSICS TOOLS TO ANALYZE FILE SYSTEMS

Examining the file system is a crucial step in digital forensics to find evidence. It is like going through an extremely well-kept archive, only with digital traces in place of dusty documents. File system analysis is crucial to investigations in revealing the digital tale. File systems carefully safeguard information about files in addition to storing them. This metadata consists of user rights, file size, creation dates, and last accessed timestamps. Investigators can create a history of activity, determine who visited files, and possibly find hidden files by examining this data. Even deleted files can still be found. File carving techniques can be utilized by file system analysis tools to discover these remnants in unallocated space, with the possibility of retrieving erased data that may provide important evidence. There are other storytellers than the file system.

File system analysis can also uncover artifacts such as email correspondence, chat logs, online browser history, and registry entries (on Windows computers), in addition to files. These digital crumbs can provide a clear picture of what people have been doing. One of the main components of digital forensics is file system examination. Investigators can find a plethora of evidence, reconstruct events, and find any misconduct by closely examining this digital world. Although it is a tedious process, it might be vital for exposing cybercrimes. An image file and file system data that have been forensically collected can be investigated and examined by a forensic investigator using the Sleuth Kit, a set of command-line tools. The examination of disk image files with Autopsy is covered in this section.

File Systems for Windows

For storing and organizing data, Windows primarily uses three file systems FAT, FAT32, and NTFS. The Master File Table (MFT) is a system file that NTFS uses to hold metadata about files and directories. Information of forensic importance, such as file names, locations, and MAC timings, can be obtained by looking through the $MFT file. To assist them in recovering lost data during an investigation, forensic investigators should also be knowledgeable about file allocation and deletion.

File Allocation Table (FAT)

FAT is the first entry in a volume and stores all the files. It is named after the manner it arranges folders and is intended for tiny hard drives with a straightforward folder structure. The sizes of the entries in the FAT structure vary from FAT12 to FAT32. FAT is compatible with a greater variety of operating systems and older devices because it is a relatively simple file system. Because FAT has a simpler design than NTFS, it can occasionally perform better for basic read/write tasks. FAT has few security measures and few methods for controlling access. To prevent harm to the volume, FAT duplicates the file allocation table twice. The root folder and file allocation table are kept in a permanent location. The size of the formatted volume determines the size of the cluster formed by the FAT file system-formatted volume. The system compresses the cluster number—which is a power of two—into 16 bits for the FAT file system. Devices that use the FAT file system include flash memory, digital cameras, and portable electronics. Nearly every operating system that is installed on personal computers uses the FAT file system.

New Technology File System (NTFS)

NTFS is the most widely used file system for internal hard drives on modern Windows systems (Windows NT and later). Designed to address the inadequacies of the File Allocation Table (FAT), it offers several advantages in terms of reliability, security, and functionality. One of the most recent file systems that Windows supports is NTFS. High-performance, self-repairing file system with many cutting-edge features, including compression, auditing, and file-level security. Large and potent volume storage options, such as self-recovering drives, are also supported. Since NTFS can encrypt and decrypt files, directories, and data, it offers data security. For file and folder naming, it employs a 16-bit Unicode character set. This feature of NTFS enables file management in the native languages of users all over the world. Additionally, the file system offers failure tolerance. When a user modifies a file, NTFS logs all of the modifications in specially defined log files. When a hard drive fails, NTFS uses these log files to restore the disk with the least amount of data loss. NTFS also makes use of master file structures and metadata. Metadata contains information about the data that is stored on the computer. The identical information is also calculated in a master file table; however, this table has less data storage capacity than metadata. Because of its extensive feature set, NTFS is the recommended file system for internal hard drives on Windows systems. It provides an excellent mix of performance, dependability, security, and usability for daily use. On contemporary Windows systems, NTFS is the reliable and secure file system that serves as the basis for data storage. Description is shown in Table **3**. It is the recommended option for internal hard drives due to its emphasis on security, dependability, and support for huge files.

Table 3. NTFS System files

File Name	Description
$attrdef	Explains each of the user- and system-defined volume attributes.
$badclus	The firmware on your hard drive usually designates a sector as defective when it malfunctions and is unable to retain data consistently. The file system uses $badclus as a list or map to keep track of these bad sectors.
$bitmap	Contains the volume's complete bitmap.
$boot	Contains the bootstrap for the volume.
$logfile	used as a means of recovery

(Table 3) cont.....

File Name	Description
$mft	Includes a record for each file.
$mftmirr	The MFT mirror that is utilized to retrieve files
$quota	Shows the disk quota for every user.
$upcase	Transforms characters into Unicode uppercase
$volume	Contains the version number and volume name.

USE CASES AND EXAMPLES

Autopsy is a digital forensics tool that may be downloaded for free. With capabilities like multi-user situations, timeline analysis, registry analysis, keyword search, email analysis, video playback, EXIF analysis, potentially dangerous file detection, and much more, it is a powerful and free hard drive inspection tool. Its plug-in architecture allows for extension *via* user-developed or custom modules. Autopsy is essential to the needs of hundreds of thousands of professionals in law enforcement, national security, corporate investigations, and litigation support. It is even capable of retrieving images from the memory card of a camera. Autopsy is a comprehensive platform that includes both proprietary and in-built modules.

The functions listed below are offered by a few modules:

- High-tech graphical event viewer interface for chronological analysis
- Hash filtering: Identifies and marks as malicious files while ignoring legitimate files.
- Keyword search: To locate files that include pertinent terms, use an index.
- Web artifacts: reveals the history, bookmarks, and cookies from Internet Explorer, Firefox, and Chrome.
- Data carving: uses PhotoRec to recover deleted files from unallocated space.
- Multimedia: eliminates Exif information from images and videos
- Compromise indicators: Utilizing Structured Threat Information Expression (STIX), a computer is scanned

Installing Autopsy

Step 1: Click to download Autopsy from https://www.autopsy.com/download/.

Step 2: Open the Autopsy MSI installer to begin the process.

Step 3: Click Yes if prompted by Windows.

Step 4: Go through the dialog boxes by clicking each one until you find the "Finish" button. As shown in Fig. (**12**).

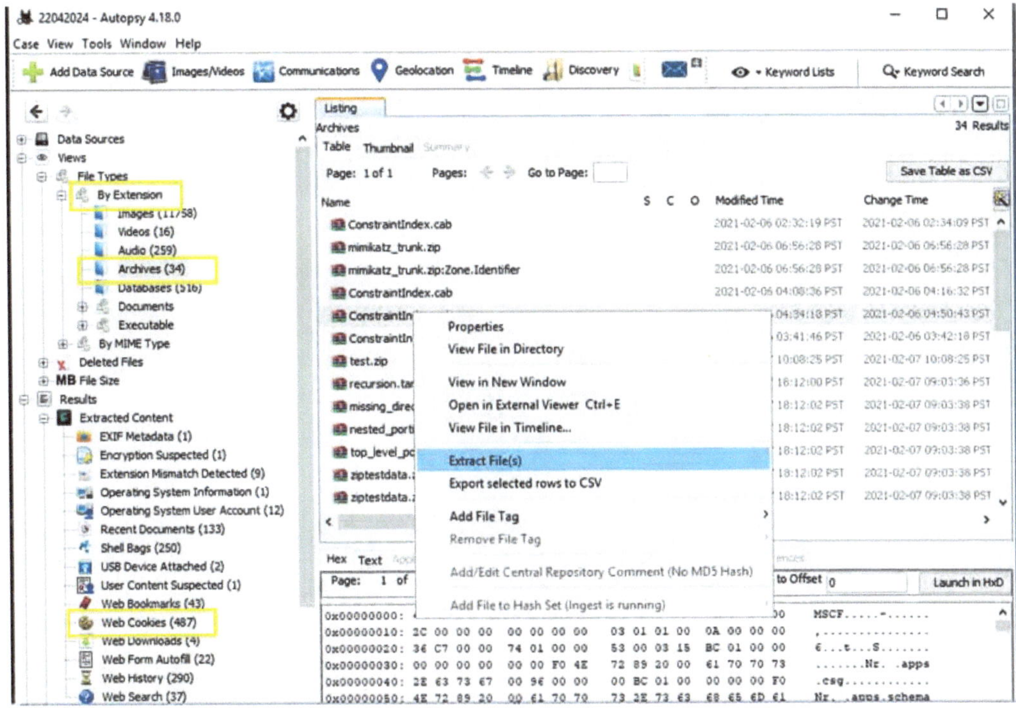

Fig. (12). Autopsy interface.

Conduct Investigations using Autopsy

We will now look at how to utilize Autopsy to examine a hard drive. To do that, we will examine a common scenario that most of us encounter when studying digital forensics.

Scenario: This system is suspected of being used for hacking, even if it cannot be linked to Greg Schardt, a hacking suspect. Known online as "Mr. Evil," Schardt is said to be well-known among some of his coworkers for frequently parking his automobile near wireless access points. He would then allegedly try to get usernames, passwords, and credit card information by intercepting internet traffic. Keep an eye out for any software that has been hacked, as well as any created data and proof of its usage. Consider making a connection between the computer and Greg Schardt, the suspect [3].

Step 1: Open Autopsy, then click New Case as shown in Fig. (**13**).

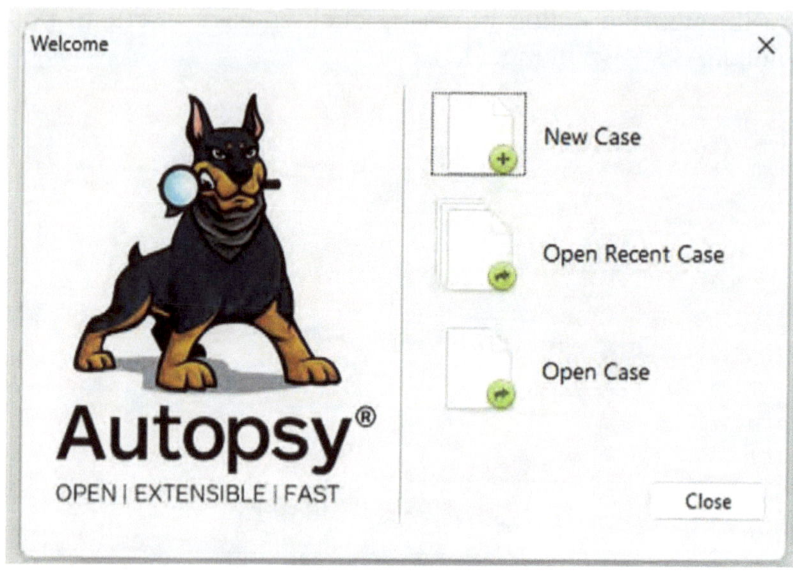

Fig. (13). Choose a new case.

Step 2: Give the directory where the case file will be stored along with the case name. Press the Next button as shown in Fig. (**14**).

New Case Information

Steps
1. Case Information
2. Optional Information

Case Information

Case Name: 29042024

Base Directory: D:\autopsy\ Browse

Case Type: Single-User Multi-User

Case data will be stored in the following directory:

D:\autopsy\29042024

< Back Next > Finish Cancel Help

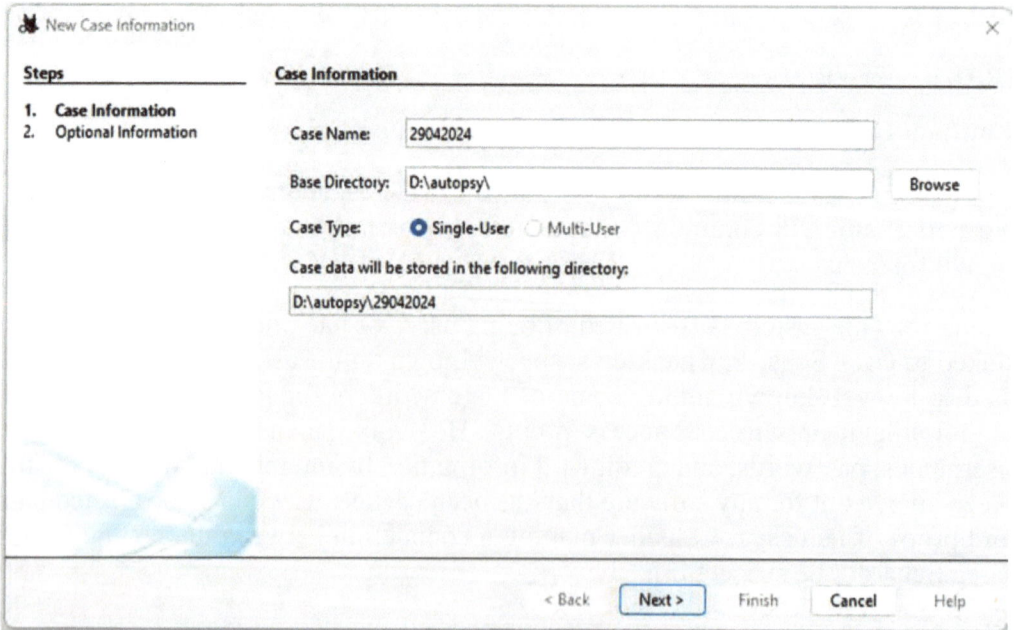

Fig. (14). Base directory for the case.

Step 3: After adding the Examiner's information and the Case Number, click Finish as shown in Fig. (**15**).

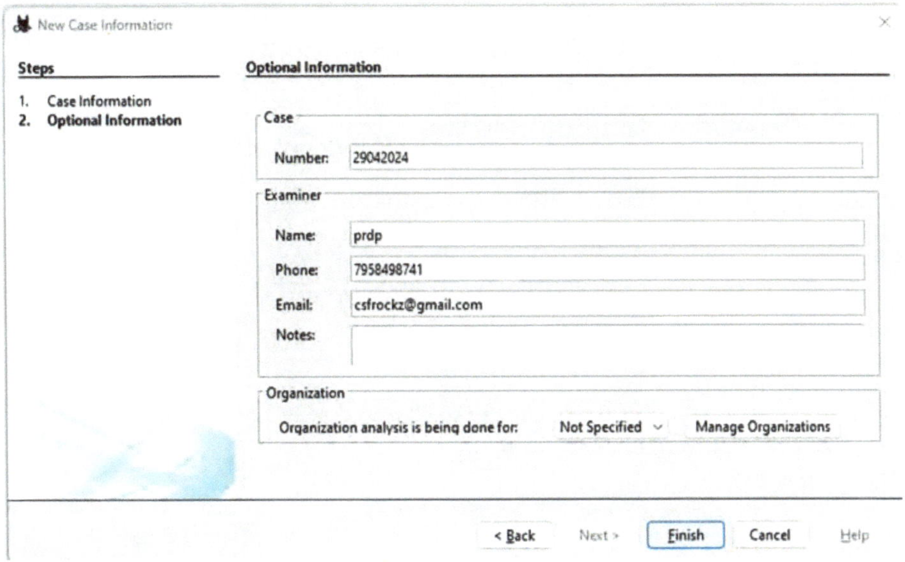

Fig. (15). Optional information.

Step 4: Press next after choosing the proper kind of data source, the disk image in this case as shown in Fig. (**16**).

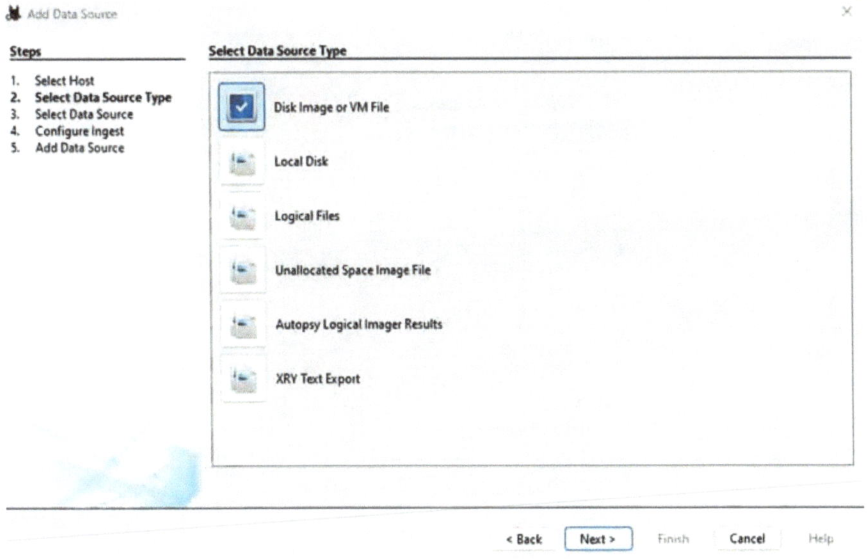

Fig. (16). Data source.

Step 5: Once you have entered the data source path, select “Next.” After inserting the data source, click Finish as shown in Fig. (**17**).

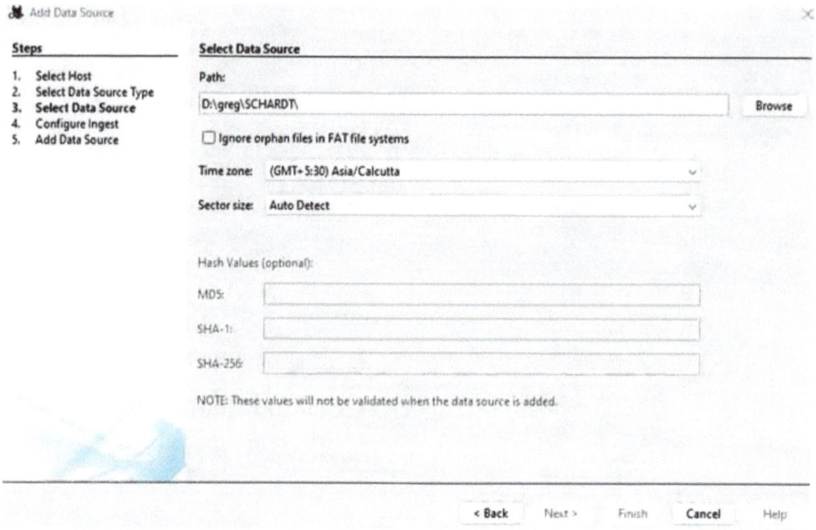

Fig. (17). Select the data source image.

Step 6: You reach here when you have used up every module. You can begin investigating, but we suggest waiting until the analysis and integrity check are complete as shown in Fig. (**18**).

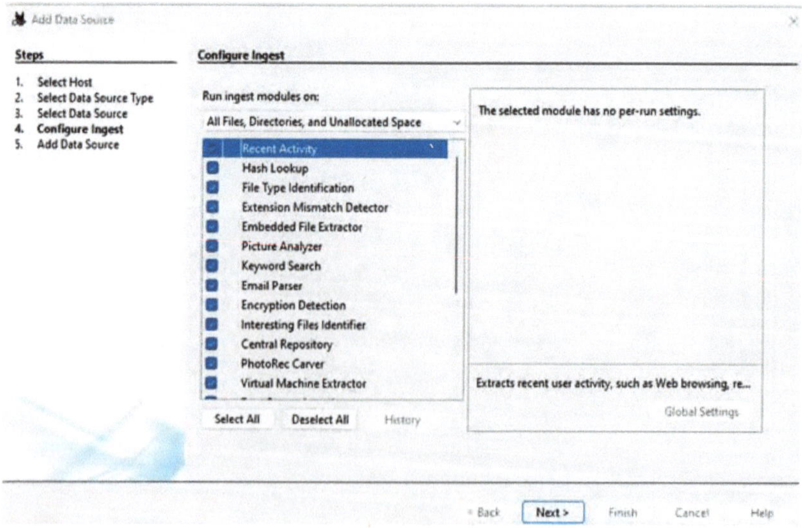

Fig. (18). Configure ingest.

While there are many avenues, we may explore to address the situation previously outlined, in this chapter we will focus on addressing the questions that follow.

Investigation 1: Hash of the image → aee4fcd9301c03b3b054623ca261959a

Click on the image to view the File Metadata tab and verify the hash of the image. To make sure it matches the hash generated when the image was created, we compare the hash of the image as shown in Fig. (**19**).

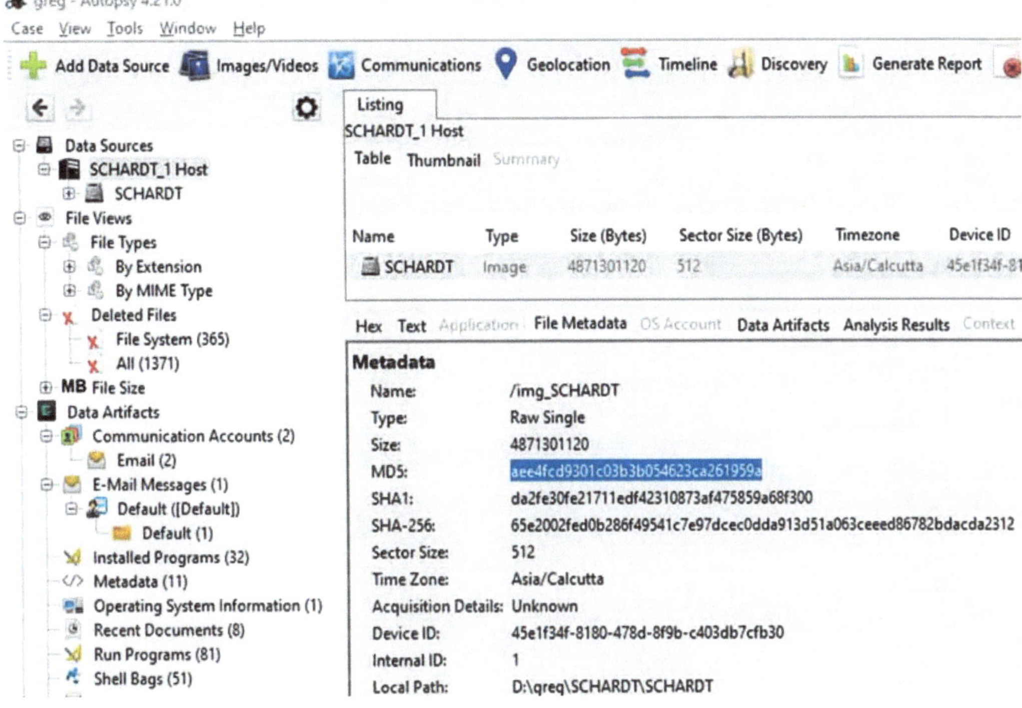

Fig. (19). Image hash value.

Investigation 2: The OS of the machine → Microsoft Windows XP as shown in Fig. (**20**).

Investigation 3: OS installation date → Thursday, August 19, 2004, 10:48:27 PM as shown in Fig. (**21**). The registry value contains a time value that is formatted in UNIX time. Thus, we have converted it as shown in Fig. (**22**).

Investigation 4: Registered owner→ Greg Schardt is the registered owner as shown in Fig. (**23**).

Operating System Information

Table Thumbnail

Source Name	S	C	O	Name	Program Name	Processor Architecture	Temporary Files Directory	Path	Product ID	Owner	Organization	Data Source
SCHARDT				N-1A9ODN6ZXK4LQ	Microsoft Windows XP	x86	%SystemRoot%\TEMP	C:\WINDOWS	55274-640-0147306-23684	Greg Schardt	N/A	SCHARDT

Hex Text Source File Metadata Data Artifacts Annotations Other Occurrences

Result: 1 of 1 Result

Type	Value	Source(s)
Name	N-1A9ODN6ZXK4LQ	Recent Activity
Program Name	Microsoft Windows XP	Recent Activity
Processor Architecture	x86	Recent Activity
Temporary Files Directory	%SystemRoot%\TEMP	Recent Activity
Path	C:\WINDOWS	Recent Activity
Product ID	55274-640-0147306-23684	Recent Activity
Owner	Greg Schardt	Recent Activity
Organization	N/A	Recent Activity
Source File Path	/img_SCHARDT	
Artifact ID	-9223372036854775710	

Fig. (20). Operating system information.

1092955707 Timestamp to Human date [batch convert]

Supports Unix timestamps in seconds, milliseconds, microseconds and nanoseconds.

Assuming that this timestamp is in **seconds**:

GMT : Thursday, August 19, 2004 10:48:27 PM

Your time zone : Friday, August 20, 2004 4:18:27 AM GMT+05:30

Fig. (21). Time conversion UNIX to GMT.

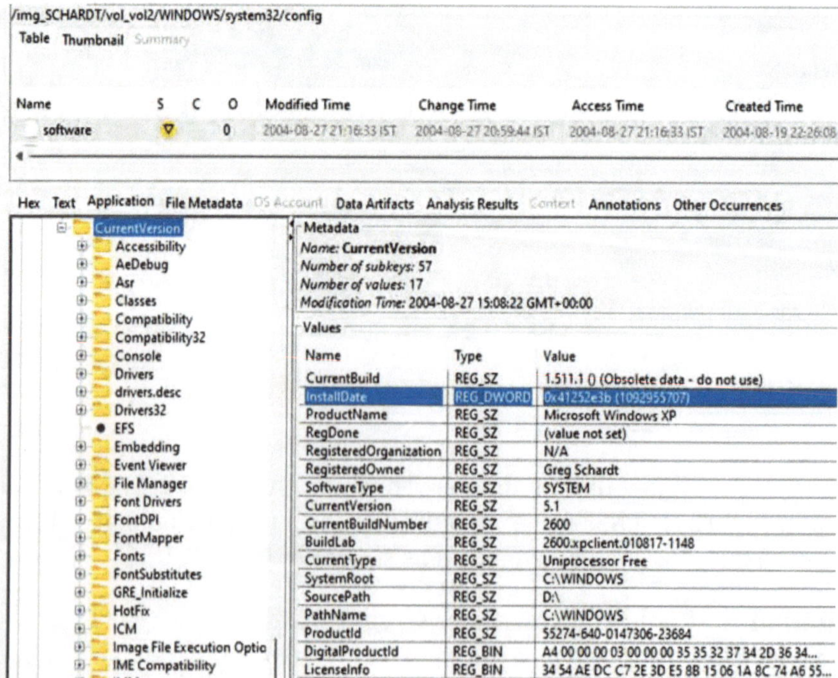

Fig. (22). Operating system installation date.

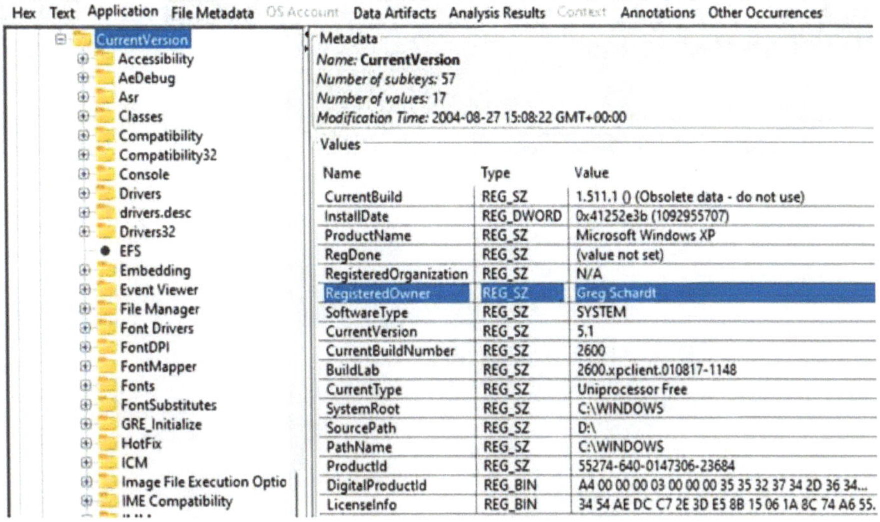

Hex Text Application File Metadata OS Account Data Artifacts Analysis Results Context Annotations Other Occurrences

CurrentVersion: Accessibility, AeDebug, Asr, Classes, Compatibility, Compatibility32, Console, Drivers, drivers.desc, Drivers32, EFS, Embedding, Event Viewer, File Manager, Font Drivers, FontDPI, FontMapper, Fonts, FontSubstitutes, GRE_Initialize, HotFix, ICM, Image File Execution Optio, IME Compatibility

Metadata

Name: **CurrentVersion**
Number of subkeys: 57
Number of values: 17
Modification Time: 2004-08-27 15:08:22 GMT+00:00

Values

Name	Type	Value
CurrentBuild	REG_SZ	1.511.1 () (Obsolete data - do not use)
InstallDate	REG_DWORD	0x41252e3b (1092955707)
ProductName	REG_SZ	Microsoft Windows XP
RegDone	REG_SZ	(value not set)
RegisteredOrganization	REG_SZ	N/A
RegisteredOwner	REG_SZ	Greg Schardt
SoftwareType	REG_SZ	SYSTEM
CurrentVersion	REG_SZ	5.1
CurrentBuildNumber	REG_SZ	2600
BuildLab	REG_SZ	2600.xpclient.010817-1148
CurrentType	REG_SZ	Uniprocessor Free
SystemRoot	REG_SZ	C:\WINDOWS
SourcePath	REG_SZ	D:\
PathName	REG_SZ	C:\WINDOWS
ProductId	REG_SZ	55274-640-0147306-23684
DigitalProductId	REG_BIN	A4 00 00 00 03 00 00 00 35 35 32 37 34 2D 36 34...
LicenseInfo	REG_BIN	34 54 AE DC C7 2E 3D E5 8B 15 06 1A 8C 74 A6 55.

Fig. (23). Registered owner information.

Investigation 5: Name of the computer account→ Default username Mr. Evil as shown in Fig. (**24**).

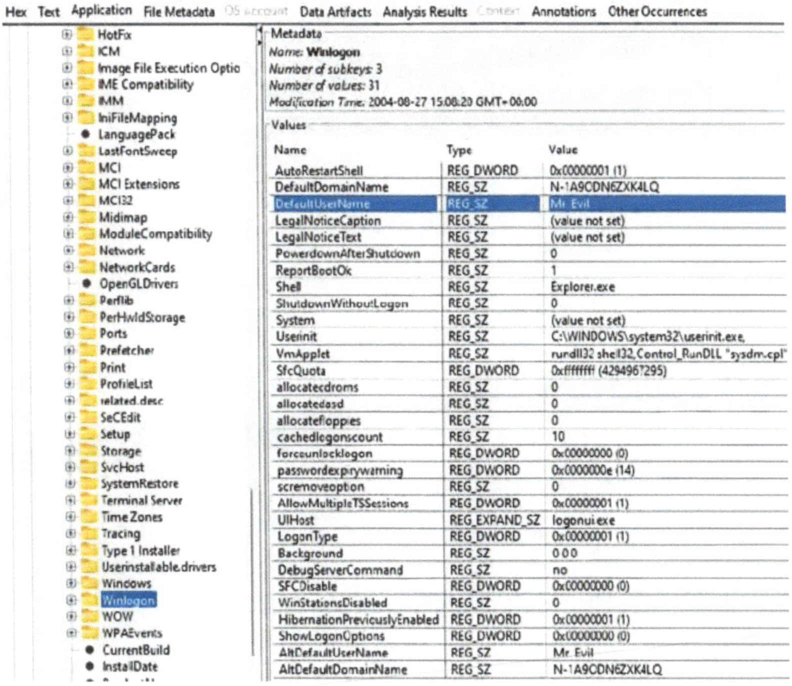

Hex Text Application File Metadata OS Account Data Artifacts Analysis Results Context Annotations Other Occurrences

HotFix, ICM, Image File Execution Optio, IME Compatibility, IMM, IniFileMapping, LanguagePack, LastFontSweep, MCI, MCI Extensions, MCI32, Midimap, ModuleCompatibility, Network, NetworkCards, OpenGLDrivers, Perflib, PerHwIdStorage, Ports, Prefetcher, Print, ProfileList, related.desc, SeCEdit, Setup, Storage, SvcHost, SystemRestore, Terminal Server, Time Zones, Tracing, Type 1 Installer, Userinstallable.drivers, Windows, Winlogon, WOW, WPAEvents, CurrentBuild, InstallDate

Metadata

Name: **Winlogon**
Number of subkeys: 3
Number of values: 31
Modification Time: 2004-08-27 15:08:20 GMT+00:00

Values

Name	Type	Value
AutoRestartShell	REG_DWORD	0x00000001 (1)
DefaultDomainName	REG_SZ	N-1A9ODN6ZXK4LQ
DefaultUserName	REG_SZ	Mr. Evil
LegalNoticeCaption	REG_SZ	(value not set)
LegalNoticeText	REG_SZ	(value not set)
PowerdownAfterShutdown	REG_SZ	0
ReportBootOk	REG_SZ	1
Shell	REG_SZ	Explorer.exe
ShutdownWithoutLogon	REG_SZ	0
System	REG_SZ	(value not set)
Userinit	REG_SZ	C:\WINDOWS\system32\userinit.exe,
VmApplet	REG_SZ	rundll32 shell32,Control_RunDLL "sysdm.cpl"
SfcQuota	REG_DWORD	0xffffffff (4294967295)
allocatecdroms	REG_SZ	0
allocatedasd	REG_SZ	0
allocatefloppies	REG_SZ	0
cachedlogonscount	REG_SZ	10
forceunlocklogon	REG_DWORD	0x00000000 (0)
passwordexpirywarning	REG_DWORD	0x0000000e (14)
scremoveoption	REG_SZ	0
AllowMultipleTSSessions	REG_DWORD	0x00000001 (1)
UIHost	REG_EXPAND_SZ	logonui.exe
LogonType	REG_DWORD	0x00000001 (1)
Background	REG_SZ	0 0 0
DebugServerCommand	REG_SZ	no
SFCDisable	REG_DWORD	0x00000000 (0)
WinStationsDisabled	REG_SZ	0
HibernationPreviouslyEnabled	REG_DWORD	0x00000001 (1)
ShowLogonOptions	REG_DWORD	0x00000000 (0)
AltDefaultUserName	REG_SZ	Mr. Evil
AltDefaultDomainName	REG_SZ	N-1A9ODN6ZXK4LQ

Fig. (24). Computer name information.

Investigation 6: Primary domain name→ Default domain name **N-1A9ODN6ZXK4LQ** as shown in Fig. (**25**).

Hex Text Application File Metadata OS Account Data Artifacts Analysis Results Context Annotations Other Occurrences

LanguagePack, LastFontSweep, MCI, MCI Extensions, MCI32, Midimap, ModuleCompatibility, Network, NetworkCards, OpenGLDrivers, Perflib, PerHwIdStorage, Ports, Prefetcher, Print, ProfileList, related.desc, SeCEdit, Setup, Storage, SvcHost, SystemRestore, Terminal Server, Time Zones, Tracing, Type 1 Installer, Userinstallable.drivers, Windows, Winlogon, WOW

Metadata

Name: **Winlogon**
Number of subkeys: 3
Number of values: 31
Modification Time: 2004-08-27 15:08:20 GMT+00:00

Values

Name	Type	Value
AutoRestartShell	REG_DWORD	0x00000001 (1)
DefaultDomainName	REG_SZ	N-1A9ODN6ZXK4LQ
DefaultUserName	REG_SZ	Mr. Evil
LegalNoticeCaption	REG_SZ	(value not set)
LegalNoticeText	REG_SZ	(value not set)
PowerdownAfterShutdown	REG_SZ	0
ReportBootOk	REG_SZ	1
Shell	REG_SZ	Explorer.exe
ShutdownWithoutLogon	REG_SZ	0
System	REG_SZ	(value not set)
Userinit	REG_SZ	C:\WINDOWS\system32\userinit.exe,
VmApplet	REG_SZ	rundll32 shell32,Control_RunDLL "sysdm.cpl"
SfcQuota	REG_DWORD	0xffffffff (4294967295)
allocatecdroms	REG_SZ	0
allocatedasd	REG_SZ	0
allocatefloppies	REG_SZ	0
cachedlogonscount	REG_SZ	10
forceunlocklogon	REG_DWORD	0x00000000 (0)
passwordexpirywarning	REG_DWORD	0x0000000e (14)
scremoveoption	REG_SZ	0
AllowMultipleTSSessions	REG_DWORD	0x00000001 (1)
UIHost	REG_EXPAND_SZ	logonui.exe

Fig. (25). Primary domain name information.

Investigation 7: Last time or date that computer was shut down→ Exit Time **2004/08/27-10:46:27** as shown in Fig. (**26**).

Hex Text Application File Metadata OS Account Data Artifacts Analysis Results Context Annotations Other Occurrences

IME Compatibility, IMM, IniFileMapping, LanguagePack, LastFontSweep, MCI, MCI Extensions, MCI32, Midimap, ModuleCompatibility, Network, NetworkCards, OpenGLDrivers, Perflib, PerHwIdStorage, Ports, Prefetcher, Print

Metadata

Name: **Prefetcher**
Number of subkeys: 0
Number of values: 10
Modification Time: 2004-08-27 15:46:28 GMT+00:00

Values

Name	Type	Value
Version	REG_DWORD	0x00000011 (17)
StartTime	REG_SZ	2004/08/27-10:08:25
TracesProcessed	REG_DWORD	0x00000016 (22)
TracesSuccessful	REG_DWORD	0x00000016 (22)
LastTraceFailure	REG_DWORD	0x00000000 (0)
ExitCode	REG_DWORD	0x00000000 (0)
ExitTime	REG_SZ	2004/08/27-10:46:27
BootFilesOptimized	REG_DWORD	0x00000001 (1)
LastDiskLayoutTime	REG_BIN	B0 D0 7B D3 83 8B C4 01
LastDiskLayoutTimeString	REG_SZ	2004/08/26-10:46:17

Fig. (26). Information about shutdown.

Investigation 8: Logged onto the computer most recently→ the person that logged on recently is **Mr. Evil**. As illustrated in Fig. (**27**).

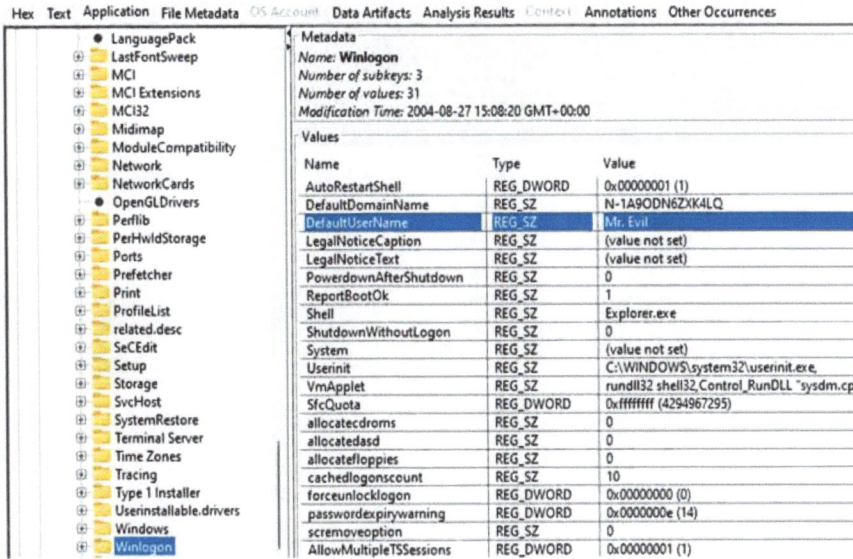

Hex Text Application File Metadata OS Account Data Artifacts Analysis Results Context Annotations Other Occurrences

LanguagePack, LastFontSweep, MCI, MCI Extensions, MCI32, Midimap, ModuleCompatibility, Network, NetworkCards, OpenGLDrivers, Perflib, PerHwIdStorage, Ports, Prefetcher, Print, ProfileList, related.desc, SeCEdit, Setup, Storage, SvcHost, SystemRestore, Terminal Server, Time Zones, Tracing, Type 1 Installer, Userinstallable.drivers, Windows, Winlogon

Metadata
Name: **Winlogon**
Number of subkeys: 3
Number of values: 31
Modification Time: 2004-08-27 15:08:20 GMT+00:00

Values

Name	Type	Value
AutoRestartShell	REG_DWORD	0x00000001 (1)
DefaultDomainName	REG_SZ	N-1A9ODN6ZXK4LQ
DefaultUserName	REG_SZ	Mr. Evil
LegalNoticeCaption	REG_SZ	(value not set)
LegalNoticeText	REG_SZ	(value not set)
PowerdownAfterShutdown	REG_SZ	0
ReportBootOk	REG_SZ	1
Shell	REG_SZ	Explorer.exe
ShutdownWithoutLogon	REG_SZ	0
System	REG_SZ	(value not set)
Userinit	REG_SZ	C:\WINDOWS\system32\userinit.exe,
VmApplet	REG_SZ	rundll32 shell32,Control_RunDLL "sysdm.cpl"
SfcQuota	REG_DWORD	0xffffffff (4294967295)
allocatecdroms	REG_SZ	0
allocatedasd	REG_SZ	0
allocatefloppies	REG_SZ	0
cachedlogonscount	REG_SZ	10
forceunlocklogon	REG_DWORD	0x00000000 (0)
passwordexpirywarning	REG_DWORD	0x0000000e (14)
scremoveoption	REG_SZ	0
AllowMultipleTSSessions	REG_DWORD	0x00000001 (1)

Fig. (27). Details regarding the user's most recent login.

Investigation 9: Who uses the computer the most, and their account name→ Mr. Evil as shown in Fig. (**28**) count 15 times.

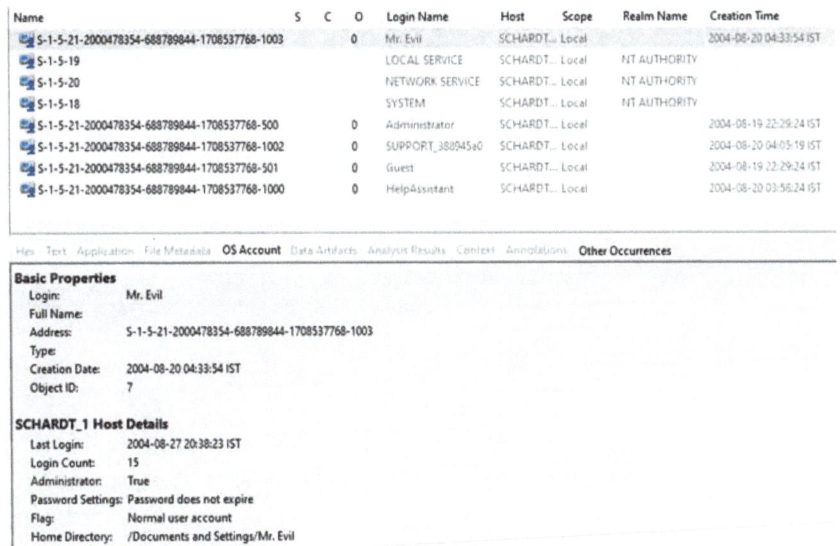

Name	S	C	O	Login Name	Host	Scope	Realm Name	Creation Time
S-1-5-21-2000478354-688789844-1708537768-1003			0	Mr. Evil	SCHARDT...	Local		2004-08-20 04:33:54 IST
S-1-5-19				LOCAL SERVICE	SCHARDT...	Local	NT AUTHORITY	
S-1-5-20				NETWORK SERVICE	SCHARDT...	Local	NT AUTHORITY	
S-1-5-18				SYSTEM	SCHARDT...	Local	NT AUTHORITY	
S-1-5-21-2000478354-688789844-1708537768-500			0	Administrator	SCHARDT...	Local		2004-08-19 22:29:24 IST
S-1-5-21-2000478354-688789844-1708537768-1002			0	SUPPORT_388945a0	SCHARDT...	Local		2004-08-20 04:05:19 IST
S-1-5-21-2000478354-688789844-1708537768-501			0	Guest	SCHARDT...	Local		2004-08-19 22:29:24 IST
S-1-5-21-2000478354-688789844-1708537768-1000			0	HelpAssistant	SCHARDT...	Local		2004-08-20 03:56:24 IST

Hex Text Application File Metadata OS Account Data Artifacts Analysis Results Context Annotations Other Occurrences

Basic Properties
Login: Mr. Evil
Full Name:
Address: S-1-5-21-2000478354-688789844-1708537768-1003
Type:
Creation Date: 2004-08-20 04:33:54 IST
Object ID: 7

SCHARDT_1 Host Details
Last Login: 2004-08-27 20:38:23 IST
Login Count: 15
Administrator: True
Password Settings: Password does not expire
Flag: Normal user account
Home Directory: /Documents and Settings/Mr. Evil

Fig. (28). Information about the person who uses the computer the most.

Investigation 10: Total number of recorded accounts→ Five (Mr. Evil, Administrator, Support_388945a0, Guest, HelpAssistant) as shown in Fig. (**29**).

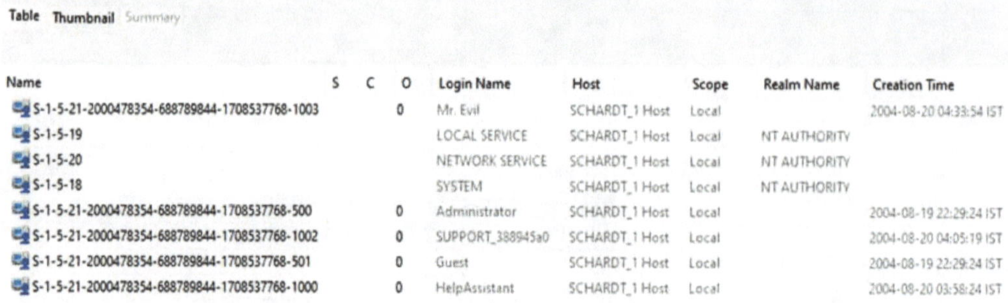

Table Thumbnail Summary

Name	S	C	O	Login Name	Host	Scope	Realm Name	Creation Time
S-1-5-21-2000478354-688789844-1708537768-1003			0	Mr. Evil	SCHARDT_1 Host	Local		2004-08-20 04:33:54 IST
S-1-5-19				LOCAL SERVICE	SCHARDT_1 Host	Local	NT AUTHORITY	
S-1-5-20				NETWORK SERVICE	SCHARDT_1 Host	Local	NT AUTHORITY	
S-1-5-18				SYSTEM	SCHARDT_1 Host	Local	NT AUTHORITY	
S-1-5-21-2000478354-688789844-1708537768-500			0	Administrator	SCHARDT_1 Host	Local		2004-08-19 22:29:24 IST
S-1-5-21-2000478354-688789844-1708537768-1002			0	SUPPORT_388945a0	SCHARDT_1 Host	Local		2004-08-20 04:05:19 IST
S-1-5-21-2000478354-688789844-1708537768-501			0	Guest	SCHARDT_1 Host	Local		2004-08-19 22:29:24 IST
S-1-5-21-2000478354-688789844-1708537768-1000			0	HelpAssistant	SCHARDT_1 Host	Local		2004-08-20 03:58:24 IST

Fig. (29). Information about the accounts that have been recorded.

Investigation 11: Identify the network cards that are used by the machine→ Compaq WL110 Wireless LAN PC Card and Xircom CardBus Ethernet 100 + Modem 56 are the two network cards. As shown in Fig. (**30**).

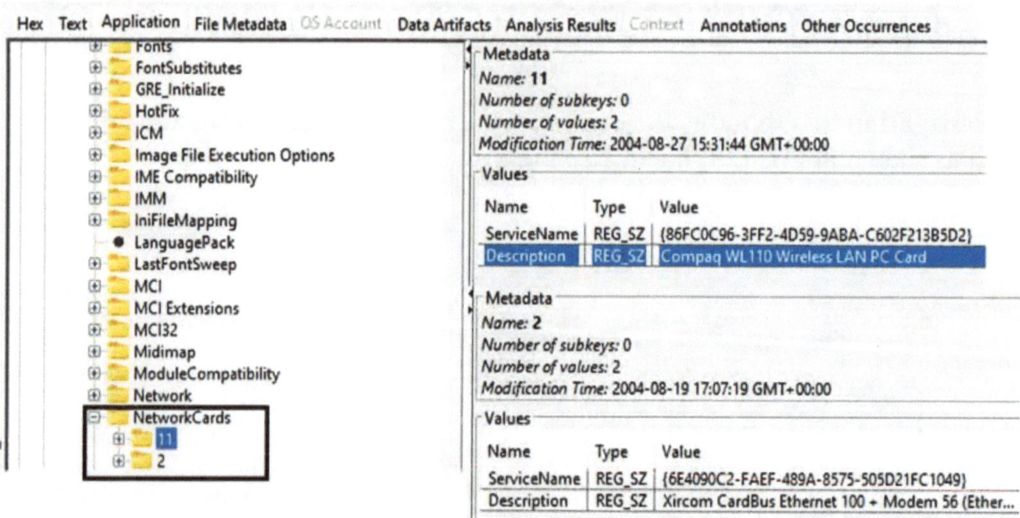

Fig. (30). Network card information.

Investigation 12: IP Address→ 192.168.1.111, MAC→ 00:10:a4:93:3e:09 are the computer's MAC and IP addresses, respectively as shown in Fig. (**31**).

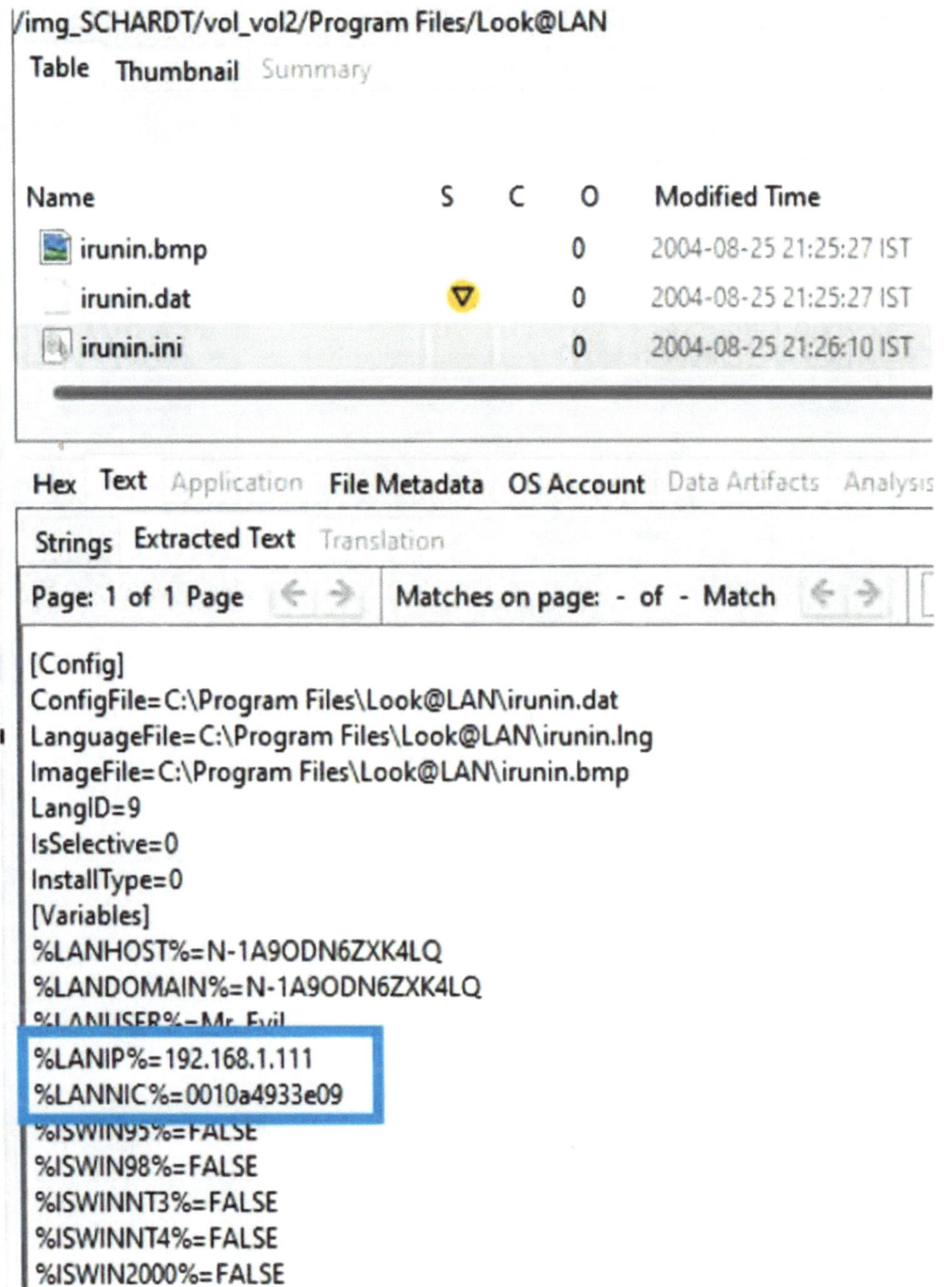

Fig. (31). IP and MAC address.

Investigation 13: Installed applications with potential for hacking usage as shown in Fig. (**32**).

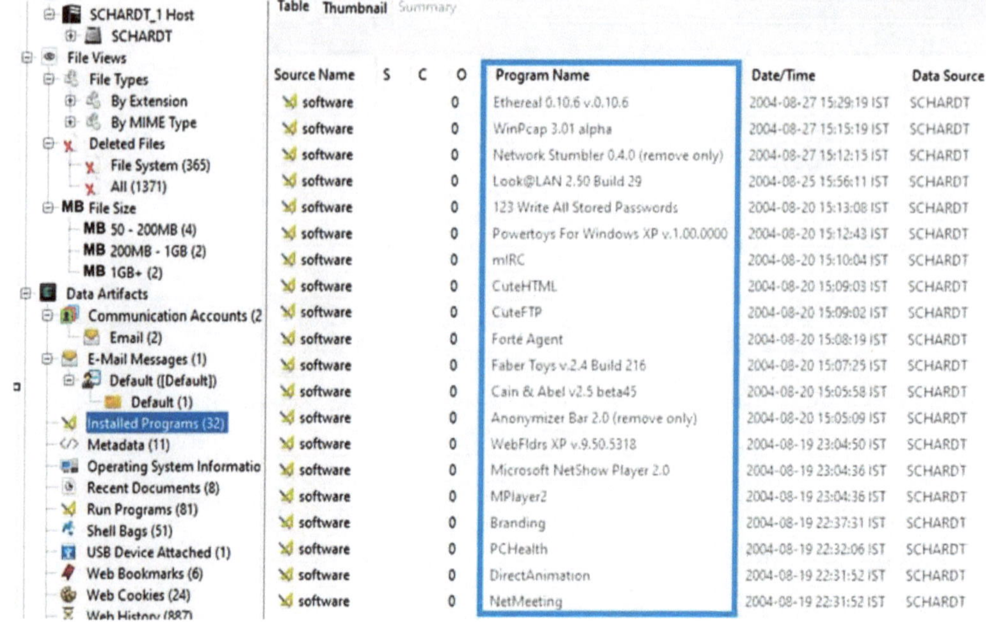

Source Name	S	C	O	Program Name	Date/Time	Data Source
software			0	Ethereal 0.10.6 v.0.10.6	2004-08-27 15:29:19 IST	SCHARDT
software			0	WinPcap 3.01 alpha	2004-08-27 15:15:19 IST	SCHARDT
software			0	Network Stumbler 0.4.0 (remove only)	2004-08-27 15:12:15 IST	SCHARDT
software			0	Look@LAN 2.50 Build 29	2004-08-25 15:56:11 IST	SCHARDT
software			0	123 Write All Stored Passwords	2004-08-20 15:13:08 IST	SCHARDT
software			0	Powertoys For Windows XP v.1.00.0000	2004-08-20 15:12:43 IST	SCHARDT
software			0	mIRC	2004-08-20 15:10:04 IST	SCHARDT
software			0	CuteHTML	2004-08-20 15:09:03 IST	SCHARDT
software			0	CuteFTP	2004-08-20 15:09:02 IST	SCHARDT
software			0	Forte Agent	2004-08-20 15:08:19 IST	SCHARDT
software			0	Faber Toys v.2.4 Build 216	2004-08-20 15:07:25 IST	SCHARDT
software			0	Cain & Abel v2.5 beta45	2004-08-20 15:05:58 IST	SCHARDT
software			0	Anonymizer Bar 2.0 (remove only)	2004-08-20 15:05:09 IST	SCHARDT
software			0	WebFldrs XP v.9.50.5318	2004-08-19 23:04:50 IST	SCHARDT
software			0	Microsoft NetShow Player 2.0	2004-08-19 23:04:36 IST	SCHARDT
software			0	MPlayer2	2004-08-19 23:04:36 IST	SCHARDT
software			0	Branding	2004-08-19 22:37:31 IST	SCHARDT
software			0	PCHealth	2004-08-19 22:32:06 IST	SCHARDT
software			0	DirectAnimation	2004-08-19 22:31:52 IST	SCHARDT
software			0	NetMeeting	2004-08-19 22:31:52 IST	SCHARDT

Fig. (32). Installed program.

Investigation 14: Mr. Evil's subscriptions to newsgroups as shown in Fig. (**33**).

/img_SCHARDT/vol_vol2/Documents and Settings/Mr. Evil/Local Settings/Application Data/Identities/{EF086998-1115-4ECD-9B13-9ADC067B4929}/Microsoft/Outlook Express

Table Thumbnail Summary

Name	S	C	O	Modified Time	Change Time	Access Time	Created Time
[current folder]				2004-08-21 02:44:23 IST	2004-08-21 02:44:23 IST	2004-08-21 02:45:52 IST	2004-08-21 02:43:25 IST
[parent folder]				2004-08-21 02:43:25 IST	2004-08-21 02:43:25 IST	2004-08-21 02:43:25 IST	2004-08-21 02:43:25 IST
alt.2600.cardz.dbx			0	2004-08-21 02:57:17 IST	2004-08-21 02:57:17 IST	2004-08-21 02:57:17 IST	2004-08-21 02:48:41 IST
alt.2600.codez.dbx			0	2004-08-21 02:57:16 IST	2004-08-21 02:57:16 IST	2004-08-21 02:57:16 IST	2004-08-21 02:48:44 IST
alt.2600.crackz.dbx			0	2004-08-21 02:57:16 IST	2004-08-21 02:57:16 IST	2004-08-21 02:57:16 IST	2004-08-21 02:48:46 IST
alt.2600.dbx			0	2004-08-21 02:57:23 IST	2004-08-21 02:57:23 IST	2004-08-21 02:57:23 IST	2004-08-21 02:48:32 IST
alt.2600.hackerz.dbx			0	2004-08-21 02:57:16 IST	2004-08-21 02:57:16 IST	2004-08-21 02:57:16 IST	2004-08-21 02:55:57 IST
alt.2600.moderated.dbx			0	2004-08-21 02:49:20 IST	2004-08-21 02:49:20 IST	2004-08-21 02:49:20 IST	2004-08-21 02:49:15 IST
alt.2600.phreakz.dbx			0	2004-08-21 02:57:10 IST	2004-08-21 02:57:10 IST	2004-08-21 02:57:10 IST	2004-08-21 02:55:09 IST
alt.2600.programz.dbx			0	2004-08-21 02:57:16 IST	2004-08-21 02:57:16 IST	2004-08-21 02:57:16 IST	2004-08-21 02:54:25 IST
alt.binaries.hacking.beginner.dbx			0	2004-08-21 02:53:41 IST	2004-08-21 02:53:41 IST	2004-08-21 02:53:41 IST	2004-08-21 02:52:54 IST
alt.binaries.hacking.computers.dbx			0	2004-08-21 02:50:55 IST	2004-08-21 02:50:55 IST	2004-08-21 02:50:55 IST	2004-08-21 02:50:36 IST
alt.binaries.hacking.utilities.dbx			0	2004-08-21 02:49:24 IST	2004-08-21 02:49:24 IST	2004-08-21 02:49:24 IST	2004-08-21 02:49:22 IST
alt.binaries.hacking.websites.dbx			0	2004-08-21 02:50:50 IST	2004-08-21 02:50:50 IST	2004-08-21 02:50:50 IST	2004-08-21 02:50:42 IST
alt.dss.hack.dbx			0	2004-08-21 02:52:54 IST	2004-08-21 02:52:54 IST	2004-08-21 02:52:54 IST	2004-08-21 02:50:55 IST
alt.hacking.dbx			0	2004-08-21 02:57:07 IST	2004-08-21 02:57:07 IST	2004-08-21 02:57:07 IST	2004-08-21 02:53:41 IST
alt.nl.binaries.hack.dbx			0	2004-08-21 02:50:34 IST	2004-08-21 02:50:34 IST	2004-08-21 02:50:34 IST	2004-08-21 02:49:52 IST
alt.stupidity.hackers.malicious.dbx			0	2004-08-21 02:49:27 IST	2004-08-21 02:49:27 IST	2004-08-21 02:49:27 IST	2004-08-21 02:49:25 IST
cleanup.log			0	2004-08-21 02:43:58 IST	2004-08-21 02:43:58 IST	2004-08-21 02:43:58 IST	2004-08-21 02:43:55 IST
Deleted Items.dbx			0	2004-08-21 02:48:30 IST	2004-08-21 02:48:30 IST	2004-08-21 02:48:30 IST	2004-08-21 02:48:30 IST
Folders.dbx			0	2004-08-21 02:55:59 IST	2004-08-21 02:55:59 IST	2004-08-21 02:43:57 IST	2004-08-21 02:43:25 IST
free.binaries.hackers.malicious.dbx			0	2004-08-21 02:49:31 IST	2004-08-21 02:49:31 IST	2004-08-21 02:49:31 IST	2004-08-21 02:49:29 IST
free.binaries.hacking.beginner.dbx			0	2004-08-21 02:50:14 IST	2004-08-21 02:50:14 IST	2004-08-21 02:50:14 IST	2004-08-21 02:50:09 IST

Fig. (33). Newsgroups information.

Investigation 15: An IRC (Internet Relay Chat) program called MIRC was launched. The user settings that appeared in a chat channel while the user was online as shown in Fig. (**34**).

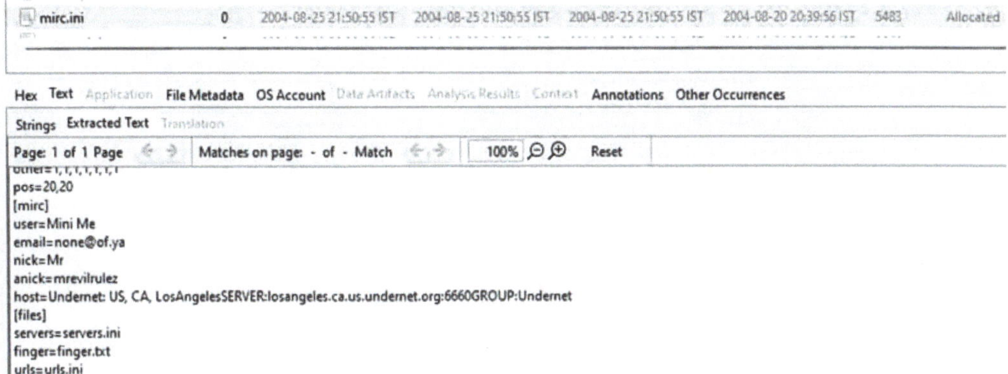

Fig. (34). MIRC application.

Investigation 16: The IRC software can record conversations. The user of this machine accessed three IRC channels as shown in Fig. (**35**).

/img_SCHARDT/vol_vol2/Program Files/mIRC/logs

Table Thumbnail Summary

Name	S	C	O	Modified Time	Change Time	Access Time	Created Time
[current folder]				2004-08-20 20:54:48 IST	2004-08-20 20:54:48 IST	2004-08-27 20:44:45 IST	2004-08-20 20:54:48 IST
[parent folder]				2004-08-25 21:50:55 IST	2004-08-25 21:50:55 IST	2004-08-27 20:44:45 IST	2004-08-20 20:39:53 IST
#Chataholics.UnderNet.log	▽		0	2004-08-20 21:24:11 IST	2004-08-20 21:24:11 IST	2004-08-20 21:24:11 IST	2004-08-20 21:22:09 IST
#CyberCafe.UnderNet.log	▽		0	2004-08-21 00:32:55 IST	2004-08-21 00:32:55 IST	2004-08-21 00:32:55 IST	2004-08-20 21:24:21 IST
#Elite.Hackers.UnderNet.log			0	2004-08-20 21:19:05 IST	2004-08-20 21:19:05 IST	2004-08-20 21:19:05 IST	2004-08-20 21:15:34 IST
#evilfork.EFnet.log	▽		0	2004-08-20 21:01:07 IST	2004-08-20 21:01:07 IST	2004-08-20 21:01:07 IST	2004-08-20 21:00:18 IST
#funny.UnderNet.log			0	2004-08-21 00:58:14 IST	2004-08-21 00:58:14 IST	2004-08-21 00:58:14 IST	2004-08-21 00:56:18 IST
#houston.UnderNet.log			0	2004-08-20 21:22:01 IST	2004-08-20 21:22:01 IST	2004-08-20 21:22:01 IST	2004-08-20 21:18:59 IST
#ISO-WAREZ.EFnet.log			0	2004-08-20 20:59:42 IST	2004-08-20 20:59:42 IST	2004-08-20 20:59:42 IST	2004-08-20 20:59:01 IST
#LuxShell.UnderNet.log			0	2004-08-20 21:13:21 IST	2004-08-20 21:13:21 IST	2004-08-20 21:13:21 IST	2004-08-20 21:12:03 IST
#mp3xserv.UnderNet.log			0	2004-08-20 21:14:32 IST	2004-08-20 21:14:32 IST	2004-08-20 21:14:32 IST	2004-08-20 21:13:16 IST
#thedarktower.AfterNET.log	▽		0	2004-08-21 00:46:23 IST	2004-08-21 00:46:23 IST	2004-08-21 00:46:23 IST	2004-08-21 00:44:45 IST
#ushells.UnderNet.log			0	2004-08-20 21:15:07 IST	2004-08-20 21:15:07 IST	2004-08-20 21:15:07 IST	2004-08-20 21:14:49 IST
m5tar.UnderNet.log			0	2004-08-20 21:30:08 IST	2004-08-20 21:30:08 IST	2004-08-20 21:30:08 IST	2004-08-20 21:24:55 IST

Fig. (35). mIRC logs.

Investigation 17: There was also an installation of Ethereal, a popular "sniffing" application for obtaining wired and wireless internet connections. Upon collecting and reassembling TCP packets, the file name containing the intercepted data is saved by default in the user's /My Documents directory, as illustrated in Fig. (**36**).

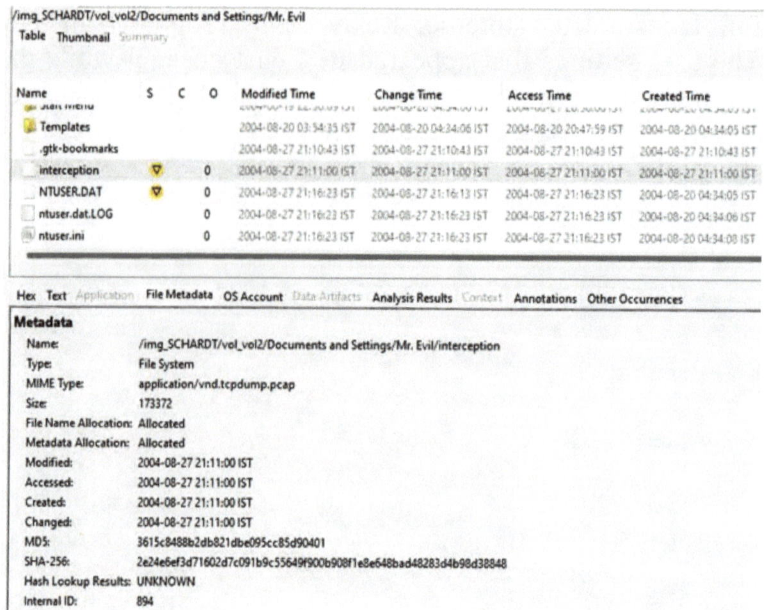

Fig. (36). Intercepting application.

Investigation 18: Websites victim was accessing as shown in Fig. (**37**).

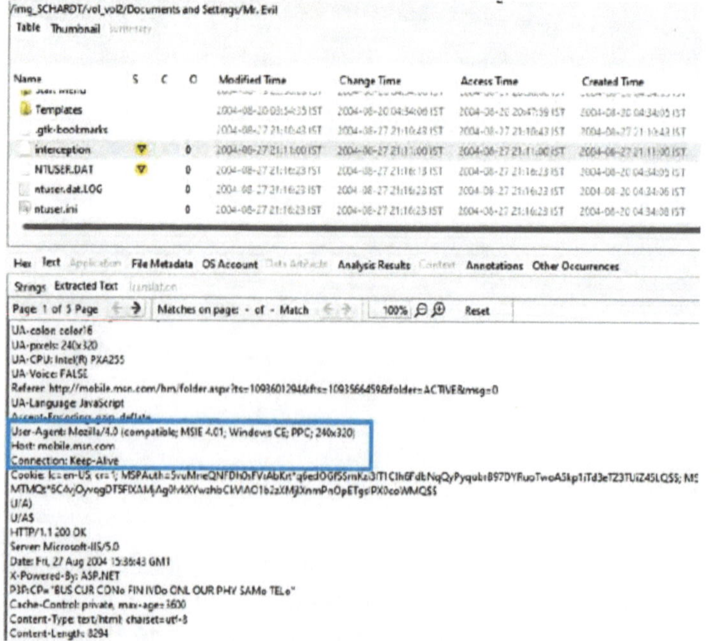

Fig. (37). Website victim accessing.

Investigation 19: Email address for the main user on the web discovered in web history as shown in Fig. (**38**).

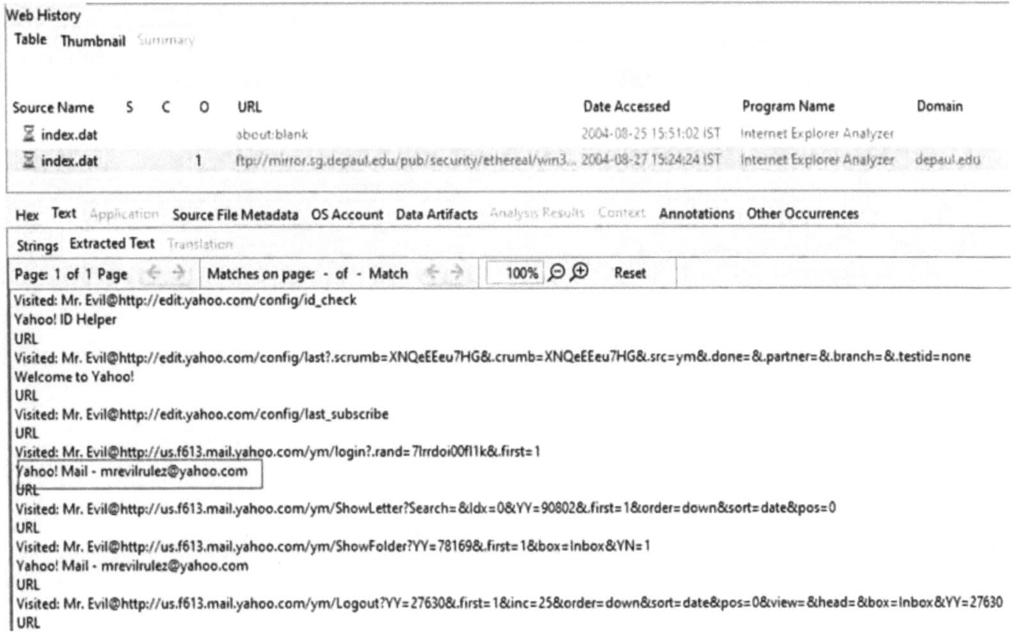

Fig. (38). Web history log.

Investigation 20: The following four executable files are in the recycle bin: the files Dc1.exe, Dc2.exe, Dc3.exe, and Dc4.exe. as shown in Fig. (**39**).

/img_SCHARDT/vol_vol2/RECYCLER/S-1-5-21-2000478354-688789844-1708537768-1003

Table Thumbnail Summary

Name	S	C	O	Modified Time	Change Time	Access Time	Created Time	Size
[current folder]				2004-08-27 20:59:58 IST	2004-08-27 20:59:58 IST	2004-08-27 20:59:58 IST	2004-08-25 21:48:25 IST	56
[parent folder]				2004-08-25 21:48:25 IST	2004-08-25 21:48:25 IST	2004-08-27 20:42:30 IST	2004-08-25 21:48:25 IST	328
Dc1.exe			0	2004-08-25 21:21:23 IST	2004-08-25 21:48:25 IST	2004-08-25 21:26:08 IST	2004-08-25 21:21:24 IST	2160043
Dc2.exe			0	2004-08-27 20:41:07 IST	2004-08-27 20:42:30 IST	2004-08-27 20:42:18 IST	2004-08-27 20:41:07 IST	1324940
Dc3.exe			0	2004-08-27 20:44:20 IST	2004-08-27 20:45:26 IST	2004-08-27 20:45:16 IST	2004-08-27 20:44:20 IST	442417
Dc4.exe			0	2004-08-27 20:54:24 IST	2004-08-27 20:59:58 IST	2004-08-27 20:59:47 IST	2004-08-27 20:54:24 IST	8460502
desktop.ini			0	2004-08-25 21:48:25 IST	2004-08-25 21:48:25 IST	2004-08-27 20:42:30 IST	2004-08-25 21:48:25 IST	65
INFO2			0	2004-08-27 21:16:17 IST	2004-08-27 21:16:17 IST	2004-08-27 21:16:17 IST	2004-08-25 21:48:25 IST	3220

Fig. (39). Recycle files.

Investigation 21: Virus on the system Unix_hack.tgz, a zip bomb, is present which is shown in Fig. (**40**).

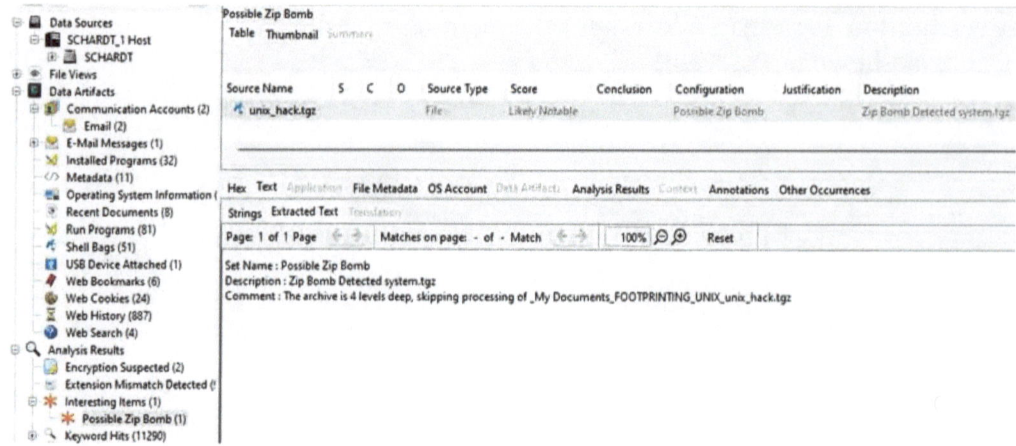

Fig. (40). Virus information.

CONCLUSION

Understanding file system analysis is a fundamental ability for anyone entering the field of digital forensics, as file systems are the cornerstone of digital storage. Through a comprehensive understanding of file system structures, boot processes, and the use of forensics tools such as Autopsy, investigators may proficiently evaluate file systems, unearth concealed evidence, and eventually participate in fruitful investigations. File system analysis methods will develop more in tandem with technology. The fundamental ideas covered in this chapter, however, will still be helpful for successfully recovering and analyzing digital evidence as well as for navigating the constantly evolving digital landscape.

REFERENCES

[1] "Hard Drives: How Do They Work? – Techbytes." Websites.umass.edu, Available from: websites.umass.edu/Techbytes/2017/04/04/hard-drives-how-do-they-work/

[2] "EC-Council Learning," codered.eccouncil.org. Available from: https://codered.eccouncil.org/courseVideo/digital-forensics-essentials?lessonId=83bf05df-971b-441e-a814-f5e8735bb378&finalAssessment=false

[3] "CFReDS Portal," cfreds.nist.gov. Available from: Available from: https://cfreds.nist.gov/all/NIST/HackingCase (accessed Apr. 29, 2024).

CHAPTER 5

Windows Forensics and Registry Analysis

Abstract: The evidence we seek in today's digital environment frequently resides in computer systems. The basic knowledge and abilities needed to carry out an extensive Windows forensics investigation are provided to readers in this chapter. We start by building a solid foundation of the fundamentals of Windows forensics. Methods for gathering volatile data, which is kept in memory, as well as non-volatile data, such as files and system records, are investigated. We then explore the skill of interpreting this abundance of data. The chapter will teach readers how to mine a variety of Windows data sources, such as program data, system configuration files, and user activity logs, for important evidence. Turning the page, the chapter presents the Windows Registry, an essential part that protects the configuration secrets of the operating system. Methods for examining both static and dynamic registry hives are offered, enabling detectives to find concealed proof of malicious activity or system alterations. Looking into internet browser history is a necessary step in any digital inquiry. To find possible leads and user activity patterns, this chapter walks readers through the process of extracting and analyzing web browser history, cookies, and cached data. This chapter provides readers with the necessary knowledge to enable them to extract and analyze digital evidence from Windows PCs with ease. This information is crucial for forensic investigations to be clear and for finding the truth.

Keywords: Cookie, Cache data, Metadata, Registry analysis, Windows forensics.

INTRODUCTION

One crucial area of cyber security is computer forensics, which is the collection of data about activities performed on computers. It is a subset of the larger area of "Digital Forensics," which deals with the forensic study of many kinds of digital devices, including data recovery, examination, and analysis. Digital and computer forensics have a wide range of uses. In the legal field, they are employed to confirm or deny a theory in a civil or criminal case. In the private sector, they are utilized for incident and intrusion analysis, internal company investigations, and other similar tasks. The desktop operating system that is currently most widely used is Microsoft Windows. It presently has about 80% of the desktop market share and is preferred by both private users and enterprises. For anyone interested in Digital Forensics, this means that performing forensic analysis on Microsoft Windows is a crucial skill to have.

Akashdeep Bhardwaj, Pradeep Singh & Ajay Prasad

Unquestionably, the digital world is currently influencing every aspect of our lives. From business and economics to communication and entertainment, computers are used for everything. Regrettably, criminal conduct can also be enabled by this digital environment. When this kind of thing happens, computers themselves can contain important evidence. The study of cybercrimes involving Windows computers is known as Windows forensics. It entails obtaining data from a Windows computer to identify and bring charges against the person or people responsible for a cybercrime. Because Windows is one of the most used operating systems, there is a greater chance that a Windows computer will be involved in an incident. Therefore, to locate information of potential use as evidence, investigators need to have a solid understanding of the many Windows OS components, including the file system, registry, system files, and event logs [1].

The process of locating, protecting, evaluating, and presenting digital evidence from a Windows operating system is known as Windows Forensics. Recovering data in a form that is legally admissible in court is its aim. Then, using the recovered data, legal actions can be supported, criminals can be identified, and events can be rebuilt. The main features of Windows Forensics are broken down as follows:

- Identification: Identifying possible electronic evidence on a Windows platform.
- Preservation: Protecting the evidence's integrity by gathering it in a way that adheres to forensic best practices.
- Analysis: Looking through the collected data to find pertinent details.
- Presentation: Clearly and succinctly summarizing the results in a way that is appropriate for court hearings.

Windows Forensics gives detectives the instruments and methods necessary to retrieve a Windows system's digital trail, which offers insightful information about previous actions. In the current field of digital forensics, Windows Forensics is essential. The capacity to retrieve and examine digital evidence from Windows computers is becoming increasingly important as long as criminals are using these platforms for their operations.

Any digital data that may have evidence value is considered a forensic artifact. They are essentially the digital traces that programs and users on a device leave behind. These relics may be essential for piecing together historical events and identifying possible criminal conduct. 'Artifact' is a term you will frequently see in forensic analysis. Forensic artifacts are vital bits of data that demonstrate human behavior. Items such as fingerprints discovered at crime scenes, broken buttons discovered on clothing, and tools involved in the crime commission are examples of forensic artifacts [2]. With the aid of all these objects, the story of the crime's commission is rebuilt. Forensic artifacts in computer forensics might be tiny traces of past activity on the system. Because of the numerous artifacts that a Windows system generates for a particular activity, a person's activities on a Windows machine can be properly tracked down through computer forensics. Frequently, these relics are found in places that 'regular' users wouldn't go. These artifacts can serve as the trial run for an investigation of our goals if they are evaluated [3]. Here is a closer look at objects used in forensics:

- Examples: Common forensic artifacts include system logs, registry entries, file system metadata, deleted files, web browser history, email records, and temporary files.
- Worth: The ability to reveal details about the events on a device is what gives forensic artifacts their worth. A user's web browser history can disclose their online actions, whereas a deleted file record may suggest an attempt to conceal information.
- Hidden Nature: A lot of forensic artifacts have a hidden nature and are not easily visible. They can live in the memory of a computer, system files, or unallocated disk space. To locate and evaluate these artifacts in an efficient manner, forensic instruments and methods are needed.

Investigators can create a timeline of events, identify users involved, and unearth possible motivations behind illegal action by examining a variety of forensic evidence. These relics are essential to providing a complete picture of what happened on a digital device.

VOLATILE AND NON-VOLATILE DATA

A computer's memory is an ever-changing landscape that holds volatile information. It includes active processes, open connections to networks, and data stored in RAM, all of which disappear when the power is turned off. But this transient data, which offers a moment-in-time picture of the system's condition, can have enormous forensic significance [4]. When a system is turned off, volatile data, which usually resides in system RAM, is lost. From a forensics perspective, it produces useful artifacts like command history, shared resources, network-related data, process-related data, open file information, and user log-in information [5].

Hard disks and solid-state drives are examples of storage devices that hold non-volatile data. This data is more historically oriented than its volatile cousin, as it continues to exist even after a shutdown. Data that is persistent and does not disappear when a system crashes or is turned off is referred to as non-volatile information. This data is typically stored on the system's flash memory, external hard disk, or internal hard drive. From a forensics perspective, it discloses important artifacts such as data from hidden partitions, file systems, database files, external devices connected to the system, and the Windows registry.

The following section explains how information from Windows computers, both volatile and non-volatile, can be gathered by forensic investigators.

Gathering Volatile Information

During the live data-collecting process, volatile information may be obtained. A forensic investigator can analyze malware, look through log and cache files, find passwords, and other tasks with the aid of knowledge gleaned from volatile data. During a forensic inquiry, any of these could be a possible source of evidence. As previously stated, data kept in digital devices' registries, cache, and RAM is referred to as volatile information. Whenever the system is restarted or switched off, this data is typically lost or deleted. Since volatile data is dynamic and subject to change over time, investigators should be able to obtain it quickly.

The approaches investigators are employing to obtain more volatile data have the potential to alter the contents of the memory, and this is something investigators need to be completely aware of. With the volatile information gathered, investigators can determine who logged on and when, as well as the program(s) and libraries used, the timeline of a security incident [6], the files accessed and shared during a suspected attack, and other details like network information, network connections, network status, open files, process-to-port mapping, mapped drives, command history, process information, process memory, shares, and contents of the clipboard [7].

Obtaining System Time

Gathering system time is the first stage in any investigation into an incident. When an event occurs, the exact day and hour is known as system time, which is stated in Coordinated Universal Time (UTC). Applications can obtain precise time and date information from system time. The context of the data gathered in the next steps is greatly enhanced by the understanding of system time. It also helps to piece together what happened in the system. Along with the current system time, information on system uptime is quite relevant to the entire investigation process.

When logging the system time, investigators also log the wall time or actual time. The investigator can ascertain if the system clock was accurate or not by comparing the two timings. Investigators can use the net statistics server command or the date /t & time /t command to retrieve system time and date as shown in Fig. (**1**). Using the GetSystemTime function is an additional method for obtaining the system time information.

```
Administrator: Command Pro

Microsoft Windows [Version 10.0.22631.3447]
(c) Microsoft Corporation. All rights reserved.

C:\Users\Administrator>date /t & time /t
Fri 05/10/2024
02:59 PM
```

Fig. (1). Date & Time commands.

Gathering Logged-On Users

An investigator needs to compile information about every person who has logged into the suspected system while investigating. This contains details about users who accessed the system remotely (for example, through a mapped share or the net use command) in addition to those who logged on locally (using the keyboard or console). With the use of this data, an investigator can provide context to other data gathered from the system, like the owner of a file, the user context of an active process, and the most recent access times of files.

PsLoggedOn

This applet shows users who are logged on remotely as well as those who are logged on locally as shown in Fig. (**2**), if you designate a username rather than a machine. PsLoggedOn displays if the user is logged in or not by scanning the PCs in the network's area.

```
PS C:\PSTools> .\PsLoggedon.exe

PsLoggedon v1.35 - See who's logged on
Copyright (C) 2000-2016 Mark Russinovich
Sysinternals - www.sysinternals.com

Users logged on locally:
     5/10/2024 8:59:57 AM        ITLAB101_PC01\Administrator

No one is logged on via resource shares.
```

Fig. (2). Logged-in users using PsLoggedOn.

Net Sessions

To manage server computer connections, use the net sessions command. When used without any parameters, it shows details about every local computer session that is logged in. On a server, this command shows the usernames and computer names. It can assist investigators in finding out how long each user session has been in idle mode and whether users have any open files as shown in Fig. (**3**).

```
C:\Windows\system32>net sessions

Computer              User name           Client Type        Opens Idle time

-------------------------------------------------------------------------------
\\192.168.0.137       Administrator                              4 00:00:26
\\192.168.0.178       Administrator                              2 00:07:24
The command completed successfully.
```

Fig. (3). Net sessions.

Logon Sessions

On a Windows system, LogonSessions provide important details about currently running Windows login sessions as shown in Fig. (**4**).

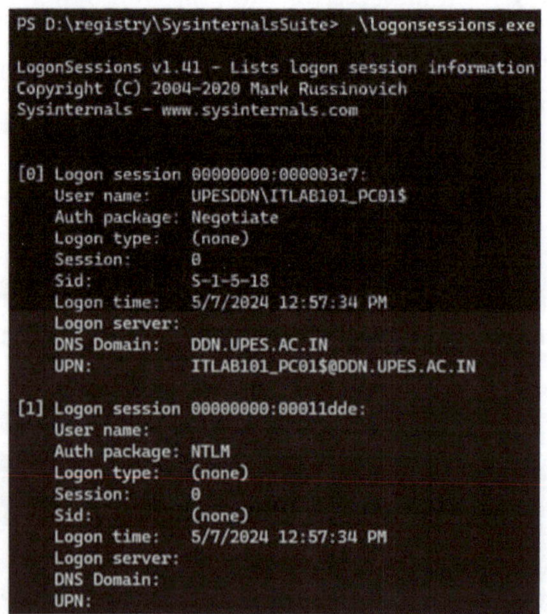

Fig. (4). Logon sessions.

Gathering Data from Networ

When hackers have remote access to a system, they frequently look for other systems that are visible to and linked to the network from the compromised system. In order to accomplish this, the hackers use the web and database servers to transmit commands to the system through browsers, which they then run as batch files. This allows them to initiate net view commands *via* SQL injection. The systems keep track of other systems that are visible to them when users connect to them *via* NetBIOS networking. It may be possible for the investigator to identify the other compromised systems in the network by looking through the contents of the cached name table. If an investigator wants to locate evidence of a possible incident, they should gather several kinds of network data. The following network data is helpful for investigation:

- Data content includes text, headers, and other information.
- Information from the sessions that are pertinent to the investigation.
- Application, server, firewall, and IDS/IPS log data.
- Results of the port scan.
- Packets from the network.

The NetBIOS name table cache maintains a list of connections established by NetBIOS networking with other systems. It contains the name and IP address of the remote system. As shown in Fig. (**5**), the NetBIOS name table cache on Windows can be inspected with the nbtstat command-line utility.

```
C:\Users\Administrator>nbtstat -c

Ethernet:
Node IpAddress: [10.9.3.148] Scope Id: []

    No names in cache
```

Fig. (5). Nbtstat command.

Gathering Network Connection Data

After the incident is reported, the investigator should try to obtain information on network connections to and from the compromised system as soon as possible, or else it may become out of date.

The system should be carefully examined by investigators to see if the attacker has logged out or is still using it. To transfer data out of the system, it is crucial to determine if the attacker has installed any worms or IRCbots. To stop malware from spreading, investigators should look for more compromised systems right away and take them offline. The Netstat utility facilitates the gathering of data regarding active network connections within a Windows operating system. This CLI software gives you a primitive overview of TCP and UDP connections, their status, and network traffic data. One of Windows OS's built-in tools is Netstat.exe. Using the -ano switch when running netstat is the most popular method. By flipping this switch, the software gets instructed to display the process identifiers (PIDs), TCP and UDP network connections, and listening ports as they are displayed in Fig. (**6**).

```
C:\Users\Administrator>netstat -ano

Active Connections

  Proto  Local Address          Foreign Address        State           PID
  TCP    0.0.0.0:22             0.0.0.0:0              LISTENING       4704
  TCP    0.0.0.0:135            0.0.0.0:0              LISTENING       1564
  TCP    0.0.0.0:445            0.0.0.0:0              LISTENING       4
  TCP    0.0.0.0:523            0.0.0.0:0              LISTENING       3396
  TCP    0.0.0.0:808            0.0.0.0:0              LISTENING       4212
  TCP    0.0.0.0:5040           0.0.0.0:0              LISTENING       7284
  TCP    0.0.0.0:7680           0.0.0.0:0              LISTENING       2024
  TCP    0.0.0.0:49664          0.0.0.0:0              LISTENING       1320
  TCP    0.0.0.0:49665          0.0.0.0:0              LISTENING       1156
  TCP    0.0.0.0:49666          0.0.0.0:0              LISTENING       2284
  TCP    0.0.0.0:49667          0.0.0.0:0              LISTENING       2452
  TCP    0.0.0.0:49668          0.0.0.0:0              LISTENING       3776
  TCP    0.0.0.0:49670          0.0.0.0:0              LISTENING       1320
  TCP    0.0.0.0:49679          0.0.0.0:0              LISTENING       1256
  TCP    0.0.0.0:49704          0.0.0.0:0              LISTENING       3024
  TCP    0.0.0.0:50000          0.0.0.0:0              LISTENING       5580
  TCP    0.0.0.0:63686          0.0.0.0:0              LISTENING       4136
  TCP    10.9.3.148:139         0.0.0.0:0              LISTENING       4
  TCP    10.9.3.148:59671       20.198.119.143:443     ESTABLISHED     4120
  TCP    10.9.3.148:59875       172.253.118.188:5228   ESTABLISHED     9600
  TCP    10.9.3.148:60189       52.111.244.0:443       ESTABLISHED     9600
  TCP    10.9.3.148:60196       52.111.252.0:443       ESTABLISHED     9600
  TCP    10.9.3.148:60253       52.111.244.0:443       ESTABLISHED     9600
  TCP    10.9.3.148:60501       40.79.197.35:443       ESTABLISHED     7808
  TCP    10.9.3.148:60502       49.44.175.65:443       CLOSE_WAIT      7808
  TCP    10.9.3.148:60527       104.18.36.252:443      ESTABLISHED     9600
  TCP    10.9.3.148:60539       35.162.243.32:443      ESTABLISHED     9600
  TCP    10.9.3.148:60550       13.107.42.14:443       ESTABLISHED     9600
  TCP    10.9.3.148:60553       172.217.166.19:443     ESTABLISHED     9600
```

Fig. (6). Netstat with -ano switch.

Using netstat with the -r switch, as illustrated in Fig. (**7**), one may view the routing table and discover whether any permanent routes are configured on the system. An investigator or even a system administrator could find this to be a helpful source of information for troubleshooting purposes.

```
C:\Users\Administrator>netstat -r
===========================================================================
Interface List
  5...f4 39 09 02 f2 41 ......Intel(R) Ethernet Connection (7) I219-LM
  1...........................Software Loopback Interface 1
===========================================================================

IPv4 Route Table
===========================================================================
Active Routes:
Network Destination        Netmask          Gateway       Interface  Metric
          0.0.0.0          0.0.0.0         10.9.1.1      10.9.3.148     25
         10.9.0.0      255.255.0.0         On-link       10.9.3.148    281
       10.9.3.148  255.255.255.255         On-link       10.9.3.148    281
     10.9.255.255  255.255.255.255         On-link       10.9.3.148    281
        127.0.0.0        255.0.0.0         On-link        127.0.0.1    331
        127.0.0.1  255.255.255.255         On-link        127.0.0.1    331
  127.255.255.255  255.255.255.255         On-link        127.0.0.1    331
        224.0.0.0        240.0.0.0         On-link        127.0.0.1    331
        224.0.0.0        240.0.0.0         On-link       10.9.3.148    281
  255.255.255.255  255.255.255.255         On-link        127.0.0.1    331
  255.255.255.255  255.255.255.255         On-link       10.9.3.148    281
===========================================================================
Persistent Routes:
  Network Address          Netmask  Gateway Address  Metric
          0.0.0.0          0.0.0.0         10.9.1.1       1
===========================================================================

IPv6 Route Table
===========================================================================
Active Routes:
 If Metric Network Destination      Gateway
  1    331 ::1/128                  On-link
  5    281 fe80::/64                On-link
  5    281 fe80::b1b9:85fd:a43a:282c/128
                                    On-link
  1    331 ff00::/8                 On-link
  5    281 ff00::/8                 On-link
===========================================================================
Persistent Routes:
  None
```

Fig. (7). Netstat with -r flag.

Process Information

Information regarding every process that is active on the system should be gathered by investigators. They can view details about each process by using the Task Manager as shown in Fig. (**8**). However, the Task Manager does not always provide all the necessary data. By searching for the information below, an investigator can find all the procedure details:

- The entire path points to the executable file (.exe).
- Command line used, if any, to initiate the procedure.
- How long the procedure has been in place.
- Security and user context in which the process is being used.
- Modules that the procedure loaded.
- Process that memory contains.

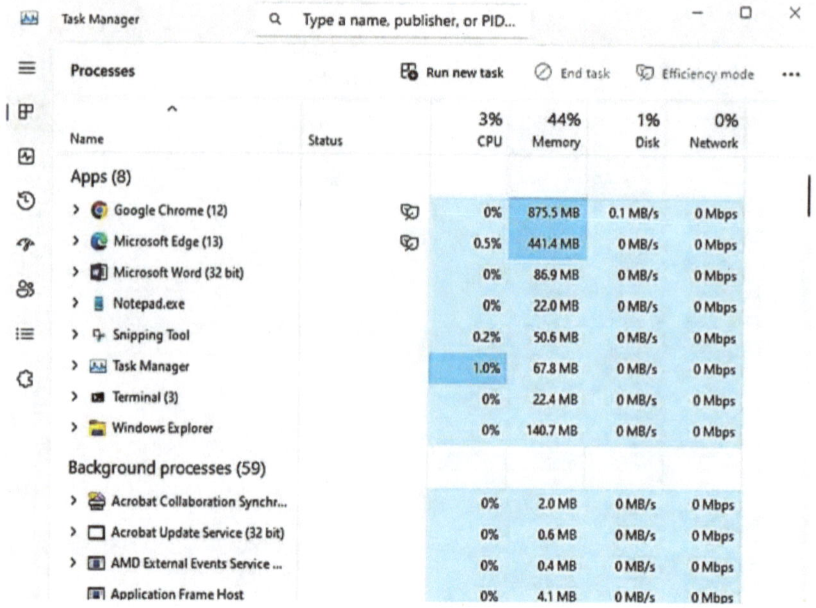

Fig. (8). Task Manager.

Therefore, to gather all relevant information about a process, investigators should become adept at using specific sources, tools, and commands. Below is a summary of several important tools and commands that are used to get comprehensive process information.

Tasklist

Tasklist.exe is a built-in program that replaces tlist.exe in Windows XP Pro and later editions. There are very slight variations between the two tools, mostly in the names and how the switches are implemented. It offers options for formatting the output, including list, CSV, and table formats. The /svc switch allows the investigator to see a list of the services connected to each process. The Tasklist utility shows the list of services and apps as well as the process IDs (PIDs) for all active tasks on locally or remotely connected computers as shown in Fig. (**9**).

```
C:\Users\Administrator>tasklist /v
Image Name                     PID Session Name        Session#    Mem Usage Status          User Name                                               CPU Time Window Title
========================= ======== ================ =========== ============ =============== ================================================== ============ ========================
System Idle Process              0 Services                   0          8 K Unknown         NT AUTHORITY\SYSTEM                                   345:49:49 N/A
System                           4 Services                   0     19,828 K Unknown         N/A                                                     0:09:19 N/A
Secure System                  140 Services                   0     40,360 K Unknown         NT AUTHORITY\SYSTEM                                     0:00:00 N/A
Registry                       196 Services                   0     44,240 K Unknown         NT AUTHORITY\SYSTEM                                     0:00:01 N/A
smss.exe                       668 Services                   0      1,160 K Unknown         NT AUTHORITY\SYSTEM                                     0:00:00 N/A
csrss.exe                      916 Services                   0      5,452 K Unknown         NT AUTHORITY\SYSTEM                                     0:00:02 N/A
wininit.exe                   1156 Services                   0      6,488 K Unknown         NT AUTHORITY\SYSTEM                                     0:00:00 N/A
services.exe                  1256 Services                   0     13,384 K Unknown         NT AUTHORITY\SYSTEM                                     0:00:33 N/A
```

Fig. (9). Tasklist with /v option.

PsList

Basic details about the processes that are currently active on a system are displayed by pslist.exe, including the duration of each process's operation (in both kernel and user modes) as shown in Fig. (**10**).

```
D:\registry\SysinternalsSuite>pslist.exe

PsList v1.41 - Process information lister
Copyright (C) 2000-2023 Mark Russinovich
Sysinternals - www.sysinternals.com

Process information for ITLAB101_PC01:

Name                Pid Pri Thd  Hnd    Priv        CPU Time    Elapsed Time
Idle                  0   0  24    0      60   346:55:24.812   140:04:37.921
System                4   8 255 4820      68     0:09:22.312   140:04:37.921
Secure System       140   8   0    0     188     0:00:00.000   140:04:47.104
Registry            196   8   4    0   16812     0:00:01.328   140:04:47.072
smss                668  11   2   58    1120     0:00:00.062   140:04:37.349
csrss               916  13  15  646    2324     0:00:02.156   140:04:21.248
wininit            1156  13   2  155    1640     0:00:00.031   140:04:18.732
services           1256   9   8  781    6284     0:00:33.703   140:04:18.476
LsaIso             1304   8   1   65    1412     0:00:00.046   140:04:18.299
lsass              1320   9  12 1836   23000     0:00:13.546   140:04:18.231
svchost            1432   8  22 15997  60164      0:00:10.296   140:04:16.89
fontdrvhost        1472   8   5   40    1612     0:00:00.000   140:04:16.691
svchost            1564   8  14 1624   11628     0:01:05.687   140:04:16.047
svchost            1628   8   6  359    2836     0:00:01.750   140:04:15.934
svchost            1736   8   1  108    1124     0:00:00.000   140:04:15.633
svchost            1796   8   2  219    2744     0:00:00.062   140:04:15.610
IntelCpHDCPSvc     1828   8   4  180    1656     0:00:00.000   140:04:15.597
```

Fig. (10). Pslist displaying active processes.

Process-to-Port Mapping

Every network connection and open port on a system are linked to a process since some processes must be utilized in order for the connection to be open. The process-to-port mapping can be obtained by the investigator using available techniques. For instance, the netstat command can obtain details on process-t--port mapping as shown in Fig. (**11**).

```
D:\registry\SysinternalsSuite>netstat -o

Active Connections

  Proto  Local Address          Foreign Address          State           PID
  TCP    10.9.3.148:7680        10.3.6.144:57747         ESTABLISHED     2024
  TCP    10.9.3.148:59671       20.198.119.143:https     ESTABLISHED     4120
  TCP    10.9.3.148:59875       sl-in-f188:5228          ESTABLISHED     9600
  TCP    10.9.3.148:60189       52.111.244.0:https       ESTABLISHED     9600
  TCP    10.9.3.148:60196       52.111.252.0:https       ESTABLISHED     9600
  TCP    10.9.3.148:60253       52.111.244.0:https       ESTABLISHED     9600
  TCP    10.9.3.148:60527       104.18.36.252:https      ESTABLISHED     9600
  TCP    10.9.3.148:60820       52.178.17.3:https        ESTABLISHED     7808
  TCP    10.9.3.148:60821       a104-90-5-195:https      CLOSE_WAIT      1457
  TCP    10.9.3.148:60823       13.107.213.48:https      CLOSE_WAIT      1457
  TCP    10.9.3.148:60824       13.107.246.68:https      CLOSE_WAIT      1457
  TCP    10.9.3.148:60951       10.3.2.192:ms-do         ESTABLISHED     2024
  TCP    10.9.3.148:60964       13.107.42.14:https       ESTABLISHED     9600
  TCP    10.9.3.148:60965       ec2-52-41-35-115:https   ESTABLISHED     960
  TCP    10.9.3.148:60966       ec2-52-41-35-115:https   TIME_WAIT       0
  TCP    10.9.3.148:60967       del03s17-in-f19:https    ESTABLISHED     9600
  TCP    10.9.3.148:60968       del11s11-in-f14:https    ESTABLISHED     9600
  TCP    10.9.3.148:60976       del11s11-in-f14:https    ESTABLISHED     9600
  TCP    10.9.3.148:60982       20.190.146.32:https      ESTABLISHED     9600
  TCP    10.9.3.148:60983       13.89.179.13:https       ESTABLISHED     9600
  TCP    10.9.3.148:60984       13.89.179.13:https       ESTABLISHED     9600
  TCP    10.9.3.148:60987       authddn:microsoft-ds     ESTABLISHED     4
```

Fig. (11). Netstat with -o option.

Time is of the essence when gathering volatile data. To safeguard the evidence before it vanishes, investigators must move quickly. To protect the chain of custody and ensure that the evidence is still admissible in court, strict protocols must also be adhered to.

Gathering Non-Volatile Information

During the static data-gathering process, non-volatile information can be obtained. When conducting a forensic investigation, information from non-volatile data can be used to help investigators recover lost or deleted data, browser information, linked device information, *etc.* When a system goes down or loses power, non-volatile data is unaffected. Several instances of spreadsheets, word processing documents, emails, and different "deleted" files are examples of non-volatile data. It is up to the investigator to determine what data needs to be taken from the registry or what data should be gathered for further research of (or from) files. It is also possible that the attacker is actively using the system to log in and obtain the data. The investigator may even choose to pursue the offender in such circumstances. It is crucial that the investigator preserves some crucial material unaltered and without additions or deletions. As the user boots up the computer, certain information may change, such as disks mapped to or from the system, services enabled, or installed programs. The investigator should note and record these adjustments because they might not last through a reboot. Hard drives are the typical location of non-volatile data; swap files, slack space, and unallocated disk space can also contain it. Smartphones, CD-ROMs, and USB storage devices are a few other non-volatile data sources.

Analyzing File Systems

When attempting to retrieve file system data or reconstruct file system events, a forensic investigator must possess a comprehensive understanding of the Windows file system. The file name, metadata, content data, file system application data, and file system data are the five elements that comprise file systems:

- **File system data:** The file system's structure, including block sizes, the number of allocated blocks, and file system and block sizes.
- **Content data:** The bulk of the file system's information is included in this data. It consists of all the data in the file system.
- **Metadata:** Metadata generally provides information about content locations, MAC timestamps, and file sizes.
- **Application data:** Application data provides details on the journal quota statistics for the file system.

By looking through these file system areas, an investigator can gather a range of information that might lead to the discovery of evidence that could help solve the case. In the command terminal, an investigator types the command dir /o:d. They can utilize this, as shown in Fig. (**12**), to confirm the OS installation date and time as well as the service packs, patches, and regularly updated subdirectories.

- **ESE Database File:** Extensible Storage Engine (ESE) is a data storage technology used by many Microsoft programs running on Windows OS. Several Microsoft-managed programs, including Windows Update Client, Windows Mail, Active Directory, and Windows Search, rely on ESE. The ESE database is significant from a forensics perspective because it houses and maintains key information about Windows OS installations and users. JET Blue is another name for the ESE.
- **Utilizing ESEDatabaseView to Examine a .edb File:** The ESEDatabaseView

utility allows forensic investigators to retrieve important evidence from .edb files. The application presents the information contained in .edb files in an easily readable and analyzed manner. A straightforward tool called ESEDatabaseView reads and shows the data kept in the ESE database. The user is shown a list of all the tables that are part of the opened database file. They can choose the table they wish to see and view each record that is contained in that table. ESEDatabaseView also simplifies the process of selecting one or more records, copying them to the clipboard, and pasting them into Excel or another spreadsheet application. An HTML, XML, tab-delimited, or comma-delimited file can be created when the records are exported.

```
D:\registry\SysinternalsSuite>dir /o:d
 Volume in drive D is New Volume
 Volume Serial Number is AAB0-C1CB

 Directory of D:\registry\SysinternalsSuite

05/10/2024  03:35 PM    <DIR>          ..
05/10/2024  03:35 PM            10,104 ctrl2cap.amd.sys
05/10/2024  03:35 PM           150,328 ctrl2cap.exe
05/10/2024  03:35 PM           154,424 ldmdump.exe
05/10/2024  03:35 PM           220,336 Listdlls64.exe
05/10/2024  03:35 PM           424,096 Listdlls.exe
05/10/2024  03:35 PM           158,896 ntfsinfo64.exe
05/10/2024  03:35 PM           139,432 ntfsinfo.exe
05/10/2024  03:35 PM           151,728 PsLoggedon.exe
05/10/2024  03:35 PM           451,392 portmon.exe
05/10/2024  03:35 PM           170,160 PsLoggedon64.exe
05/10/2024  03:35 PM            66,582 Pstools.chm
05/10/2024  03:35 PM                39 psversion.txt
05/10/2024  03:35 PM             7,903 readme.txt
05/10/2024  03:35 PM           243,888 Testlimit64.exe
05/10/2024  03:35 PM           233,640 Volumeid.exe
05/10/2024  03:35 PM           231,584 Testlimit.exe
05/10/2024  03:35 PM           169,648 Volumeid64.exe
05/10/2024  03:35 PM         2,181,688 CPUSTRES.EXE
```

Fig. (12). Dir /o:d command.

Analysis of the Windows Search Index

Windows Search Index is an index database used by Windows OS that facilitates file and other content indexing, allowing for more rapid and precise system-wide data searches. It keeps track of all the stuff that users have looked for and is indexed. Windows.edb file, which can be found in the following directory, contains the Windows Search Index. From the windows.edb file, forensic investigators can retrieve important information related to erased data, damaged disks, encrypted files, event boundaries, *etc.* Investigators should parse the data stored in the Windows.edb file to obtain evidence for their inquiry.

Slack Space

File slack, also known as slack space, describes the parts of a hard disk that might include data from files that have been deleted in the past or from space that a file is now using up. It is the area created between a stored file's end and the disk cluster's end. This occurs when the size of the file being written on the same cluster is smaller than the size of the file that was written previously. In these situations, the leftover data is left intact and, upon forensic examination, can yield important information. When files are allocated non-contiguously, there are more tail clusters and more slack space. Reading the entire cluster yields the data residue in the slack space. It would be possible to store data in slack space that one desires to keep hidden if one were unaware of the underlying file system [8]. To do this, create a file that is smaller than the slack space that is available, then use the leftover space to store the hidden data. Until it is deliberately altered, this data is invisible to the file system and stays unchanged. Nevertheless, the safest method of data hiding is not to create new files that leave slack space [9]. DriveSpy tool gathers all of a partition's free space into a file. Procedures for gathering data on slack space are shown in Fig. (**13**).

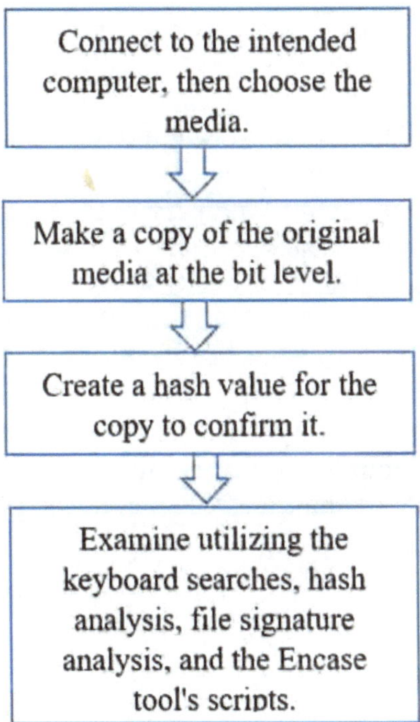

Connect to the intended computer, then choose the media.
Make a copy of the original media at the bit level.
Create a hash value for the copy to confirm it.
Examine utilizing the keyboard searches, hash analysis, file signature analysis, and the Encase tool's scripts.

Fig. (13). Procedures for gathering data on slack space.

OVERVIEW OF REGISTRY ON WINDOWS

The configuration information for the system is stored in a collection of databases called the Windows Registry. A central hierarchical database was featured in Windows 98, Windows CE, Windows NT, and Windows 2000 to store configuration information for one or more users, applications, and hardware parts. Windows continuously interacts with the Registry to store information about installed programs, user profiles, and the types of documents they can create, as well as hardware configurations, open ports, property sheet settings for folders and application icons, and other information. This configuration data may pertain to the user's personal information, the software, or the hardware. It also contains information on recently used programs, files, and system-connected devices. As you can see, this information is useful in terms of forensics. We will discover how to interpret this data in order to extract the necessary system information throughout this chapter. Regedit.exe is a built-in Windows program that allows you to view and edit the registry.

Windows' registry is made up of values and keys. Registry Keys are the directories that appear when you launch the regedit.exe application to view the registry. The information kept in these Registry Keys is called a registry value. A collection of data, keys, and sub-keys kept together in a single disk file is called a registry hive. The Registry replaces the majority of text-based.ini files used in Windows 3.x and MS-DOS configuration files, such as Autoexec.bat and Config.sys. The Registry is shared by several Windows operating systems, despite certain differences between them. A registry hive is a grouping of registry keys, subkeys, and values that have backup copies of their data kept in a number of auxiliary files. Except for HKEY_CURRENT_USER, the supporting files for Windows NT 4.0, Windows 2000, Windows XP, Windows Server 2003, and Windows Vista are found in the %SystemRoot%\System32\Config folder. %SystemRoot%\Profiles\ is where The HKEY_CURRENT_USER supporting files are in the Username folder. The file names in these folders indicate the type of data that is included within them. Furthermore, the type of data they carry may sometimes be made visible by their lack of an extension.

Registry Organization

The Windows Registry contains a record of every activity a user does on the system, making it a valuable source of information for forensic investigations. Any Windows system's registry has the following five root keys:

- **HKEY_CLASSES_ROOT:** HKEY_LOCAL_MACHINE\Software has a subkey called HKEY_CLASSES_ROOT, or HKCR. It includes a programmable identifier (ProgID), class ID (CLSID), interface ID (IID), and file extension association information. When a user accesses a file using Windows Explorer, this hive contains the essential data that ensures the right program opens. Both –HKEY_LOCAL_MACHINE and –HKEY_CURRENT_USER contain the class registration and file name extension data kept under HKEY_CLASSES_ROOT.

- **HKEY_CURRENT_USER:** The registry key for the currently logged-in user can be found in HKCU, or HKEY_CURRENT_USER. This hive controls all user-level options pertaining to the user profile, such as desktop wallpaper, screen colors, and display settings.
- **HKEY_LOCAL_MACHINE:** Most configuration information for installed applications, including Windows OS, and information about the hardware of the machine is located in HKEY_LOCAL_MACHINE, or HKLM. This data includes bus type, installed cards, memory type, startup control parameters, and device drives.
- **HKEY_USERS:** HKEY_USERS, also referred to as HKU, contains details about each user profile that is currently active on the computer. Every registry key in the HKEY_USERS hive corresponds to a computer user, whose name is derived from their security identification (SID). Environmental variables, installed printers, user-specific mapped disks, and other settings are managed *via* the registry keys and registry values under each SID.
- **HKEY_CURRENT_CONFIG:** The shorthand for HKEY_CURRENT_CONFIG, or HKCC, is where data regarding the system's current hardware profile is kept. The details kept under this hive provide an explanation of the variations between the standard configuration and the present hardware setup. The HKEY_CURRENT_CONFIG is essentially a pointer to the registry key HKEY_LOCAL_MACHINE\SYSTEM\CurrentControlSet\CurrentControlSet\Hardware Profiles\Current, which is located beneath the Software and System keys and provides details on the standard hardware configuration.

Windows Registry hives are separated into different categories based on data persistence. While the volatile hives are obtained during real-time system analysis, the non-volatile hives are stored on the hard drive as depicted in Fig. (**14**).

When the regedit.exe program is launched, you can see these keys. The registry editor can be accessed by simultaneously pressing the R and Windows keys. A run prompt similar to this one will appear as shown in Fig. (**15**).

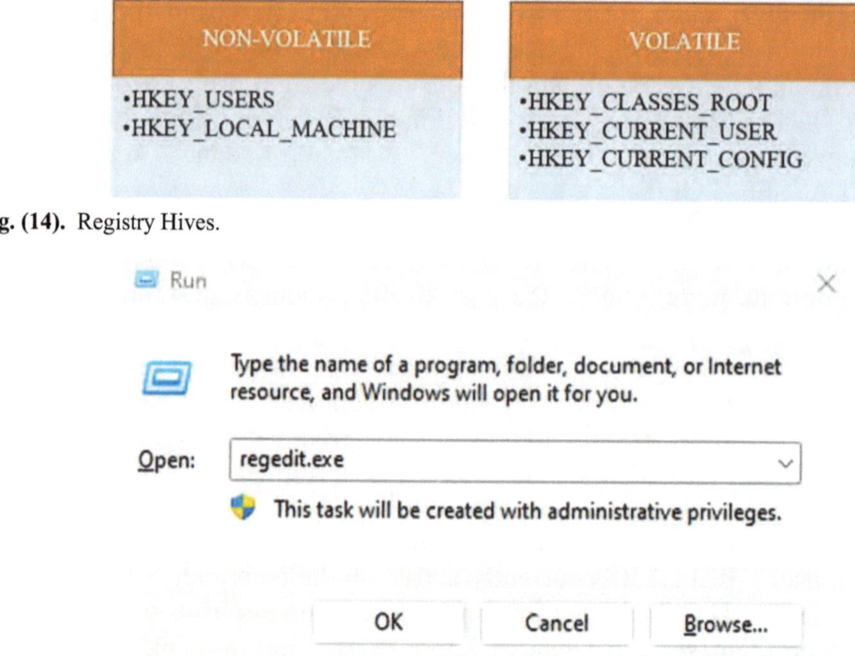

Fig. (14). Registry Hives.

Fig. (15). Regedit.

The registry editor window will appear when you type regedit.exe into this prompt. This is how it will appear as shown in Fig. (**16**).

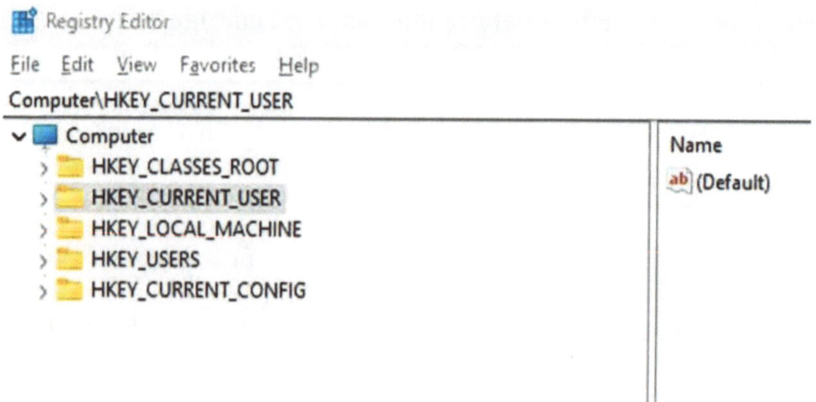

Fig. (16). Registry editor.

In a tree view that shows the included registry entries, the values of the selected key are shown in the right pane and the root keys are shown in the left pane [10]. To view the properties of the value shown in the right pane, select Properties with a right-click on the value. The Windows registry's hives are essential to the system's operation. Microsoft defines each of the root keys [11]. The preconfigured keys that the system uses are listed in the following Table **1**. A key name can have a maximum length of 255 characters.

Table 1. Description of the root keys.

Folder	Description
HKEY_CLASSES_ROOT	Is in the subkey HKEY_LOCAL_MACHINE\Software. This data makes sure that the right program opens when you open a file with Windows Explorer. This key is commonly shortened as HKCR. Beginning with Windows 2000, this information is contained in the HKEY_LOCAL_MACHINE and HKEY_CURRENT_USER keys. The default configurations in the HKEY_LOCAL_MACHINE\Software\Classes key are accessible to all local users. The HKEY_CURRENT_USER\Software\Classes key contains settings that are specific to the interactive user and override the default values. The HKEY_CLASSES_ROOT key provides an overview of the registry by combining information from these two sources. Software created for Windows versions prior to HKEY_CLASSES_ROOT can likewise be viewed in this combined manner. The interactive user's settings must be changed by making changes in HKEY_CURRENT_USER\Software\Classes, not HKEY_CLASSES_ROOT. To change the default settings, make changes at HKEY_LOCAL_MACHINE\Software\Classes. If you write keys to a key under HKEY_CLASSES_ROOT, the data is saved by the system at HKEY_LOCAL_MACHINE\Software\Classes. If you write values to a key under HKEY CLASSES ROOT and the key already exists there, the system will store the data under HKEY_CURRENT_USER\Software\Classes instead of HKEY_LOCAL_MACHINE\Software\Classes.
HKEY_CURRENT_USER	This is the loaded and active user profile of the person who is now logged in, consists of the user's current logged-in configuration information's root. This is where the user stores their folders, Control Panel preferences, and screen colors. The profile of the user is linked to this information. The key can also be abbreviated to HKCU.
HKEY_LOCAL_MACHINE	A wide range of system configuration data, including software and hardware settings, are contained in this hive. Contains specific computer configuration data (for any user). HKLM is another common abbreviation for this key.
HKEY_USERS	It includes every user profile that is currently loaded for that system. Includes every user profile that is currently loaded onto the machine. HKEY_CURRENT_USER is a subkey of HKEY_USERS. HKEY_USERS is occasionally abbreviated as HKU.
HKEY_CURRENT_CONFIG	Contains information on the hardware profile that is used by the local computer during its initial boot-up. This hive contains the system's basic hardware profile.

The Registry Structure in a Hive File

For digital forensics investigations, the Windows registry's structure into hive files offers a wealth of information. Every hive serves as a snapshot of the user preferences, installed software, and system settings. It is arranged hierarchically with keys, subkeys, and values. An investigation team may be able to construct a timeline of events by examining timestamps connected to registry alterations. Furthermore, the identification of malware can benefit from the existence of keys or values. It is imperative to bear in mind, however, that certain hives reside in memory and require volatile analysis techniques; also, safe copies must be made to preserve the original evidence's integrity during forensic registry data access [12].

A forensic investigator must possess a solid understanding of the registry's fundamental elements. They can find more information by doing keyword searches across a variety of sources and locations, including physical memory, the page file, and even unallocated regions. The forensic investigator can have a better idea of what is feasible and how to move forward by learning more about the registry structure [13]. The cells that make up the registry component cells are structured differently and include different kinds of data. The many sorts of cells are described in the following Table **2**.

Table 2. Different types of cells and descriptions.

Types of Cells	Description
Key cell	Along with offsets to adjacent cells and the key's last write time, it contains registry key information. Behave similarly to folders, with registry data organized in a hierarchical structure. Their names usually reflect what kind of data they include (*e.g.*, the “Software” key probably contains information about installed programs).
Value cell	Value cells are the foundation of the registry; they contain the real data that defines user preferences, software settings, and system behavior. Through the examination of registry key values, investigators specializing in digital forensics can obtain vital information regarding previous system operations.
Subkey list cell	To organize and reference subkeys within a key, the subkey list cell is essential. It functions as an index or pointer rather than a cell that holds data. It consists of several indexes that point to key cells; each of these indexes is a subkey that points to the parent key cell. Serving as a central hub, the subkey list cell points the registry in the direction of the specific key cells holding details on the subkeys inside a given key. Digital forensics investigators can decipher the subkey hierarchy and possibly even rebuild the registry hive's general structure by examining subkey list cells and the key cells they refer to.

(Table 2) cont.....

Types of Cells	Description
Value list cell	It consists of several indexes that lead to value cells, each of which contains the value of a common key cell. For the aim of conveniently storing and retrieving configuration data, values are arranged within keys. Analyzing values' names and structures yields useful information for digital forensics investigations.
Security descriptor cell	In order to restrict access to registry keys and their contents, the security descriptor cell is essential. It's a special cell that holds data regarding the rights given to individuals and groups to perform certain operations (read, write, delete, *etc.*) on a particular key.

PERFORM FORENSIC ANALYSIS OF THE WINDOWS REGISTRY

The investigator can get forensic artifacts including user accounts, recently accessed files, USB activity, last-run programs, and installed apps with the use of forensic analysis of the Windows registry. There are two ways that investigators can investigate the Windows registry:

- **Static Analysis:** using this technique, investigators need to look through the registry files that are in the evidence file that was taken. The subdirectory c:\windows\system32\config contains these files.
- **Live Analysis:** Investigators can extract registry files from a live system and use the integrated registry editor to evaluate it with the help of FTK imager and other tools.

FTk Imager to Capture Windows Registry Files on a Live System

Step 1: Navigate to File→ Obtain Protected Files in FTK Imager. To extract the files, select Password recovery and all registry files as shown in Fig. (**17**).

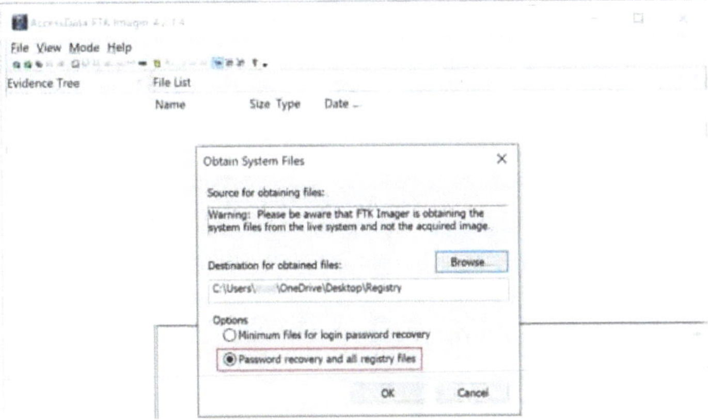

Fig. (17). Obtaining system file.

Step 2: The files displayed in Fig. (**18**) are the HKEY_LOCAL_MACHINE subkeys that were exported from a live suspicious PC using FTK Imager.

Name	Date modified
software	4/1/2024 8:56 AM
default	4/1/2024 8:56 AM
SAM	4/1/2024 8:56 AM
SECURITY	4/1/2024 8:56 AM
system	4/1/2024 8:56 AM

Fig. (18). Hkey_local_machine subkeys.

The extracted HKEY_LOCAL_MACHINE subkeys contain the following information:

- **Security Account Manager, or SAM:** This subkey contains data about users, guest accounts, administrator accounts, and cryptographic hashes of each user password, among other things.
- **Security:** Data about the current user security policy is stored in this subkey.
- **Software:** This subkey contains details on the installed software programs and the system configurations for them.
- **System:** Data about hardware driver and service configuration parameters are stored in this subkey.
- **Default:** Information about the user's default settings is stored in this subkey. Nonetheless, the default user settings are superseded by the NTUSER.dat file associated with the presently logged-on user.

Sysinternals Process Monitor

For real-time registry activity analysis, Process Monitor, a potent tool from the Microsoft Sysinternals package, is an invaluable resource. It can be applied to registry analysis as follows:

- Recording Registry Events, as a capture tool, Process Monitor keeps track of and logs all file system, registry, and process/thread activity on your computer. This covers all registry operations, including creations, reads, writes, and deletes.
- Process Monitor allows you to record in-depth information about how a program or operation interacts with the registry before you execute it or perform an action.

- The power of Process Monitor is found in its filtering powers. The recorded occurrences can be filtered using a few criteria, such as:
- Operation: Apply a filter to particular registry actions, such as RegOpenKey, RegSetValue, RegDeleteValue, and so forth.
- Path: To see how a program interacts with a specific registry key (such as HKEY_LOCAL_MACHINE\SOFTWARE), concentrate on that key.
- ***Results:*** To find possible access problems, filter for registry activities that succeeded or failed.
- Process: To view all registry activity started by a particular program, filter by the name of the process.

Process Monitor is a versatile tool for instantaneous registry inspection and can be an asset for identifying issues with the system, understanding how apps behave, and carrying out digital forensics inquiries [14].

Step 1: First, get familiar with Process Monitor's interface. You are able to get from, as shown in Fig. (**19**).

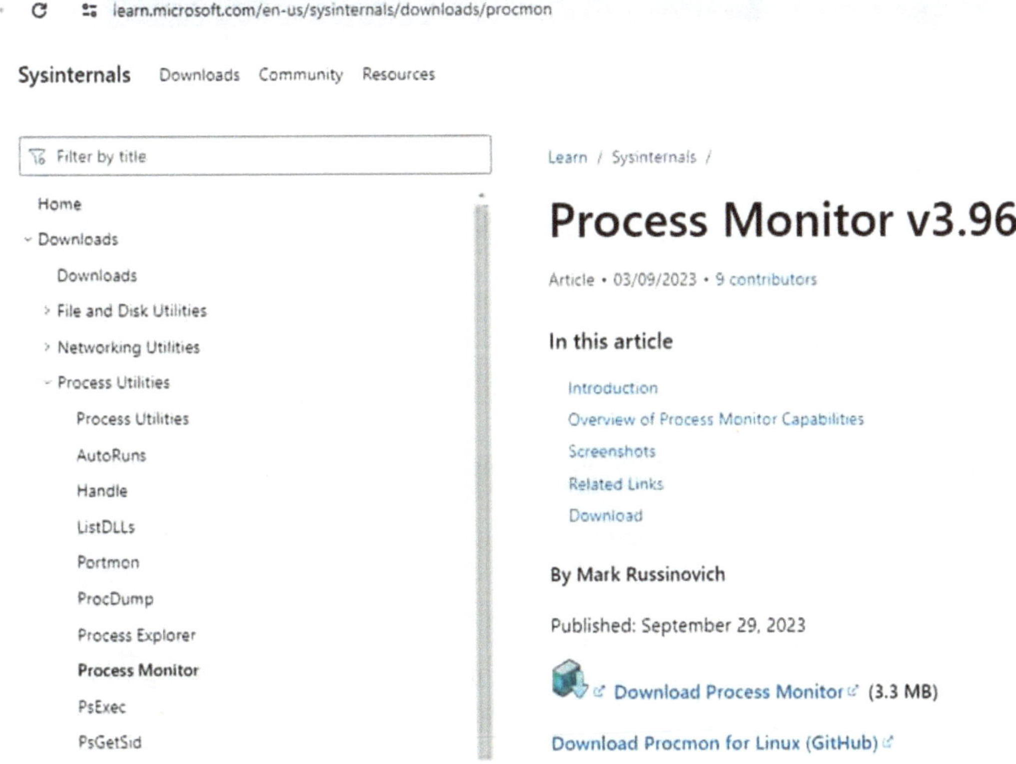

Fig. (19). Process monitor download.

Step 2: The application begins recording events on the computer as soon as it launches.

Step 3: At all times, five types of events are being recorded. This is presented in Fig. (**20**) and denoted by the top five buttons:

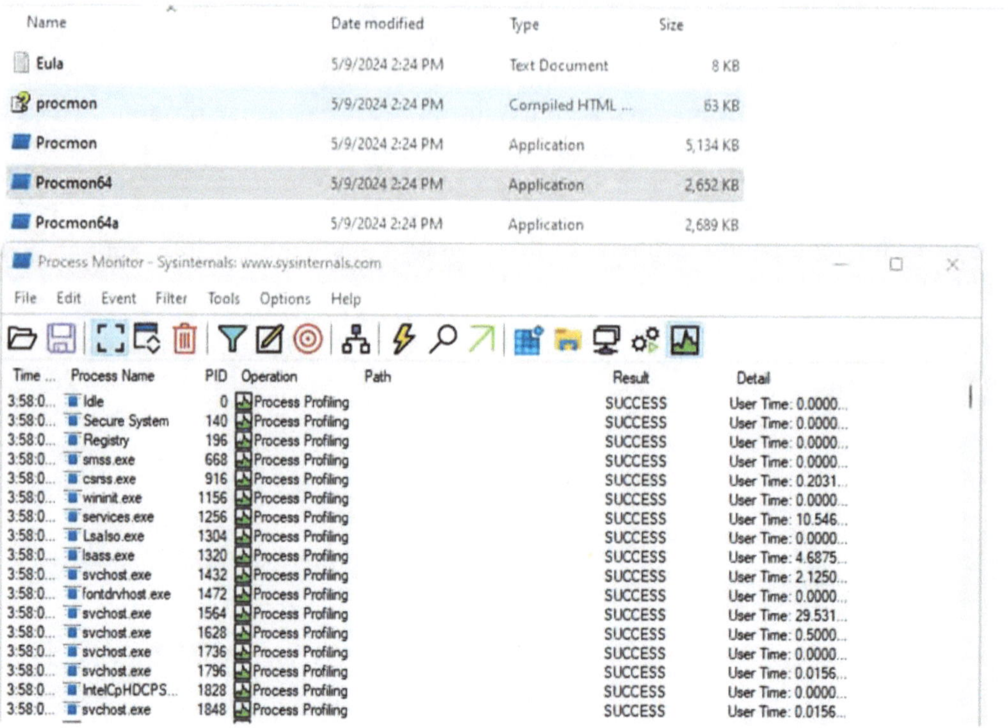

Fig. (20). Process monitor installation.

- **Registry activity:** when values and keys in the registry are added, removed, or changed.
- **File System Activity:** when directories and files are added, removed, and accessed.
- **Network Activity:** displaying the outbound connections that the process made.
- **Process and thread activity:** keeping track of when they are generated and deleted.
- **Profiling Events:** This shows how a process utilized the CPU. The "capture event" button, located third from the left, indicates that events are being recorded when it is highlighted. Just deselect this option to end the capture as shown in Fig. (**21**).

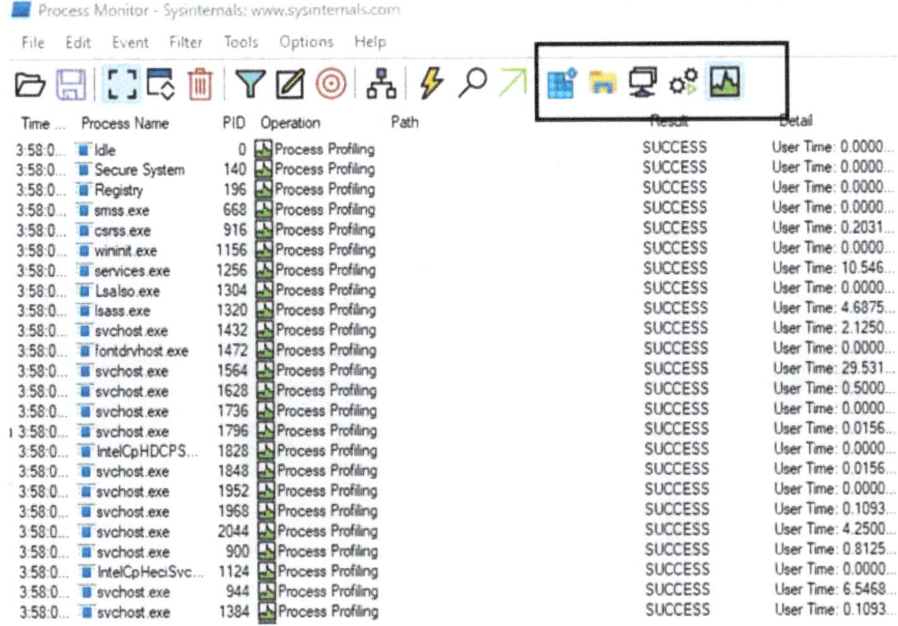

Fig. (21). Event categories.

Step 4: You can deselect the other things if a certain event is highlighted, which indicates that just the pertinent events are visible in Fig. (**22**).

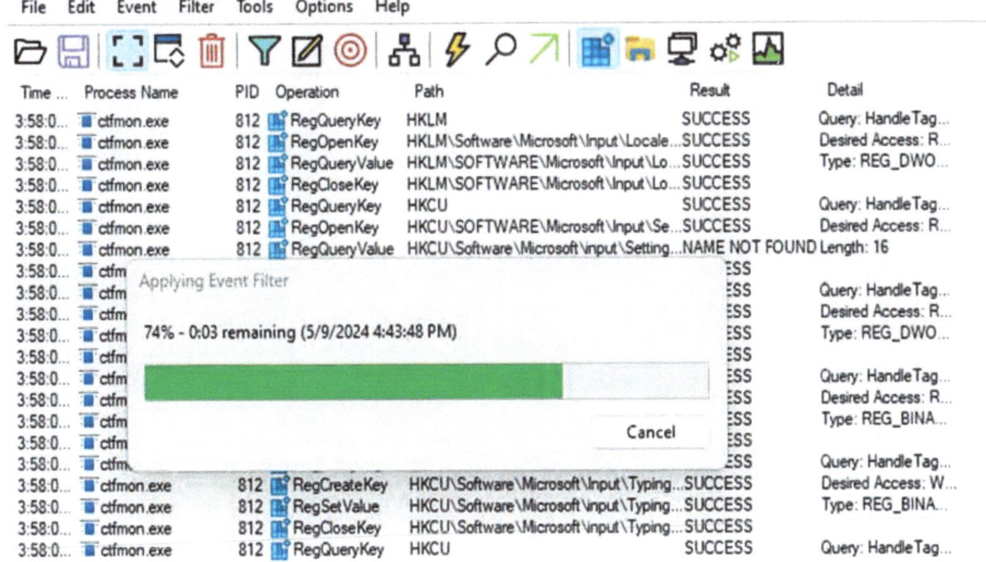

Fig. (22). Registry events displayed.

Step 5: Double clicking an event or selecting the event properties button from this page will allow you to see further details about that event. By clicking the button, you may also view the current process tree, which is useful for determining whether a target process has produced any child processes as depicted in Fig. (**23**).

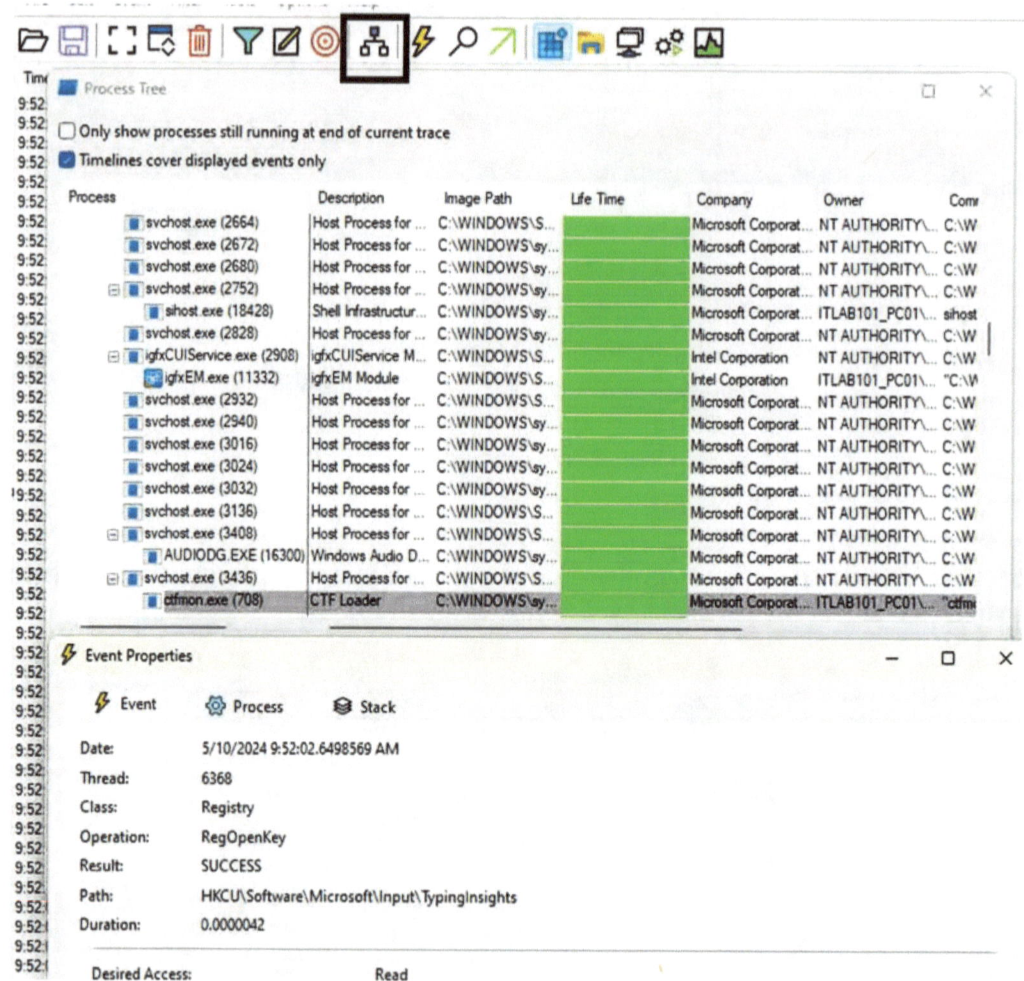

Fig. (23). Process tree of a process.

Step 6: you can view events based on a specific filter you can create custom filters as shown in Fig. (**24**).

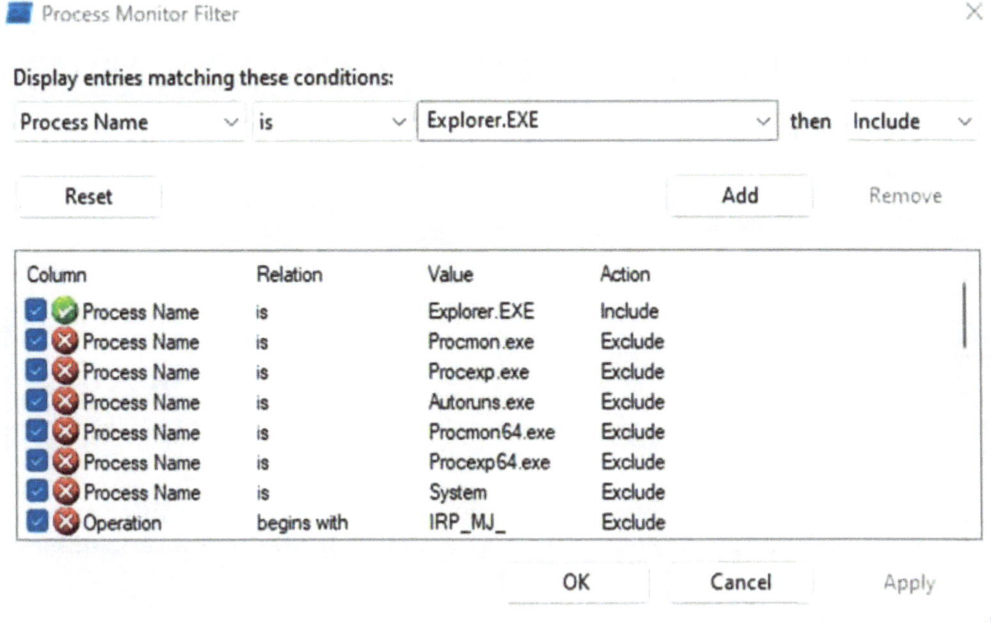

Fig. (24). Process monitor filter.

Analyze Malware Activity

Here is the selected example payment.exe has already been run, therefore use Process Monitor to record events. We have saved the event in a CSV file. Now let us analyze them we have created a filter to view only the event relevant to the malware sample. As depicted in Fig. (**25**).

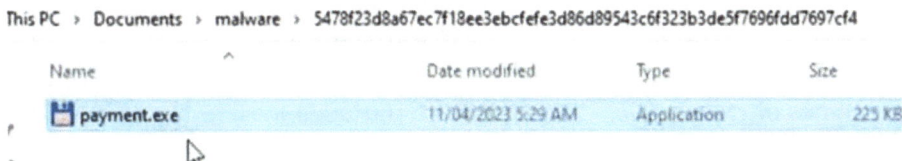

This PC › Documents › malware › 5478f23d8a67ec7f18ee3ebcfefe3d86d89543c6f323b3de5f7696fdd7697cf4

Name	Date modified	Type	Size
payment.exe	11/04/2023 5:29 AM	Application	225 KB

Fig. (25). Payement.exe analysis.

As shown in Fig. (**26**), several registry keys, including those pertaining to the.net framework, have been accessed and queried. Let us first examine just the registry activity. There's a chance that the executable was created with.net.

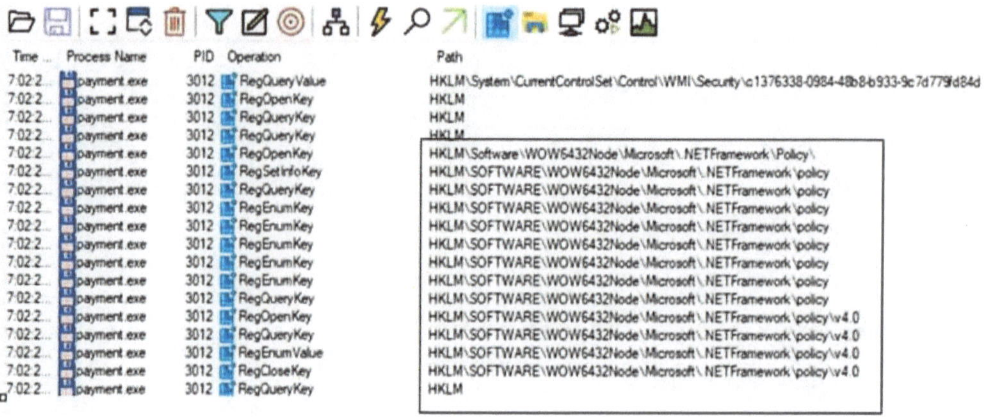

Time ...	Process Name	PID	Operation	Path
7:02:2...	payment.exe	3012	RegQueryValue	HKLM\System\CurrentControlSet\Control\WMI\Security\c1376338-0984-48b8-b933-9c7d779fd84d
7:02:2...	payment.exe	3012	RegOpenKey	HKLM
7:02:2...	payment.exe	3012	RegQueryKey	HKLM
7:02:2...	payment.exe	3012	RegQueryKey	HKLM
7:02:2...	payment.exe	3012	RegOpenKey	HKLM\Software\WOW6432Node\Microsoft\.NETFramework\Policy\
7:02:2...	payment.exe	3012	RegSetInfoKey	HKLM\SOFTWARE\WOW6432Node\Microsoft\.NETFramework\policy
7:02:2...	payment.exe	3012	RegQueryKey	HKLM\SOFTWARE\WOW6432Node\Microsoft\.NETFramework\policy
7:02:2...	payment.exe	3012	RegEnumKey	HKLM\SOFTWARE\WOW6432Node\Microsoft\.NETFramework\policy
7:02:2...	payment.exe	3012	RegEnumKey	HKLM\SOFTWARE\WOW6432Node\Microsoft\.NETFramework\policy
7:02:2...	payment.exe	3012	RegEnumKey	HKLM\SOFTWARE\WOW6432Node\Microsoft\.NETFramework\policy
7:02:2...	payment.exe	3012	RegEnumKey	HKLM\SOFTWARE\WOW6432Node\Microsoft\.NETFramework\policy
7:02:2...	payment.exe	3012	RegQueryKey	HKLM\SOFTWARE\WOW6432Node\Microsoft\.NETFramework\policy
7:02:2...	payment.exe	3012	RegOpenKey	HKLM\SOFTWARE\WOW6432Node\Microsoft\.NETFramework\policy\v4.0
7:02:2...	payment.exe	3012	RegQueryKey	HKLM\SOFTWARE\WOW6432Node\Microsoft\.NETFramework\policy\v4.0
7:02:2...	payment.exe	3012	RegEnumValue	HKLM\SOFTWARE\WOW6432Node\Microsoft\.NETFramework\policy\v4.0
7:02:2...	payment.exe	3012	RegCloseKey	HKLM\SOFTWARE\WOW6432Node\Microsoft\.NETFramework\policy\v4.0
7:02:2...	payment.exe	3012	RegQueryKey	HKLM

Fig. (26). Registry activity with .net framework.

The sample also inquires about the existence and use of Microsoft's Malicious Software Removal Tool (MRT), which is depicted in Fig. (**27**), as well as the status of antivirus software.

7:02:2...	payment.exe	3012	RegQueryKey	HKLM
7:02:2...	payment.exe	3012	RegOpenKey	HKLM\Software\Microsoft\RemovalTools\MRT
7:02:2...	payment.exe	3012	RegSetInfoKey	HKLM\SOFTWARE\Microsoft\RemovalTools\MRT
7:02:2...	payment.exe	3012	RegQueryValue	HKLM\SOFTWARE\Microsoft\RemovalTools\MRT\GUID
7:02:2...	payment.exe	3012	RegCloseKey	HKLM\SOFTWARE\Microsoft\RemovalTools\MRT
7:02:2...	payment.exe	3012	RegQueryKey	HKLM
7:02:2...	payment.exe	3012	RegOpenKey	HKLM\SOFTWARE\Policies\Microsoft
7:02:2...	payment.exe	3012	RegSetInfoKey	HKLM\SOFTWARE\Policies\Microsoft
7:02:2...	payment.exe	3012	RegQueryKey	HKLM

Fig. (27). MRT software.

Now, highlight the operation where the registry value has been set. As we can see in Fig. (**28**), there is only one entry. Scroll towards the end to see this. The sample configures a file called 'crsi' to run when the system boots up. This registry path holds the names of executables that need to be started at system boot time [15].

Next, let us look at the file system activity. We can see that a prefetch file has been created for the executable, it can also be examined to get more information about the sample. We can see a log file has been created by the CLR, which is the common language one time used by .net executables from the registry activity. As depicted in Fig. (**29**).

We observe that several keys relevant to the .net framework have been queried toward the end of the list. We can see the executable with the name 'crsi' has been created; this was the executable configured to start at system boot time. This could be a file dropped by the malware sample. We can see a batch script has also been created as a temporally file as shown in Fig. (**30**).

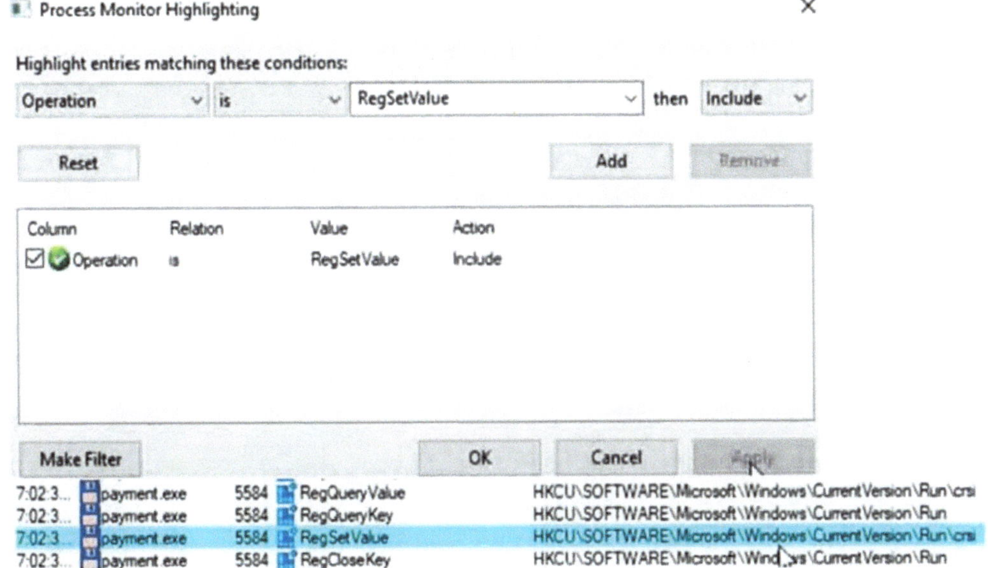

Fig. (28). Filtering operation.

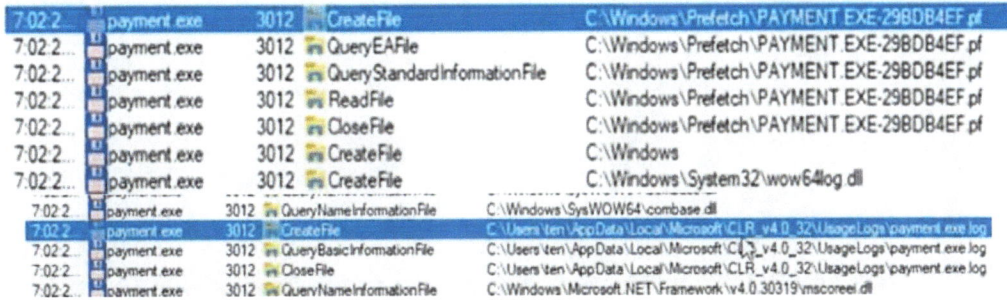

7:02:2...	payment.exe	3012	CreateFile	C:\Windows\Prefetch\PAYMENT.EXE-29BDB4EF.pf
7:02:2...	payment.exe	3012	QueryEAFile	C:\Windows\Prefetch\PAYMENT.EXE-29BDB4EF.pf
7:02:2...	payment.exe	3012	QueryStandardInformationFile	C:\Windows\Prefetch\PAYMENT.EXE-29BDB4EF.pf
7:02:2...	payment.exe	3012	ReadFile	C:\Windows\Prefetch\PAYMENT.EXE-29BDB4EF.pf
7:02:2...	payment.exe	3012	CloseFile	C:\Windows\Prefetch\PAYMENT.EXE-29BDB4EF.pf
7:02:2...	payment.exe	3012	CreateFile	C:\Windows
7:02:2...	payment.exe	3012	CreateFile	C:\Windows\System32\wow64log.dll
7:02:2...	payment.exe	3012	QueryNameInformationFile	C:\Windows\SysWOW64\combase.dll
7:02:2...	payment.exe	3012	CreateFile	C:\Users\ten\AppData\Local\Microsoft\CLR_v4.0_32\UsageLogs\payment.exe.log
7:02:2...	payment.exe	3012	QueryBasicInformationFile	C:\Users\ten\AppData\Local\Microsoft\CLR_v4.0_32\UsageLogs\payment.exe.log
7:02:2...	payment.exe	3012	CloseFile	C:\Users\ten\AppData\Local\Microsoft\CLR_v4.0_32\UsageLogs\payment.exe.log
7:02:2...	payment.exe	3012	QueryNameInformationFile	C:\Windows\Microsoft.NET\Framework\v4.0.30319\mscoreei.dll

Fig. (29). Prefetch file information.

7:02:3...	payment.exe	5584	WriteFile	C:\Users\ten\AppData\Roaming\crsi.exe
7:02:3...	payment.exe	5584	CreateFile	C:\Users\ten\AppData\Local\Temp
7:02:3...	payment.exe	5584	QueryBasicInformationFile	C:\Users\ten\AppData\Local\Temp
7:02:3...	payment.exe	5584	CloseFile	C:\Users\ten\AppData\Local\Temp
7:02:3...	payment.exe	5584	CreateFile	C:\Users\ten\AppData\Local\Temp\tmpD702.tmp
7:02:3...	payment.exe	5584	CloseFile	C:\Users\ten\AppData\Local\Temp\tmpD702.tmp
7:02:3...	payment.exe	5584	CreateFile	C:\Users\ten\AppData\Local\Temp\tmpD702.tmp.bat
7:02:3...	payment.exe	5584	WriteFile	C:\Users\ten\AppData\Local\Temp\tmpD702.tmp.bat
7:02:3...	payment.exe	5584	CloseFile	C:\Users\ten\AppData\Local\Temp\tmpD702.tmp.bat
7:02:3...	payment.exe	5584	CreateFile	C:\Users\ten\AppData\Local\Temp\tmpD702.tmp.bat
7:02:3...	payment.exe	5584	QueryBasicInformationFile	C:\Users\ten\AppData\Local\Temp\tmpD702.tmp.bat

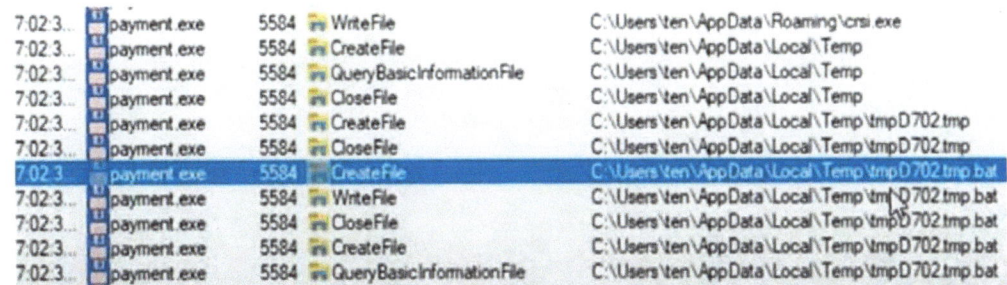

Fig. (30). Information about the batch script.

Now, let's examine the process and thread activity to see if a script has been created and run. We can see that a child process with the same name has been generated as threads have been created when the dll has been imported for use. Upon seeing the variation in the process ID, it is evident that a command prompt process has been initiated, as depicted in Fig. (**31**).

7:02:3...	payment.exe	5584	Load Image	C:\Windows\SysWOW64\cryptbase.dll
7:02:3...	payment.exe	5584	Load Image	C:\Windows\assembly\NativeImages_v4
7:02:3...	payment.exe	5584	Load Image	C:\Windows\SysWOW64\sspicli.dll
7:02:3...	payment.exe	5584	Load Image	C:\Windows\SysWOW64\crypt32.dll
7:02:3...	payment.exe	5584	Load Image	C:\Windows\SysWOW64\msasn1.dll
7:02:3...	payment.exe	5584	Load Image	C:\Windows\Microsoft.NET\assembly\G/
7:02:3...	payment.exe	5584	Load Image	C:\Windows\Microsoft.NET\assembly\G/
7:02:3...	payment.exe	5584	Load Image	C:\Windows\SysWOW64\psapi.dll
7:02:3	payment.exe	5584	Process Create	C:\WINDOWS\SysWOW64\cmd.exe
7:02:3...	payment.exe	5584	Thread Exit	

Fig. (31). Process and thread activity for cmd.exe.

When we examine the process tree as depicted in Fig. (**32**), we can observe that payment.exe has produced a child command prompt as well as a child process of the same name. This is where the executed command is displayed; it appears that the batch script has run. Command prompt typically swans the console host window as a child process timeout.exe is used to pause command processing for a specified number of seconds. It frequently appears in batch scripts. Because they have exited, the processes are grayed out.

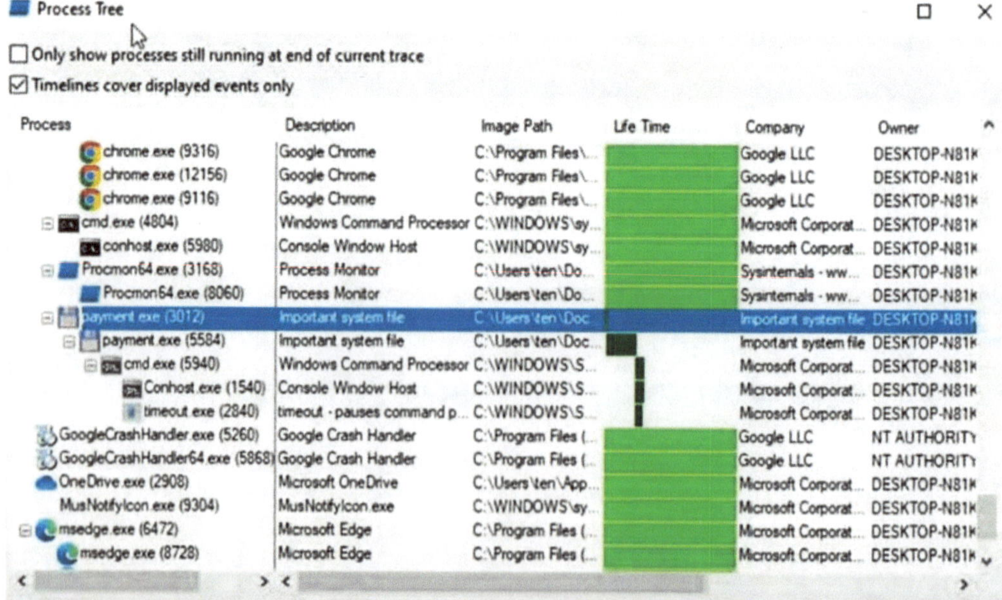

Process Tree
Only show processes still running at end of current trace
Timelines cover displayed events only
Process
Description
Image Path
Life Time
Company
Owner
chrome.exe (9316) Google Chrome C:\Program Files\... Google LLC DESKTOP-N81K
chrome.exe (12156) Google Chrome C:\Program Files\... Google LLC DESKTOP-N81K
chrome.exe (9116) Google Chrome C:\Program Files\... Google LLC DESKTOP-N81K
cmd.exe (4804) Windows Command Processor C:\WINDOWS\sy... Microsoft Corporat... DESKTOP-N81K
conhost.exe (5980) Console Window Host C:\WINDOWS\sy... Microsoft Corporat... DESKTOP-N81K
Procmon64.exe (3168) Process Monitor C:\Users\ten\Do... Sysinternals - ww... DESKTOP-N81K
Procmon64.exe (8060) Process Monitor C:\Users\ten\Do... Sysinternals - ww... DESKTOP-N81K
payment.exe (3012) Important system file C:\Users\ten\Doc... Important system file DESKTOP-N81K
payment.exe (5584) Important system file C:\Users\ten\Doc... Important system file DESKTOP-N81K
cmd.exe (5940) Windows Command Processor C:\WINDOWS\S... Microsoft Corporat... DESKTOP-N81K
Conhost.exe (1540) Console Window Host C:\WINDOWS\S... Microsoft Corporat... DESKTOP-N81K
timeout.exe (2840) timeout - pauses command p... C:\WINDOWS\S... Microsoft Corporat... DESKTOP-N81K
GoogleCrashHandler.exe (5260) Google Crash Handler C:\Program Files (... Google LLC NT AUTHORITY
GoogleCrashHandler64.exe (5868) Google Crash Handler C:\Program Files (... Google LLC NT AUTHORITY
OneDrive.exe (2908) Microsoft OneDrive C:\Users\ten\App... Microsoft Corporat... DESKTOP-N81K
MusNotifyIcon.exe (9304) MusNotifyIcon.exe C:\WINDOWS\sy... Microsoft Corporat... DESKTOP-N81K
msedge.exe (6472) Microsoft Edge C:\Program Files (... Microsoft Corporat... DESKTOP-N81K
msedge.exe (8728) Microsoft Edge C:\Program Files (... Microsoft Corporat... DESKTOP-N81K

Fig. (32). Process tree for the payment.exe.

According to observations made in the process monitor, the malware sample seems to drop two files: a batch script that was run once and an executable that is set to launch upon system boot. You can now use the Process Monitor tool to investigate the behavior of a malware sample.

WEB BROWSER - HISTORY, COOKIES, AND CACHE

Web browsers keep track of every action a user takes on them in their histories, cookies, and caches. Browsers leave a breadcrumb trail of information about our internet activities. Forensic investigators can extract valuable information from these breadcrumbs, which consist of browsing history, cookies, and cache. Through the examination of this data, forensic investigators can ascertain the online actions carried out on the system, including the websites visited, files downloaded, the last time a specific website was viewed, the frequency with which a user has visited a website, and so on. Such information can be extremely valuable as evidence in a forensic inquiry. Your browser history is a list of all the websites you have visited. It can expose a user's online behaviors, hobbies, and even possible criminal activities.

Sometimes deleted entries can be recovered by forensic tools, even if the person has tried to clean their history. Websites save little text files called cookies on your computer. They hold data on surfing habits, site preferences, and login credentials. Cookies may be used to follow a person through several websites, connect them to accounts, and even recognize the device they were using. Browsers keep temporary copies of HTML, JavaScript, and picture files in their caches. Websites load more quickly on subsequent visits thanks to the cache. Cache data, on the other hand, may also include text that you may have placed into forms and other bits of visited webpages. This might be very important evidence in an investigation [16].

Google Chrome Analysis

Like most web browsers, Google Chrome stores browsing data and improves user experience using cookies, cache, and history. The following areas are where Google Chrome keeps track of your browsing history on the system:

- Location of Cookies, Downloads, and History

C:\Users\{user-name}\AppData\Local\Google\Chrome\User Data\Default as show in the Fig. (**33**).

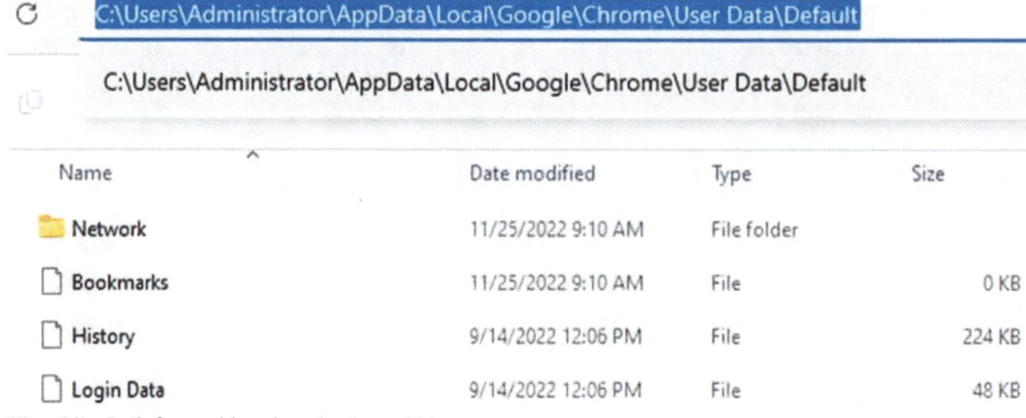

Fig. (33). Path for cookies, downloads, and history.

- Cache Location

C:\Users\{user-name}\AppData\Local\Google\Chrome\User_Data\Default\Cache as shown in Fig. (**34**).

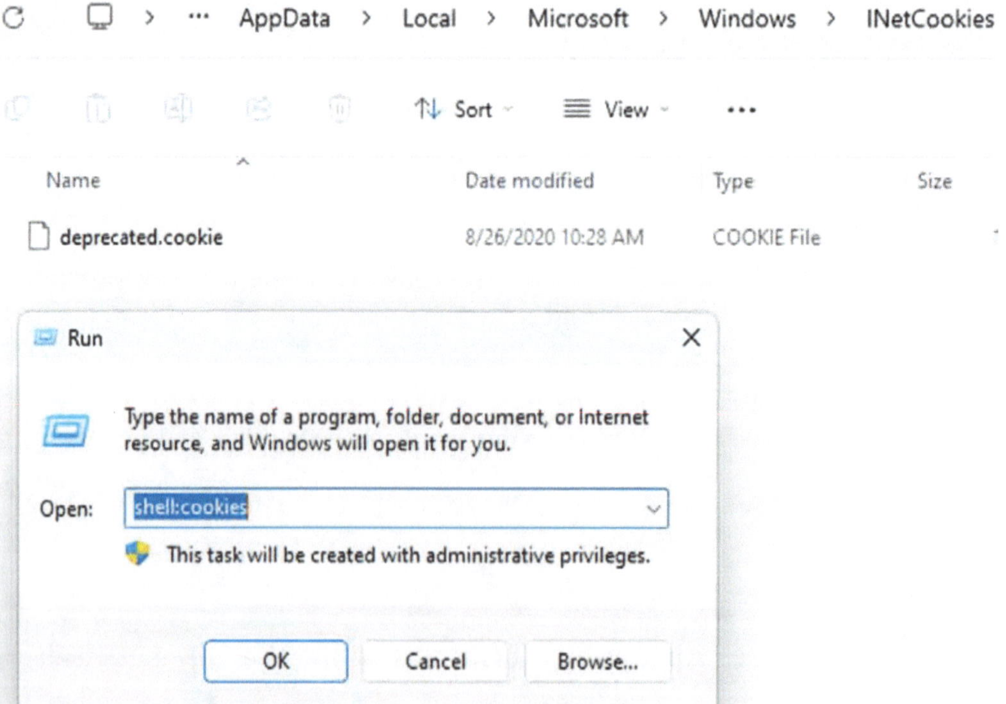

Fig. (34). Google Chrome Cookies.

WINDOWS DATA AND METADATA

It is frequently necessary for investigators to find any modifications that attackers may have made to the system's program files while looking into a Windows system. The following must be looked at by investigators to find these changes:

- **Restore Point folders:** These folders hold data on program file installations, removals, and modifications.
- **Prefetch Files:** Identifying the apps that have been used on a system can be done by looking through the Prefetch directory.
- **Metadata:** Any kind of file's metadata provides a variety of features and specifics about the creation, access, and alteration of the file.
- **Image Files and EXIF Data:** The metadata linked to JPEG images can be found by looking at the EXIF data contained in such image files.

Analysis of Windows Files

Forensic analysis of restore point log files and prefetch files can yield details about the installed and uninstalled program, including MAC timestamps, file names, sizes, and the number of times the application has been run. Analyzing Windows files on a machine that is involved in a forensic investigation might be likened to looking through digital footprints. There is a wealth of historical information regarding the system in these files. Investigators may be able to learn installation timestamps, software names, file sizes, and even how frequently programs were run by examining restore point logs and prefetch files. Moreover, timestamps on other files can provide a timeline of activity by revealing the creation, modification, and access history. Another way to determine where programs were installed or what data was downloaded is to look at the placement of files on the drive. Details regarding software settings or human behaviors may even be contained in text files, logs, and custom configurations. Furthermore, forensic methods occasionally even recover deleted file traces, maybe including installation or uninstall logs [17].

Points Of System Restore (Rp.Log Files)

The restoration point (RPxx) directory contains the restore point log file, called Rp.log. It has a value indicating the type of restore point, a descriptive name for the restore point creation event, and the 64-bit FILETIME object, which provides the time the restore point was created. The description of the restore point contains instructions on how to install or uninstall an application. System restore points are created during the installation of programs and unsigned drivers, the installation of auto updates, and restoration activities. The investigator can ascertain the date that the application was installed or removed with the help of the rp.log file, which provides a description of the event that led to the formation of the restore point. Windows System Restore is a feature that allows you to roll back your system to a previous state. Rp.log files are one piece of the puzzle. They can provide forensic investigators with important hints even though they don't immediately record software installations or uninstallations. The following is what Rp.log files reveal:

- **Timestamps:** The timestamps in these files show the dates of important system modifications. These timestamps are not exclusive to program modifications, but they might align with installations or uninstallations.
- **Restore Point Names:** Information regarding the events surrounding the creation of the restore point may be found in the name of the restore point, which can be provided by the software or the user. For instance, a restore point named "New Software Installation" is one red flag.
- File alterations are documented in the change.log files located in the restoration point directories.
- When changes are made to the files that are being monitored, the restoration point file system driver notices them and logs the original filename, sequence number, type of modification, and other information in the change.log file.

Prefetch Files

Prefetch files hold data about the programs that have been used on the system. Because the prefetch files for programs that have been launched on a system remain in the prefetch folder at C:\Windows\Prefetch, even if those applications are later deleted or uninstalled, the prefetch files can be an invaluable source of forensic evidence for investigators. The number of launches of the application is indicated by the value of the DWORD located at offset 144 in the file. The UTC-formatted DWORD value at offset 120 in the file indicates the last time the application was run. To find out who was signed in to the system, what apps they were using, and other details, information from.pf files can be compared with the registry or event log information. The Windows OS uses prefetching to accelerate the startup of applications and the system boot process. After the application process begins, the data is recorded for the first ten seconds at most. The data is written to a.pf file in the Windows\Prefetch directory after processing. Prior to beginning an examination, the forensic investigator should determine if the victim's machine has enabled the prefetching procedure. Prefetching is controlled by the following registry key:

Computer\HKEY_LOCAL_MACHINE\{SYSTEM\ControlSet001\Control\Session Manager\Memory Management\PrefetchParameters as shown in Fig. (**35**).

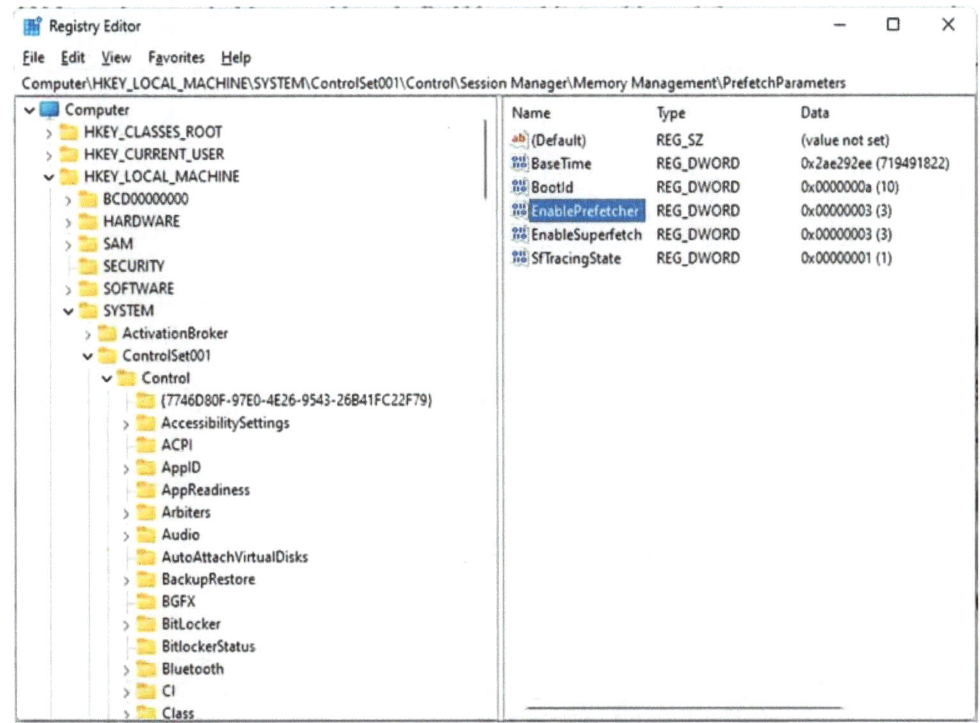

Fig. (35). Prefetch parameters.

Investigation of Metadata

Metadata from databases, word processing programs, image files, web browsers, and other sources is used in computer forensics to gather forensically valuable evidence. File names, sizes, MAC timestamps, GPS information, and other details are examples of metadata. The concealed information regarding data is essential to forensic inquiries. Comparable to looking at the minute details at a crime scene, each one may appear unimportant, but taken as a whole, they might tell a lot. Data about data is called metadata. It explains several aspects of the data, such as when and by whom it was created, accessed, or changed. Users who transfer or provide files in electronic form may unintentionally disclose sensitive information because it is not often seen. Metadata is organized information that provides details about certain aspects of electronic data, such as the date and the identity of the creator, user, and moderator. Users who transfer or provide files in electronic form run the risk of unintentionally disclosing sensitive information because it cannot be viewed without specific programs. Here are some instances of metadata:

- Name of the organization
- Name of author
- Name of computer
- Name of network
- Cells or hidden text
- Versions of documents
- Personalized views
- Template information.
- Confidential details about the document
- Who tried to alter, remove, or conceal the data.
- Related documents are sourced from multiple sources.

The file MAC times are the most widely recognized metadata about files on Windows systems. Modified, accessed, and created is what MAC stands for. The file's creation date, its last access time (when it was last opened), and its last modification date (when information was changed or added to the file) are all expressed as timestamps in the MAC timings. Although the Coordinated Universal Time (UTC) format used by the NTFS file system stores MAC times in a manner like Greenwich Mean Time (GMT), the FAT file system stores these timings according to the local time of the computer system. Files in the Portable Document Format (PDF) may include metadata like the author's name, the creation date, and the program used to produce the file. With the help of the programs pdfmeta.pl and pdfdmp.pl, PDF file metadata can be extracted. Click File→ Properties after opening the file in Adobe Reader to obtain info in another method. All the available metadata is contained in the Properties dialog box's Description tab, as shown in Fig. (**36**).

Because Word documents are built using OLE technology, which establishes a "file structure within a file," they are compound documents. Depending on how the user views the document, Word documents can include a significant amount of extra information in addition to formatting information that is hidden from view. Word documents can keep track of previous edits as well as a list of the last ten writers who have made changes to the file. This has put people and organizations in danger of information exposure. The Perl programs wmd.pl and oledmp.pl list the OLE streams and garbage bins that are part of a Word document. The following methods will allow you to access the metadata in Microsoft Word 2010 as shown in Fig. (**37**).

- Click on the File tab → Info.
- Click on the Inspect Document option.
- Make your selection and click the "Inspect" button to examine the material.

Document Properties

Description Security Fonts Custom Advanced

Description

File: Business Analytics for Managers

Title:

Author:

Subject:

Keywords:

Created: 12/14/2022 6:56:48 PM

Modified: 12/14/2022 6:56:48 PM

Application: Adobe Acrobat Pro DC (32-bit) 21.7.20099

Advanced

PDF Producer: Adobe Acrobat Pro DC (32-bit) 21.7.20099

PDF Version: 1.6 (Acrobat 7.x)

Location: C:\Users\Administrator\Downloads\

File Size: 10.91 MB (11,441,432 Bytes)

Page Size: 8.27 x 11.69 in Number of Pages: 261

Tagged PDF: No Fast Web View: Yes

OK Cancel

Fig. (36). Document properties.

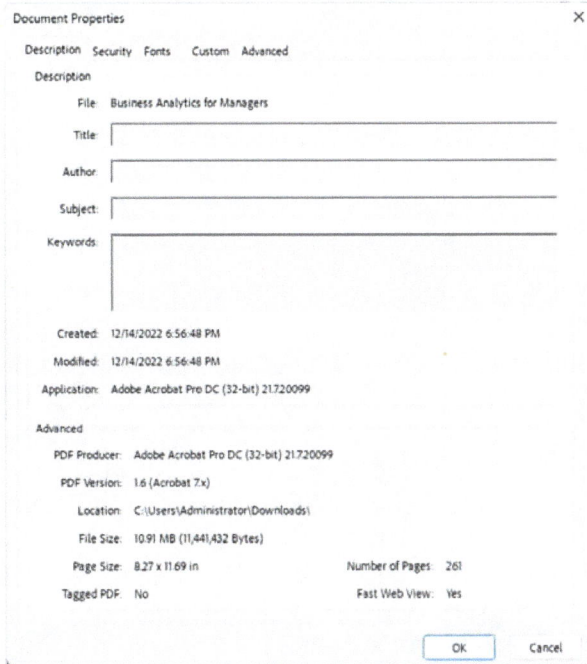

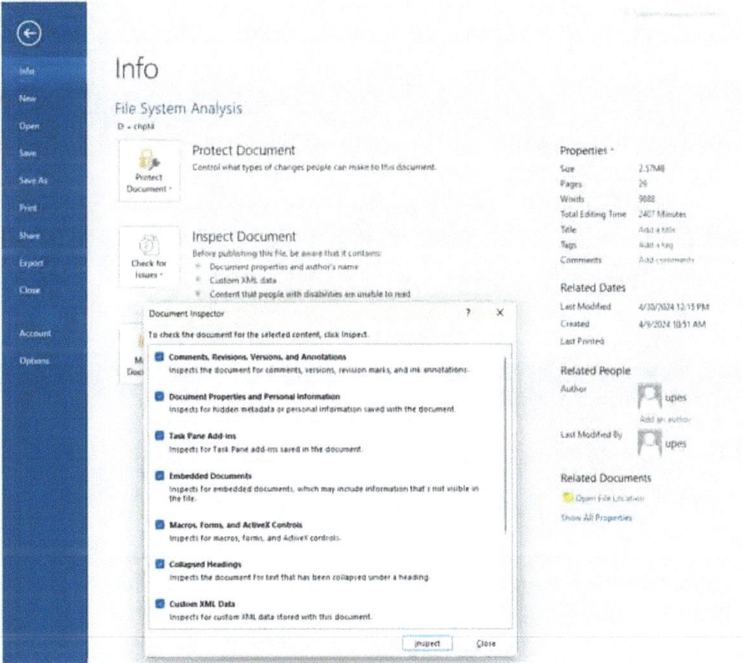

Fig. (37). Analyzing word document metadata.

Analyzing Windows files and information is an effective forensic method. Even while a single piece of data or metadata may not appear important, when combined, they can provide a valuable window into the history of a system. With the use of this method, detectives may put together digital histories, find buried evidence, and possibly even identify the perpetrators of digital crimes.

CONCLUSION

With the resources in this chapter, you will be well-equipped to take on Windows forensics' investigations. We gave a thorough introduction at the outset, emphasizing the significance of gathering and reviewing digital evidence from Windows PCs. The essential ideas of volatile and non-volatile data were then covered, emphasizing the necessity of gathering both in order to create a comprehensive picture. We then looked around the Windows registry, which is a treasure trove of data on installed apps, user behavior, and the system. The importance of timestamps in creating event timelines was emphasized by introducing techniques for registry analysis. We looked at the abundance of data concealed in web browsers after moving past the registry. We looked at techniques for prying into a user's online activity and possibly even their login credentials by examining their browsing history, cookies, and cache. We emphasized the significance of looking at both data and metadata in our final point. We talked about how metadata (creation date, author) combined with data (documents, emails) can provide important information about the provenance of a file and possible efforts at modification. By grasping these fundamental ideas, you have established a solid framework for additional research into particular forensic methods and technologies.

REFERENCES

[1] "Digital Forensics and Advanced Data Triage." FOR500: Windows Forensics Analysis Class | SANS Institute, Available from: www.sans.org/cyber-security-courses/windows-forensic-analysis/ Accessed 16 May 2024.

[2] A. Bhardwaj, F. Al-Turjman, M. Kumar, T. Stephan, and L. Mostarda, "Capturing-the-Invisible (CTI): Behavior-Based Attacks Recognition in IoT-Oriented Industrial Control Systems", *IEEE Access,* vol. 8, pp. 104956-104966, 2020. [http://dx.doi.org/10.1109/ACCESS.2020.2998983]

[3] Psmth. "Contents." GitHub, 16 Apr. 2023, Available from: github.com/Psmths/windows-forensi--artifacts

[4] A. Bhardwaj, F. Al-Turjman, V. Sapra, M. Kumar, and T. Stephan, "Privacy-aware detection framework to mitigate new-age phishing attacks", *Comput. Electr. Eng.,* vol. 96, p. 107546, 2021. [http://dx.doi.org/10.1016/j.compeleceng.2021.107546]

[5] Managing Volatile Memory with Memkind. (n.d.). Intel. Retrieved May 16, 2024, Available from: https://www.intel.com/content/www/us/en/developer/videos/managing-volatile-memory-w-th-memkind.html

[6] A. Bhardwaj, V. Avasthi, and S. Goundar, "Cyber security attacks on robotic platforms", *Netw. Secur.,*

vol. 2019, no. 10, pp. 13-19, 2019.
[http://dx.doi.org/10.1016/S1353-4858(19)30122-9]

[7] Volatile data collection from Window system. (2020, March 2). GeeksforGeeks Available from: https://www.geeksforgeeks.org/volatile-data-collection-from-window-system/

[8] K. Kaushik, A. Bhardwaj, M. Kumar, S. K. Gupta, and A. Gupta, "A novel machine learning-based framework for detecting fake Instagram profiles", *Concurrency and Computation: Practice and Experience,* vol. 34, no. 28, p. e7349, 2022.
[http://dx.doi.org/10.1002/cpe.7349]

[9] Slacking Off Slack Artefacts on Windows | SANS Institute. (n.d.). 2024. Available from: https://www.sans.org/presentations/slacking-off-slack-artefacts-on-windows/

[10] A. Bhardwaj, S. Bharany, A. Almogren, A. Ur Rehman, and H. Hamam, "Proactive threat hunting to detect persistent behaviour-based advanced adversaries", *Egyptian Informatics Journal,* vol. 27, p. 100510, 2024.
[http://dx.doi.org/10.1016/j.eij.2024.100510]

[11] Deland-Han. “Windows Registry for Advanced Users - Windows Server.” Learn.microsoft.com, 8 Mar. 2023 Available from: learn.microsoft.com/en-us/troubleshoot/window--server/performance/windows-registry-advanced-users

[12] Stevewhims. (2021, June 2). Structure of the Registry - Win32 apps. Learn.microsoft.com. Available from: https://learn.microsoft.com/en-us/windows/win32/sysinfo/structure-of-the-registry

[13] stevewhims. (n.d.). Registry Hives - Win32 apps. Learn.microsoft.com. Available from: https://learn.microsoft.com/en-us/windows/win32/sysinfo/registry-hives

[14] Mark Russinovich. (2023, March 9). Process Monitor - Windows Sysinternals. Learn.microsoft.com. Available from: https://learn.microsoft.com/en-us/sysinternals/downloads/procmon

[15] Baker, K. (2023, April 17). Malware Analysis Explained | Steps & Examples | CrowdStrike. Crowdstrike.com. Available from: https://www.crowdstrike.com/cybersecurity-101/malware/malwar--analysis/

[16] Ec-council official curricula PROFESSIONAL SERIES. (n.d.). Available from: https://eccommonstorage.blob.core.windows.net/codered/uploads/lessons/resources/Wi2AAO2spyMJTIZhyUk9slJArombZYwY6wlYmuRK.pdf

[17] Drewbatgit. (2023, June 20). Metadata Features - Win32 apps. Learn.microsoft.com. Available from: https://learn.microsoft.com/en-us/windows/win32/wmformat/metadata-features

CHAPTER 6

Network Forensics

Abstract: In the ever-expanding digital landscape, network security breaches pose a significant threat. Network forensics emerges as a vital weapon in the cybersecurity arsenal, enabling the investigation and analysis of network traffic to uncover evidence of malicious activity. This chapter delves into the core principles of network forensics, outlining the four-stage process: acquisition, preservation, analysis, and reporting. It equips readers with the knowledge to identify and collect various types of network evidence, including packet headers, network logs, and flow data. The chapter explores a range of open-source tools readily available on platforms like GitHub, empowering readers with the ability to capture and analyze network traffic using Wireshark and Bro. Furthermore, it acknowledges the inherent challenges faced in network forensics, such as the fleeting nature of network data and the growing use of encryption. To ensure the legality and effectiveness of investigations, the chapter emphasizes the importance of adhering to relevant laws and regulations. By understanding these essential concepts, readers gain valuable insights into how network forensics empowers cybersecurity professionals to combat digital crimes and safeguard network security.

Keywords: Digital forensics, Network forensics, Network traffic analysis, Open-source tools, Security onion, Wireshark.

INTRODUCTION

In today's hyper-connected world, data traverses networks at an unprecedented pace. While this interconnectedness fosters innovation and collaboration, it also creates vulnerabilities that cybercriminals exploit. Network forensics emerges as a critical discipline within cybersecurity, playing a detective-like role in uncovering evidence of malicious activity on a network. Network forensics can be defined as the application of scientific and investigative techniques to analyze network traffic for the purpose of identifying, collecting, preserving, and analyzing evidence of criminal or unauthorized activity. It is a specialized branch of digital forensics, focusing specifically on the data flowing across a network rather than data stored on individual devices.

Within the vast realm of digital forensics, two distinct disciplines illuminate the shadows cast by cybercrime: computer forensics and network forensics. While both share the overarching goal of uncovering evidence, their methods and areas

Akashdeep Bhardwaj, Pradeep Singh & Ajay Prasad

of focus diverge significantly. Understanding these differences is crucial for effectively investigating and combating security incidents.

Traditional computer forensics, the more established discipline, delves into the digital devices themselves. Imagine a meticulous investigator meticulously examining a computer, hard drive, or mobile phone. Their goal: is to identify traces of criminal activity, such as deleted files, hidden folders, malware remnants, and browsing history. The data source for this investigation lies within the storage media of these devices – hard drives, SSDs, and USB drives. This data is primarily static, consisting of files, system logs, and registry entries. The investigator's crucial first step involves creating a forensic image, a bit-by-bit copy of the storage media, to preserve the data in its original state. Following this, specialized forensic tools are employed to examine the image for evidence, a process that may involve data carving, file system analysis, and registry examination. Finally, the findings of the investigation are documented in a detailed report, outlining the methodology employed, the evidence collected, and the conclusions reached.

Network forensics, on the other hand, shifts the focus to the dynamic realm of network traffic. Imagine a detective following the flow of information through a network, instead of examining individual devices. Here, the investigator seeks to capture, analyze, and preserve network traffic data for the purpose of identifying and investigating suspicious activity. The data source for network forensics is the ever-flowing stream of information traversing the network, captured in the form of packets transmitted across it. Unlike the static data of computer forensics, this data is dynamic, consisting of protocols, IP addresses, and even the content of communications (if not encrypted). The investigator's challenge lies in the very nature of network traffic – its volatility. Unlike data on a storage device, once a packet is transmitted, it is gone unless captured beforehand. This fleeting nature necessitates proactive measures such as continuous traffic capture. The process of network forensics follows a similar structured approach: capturing the traffic data using specialized tools, preserving it in a forensically sound manner, analyzing it using network forensic tools to identify protocols, content, and potentially malicious activity, and finally, documenting the findings in a detailed report.

As cybercriminals develop increasingly sophisticated tactics, organizations require a robust arsenal of tools and techniques to combat these threats. Network forensics emerges as an indispensable weapon in this fight, acting as a digital detective meticulously examining the cybercrime scene – the network traffic itself. By analyzing captured network data, investigators can uncover evidence of malicious activity, reconstruct the timeline of attacks, and ultimately, identify the perpetrators. This understanding empowers security teams to effectively respond to incidents, mitigate damage, and fortify their defenses against future attacks. The importance of network forensics stems from the very nature of today's digital landscape.

Traditional cyberattacks often involve physical access or targeted malware on individual devices. Today, the focus has shifted towards network-based attacks. Exploits leverage vulnerabilities in network protocols and configurations, allowing attackers to gain access to systems and data without ever physically setting foot on-site. For instance, the infamous SolarWinds supply chain attack compromised a network management software platform, allowing attackers to gain access to numerous organizations through software updates. Network forensics becomes crucial in such scenarios, as it allows investigators to identify the malicious network traffic used by attackers to compromise systems.

Unlike physical crimes that leave tangible evidence behind, cybercrimes often occur in the virtual realm, leaving behind faint digital footprints. Network forensics provides the tools and techniques to capture and analyze these fleeting traces of activity, enabling investigators to reconstruct the sequence of events and identify the perpetrators. Data is the lifeblood of modern organizations. As its value continues to rise, so do the threats targeting it. Network forensics plays a crucial role in investigating data breaches and exfiltration attempts. By analyzing network traffic patterns, investigators can identify unauthorized access attempts and pinpoint the data that might have been stolen. For instance, the Equifax data breach resulted in the compromise of sensitive personal information of millions of individuals. Network forensics analysis of the attacker's network traffic could potentially reveal the types of data exfiltrated and the methods used for data transfer.

Modern networks are complex ecosystems, encompassing a diverse range of devices, applications, and protocols. This complexity creates blind spots for security teams and provides potential avenues for attackers to exploit. Network forensic tools offer deep visibility into network traffic, enabling investigators to identify anomalies and suspicious activity that might otherwise go unnoticed. Imagine a large healthcare organization with a sprawling network connecting various medical devices, patient databases, and administrative systems. Network forensics can be used to analyze traffic patterns within this complex network, potentially revealing unauthorized access attempts from unauthorized medical devices or unusual communication patterns that might indicate a malware outbreak.

The increasing adoption of cloud computing presents both opportunities and challenges for network forensics. While cloud providers offer robust security measures, gaining visibility into network traffic traversing the cloud can be complex. Security teams will need to leverage specialized cloud-based network forensic tools to maintain visibility and effectively investigate incidents within cloud environments. The widespread adoption of encryption poses a challenge for traditional network forensics techniques that rely on analyzing the content of network traffic. Security teams will need to embrace new approaches like decryption techniques and advanced traffic analysis to glean valuable insights even from encrypted traffic. The ever-growing volume of network traffic necessitates the integration of automation and machine learning into network forensics workflows. Automation can streamline tasks like data acquisition, analysis, and anomaly detection, allowing security teams to focus on more strategic aspects of investigations. Machine learning algorithms can be trained to identify complex patterns and anomalies in network traffic, potentially uncovering threats that might evade traditional detection methods.

As the value of network forensics continues to grow, the demand for skilled network forensic investigators will rise. Organizations will need to invest in training their security teams in network forensics principles and methodologies. Additionally, collaboration between network forensic investigators and other security professionals, such as incident responders and threat hunters, will be crucial for a holistic approach to cybersecurity. By meticulously examining the digital footprints left behind in network traffic, investigators can uncover the truth behind cyberattacks, identify perpetrators, and ultimately, strengthen defenses against future threats. As the digital landscape continues to evolve, network forensics will adapt and expand, remaining an indispensable tool for organizations navigating the complex and ever-changing world of cybersecurity.

ROLE OF NETWORK FORENSICS IN CYBERSECURITY

Network forensics offers a unique perspective into the clandestine world of cyberattacks. Unlike traditional computer forensics, which focuses on the static data residing on individual devices, network forensics delves into the dynamic realm of network traffic. This flowing stream of data, comprised of packets containing information like IP addresses, protocols used, and even the content of communications (if not encrypted), becomes a treasure trove of forensic evidence for investigators. Some of the key areas where network forensics has been proven invaluable are discussed below.

Incident Response

When a security breach occurs, network forensics plays a pivotal role in understanding the attack and formulating an effective response. Captured network traffic data can reveal the source of the attack, the attacker's methods, and the scope of the breach. By analyzing this data, investigators can identify compromised systems, determine what data might have been exfiltrated, and take decisive steps to contain the damage and prevent further exploitation. Imagine a scenario where a company experiences a ransomware attack. Network forensics can pinpoint the initial point of entry, such as a phishing email with a malicious attachment, and subsequently track the attacker's movements within the network, identifying the servers that were encrypted. This information is crucial for restoring affected systems and preventing further disruptions. For instance, the 2017 WannaCry ransomware [1] attack wreaked havoc across the globe, infecting millions of computers. Network forensics played a crucial role in understanding the attack vector, allowing security researchers to develop a decryption tool to help mitigate the damage.

In the high-stakes world of cybersecurity [2], a successful incident response hinges on the ability to gather irrefutable evidence and reconstruct the timeline of an attack. This is where network forensics emerges as an indispensable tool, providing a wealth of valuable insights for investigators. Unlike traditional computer forensics which focuses on individual devices, network forensics delves into the dynamic realm of network traffic, offering a unique perspective into the attacker's methods and movements.

Captured network traffic can reveal the attacker's IP address, allowing investigators to trace the origin of the attack and potentially identify the culprit. Imagine a scenario where a company experiences a data breach. Network forensics can analyze traffic patterns, identifying unusual outbound data transfers that might point toward the attacker's location. By analyzing the volume and types of network traffic during the attack, investigators can determine the extent of the breach. Network traffic data can reveal if the attacker accessed specific servers, stole sensitive data, or attempted to pivot laterally within the network. For example, a sudden spike in traffic directed towards a specific database server during a suspected data breach could be a red flag, indicating unauthorized access attempts.

Network forensics allows investigators to meticulously reconstruct the timeline of the attack. Captured packets can be used to identify the initial point of entry, the attacker's movements within the network, and the time of data exfiltration (if applicable). This timeline becomes crucial for understanding the attack methodology and identifying potential vulnerabilities exploited by the attacker. Imagine a network intrusion attempt. Analyzing the captured traffic can reveal the initial reconnaissance phase where the attacker scans for vulnerabilities, followed by attempts to exploit those vulnerabilities and gain access to the network.

Network forensic tools can be used to analyze network traffic for anomalies and signs of malicious activity. Techniques like anomaly detection and traffic reconstruction can help identify malware communication patterns, unauthorized access attempts, and command-and-control (C2) [3] server communication. For instance, network traffic analysis might reveal unusual communication patterns with known malicious IP addresses, indicating potential malware communication. Network traffic data captured during an incident can serve as crucial forensic evidence. This evidence can be used in legal proceedings against attackers or to improve future security defenses. Captured packets [4] can reveal the attacker's methods and tools, providing valuable insights for security teams to strengthen their defenses.

Pseudocode to illustrate Anomaly Detection in Network Forensics:

```
# Function to identify unusual traffic patterns
def detect_anomalies(traffic_data):
# Define baseline traffic patterns based on historical data
baseline_traffic = get_baseline_traffic()
# Iterate through captured packets
for packet in traffic_data:
# Extract relevant features from the packet (source IP, destination IP, protocol, etc.)
packet_features = extract_features(packet)
# Compare features with baseline and calculate deviation score
deviation_score = calculate_deviation(packet_features, baseline_traffic)
# If deviation score exceeds a predefined threshold, flag as anomaly
if deviation_score > threshold:
flag_anomaly(packet)
# Return list of identified anomalies
return anomalies
# This function retrieves historical traffic data to establish a baseline
def get_baseline_traffic():
# (Implementation details for retrieving baseline data omitted for brevity)
# This function extracts relevant features from each network packet
def extract_features(packet):
# (Implementation details for feature extraction omitted for brevity)
# This function calculates the deviation score between current traffic and baseline
def calculate_deviation(packet_features, baseline_traffic):
# (Implementation details for deviation calculation omitted for brevity)
# This function flags a packet as an anomaly based on the deviation score
def flag_anomaly(packet):
# (Implementation details for anomaly flagging omitted for brevity)
```

By leveraging network forensics techniques, security teams can gain a deeper understanding of cyberattacks, improve their incident response capabilities, and ultimately, secure their networks more effectively.

Investigation and Threat Detection

Network forensics goes beyond responding to active incidents and plays a crucial role in proactive threat detection. Security teams can leverage network forensic tools to continuously monitor network traffic and identify suspicious activity. Anomaly detection techniques can be employed to detect deviations from normal traffic patterns, potentially indicating malware communication or unauthorized access attempts. Additionally, network traffic analysis can help identify known attack signatures and malicious communication with command-and-control (C2) servers. Early detection allows for swift intervention and minimizes the potential damage caused by cyberattacks.

Network forensics plays a crucial role in various stages of an investigation, providing invaluable insights for security professionals. Imagine a scenario where a company experiences a data breach. Network forensics can be instrumental in identifying the source of the attack. Captured traffic data can reveal the attacker's IP address, potentially leading to their location or providing clues about the attacker's network infrastructure. By analyzing the source IP addresses and correlating them with known malicious actors or geographic locations, investigators can narrow down the suspect pool. In the case of the 2014 Target data breach [5], network forensics analysis of captured traffic helped investigators understand how attackers gained access to the network and subsequently compromised payment card data. This evidence was instrumental in holding the perpetrators accountable.

The extent of the damage caused by a security incident is crucial information for security teams. Network forensics helps to understand the scope of the attack by analyzing the volume and types of network traffic [6] during the attack period. Investigators can identify specific servers or systems that were targeted, pinpoint data exfiltration attempts (if applicable), and determine the overall impact on the network. For example, a sudden spike in outbound traffic directed towards a specific database server during a suspected data breach could be a red flag, indicating unauthorized access and potential data extraction.

Network forensics allows investigators to meticulously reconstruct the timeline of an attack. By analyzing the timestamps and sequence of captured packets, a chronological narrative of the attack unfolds. This timeline reveals the initial point of entry, the attacker's movements within the network (lateral movement), and the time of data exfiltration (if applicable). Understanding the attack sequence allows security teams to identify vulnerabilities exploited by the attacker and implement targeted security measures to prevent similar attacks in the future. Imagine a network intrusion attempt. Analyzing the captured traffic can reveal the initial reconnaissance phase where the attacker scans for vulnerabilities, followed by attempts to exploit those vulnerabilities and gain access to the network. Tracing this sequence helps security teams identify the exploited weakness and prioritize patching or implementing additional controls.

Security teams can leverage network forensic tools for continuous network traffic monitoring to identify suspicious activity in real time. Techniques like anomaly detection can be employed to detect deviations from normal traffic patterns, potentially indicating malware communication or unauthorized access attempts. Additionally, traffic analysis can help identify known attack signatures and communication with C2 servers used by malicious actors. Early detection is crucial for swift intervention and minimizes potential damage caused by cyberattacks. For instance, network traffic analysis might reveal unusual communication patterns with known malicious IP addresses, indicating potential malware communication. This early detection allows security teams to isolate compromised systems and prevent further spread of the threat.

Network traffic data captured during an incident can serve as crucial forensic evidence. This evidence can be used in legal proceedings against attackers or to improve future security defenses. Captured packets can reveal the attacker's methods and tools, providing valuable insights for security teams to strengthen their defenses. Imagine legal proceedings against a cybercriminal who launched a ransomware attack. Network forensics can provide evidence of the attacker's initial entry point, the specific systems encrypted, and any communication with the C2 server used to control the ransomware. This evidence can be used to build a strong case against the attacker.

Pseudocode to illustrate Anomaly Traffic Detection:

```
# Function to identify unusual traffic patterns
def detect_anomalies(traffic_data):
# Define baseline traffic patterns based on historical data
baseline_traffic = get_baseline_traffic()
# Iterate through captured packets
for packet in traffic_data:
# Extract relevant features from the packet (source IP, destination IP, protocol, etc.)
packet_features = extract_features(packet)
# Compare features with baseline and calculate deviation score
deviation_score = calculate_deviation(packet_features, baseline_traffic)
# If deviation score exceeds a predefined threshold, flag as anomaly
if deviation_score > threshold:
flag_anomaly(packet)
# Return list of identified anomalies
return anomalies
# This function retrieves historical traffic data to establish a baseline
def get_baseline_traffic():
# (Implementation details for retrieving baseline data omitted for brevity)
# This function extracts relevant features from each network packet
def extract_features(packet):
# (Implementation details for feature extraction omitted
```

Evidence Collection and Analysis

Network forensics provides a systematic approach to collecting and analyzing digital evidence from network traffic. Captured packets can reveal valuable information such as IP addresses, ports used, protocols employed, and even the content of communications (if not encrypted). This evidence can be used to identify attackers, build a case for prosecution, and provide insights into the attacker's methods.

The first step involves capturing network traffic data. Specialized tools like network taps, mirroring ports, or dedicated capture tools are employed to capture packets traversing the network. The choice of method depends on factors like the type of investigation, network architecture, and available resources. Captured traffic data serves as the raw material for further analysis. Imagine a scenario where a company suspects a data breach. Network forensics tools can be deployed to capture all network traffic during a specific timeframe, potentially revealing unauthorized data exfiltration attempts.

Once captured, network traffic data needs to be preserved in a manner that ensures its integrity and admissibility in a court of law. This involves creating a forensic image of the captured data, maintaining a chain of custody (a documented record tracking the movement and handling of evidence), and ensuring data is stored securely. Maintaining a chain of custody is crucial for establishing the authenticity of the evidence and preventing allegations of tampering.

Network forensic tools are used to dissect captured packets, identify protocols used, analyze content (if not encrypted), and correlate events to build a timeline of activity. Techniques like anomaly detection and traffic reconstruction can help identify suspicious activity and piece together the sequence of events. For instance, analyzing timestamps within captured packets can reveal the chronological sequence of events during an attack, potentially identifying the initial point of entry and the time of data exfiltration.

Extracting relevant information from the captured traffic data is crucial. This might include the IP addresses of attackers, communication patterns with malicious servers (C2 servers), and even the content of communications (if not encrypted). This information can be used to identify the source of the attack and potentially lead to the perpetrators. Imagine network traffic analysis revealing communication with a known malicious IP address associated with a specific cybercrime group. This information can be linked to existing intelligence and potentially aid in identifying the attackers.

Pseudocode to illustrate Evidence Extraction:

```
# Function to extract evidence from captured network traffic
def extract_evidence(traffic_data):
# Initialize empty lists to store evidence
source_ips = [ ]
destination_ips = [ ]
timestamps = [ ]
communication_patterns = [ ]
# (Optional) content (if traffic not encrypted)
# Iterate through captured packets
for packet in traffic_data:
# Extract relevant information from each packet
source_ip = packet.get_source_ip()
destination_ip = packet.get_destination_ip()
timestamp = packet.get_timestamp()
protocol = packet.get_protocol()
# (Optional) content = packet.get_content() # For non-encrypted traffic
# Analyze protocol and content for potential evidence
if protocol in suspicious_protocols: # Define list of suspicious protocols
communication_patterns.append((source_ip, destination_ip, protocol))
# (Optional) Analyze content for keywords or indicators of compromise (IOCs)
# Add extracted information to respective lists
source_ips.append(source_ip)
destination_ips.append(destination_ip)
timestamps.append(timestamp)
# Return extracted evidence as a dictionary
return {
"source_ips": source_ips,
"destination_ips": destination_ips,
"timestamps": timestamps,
"communication_patterns": communication_patterns,
# (Optional) "content": content # For non-encrypted traffic
}
```

By meticulously collecting and analyzing network traffic data, investigators can build a strong case and hold perpetrators accountable. Network forensics evidence can be used in various legal proceedings, including:

- Civil Litigation: In cases of intellectual property theft or cyberattacks that cause financial damage, network forensics evidence can be used to demonstrate the nature and scope of the attack, potentially aiding in civil lawsuits against the attackers.
- Criminal Investigations: Network forensics evidence plays a crucial role in criminal investigations involving cybercrime. Captured traffic data can reveal:
- Attack Source: By analyzing IP addresses and other network indicators,

investigators can potentially identify the location of the attackers or at least narrow down the suspect pool.

- Methods used: Examining communication patterns and protocols used in the attack can reveal the attacker's techniques and tools, potentially leading to the identification of specific malware or exploits.
- Scope of the attack: Analyzing the volume and types of network traffic during the attack can help determine the extent of the damage caused, such as compromised systems or exfiltrated data.

This evidence can be instrumental in building a strong case against cyber criminals and bringing them to justice. Imagine a law enforcement investigation into a cyberattack on a financial institution. Network forensics analysis of captured traffic from the bank's network might reveal communication with known malicious IP addresses associated with a specific cybercrime group. Additionally, the analysis might identify unusual outbound traffic patterns toward offshore servers, potentially indicating data exfiltration. This evidence, combined with other investigative findings, can be used to build a case against the cybercrime group and hold them accountable for the attack.

Network Security Monitoring and Analysis

Network forensic tools can be used for continuous monitoring and analysis of network traffic. This allows security professionals to identify potential security vulnerabilities and suspicious activity in real time. By analyzing long-term trends in network traffic, organizations can gain valuable insights into attack patterns and develop more effective security strategies.

Network forensics empowers security teams to leverage captured network traffic data to gain deeper insights into network activity, detect anomalies, and identify potential security risks. This proactive approach allows security teams to take preventive measures and fortify their defenses before a major security incident occurs. Network forensics tools can be used to establish a baseline of normal network traffic patterns. This baseline serves as a benchmark for identifying deviations that might indicate suspicious activity. Techniques like statistical analysis and traffic classification can be employed to create a comprehensive picture of normal network behavior. Imagine a scenario where a company monitors its network traffic patterns. Network forensic analysis can establish a baseline for typical network usage, including bandwidth consumption, types of traffic protocols used, and communication patterns with known business partners.

By continuously monitoring network traffic for deviations from the established baseline, security teams can proactively identify potential threats. Network forensic tools can employ anomaly detection algorithms to flag unusual traffic patterns, such as sudden spikes in traffic, communication with known malicious IP addresses, or attempts to exploit network vulnerabilities. This allows security teams to investigate these anomalies further and potentially identify threats before they escalate into major security incidents. For instance, network traffic analysis might reveal a surge in outbound traffic towards a specific domain known for hosting malware distribution. This anomaly can be investigated further to determine if malware is being downloaded onto the network.

Network forensic tools can assist in reconstructing the flow of network traffic, providing a visual representation of communication patterns and potential attack vectors. This visualization allows security teams to understand how different network devices are communicating and identify potential vulnerabilities or unauthorized connections. Imagine a network security team investigating suspicious activity on a specific server, network traffic reconstruction can visualize the server's communication with other devices on the network, potentially revealing unauthorized connections from compromised systems or external attackers.

Network forensic analysis provides valuable insights for security teams preparing for potential security incidents. By understanding historical attack patterns and analyzing past incidents through the lens of network forensics, security teams can develop more effective incident response strategies and improve their preparedness for future threats. Imagine an organization that has experienced a ransomware attack in the past. Network forensic analysis of the captured traffic from that attack can be used to identify the attacker's methods and entry points. This knowledge can be used to strengthen security measures and prevent similar attacks in the future.

Pseudocode to illustrate Network Security monitoring:

```
# Function to identify unusual traffic patterns for network security monitoring
def detect_anomalies(traffic_data, baseline_traffic):
# Iterate through captured packets
for packet in traffic_data:
# Extract relevant features from the packet (source IP, destination IP, protocol, etc.)
packet_features = extract_features(packet)
# Calculate deviation score by comparing features with baseline
deviation_score = calculate_deviation(packet_features, baseline_traffic)
# If deviation score exceeds a predefined threshold, flag as anomaly
if deviation_score > threshold:
flag_anomaly(packet)
# Return list of identified anomalies
return anomalies
# This function retrieves historical traffic data to establish a baseline
def get_baseline_traffic():
```

```
# (Implementation details for retrieving baseline data omitted for brevity)
# This function extracts relevant features from each network packet
def extract_features(packet):
# (Implementation details for feature extraction omitted for brevity)
# This function calculates the deviation score between current traffic and baseline
def calculate_deviation(packet_features, baseline_traffic):
# (Implementation details for deviation calculation omitted for brevity)
# This function flags a packet as an anomaly based on the deviation score
def flag_anomaly(packet):
# (Implementation details for anomaly flagging omitted for brevity)
```

By leveraging network forensics for continuous network security monitoring, security teams can gain deeper visibility into network activity, proactively identify potential threats and vulnerabilities, improve their incident response preparedness, and strengthen their overall network security posture.

NETWORK FORENSICS PROCESS

Network investigations and analysis follows a structured, four-stage process:

Acquisition

The first step involves capturing network traffic data. This can be done passively by mirroring traffic on a network segment or actively by deploying tools that capture specific types of traffic based on pre-defined filters. Security professionals have an arsenal of techniques at their disposal to capture network traffic for forensic analysis:

- Network Taps: These hardware devices act as transparent bridges, replicating all network traffic flowing through a specific cable segment. Captured traffic is then directed to a dedicated forensic capture tool for further analysis. Imagine a network security team investigating suspicious activity in a specific network segment. A network tap can be deployed on that segment to capture all traffic flowing through it, providing a comprehensive view of network activity for forensic analysis.
- Port Mirroring: This technique leverages a configuration setting on network switches. By enabling port mirroring on a specific switch port, all traffic traversing that port is duplicated and sent to another designated port for capture by a forensic tool. This method is like network taps but offers more flexibility within managed switch environments.
- Promiscuous Mode Network Interfaces: Network interface cards (NICs) on computers can be configured to operate in promiscuous mode. In this mode, the NIC captures all network traffic it detects on the connected network segment,

regardless of whether it's addressed specifically to the computer itself. This method is often used for forensic investigations on individual devices but can be less scalable for capturing traffic across entire network segments.

- Full Packet Capture (FPC) Appliances: Dedicated network appliances specifically designed for capturing and storing network traffic are also employed. These appliances offer high-performance capture capabilities, extensive storage capacity, and centralized management for large-scale network forensic investigations. Imagine a large organization with a complex network infrastructure. FPC appliances can be strategically deployed at key points within the network to capture traffic for forensic analysis.

Pseudocode depicting Network tap configuration process:

```
# Function to configure a network tap for traffic acquisition
def configure_network_tap(tap_device, target_segment):
# Connect the tap device to the target network segment
connect_tap_hardware(tap_device)
# Configure the tap device to mirror traffic from the target segment
set_mirroring_mode(tap_device, INGRESS, EGRESS) # Capture both incoming and outgoing traffic
# Specify the network interface card (NIC) to receive mirrored traffic
set_destination_nic(tap_device, forensic_capture_nic)
# Start traffic capture on the forensic capture NIC
start_capture(forensic_capture_nic)
```

Several factors need to be considered when planning network traffic acquisition for network forensics:

- Target Network Segment: Identifying the specific network segment where suspicious activity is suspected is crucial. Focusing the capture on relevant traffic reduces the volume of data to be analyzed and streamlines the investigation process.
- Network Traffic Volume: The volume of network traffic on the target segment can significantly impact the acquisition process. High-bandwidth networks might require specialized capture appliances to handle the data load without compromising capture fidelity.
- Capture Duration: The duration of traffic capture depends on the investigation timeframe. Security teams need to capture traffic for a period encompassing the suspected attack window or suspicious activity.
- Legal Considerations: Network traffic acquisition might be subject to legal regulations regarding data privacy and network monitoring policies. Security teams need to ensure they have the necessary authorization to capture traffic on specific network segments.

While the specifics of network traffic capture algorithms are proprietary to specific forensic tools, here's a simplified conceptual overview:

- Packet Parsing: Captured network traffic consists of raw data streams. Parsing algorithms dissect these streams into individual packets, identifying headers containing information like source and destination IP addresses, protocols used, and payload data (if not encrypted).
- Time Stamping: Captured packets are assigned timestamps during the acquisition process. These timestamps are crucial for forensic analysis, allowing investigators to reconstruct the chronological sequence of network activity.
- Filtering and Buffering: Depending on the investigation focus, captured traffic might be filtered based on specific protocols, IP addresses, or other criteria. Buffering algorithms manage the incoming data stream, ensuring efficient storage and retrieval for further analysis.

Preservation

Once captured, the network traffic data needs to be preserved in a manner that ensures its integrity and admissibility in a court of law. This involves creating a forensic image of the captured data, maintaining a chain of custody, and ensuring data is stored securely. Preserving network traffic data meticulously is paramount for several reasons:

- Evidence Admissibility: In legal proceedings, network traffic data can serve as crucial evidence against cybercriminals. To be admissible in court, the data needs to be preserved in a manner that ensures its authenticity and prevents allegations of tampering.
- Forensic Analysis: Network traffic data forms the raw material for forensic analysis. Investigators rely on the integrity of this data to reconstruct the timeline of events, identify attackers, and uncover the scope of an attack. Tampered or corrupt data can lead to inaccurate conclusions and hinder the investigation process.
- Incident Response: During incident response, security teams might need to revisit captured traffic data to identify missed clues or investigate new leads that emerge during the investigation. Preserving the data ensures its availability for future analysis.

Security professionals employ various techniques to ensure the integrity and chain of custody of captured network traffic data:

- Forensic Imaging: Creating a forensic image of the captured traffic data is a common practice. This image serves as a bit-by-bit copy of the original data, ensuring its authenticity and preventing accidental or malicious modifications. Imagine a network security team investigating a data breach. They would likely create a forensic image of the captured network traffic data to preserve its original state for potential legal proceedings.
- Secure Storage: The forensic image of the captured traffic data needs to be stored securely. This typically involves dedicated forensic storage servers with access controls and encryption measures to prevent unauthorized access and data manipulation.
- Chain of Custody: Maintaining a documented record of the movement and handling of the captured traffic data is crucial. This chain of custody establishes a clear audit trail and bolsters the admissibility of the evidence in court. Imagine a chain of custody documents recording the date and time the traffic data was captured, who captured it, where it was stored, and who accessed it during the investigation.

Pseudocode depicting Network Forensic imaging process:

```
# Function to create a forensic image of captured network traffic data
def create_forensic_image(source_data, destination_image):
# Open the source data file containing the captured traffic
with open(source_data, 'rb') as source_file:
# Open the destination image file for writing
with open(destination_image, 'wb') as image_file:
# Read data from the source file in chunks
data_chunk = source_file.read(block_size)
# While data is still being read
while data_chunk:
# Write the data chunk to the destination image file
image_file.write(data_chunk)
# Read the next chunk of data
data_chunk = source_file.read(block_size)
# Close both files after completing the copy process
source_file.close()
image_file.close()
```

Network forensic tools often employ cryptographic hashing algorithms to ensure the integrity of the captured traffic data. These algorithms generate a unique mathematical fingerprint (hash) of the data. Any modification to the data will result in a different hash value, raising a red flag and preventing the use of tampered evidence. The conceptual overview of hashing algorithms work in network traffic data preservation is presented below.

- Hashing the Captured Data: When the network traffic data is captured, a hashing algorithm calculates its unique hash value. This hash value is stored alongside the captured data.
- Verifying Data Integrity: Before forensic analysis, the hash value of the captured data is recalculated. This recalculated hash value is then compared to the original hash value stored during capture.
- Detecting Tampering: If the two hash values match, it indicates that the data hasn't been tampered with. However, if the hash values differ, it signals a potential modification of the data, rendering it potentially unreliable for forensic analysis.

Analysis

The heart of the investigation lies in analyzing the captured network traffic. Network forensic tools are used to dissect packets, identify protocols used, analyze content (if not encrypted), and correlate events to build a timeline of the activity. Advanced techniques like anomaly detection and traffic reconstruction can assist in identifying malicious activity. Following the crucial steps of network traffic acquisition and preservation, we delve into the heart of network forensics – data analysis. This digital detective work involves meticulously dissecting captured traffic to identify anomalies, reconstruct the timeline of events, and ultimately, uncover the culprit behind a cyberattack. Here, we explore the intricacies of network traffic data analysis, along with practical examples, illustrative pseudocode, and algorithmic insights.

Security professionals leverage a combination of tools and techniques to glean valuable insights from captured traffic:

- Traffic Visualization: Network forensic tools offer visualization capabilities to depict network traffic patterns. This visual representation helps identify unusual traffic flows, communication patterns with suspicious domains or IP addresses, and potential bottlenecks within the network. Imagine a network security team investigating a data breach. Traffic visualization tools might reveal a surge in outbound traffic towards an unknown server, potentially indicating exfiltration of sensitive data.
- Protocol Analysis: Network traffic consists of data packets that adhere to specific communication protocols. Analyzing these protocols (*e.g.*, TCP, UDP, HTTP) can reveal the nature of communication and potential vulnerabilities exploited by attackers. For instance, analyzing HTTP traffic during a suspected web application attack might reveal malicious code injection attempts or unauthorized access attempts to specific web pages.
- Content Analysis (if not encrypted): When dealing with non-encrypted traffic,

content analysis can provide valuable insights. Examining the actual content of packets might reveal sensitive information being transmitted, malware payloads being downloaded, or communication between compromised systems. However, the widespread adoption of encryption poses challenges for traditional content analysis techniques.

- Traffic Anomaly Detection: Network forensic tools employ anomaly detection algorithms to identify deviations from established baseline network traffic patterns. These deviations might indicate suspicious activity, such as port scans, unauthorized access attempts, or distributed denial-of-service (DDoS) attacks. Imagine a scenario where a security team monitors a network with established baseline traffic patterns. Anomaly detection algorithms might flag sudden spikes in network traffic volume or communication attempts with known malicious IP addresses.
- Timeline Reconstruction: By analyzing timestamps within captured packets, investigators can reconstruct the chronological sequence of events during an attack. This timeline helps identify the initial point of entry, the attacker's actions within the network, and the time of data exfiltration (if applicable). Imagine a network forensic investigation revealing a series of login attempts followed by unauthorized access to specific servers and subsequent data exfiltration attempts.

Pseudocode for Network Traffic visualization:

```
# Function to visualize network traffic patterns
def visualize_traffic(traffic_data):
# Extract relevant information from captured packets (source IP, destination IP, protocol, etc.)
traffic_flows = extract_traffic_flows(traffic_data)
# Create a visual representation of traffic flows using a network graph library
graph = create_network_graph()
for flow in traffic_flows:
add_node_to_graph(graph, flow.source_ip)
add_node_to_graph(graph, flow.destination_ip)
add_edge_to_graph(graph, flow.source_ip, flow.destination_ip, weight=flow.packet_count)
# Display the visualized network traffic patterns using a visualization library
display_graph(graph)
```

Network traffic analysis leverages various algorithms to automate tasks and facilitate efficient investigation:

- Traffic Classification Algorithms: These algorithms categorize network traffic based on protocols used, port numbers, and other characteristics. This classification helps investigators quickly identify specific types of traffic, such as web traffic, email traffic, or file transfer traffic.

- Statistical Anomaly Detection Algorithms: These algorithms analyze network traffic statistics like packet size, volume, and inter-arrival times. Deviations from established statistical baselines can indicate suspicious activity.
- Machine Learning Algorithms: Advanced network forensic tools employ machine learning algorithms trained on historical data to identify complex patterns and anomalies that might evade traditional detection methods. These algorithms can continuously learn and improve their accuracy over time.

Reporting

The final stage involves documenting the findings of the investigation in a clear and concise report. This report should detail the methodology used, the evidence collected, the analysis performed, and the conclusions reached. The report should be written in a manner that is understandable by both technical and non-technical audiences. Network traffic data reporting marks the culmination of the network forensics process. After meticulously acquiring, preserving, and analyzing captured network traffic, the findings need to be documented in a clear, concise, and compelling report. This 'digital storytelling' serves several crucial purposes, from informing stakeholders about the incident to providing evidence for legal action.

Network traffic data reporting plays a vital role in several aspects of network forensics investigations:

- Incident Communication: A well-crafted report effectively communicates the findings of the investigation to stakeholders, including security teams, management, and potentially law enforcement. This communication helps stakeholders understand the scope and impact of the incident, enabling them to take appropriate action.
- Legal Documentation: Network traffic data reports can serve as vital documentation for legal proceedings. The report can be used to demonstrate the nature of the attack, the attacker's methods, and the potential damages incurred. This evidence can be instrumental in holding attackers accountable.
- Future Reference: Network traffic data reports serve as a valuable historical record of security incidents. These reports can be referenced during future investigations to identify trends, improve security strategies, and prevent similar attacks from occurring again.

The comprehensive network traffic data report typically includes the following elements:

- Executive Summary: A concise overview of the incident, highlighting the key findings and recommendations.
- Incident Details: A detailed description of the incident, including the date and time of occurrence, the affected systems, and the suspected attack methods.
- Network Traffic Analysis: This section details the analysis performed on the captured traffic data, including the tools used, anomalies identified, and evidence extracted. Techniques like traffic visualization, protocol analysis, and anomaly detection might be mentioned here.
- Timeline: A chronological reconstruction of the events during the attack, based on timestamps within captured packets. This timeline helps visualize the attacker's actions and identify potential points of intervention.
- Impact Assessment: An evaluation of the impact of the incident, including compromised systems, data loss, and potential financial damage.
- Recommendations: Actionable recommendations for improving security posture and preventing similar incidents in the future. These might include patching vulnerabilities, implementing stronger access controls, or user awareness training.
- Appendix: This section might include raw data extracts, screenshots from visualization tools, and detailed logs for further reference.

Pseudocode outlining the report generation process:

```
# Function to generate a network traffic data report
def generate_report(analysis_results, timeline, impact_assessment, recommendations):
# Create a report document
report = create_report_document()
# Add executive summary section
add_section_to_report(report, "Executive Summary", summarize_findings(analysis_results))
# Add incident details section
add_section_to_report(report, "Incident Details", describe_incident(timeline))
# Add network traffic analysis section
add_section_to_report(report, "Network Traffic Analysis", analyze_traffic(analysis_results))
# Add timeline section
add_section_to_report(report, "Timeline", visualize_timeline(timeline))
# Add impact assessment section
add_section_to_report(report, "Impact Assessment", evaluate_impact(impact_assessment))
# Add recommendations section
add_section_to_report(report, "Recommendations", suggest_improvements(recommendations))
# Add appendix section (optional)
# ... (code to add appendix content omitted for brevity)
# Finalize and save the report
finalize_report(report)
```

While the specifics of report generation algorithms are proprietary to specific forensic tools, the conceptual overview of how they might assist is presented below.

- Data Aggregation and Formatting: Algorithms can aggregate data from various analysis tools and format it into a cohesive and readable report structure.
- Timeline Visualization: Algorithms can process timestamps within captured packets and generate visual representations of the attack timeline.
- Anomaly Summarization: Algorithms can analyze anomaly detection results and summarize the identified suspicious activities within the report.

TOOLS OF THE TRADE

Network forensics leverages a variety of tools to capture, analyze, and interpret network traffic data. Here are some popular open-source options available on platforms like GitHub:

Packet Capture

Wireshark

Wireshark [7] is a free and open-source packet analyzer, considered an industry standard tool for network traffic analysis. It's like a microscope for your network, allowing you to see the individual packets of data flowing through your network cables or wireless connections as illustrated in Fig. (**1**). The capabilities of Wireshark include the following:

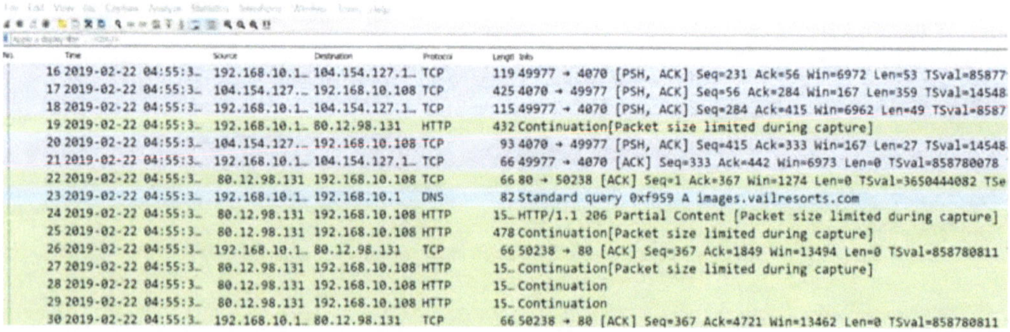

Fig. (1). Wireshark displayed captured network packets.

- Packet Capture: Wireshark can capture network traffic flowing through your network interface card (NIC). You can choose to capture traffic from your entire network interface or specific applications.
- Packet Inspection: Once captured, Wireshark allows you to inspect individual

packets in detail. You can see the source and destination IP addresses, ports used, protocols involved (like TCP/IP, HTTP, DNS), and even the actual data payload (if not encrypted).

- Traffic Analysis: Wireshark provides various tools for analyzing captured traffic. You can filter packets based on various criteria, such as IP addresses, protocols, or keywords within the data payload. You can also visualize traffic patterns and identify anomalies.
- Troubleshooting: Wireshark is a valuable tool for troubleshooting network connectivity issues. By analyzing captured traffic, you can identify potential problems like packet loss, latency, or routing issues.
- Security Monitoring: Wireshark can be used to monitor network traffic for suspicious activity. You can identify malware communication patterns, unauthorized access attempts, or data exfiltration attempts.

TCPdump

TCPdump [8] is a command-line utility used for capturing network traffic on Unix-based operating systems (including Linux and macOS). It's a powerful tool for network administrators, security professionals, and anyone who needs to analyze network activity as presented in Fig. (**2**).

```
:~# tcpdump -i eth0 -v
tcpdump: listening on eth0, link-type EN10MB (Ethernet), capture size 262144 bytes
04:42:05.006266 ARP, Ethernet (len 6), IPv4 (len 4), Request who-has 192.168.1.104 tell _gateway, length 46
04:42:05.006915 IP (tos 0x0, ttl 64, id 39077, offset 0, flags [DF], proto UDP (17), length 72)
    kali.59209 > _gateway.domain: 31573+ PTR? 104.1.168.192.in-addr.arpa. (44)
04:42:05.013667 IP (tos 0x0, ttl 62, id 30581, offset 0, flags [none], proto UDP (17), length 72)
    _gateway.domain > kali.59209: 31573 NXDomain 0/0/0 (44)
04:42:05.014283 IP (tos 0x0, ttl 64, id 39078, offset 0, flags [DF], proto UDP (17), length 70)
    kali.33221 > _gateway.domain: 65048+ PTR? 1.1.168.192.in-addr.arpa. (42)
04:42:05.018895 IP (tos 0x0, ttl 62, id 30582, offset 0, flags [none], proto UDP (17), length 70)
```

Fig. (2). TCPDump capturing wide variety of data.

TCPdump's functionalities are presented below.

- Packet Capture: tcpdump captures network traffic flowing through a specific network interface on your system. You can choose to capture traffic on your entire network interface (like eth0) or specific ports.
- Packet Filtering: tcpdump allows filtering captured packets based on various criteria. You can filter by IP addresses (source or destination), protocols (TCP, UDP, HTTP, *etc.*), ports, or even keywords within the data payload (if not encrypted).
- Offline Analysis: Unlike Wireshark, tcpdump primarily captures traffic to a file. You can then use other tools to analyze the captured packets offline. Popular tools for offline analysis include Wireshark itself (which can open tcpdump capture files) and Tshark (a command-line companion to Wireshark).

Traffic Analysis

Bro

Bro [9] previously known as Zeek, is a powerful open-source network traffic analysis framework used for network security monitoring and intrusion detection. While it's not strictly a traditional packet capture tool like Wireshark or tcpdump, Bro offers a comprehensive approach to network security by analyzing traffic in real-time and providing deep insights into network activity as illustrated in Fig. (**3**).

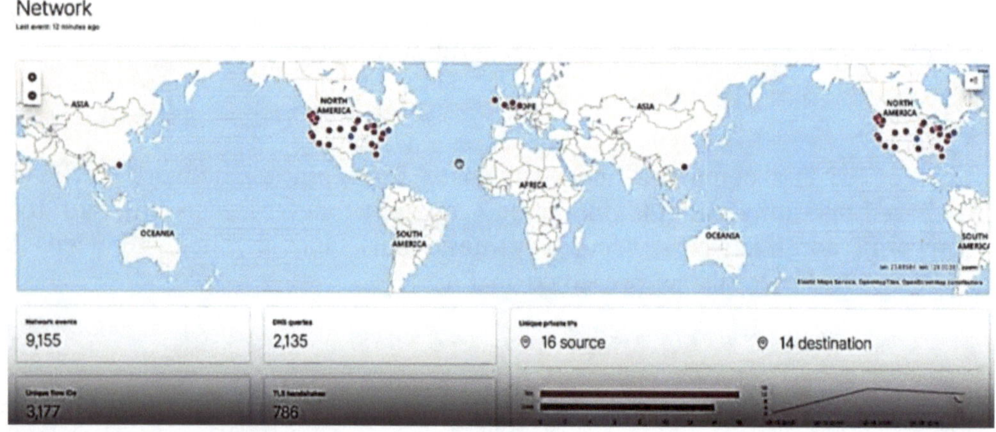

Fig. (3). Bro Network Monitoring.

Bro's functionalities are different from traditional packet capture tools:

- Real-time Analysis: Bro analyzes network traffic as it flows through the network, providing real-time insights into potential threats and suspicious activity.
- Protocol Analysis: Bro can decode and analyze a wide range of network protocols, allowing it to identify potential vulnerabilities and exploit attempts.
- Application Layer Analysis: Bro goes beyond traditional packet inspection and analyzes traffic at the application layer, providing deeper visibility into what applications are communicating and what data is being exchanged.
- Event Generation: Bro generates security events based on its analysis of network traffic. These events can be used to trigger alerts, automate security responses, and feed into Security Information and Event Management (SIEM) systems.
- Script-based Extensibility: Bro allows you to write custom scripts to extend its functionality and tailor it to your specific needs.

While Wireshark and tcpdump focus on capturing and analyzing individual packets, Bro focuses on real-time analysis of traffic flows and generating security events. Wireshark and tcpdump primarily capture traffic to a file for later analysis. Bro analyzes traffic in real-time but can also be configured to log captured data for further investigation. Bro requires some scripting knowledge for advanced configuration and analysis, while Wireshark and tcpdump offer a more user-friendly interface for basic traffic inspection.

Bro's real-time analysis allows for the proactive identification of threats and suspicious activity before they escalate into major security incidents. Bro's ability to analyze application layer traffic provides deeper insights into what's happening on your network and helps identify application-specific threats. Bro can trigger automated security responses based on detected threats, speeding up incident response times and reducing manual intervention. Bro can be deployed on a single system for basic network monitoring or scaled to handle large network traffic volumes.

NetworkMiner

NetworkMiner [10] is not specifically designed for real-time network monitoring, yet this is also a powerful tool for network forensics, particularly adept at post-incident investigation and evidence extraction from captured network traffic as illustrated in Fig. (**4**).

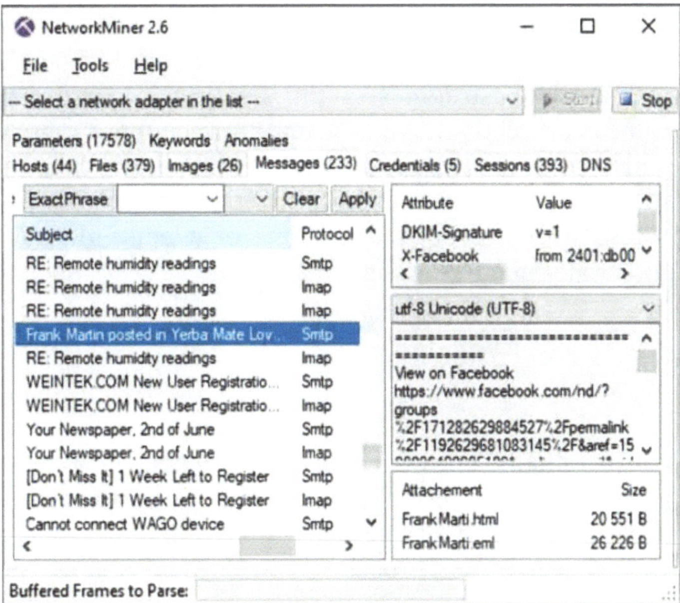

Fig. (4). NetworkMiner.

NetworkMiner's functionalities relevant to network forensics include:

- Network Traffic Analysis: NetworkMiner can analyze captured network traffic (typically in pcap format) to identify communication patterns, protocols used, and potential anomalies.
- File Extraction: NetworkMiner excels at extracting various file types (documents, images, executables) from captured traffic, even if embedded within protocols or data streams. This can be crucial for recovering evidence of data exfiltration or malware transfer during an attack.
- Email Analysis: NetworkMiner can parse captured traffic to identify email communication, including sender, recipient, subject line, and potentially even email content (if not encrypted). This can be valuable for investigating phishing campaigns or unauthorized data leaks.
- Password Extraction: NetworkMiner can sometimes identify and extract passwords transmitted over the network. However, it's important to note that this is typically limited to non-encrypted login attempts or weak encryption protocols. Strong encryption methods like HTTPS render password extraction infeasible.

NetworkMiner can passively capture live network traffic on your network interface for basic analysis. However, it's primarily designed to work with pre-captured traffic data in the pcap format. NetworkMiner supports a wide range of network protocols, allowing it to dissect captured packets and extract relevant information. NetworkMiner can analyze the content of captured packets, but this ability is limited by encryption. It can effectively extract content from unencrypted traffic but struggles with encrypted data streams. While NetworkMiner doesn't directly serve as a real-time network monitoring tool, the insights it provides from analyzing captured traffic are invaluable for network forensics investigations. By dissecting past network activity, NetworkMiner helps security professionals reconstruct the timeline of events, identify the attackers' methods, and potentially uncover stolen data.

Log Analysis

ELK Stack

ELK Stack [11] (originally known as the ELK Stack, now referred to as the Elastic Stack) has become a popular open-source platform for log analysis, particularly in the realm of network security. It's a combination of three powerful tools that work together to ingest, process, analyze, and visualize network log data as presented in Fig. (**5**).

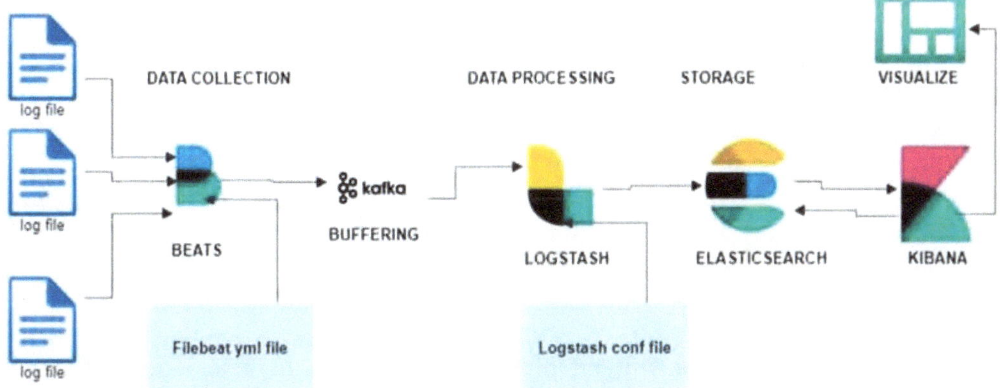

Fig. (5). ELK Stack.

Elasticsearch is a distributed, scalable search and analytics engine built on Apache Lucene. It efficiently stores and retrieves large volumes of log data, allowing for fast and flexible search queries. Logstash is a data collection pipeline that acts as the central intake point for log data. It can collect logs from various sources (network devices, firewalls, web servers, *etc.*), parse them into a structured format, and ship them to Elasticsearch for storage and indexing. While Kibana is a user-friendly visualization platform that sits on top of Elasticsearch. It allows users to explore, analyze, and visualize log data through interactive dashboards, charts, and graphs.

Logstash can ingest logs from diverse sources using various input plugins [12]. These plugins can connect to network devices *via* protocols like Syslog or SNMP or read log files directly from your system. Once collected, Logstash can parse log data using filters and codecs. Filters can extract relevant information from logs (*e.g.*, timestamps, IP addresses, usernames), while codecs convert logs into a structured format that Elasticsearch understands (*e.g.*, JSON). Logstash can also enrich log data by adding additional information. For example, it might look up IP addresses in a geolocation database to identify the source country of a log entry.

Elasticsearch stores logs in a structured format, allowing for efficient retrieval and querying. Each log entry becomes a document with indexed fields for easier search and filtering. Elasticsearch is horizontally scalable, meaning you can add more nodes to your cluster to handle increasing log volumes. This ensures efficient performance even when dealing with massive amounts of network log data. Users can leverage Elasticsearch's powerful search capabilities to query log data based on specific criteria (*e.g.*, timestamps, IP addresses, error messages). Additionally, aggregations allow users to group and summarize log data for analysis (*e.g.*, counting failed login attempts per user) [13].

Kibana provides a user-friendly interface for creating interactive dashboards and visualizations. Users can build dashboards displaying key network security metrics, such as the number of security events per day, distribution of source IP addresses, or trends in specific log messages. Kibana allows for near real-time visualization of log data, enabling security professionals to monitor network activity and identify potential threats as they occur. Kibana can be configured to generate alerts based on pre-defined conditions within log data. For instance, it can send an alert if it detects a surge in failed login attempts or suspicious network traffic patterns.

ELK Stack provides a centralized platform for collecting and storing log data from various network devices and systems. This eliminates the need to manage logs on individual devices, simplifying log management and analysis. The distributed nature of ELK Stack allows it to handle large volumes of network log data efficiently. Kibana's visualization capabilities enable real-time monitoring of network activity and faster identification of security threats. Users can create customized dashboards that display the most relevant network security metrics for their specific needs. ELK Stack's open-source nature makes it a cost-effective solution for network log analysis.

Security Onion

Security Onion, while not solely focused on network log analysis, incorporates powerful tools that make it a valuable platform for this purpose. It goes beyond basic log collection and offers functionalities for log processing, analysis, and visualization as displayed in Fig. (**6**).

Security Onion is a Linux distribution pre-configured with a collection of open-source security tools. These tools work together to provide comprehensive security monitoring and analysis capabilities like:

- Logstash: This plays a central role in collecting logs from various network devices and systems. Security Onion typically includes pre-configured Logstash pipelines to collect logs from common sources like firewalls, web servers, and intrusion detection systems (IDS).
- Elasticsearch: Security Onion integrates Elasticsearch to store, and index collected log data. This allows for efficient search and retrieval of logs for analysis purposes.
- Kibana: The Security Onion environment provides Kibana for log data visualization. Users can create dashboards to monitor key security metrics, identify trends, and investigate potential threats.

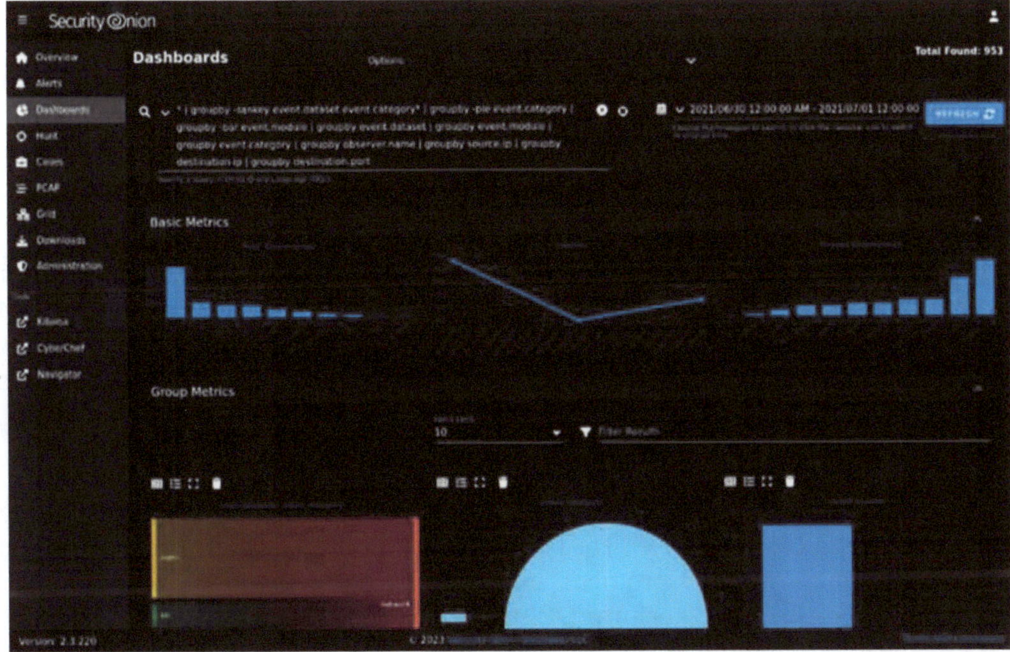

Fig. (6). Security Onion.

Security Onion offers a central location for collecting, storing, and analyzing logs from diverse network sources. This eliminates the need to manage logs on individual devices and simplifies security monitoring. Security Onion comes with pre-built Kibana dashboards that display essential network security metrics. These dashboards provide insights into firewall events, IDS alerts, system logs, and network traffic analysis (using tools like Bro). The SOC interface provides a central hub for managing and interacting with Security Onion's various security tools. Users can access Kibana dashboards, view real-time alerts, and investigate security incidents through the SOC console.

Security Onion comes pre-configured with all the necessary tools for network log analysis, making it a faster and easier solution to deploy compared to setting up a custom ELK Stack environment. Security Onion offers pre-built dashboards and functionalities specifically tailored towards network security monitoring, saving time on configuration and customization. Security Onion integrates other security tools like Bro for network traffic analysis, providing a more comprehensive view of network activity beyond just log data. Like ELK Stack, Security Onion is an open-source platform, making it a cost-effective solution for network log analysis.

Security Onion can be resource-intensive, especially when dealing with large volumes of network log data. Ensure your system has sufficient hardware resources to run Security Onion effectively. While Security Onion offers pre-configured tools, some technical expertise is needed to understand log data and utilize the platform's full potential.

Network Threat Detection - Suricata

Suricata stands as a prominent open-source network threat detection engine, offering real-time intrusion detection and prevention (IDS/IPS) capabilities. Suricata can capture network traffic flowing through your network interface or ingest pre-captured traffic files. It then inspects each packet against a rule set containing signatures for known threats and suspicious activities. Suricata relies on a rule set that defines patterns associated with malicious activity. These rules can identify various threats, including malware communication, network exploits, unauthorized access attempts, and denial-of-service (DoS) attacks.

Suricata can analyze traffic across a wide range of network protocols, including common ones like TCP, UDP, HTTP, DNS, and more. This allows it to detect threats regardless of the protocol used by attackers. Beyond basic header information, Suricata can perform DPI to inspect the payload section of packets. This enables it to identify malicious content embedded within data streams, such as exploit code or malware payloads as presented in Fig. (7).

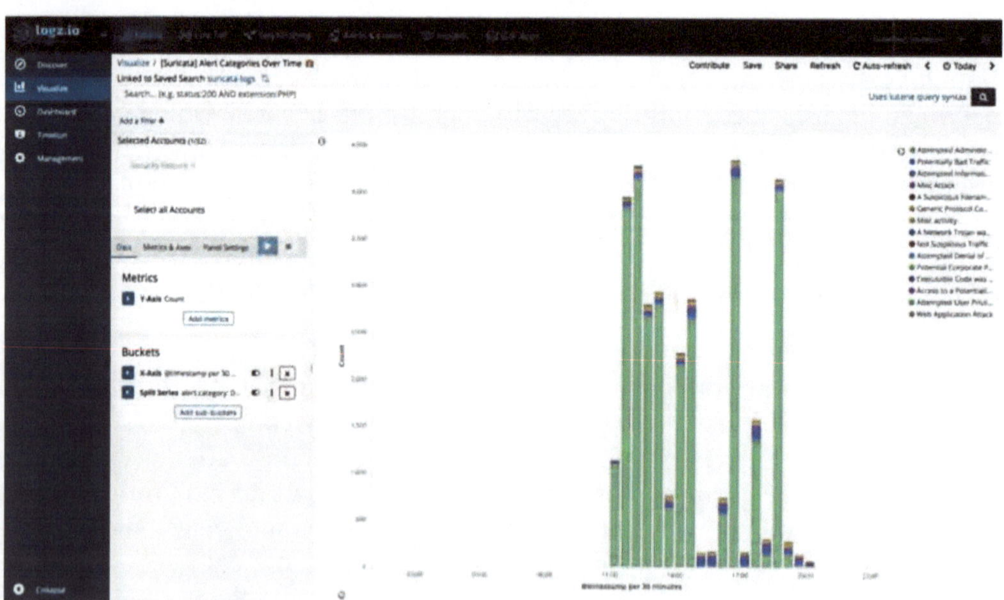

Fig. (7). Suricata Dashboard.

Suricata's Detection Modes

- IDS Mode (Detection): In this mode, Suricata detects suspicious activity based on its rule set and generates alerts for security teams to investigate. This allows for proactive identification of potential threats before they can cause significant damage.
- IPS Mode (Prevention): Suricata can also operate in IPS mode, where it actively blocks malicious traffic based on its rule set. This can involve dropping packets, resetting connections, or redirecting traffic to a quarantine zone.
- Advanced Capabilities: Suricata integrates with YARA, a powerful pattern-matching engine, allowing users to create custom rules to detect emerging threats and zero-day attacks.
- Flow Monitoring: Suricata can analyze network traffic flows to identify potential threats based on traffic patterns and anomalies.
- Network Traffic Analysis (NTA): Suricata can be integrated with NTA tools to provide a more comprehensive view of network activity and potential threats.

Suricata's open-source nature makes it a cost-effective solution for network threat detection. Suricata is known for its efficient performance, allowing it to analyze large volumes of network traffic in real-time. The tool offers a wide range of community-developed rule sets, constantly updated to keep pace with evolving threats. Users can create custom rules with YARA to address specific security concerns within their network environment. Suricata can operate in both IDS and IPS modes, offering flexibility in threat detection and prevention strategies.

NETWORK FORENSIC EVIDENCE

Network evidence encompasses digital artifacts and information collected from a network that can be used to reconstruct events, identify attackers, and potentially serve as legal proof in investigations. Different types of network evidence commonly encountered in network forensics are discussed below.

- Network Traffic Data is the primary source of evidence in network forensics. It consists of captured packets flowing through the network, containing information like Source and destination IP addresses, Port numbers, Protocols used (TCP, UDP, HTTP, *etc.*), Data payload (if not encrypted). Captured traffic data can be analyzed to identify suspicious activity, malware communication, unauthorized access attempts, and data exfiltration. Tools like Wireshark (for capture and analysis) and Suricata (for real-time threat detection) play a crucial role in dealing with network traffic data as evidence.
- Network Devices like routers, firewalls, and switches generate logs that record events, errors, and security-related messages. These logs can provide valuable

insights into network activity and potential security incidents. Tools like Security Onion (pre-configured with log analysis tools) and ELK Stack (customizable log analysis platform) can be used to collect, analyze, and correlate network device logs for forensic purposes. Security-relevant logs might include:

o Firewall logs: Recording allowed, blocked, and dropped connections.

o Syslogs: System logs from network devices containing informational, warning, and error messages.

o Authentication logs: Recording successful and failed login attempts.

- Network Flow Data and flow analysis (NFA) tools like NetFlow (Cisco), sFlow (open source), and IPFIX (IETF standard) collect aggregated network traffic data at a flow level. Flow represents a series of packets between two endpoints, characterized by source and destination IP addresses, ports, and protocol used. Network flow data can be helpful for identifying:

o High bandwidth consumers potentially indicative of malware or data exfiltration.

o Traffic patterns during a security incident to understand the scope and attack methods.

o Baselining network traffic patterns for anomaly detection.

- DNS (Domain Name System) records map human-readable domain names (like https://www.example.com to machine-readable IP addresses. Analyzing DNS logs can reveal domains accessed by compromised systems, potentially indicating malware communication or phishing attempts and unusual DNS queries outside the organization's typical browsing patterns.
- Email Server Logs record activities related to email sending and receiving. These logs can be crucial for investigations involving phishing campaigns, spam emails, or data leaks *via* email. Email server logs might contain details like:

o Sender and recipient email addresses.

o Subject lines and timestamps of emails.

o Instances of suspicious attachments or malware delivery attempts.

- Web Server Logs record information about user requests to a web server. They can be helpful in identifying unauthorized access attempts to web applications, Denial-of-service (DoS) attacks targeting web servers, and Web application vulnerabilities exploited by attackers. Web server logs typically include details like:

o IP addresses of users accessing the web server.

o URLs requested by users.

o HTTP status codes indicate successful or failed requests.

- Network Metadata refers to additional information associated with network traffic, such as timestamps, packet sizes, and Time-to-Live (TTL) values. Analyzing network metadata can be helpful for identifying the source of an attack based on IP address geolocation (though not always reliable), correlating events happening at different times on the network based on timestamps, understanding the nature of traffic based on packet sizes (*e.g.*, large file transfers).
- Network Configuration Files define how network devices operate and interact. Examining these files can reveal misconfigurations that might have created security vulnerabilities and intentional changes made by attackers to compromise network security.

NETWORK FORENSICS CHALLENGES

Despite its immense value, network forensics evidence collection and analysis present several challenges:

- Network Traffic Volatility: Unlike data stored on devices, network traffic is fleeting. Once a packet is transmitted, it's gone unless captured beforehand. This necessitates proactive measures like continuous traffic capture to ensure relevant evidence isn't lost.
- Encryption: The widespread adoption of encryption poses a challenge for traditional network forensic techniques that rely on analyzing the content of network traffic. Security teams might need to leverage decryption techniques or focus on other analysis methods like traffic reconstruction and anomaly detection.
- Data Volume: The ever-growing volume of network traffic can overwhelm investigators. Utilizing automation and machine learning algorithms can help streamline analysis and identify potential anomalies or suspicious activity.
- Legal Considerations: Network forensic investigations must adhere to legal

requirements regarding data privacy and chain of custody to ensure the admissibility of evidence in court. Security teams need to be familiar with relevant legal frameworks and ensure proper procedures are followed during evidence collection and analysis.

CONCLUSION

The ever-evolving threat landscape necessitates robust cybersecurity measures, and network forensics has become an indispensable tool in this fight. This chapter has provided a comprehensive foundation for network forensics, equipping readers with the knowledge to navigate the crucial stages of an investigation and leverage the power of open-source tools. From capturing network traffic with Wireshark to analyzing it with Bro, readers gain the ability to identify and understand digital evidence. The chapter acknowledges the challenges inherent in network forensics, such as data volatility and encryption, highlighting the importance of staying ahead of the curve. Furthermore, it underscores the critical role of legal considerations during investigations. By embracing the power of network forensics and adhering to legal guidelines, cybersecurity professionals can ensure a secure digital environment. As cyber threats continue to evolve, the ability to effectively analyze network traffic will remain paramount for successful incident response and investigations.

REFERENCES

[1] Kaspersky, “What is WannaCry ransomware?,” *Kaspersky.com*, 2019. 2019https://www.kaspersky.com/resource-center/threats/ransomware-wannacry

[2] A. Bhardwaj, F. Al-Turjman, M. Kumar, T. Stephan, and L. Mostarda, "Capturing-the-Invisible (CTI): Behavior-Based Attacks Recognition in IoT-Oriented Industrial Control Systems", *IEEE Access,* vol. 8, pp. 104956-104966, 2020. [http://dx.doi.org/10.1109/ACCESS.2020.2998983]

[3] R. Grimmick, https://www.varonis.com/blog/what-is-c2 “What is C2? Command and Control Infrastructure Explained,” www.varonis.com, Aug. 08, 2022. Available from: www.varonis.com

[4] A. Bhardwaj, F. Al-Turjman, V. Sapra, M. Kumar, and T. Stephan, "Privacy-aware detection framework to mitigate new-age phishing attacks", *Comput. Electr. Eng.,* vol. 96, p. 107546, 2021. [http://dx.doi.org/10.1016/j.compeleceng.2021.107546]

[5] M. McGrath, “Target Data Breach Spilled Info On As Many As 70 Million Customers,” Forbes. Available from: https://www.forbes.com/sites/maggiemcgrath/2014/01/10/target-data-breach-spilled-info-on-as-many-as-70-million-customers/?sh=3edb73d2e795 (accessed May 22, 2024).

[6] A. Bhardwaj, V. Avasthi, and S. Goundar, "Cyber security attacks on robotic platforms", *Netw. Secur.,* vol. 2019, no. 10, pp. 13-19, 2019. [http://dx.doi.org/10.1016/S1353-4858(19)30122-9]

[7] CompTIA, “What Is Wireshark and How to Use It,” CompTIA, 2020. Available from: https://www.comptia.org/content/articles/what-is-wireshark-and-how-to-use-it

[8] R. Gerardi, “An introduction to using tcpdump at the Linux command line,” Opensource.com, Sep. 01, 2020. Available from: https://opensource.com/article/18/10/introduction-tcpdump

[9] "The Zeek Network Security Monitor," Zeek. Available from: https://zeek.org/

[10] Netresec, "NetworkMiner - The NSM and Network Forensics Analysis Tool □," Netresec, 2019. Available from: https://www.netresec.com/?page=networkminer

[11] "What is the ELK stack? - Elastisearch, Logstash, Kibana Stack Explained - AWS," Amazon Web Services, Inc. Available from https://aws.amazon.com/what-is/elk-stack

[12] A. Bhardwaj, S. Bharany, A. Almogren, A. Ur Rehman, and H. Hamam, "Proactive threat hunting to detect persistent behaviour-based advanced adversaries", *Egyptian Informatics Journal,* vol. 27, p. 100510, 2024. [http://dx.doi.org/10.1016/j.eij.2024.100510]

[13] K. Kaushik, A. Bhardwaj, M. Kumar, S.K. Gupta, and A. Gupta, "A novel machine learning-based framework for detecting fake Instagram profiles", *Concurrency and Computation: Practice and Experience,* vol. 34, no. 28, p. e7349, 2022. [http://dx.doi.org/10.1002/cpe.7349]

CHAPTER 7

Unmasking Web Browser Artifacts

Abstract: Web browser forensics plays a crucial role in digital investigations, offering insights into an individual's online activities and behavior. This chapter delves into the intricacies of web browser forensics, exploring methodologies, tools, and challenges encountered in extracting and analysing data from various browsers. Through a comprehensive examination, this chapter aims to equip forensic professionals and researchers with the necessary knowledge and techniques to effectively conduct investigations involving web browsers. This chapter provides a comprehensive overview of web browser forensics, encompassing methodologies, tools, challenges, and best practices. By equipping forensic professionals and researchers with the requisite knowledge and techniques, this chapter aims to enhance the efficacy and accuracy of investigations involving web browsers, ultimately contributing to the advancement of the forensic field.

Keywords: Acquisition, Analysis, Browser artefact, Parsing, Presentation, Reporting, Timeline.

INTRODUCTION

Web browsers have become integral components of modern computing, serving as gateways to the vast expanse of the internet. With the proliferation of online activities ranging from communication and commerce to entertainment and education, web browsers store a treasure trove of digital evidence crucial for forensic investigations. The examination of web browser artifacts [1] has emerged as a specialized field within digital forensics, enabling investigators to reconstruct an individual's online behavior, and uncover vital clues and insights. This introduction serves as a comprehensive primer on web browser forensics, elucidating key concepts, methodologies, and challenges encountered [2] in the analysis of browser-related data. It begins by elucidating the significance of web browser forensics in contemporary digital investigations, highlighting its relevance in uncovering evidence pertinent to criminal cases, cybersecurity incidents, and corporate misconduct. Subsequently, the introduction delves into the fundamental components of web browsers, elucidating their architecture and the mechanisms underlying data storage and retrieval.

Akashdeep Bhardwaj, Pradeep Singh & Ajay Prasad

Detailed examination of browser artifacts follows in subsequent sections, encompassing cookies, browsing history, cache files, bookmarks, and download records, among others. Through illustrative examples and case studies, this introduction underscores the pivotal role of web browser forensics in elucidating the digital footprints left behind by users, thereby facilitating the reconstruction of events and aiding in the attribution of activities to specific individuals or entities. Finally, the introduction delineates the overarching structure of the chapter, providing a roadmap for subsequent discussions on methodologies, tools, challenges, and future directions in web browser forensics.

It is imperative to delve deeper into the methodologies employed in web browser forensics. This involves elucidating the processes and techniques utilized to extract, analyse, and interpret browser artifacts effectively. Methodologies in web browser forensics encompass both manual and automated approaches, each with its advantages and limitations. Manual analysis involves the meticulous examination of browser data through forensic tools and scripts, allowing investigators to scrutinize artifacts in detail and uncover hidden traces left behind by user activities. Conversely, automated analysis leverages specialized tools and software to expedite the extraction and analysis of browser artifacts, enabling investigators to process large volumes of data efficiently. However, automated approaches may overlook nuanced details that could be crucial in certain investigations, highlighting the importance of a balanced approach that integrates both manual and automated techniques.

Moreover, the chapter delves into the diverse array of forensic tools available for web browser analysis, ranging from open-source utilities to commercial software suites. These tools facilitate the acquisition, parsing, and visualization of browser data, enabling investigators to navigate through complex datasets and derive actionable insights. Additionally, considerations pertaining to data integrity, preservation, and chain of custody are addressed, underscoring the importance of adhering to best practices and legal standards throughout the forensic process. Furthermore, the chapter explores the challenges encountered in web browser forensics, including encryption, anti-forensic techniques, and platform-specific idiosyncrasies. Encryption mechanisms employed by modern browsers pose significant hurdles to forensic analysis, necessitating innovative approaches to circumvent encryption barriers and recover encrypted data. Likewise, the proliferation of anti-forensic tools and techniques complicates the forensic landscape, requiring forensic examiners to adapt and evolve their methodologies continually.

BROWSER ARTIFACTS

Web browser artifacts [3] are the digital footprints left behind by users as they interact with web browsers. These artifacts encompass a diverse range of data elements stored by browsers during typical browsing activities [4]. Understanding and analysing these artifacts is crucial in digital forensic investigations, as they can provide valuable insights into an individual's online behavior, preferences, and activities. In this section, we delve into the intricacies of web browser artifacts, examining their types, locations, significance, and methodologies for extraction and analysis.

Types of Web Browser Artifacts

Cookies

Cookies [5] are small text files stored on a user's device by websites they visit. They contain information such as site preferences, login credentials, and tracking data. Cookies play a crucial role in web browser forensics, as they can reveal a user's browsing history, interests, and interactions with specific websites.

Browsing History

Browsing history [6] records the URLs of web pages visited by the user, along with timestamps. Analyzing browsing history can provide insights into the user's online activities, interests, and the chronology of their browsing sessions.

Cache Files

Cache files [7] store copies of web pages, images, and other resources locally on the user's device to expedite subsequent page loads. Examining cache files can reveal the websites visited by the user, even if the browsing history has been cleared.

Download History

Download history [8] records the files downloaded by the user through the browser. This artifact can provide information about the types of files accessed by the user and their sources.

Bookmarks

Bookmarks [9], also known as favourites, are shortcuts to specific web pages saved by the user for easy access. Analyzing bookmarks can offer insights into the user's interests, frequently visited websites, and organizational preferences.

Form Data

Form data [10] includes information entered by the user into web forms, such as login credentials, search queries, and personal details. Examining form data can reveal sensitive information about the user's online activities and interactions.

Session Data

Session data [11] encompasses temporary data generated during browsing sessions, such as session cookies, authentication tokens, and temporary files. Analyzing session data can provide insights into active user sessions and interactions with websites.

Autofill Data

Autofill data [12] consists of information automatically populated by the browser in web forms, such as usernames, passwords, and addresses. Autofill data can be valuable in reconstructing the user's online interactions and activities.

Locations of Web Browser Artifacts

Web browser artifacts are typically stored in specific locations on the user's device, depending on the browser and operating system. Common locations include:

Browser Profile Directories

Each browser maintains a profile directory containing configuration files, databases, and other data related to user preferences and activities. These directories are typically located within the user's home directory or application data folder.

Browser Cache Directory

Cache files are stored in a designated directory on the user's device, often within the browser's profile directory. Cache directories may contain subdirectories corresponding to different websites visited by the user.

Cookies Database

Cookies are stored in a database file maintained by the browser. The location of the cookies database varies depending on the browser and operating system but is typically found within the browser's profile directory.

History Database

Browsing history is stored in a database file maintained by the browser. The location of the history database varies depending on the browser and operating system but is often located within the browser's profile directory.

Bookmarks File

Bookmarks are typically stored in a file maintained by the browser, which may be in a proprietary format or a standard format such as HTML. The location of the bookmarks file varies depending on the browser and operating system.

Download History Database

Download history is stored in a database file maintained by the browser. The location of the download history database varies depending on the browser and operating system.

Form Data Database

Form data is stored in a database file maintained by the browser. The location of the form data database varies depending on the browser and operating system.

Autofill Data Database

Autofill data is stored in a database file maintained by the browser. The location of the autofill data database varies depending on the browser and operating system.

These artifacts are files stored inside specific folders in the operating system. Each browser stores its files in a different place than other browsers and they all have different names, but they all store (most of the time) the same type of data (artifacts) as discussed in the below sections.

Mozilla Firefox

Mozilla Firefox uses its rendering engine called Gecko. This engine is responsible for interpreting web page code (HTML, CSS, JavaScript) and displaying it in a user-friendly format on your screen. Gecko prioritizes adhering to current and upcoming web standards to ensure compatibility with most websites. Firefox is available for a wide range of operating systems: Windows 10 and later, macOS, and Linux. Unofficial versions are also available for some Unix-based systems like FreeBSD and OpenBSD. Mobile versions exist for Android and iOS. It is important to note that due to Apple's restrictions, the iOS version utilizes the

WebKit layout engine instead of Firefox's Gecko engine.

Firefox is known for its focus on customization. Users can install extensions to add new features and functionality to the browser. Themes are also available to change the visual appearance. Security is a major selling point for Firefox. The browser prioritizes user privacy and offers features like blocking tracking cookies and preventing websites from fingerprinting users. Regular updates ensure the browser stays secure and implements the latest web technologies. For more in-depth details, you can refer to the official Firefox pages on features and technical specifications:

• Firefox Features [13]

• What is a web browser [14]

• Profile Path: Contains the profile data and majority of the artifacts as shown in Fig. (**1**).

C:\Users\XXX\AppData\Roaming\Mozilla\Firefox\Profiles\[profileID].default\C:\Users\XXX\AppData\Local\Mozilla\Firefox\Profiles\[profileID].default

Fig. (1). Profile Path (Mozilla).

• Navigation History + Bookmarks [SQLite Database] as presented in Fig. (**2**).

C:\Users\XXX\AppData\Roaming\Mozilla\Firefox\Profiles\[profileID].default\places.sqlite

Fig. (2). SQLite Database (Mozilla).

• Bookmarks Backups [Folder /.jsonlz4 Files] as illustrated in Fig. (**3**).

C:\Users\XXX\AppData\Roaming\Mozilla\Firefox\Profiles\[profileID].default\bookmarkbackups\

Fig. (3). Bookmarks Backups (Mozilla).

• Cookies [SQLite Database] as shown in Fig. (**4**).

C:\Users\XXX\AppData\Roaming\Mozilla\Firefox\Profiles\[profileID].default\cookies.sqlite

Fig. (4). Cookies (Mozilla).

• Cache [Multiple Types of Data] as displayed in Fig. (**5**).

C:\Users\XXX\AppData\Local\Mozilla\Firefox\Profiles\[profileID].default\cache2\entries
C:\Users\XXX\AppData\Local\Mozilla\Firefox\Profiles\[profileID].default\startupCache

Fig. (5). Cache (Mozilla).

• Form History [SQLite Database] as displayed in Fig. (**6**).

C:\Users\XXX\AppData\Roaming\Mozilla\Firefox\Profiles\[profileID].default\formhistory.sqlite

Fig. (6). Form History (Mozilla).

• Addons + Extensions [SQLite Database] are presented in Fig. (**7**) that displays the data about the installed add-ons in the browser.

C:\Users\XXX\AppData\Roaming\Mozilla\Firefox\Profiles\[profileID].default\addons.sqlite
C:\Users\XXX\AppData\Roaming\Mozilla\Firefox\Profiles\[profileID].default\extensions.sqlite

Fig. (7). Addons + Extensions (Mozilla).

• Favicons [SQLite Database] as illustrated in Fig. (**8**).

C:\Users\XXX\AppData\Roaming\Mozilla\Firefox\Profiles\[profileID].default\favicons.sqlite

Fig. (8). Favicons (Mozilla).

• Settings and Preferences as presented in Fig. (**9**).

C:\Users\XXX\AppData\Roaming\Mozilla\Firefox\Profiles\[profileID].default\prefs.js

Fig. (9). Settings & Preferences.

• Logins + Passwords [JSON File]

o Logins as shown in Fig. (**10**).

C:\Users\XXX\AppData\Roaming\Mozilla\Firefox\Profiles\[profileID].default\logins.json

C:\Users\XXX\AppData\Roaming\Mozilla\Firefox\Profiles\[profileID].default\logins.json

Fig. (10). Logins (Mozilla).

o Passwords present Key4.db and Key3.db for older versions as shown in Fig. (**11**).

C:\Users\XXX\AppData\Roaming\Mozilla\Firefox\Profiles\[profileID].default\key4.db

C:\Users\XXX\AppData\Roaming\Mozilla\Firefox\Profiles\[profileID].default\key3.db

Fig. (11). Passwords (Mozilla).

• Sessions Data [jsonlz4 File] contains data about the current session (Tabs and Websites opened) as illustrated in Fig. (**12**).

C:\Users\XXX\AppData\Roaming\Mozilla\Firefox\Profiles\[profileID].default\sessionstore.jsonlz4
C:\Users\XXX\AppData\Roaming\Mozilla\Firefox\Profiles\[profileID].default\sessionstore-backups\

Fig. (12). Session Data (Mozilla).

• Downloads [SQLite Database]: List of downloaded files from Firefox in Fig. (**13**).

C:\Users\XXX\AppData\Roaming\Mozilla\Firefox\Profiles\[profileID].default\downloads.sqlite

Fig. (13). Downloads (Mozilla).

• Thumbnails: Folder containing the images shown when we open the "about:newtab" page as shown in Fig. (**14**).

C:\Users\XXX\AppData\Local\Mozilla\Firefox\Profiles\[profileID].default\thumbnails

Fig. (14). Thumbnails (Mozilla).

Google Chrome

Google Chrome is a dominant web browser that boasts a feature-rich experience built on a solid technical foundation. Chrome leverages the open-source Chromium project as its foundation. Chromium provides the core functionality and rendering engine, Blink. Blink is a web rendering engine responsible for translating web page code (HTML, CSS, JavaScript) into visuals displayed on your screen. It prioritizes speed and adherence to web standards. Chrome is available for a vast array of platforms, including Windows (versions 7 and later), macOS, Linux distributions, Android, and iOS.

Chrome employs a security concept called sandboxing. This isolates processes for individual tabs and extensions, preventing malware or vulnerabilities on one webpage from compromising your entire system. Regular updates ensure Chrome stays patched against the latest security threats and incorporates new features.

Chrome popularized the now-standard tabbed browsing interface, allowing users to manage multiple web pages within a single window. The address bar doubles as a search bar (Omnibox). Users can seamlessly enter website URLs or search queries directly. Chrome offers a robust extension store with a vast library of extensions for adding functionalities and customizing the browser experience. Themes allow users to personalize visual appearance. Chrome utilizes a high-performance JavaScript engine named V8 for efficient execution of JavaScript code on web pages. Incognito mode allows for private browsing sessions where browsing history and cookies are not saved by default. If you like to delve deeper, you can explore these resources:

• Google Chrome - Wikipedia [15]

• What is Google Chrome browser? | Definition from TechTarget [16]

• Profile Path: Contains the profile data and the majority of the artifacts as shown in Fig. (**15**).

C:\Users\XXX\AppData\Local\Google\Chrome\User Data\Default
C:\Users\XXX\AppData\Local\Google\Chrome\User Data\ChromeDefaultData

Fig. (15). Profile Path (Chrome).

• Navigation History + Downloads + Search History [SQLite Database] as displayed in Fig. (**16**).

C:\Users\XXX\AppData\Local\Google\Chrome\User Data\Default\History
C:\Users\XXX\AppData\Local\Google\Chrome\User Data\ChromeDefaultData\History

Fig. (16). Navigation History, Downloads & Search History (Chrome).

• Cookies [SQLite Database] as shown in Fig. (**17**).

C:\Users\XXX\AppData\Local\Google\Chrome\User Data\Default\Cookies
C:\Users\XXX\AppData\Local\Google\Chrome\User Data\ChromeDefaultData\Cookies

Fig. (17). Cookies (Chrome).

• Cache [Multiple Types] as shown in Fig. (**18**).

C:\Users\XXX\AppData\Local\Google\Chrome\User Data\Default\Cache
C:\Users\XXX\AppData\Local\Google\Chrome\User Data\ChromeDefaultData\Cache

Fig. (18). Cache (Chrome).

• Bookmarks [JSON] as displayed in Fig. (**19**).

C:\Users\XXX\AppData\Local\Google\Chrome\User Data\Default\Bookmarks
C:\Users\XXX\AppData\Local\Google\Chrome\User Data\ChromeDefaultData\Bookmarks

Fig. (19). Bookmarks (Chrome).

• Form History [SQLite Database] as displayed in Fig. (**20**).

C:\Users\XXX\AppData\Local\Google\Chrome\User Data\Default\Web Data
C:\Users\XXX\AppData\Local\Google\Chrome\User Data\ChromeDefaultData\Web Data

Fig. (20). Form History (Chrome).

• Favicons [SQLite Database] as illustrated in Fig. (**21**).

C:\Users\XXX\AppData\Local\Google\Chrome\User Data\Default\Favicons
C:\Users\XXX\AppData\Local\Google\Chrome\User Data\ChromeDefaultData\Favicons

Fig. (21). Favicons (Chrome).

• Logins [SQLite Database] as shown in Fig. (**22**).

C:\Users\XXX\AppData\Local\Google\Chrome\User Data\ChromeDefaultData\Login Data

Fig. (22). Logins (Chrome).

Sessions Data

o Current Sessions / Tabs as shown in Fig. (**23**).

C:\Users\XXX\AppData\Local\Google\Chrome\User Data\Default\Current Session
C:\Users\XXX\AppData\Local\Google\Chrome\User Data\ChromeDefaultData\Current Session
C:\Users\XXX\AppData\Local\Google\Chrome\User Data\Default\Current Tabs
C:\Users\XXX\AppData\Local\Google\Chrome\User Data\ChromeDefaultData\Current Tabs

Fig. (23). Current Sessions Data (Chrome).

o Last (Previous) Sessions / Tabs as displayed in Fig. (**24**).

C:\Users\XXX\AppData\Local\Google\Chrome\User Data\Default\Last Session
C:\Users\XXX\AppData\Local\Google\Chrome\User Data\ChromeDefaultData\Last Session
C:\Users\XXX\AppData\Local\Google\Chrome\User Data\Default\Last Tabs
C:\Users\XXX\AppData\Local\Google\Chrome\User Data\ChromeDefaultData\Last Tabs

Fig. (24). Last Sessions Data (Chrome).

• Addons + Extensions [Folders] as illustrated in Fig. (**25**).

C:\Users\XXX\AppData\Local\Google\Chrome\User Data\Default\Extensions
C:\Users\XXX\AppData\Local\Google\Chrome\User Data\ChromeDefaultData\Extensions
Thumbnails [SQLite Database]
C:\Users\XXX\AppData\Local\Google\Chrome\User Data\Default\Top Sites
C:\Users\XXX\AppData\Local\Google\Chrome\User Data\Default\Thumbnails (Older versions)

Fig. (25). Addons & Extensions (Chrome).

Microsoft Edge

Microsoft Edge has undergone a significant technical transformation in recent times. Edge leverages the Chromium project as its base. This open-source project provides the core functionalities and the web rendering engine, Blink, which as we discussed earlier, translates web page code (HTML, CSS, JavaScript) into visuals displayed on user screens and prioritizes speed and adherence to web standards [2]. Edge boasts a wide reach, being available on Windows (versions 10 and later), macOS, Linux distributions, Android, and iOS.

Edge utilizes sandboxing to isolate processes for individual tabs and extensions. This prevents vulnerabilities on one webpage from compromising your entire system. Regular updates ensure Edge receives the latest security patches and incorporates new features. Edge offers the standard tabbed browsing interface, allowing you to manage multiple web pages within a single window. The address bar doubles as a search bar, enabling you to directly enter website URLs or search queries. Edge provides an extension store with a vast library for adding functionalities and personalizing the browsing experience with themes. Like Chrome, Edge utilizes the V8 JavaScript engine for efficient execution of JavaScript code on webpages. Incognito mode allows for private browsing sessions where browsing history and cookies are not saved by default. Microsoft Edge, with its chromium base and additional security features, aims to deliver a secure and feature-rich browsing experience.

• Profile Path as displayed in Fig. (**26**).

C:\Users\XX\AppData\Local\Packages\Microsoft.MicrosoftEdge_XXX\AC

Fig. (26). Profile Path (Edge).

• History + Cookies + Downloads [ESE Database] as shown in Fig. (**27**).

C:\Users\XX\AppData\Local\Microsoft\Windows\WebCache\WebCacheV01.dat

Fig. (27). History, Cookies & Downloads (Edge).

• Settings + Bookmarks + Reading List [ESE Database] as shown in Fig. (**28**).

C:\Users\XX\AppData\Local\Packages\Microsoft.MicrosoftEdge_XXX\AC\MicrosoftEdge\User\Default\DataStore\Data\nouser1\XXX\DBStore\spartan.edb

Fig. (28). Settings, Bookmarks & Reading List (Edge).

• Cache location as displayed in Fig. (**29**).

C:\Users\XXX\AppData\Local\Packages\Microsoft.MicrosoftEdge_XXX\AC\#!XXX\MicrosoftEdge\Cache

Fig. (29). Cache location (Edge).

• Last Active Session is displayed in Fig. (**30**).

C:\Users\XX\AppData\Local\Packages\Microsoft.MicrosoftEdge_XXX\AC\MicrosoftEdge\User\Default\Recovery\Active

Fig. (30). Last Active Session.

Significance of Web Browser Artifacts

Web browser artifacts play a significant role in digital forensic investigations for several reasons:

- Evidence of Online Activities: Browser artifacts provide tangible evidence of a user's online activities, including [17] websites visited, searches conducted, files downloaded, and interactions with web forms.
- Chronological Timeline: Browsing history and other artifacts can be used to reconstruct a chronological timeline of the user's online sessions, facilitating the investigation of cybercrimes, unauthorized access, and other illicit activities [18]. User Behavior Analysis: Analysis of browser artifacts enables forensic examiners to gain insights into the user's behavior, preferences, interests, and patterns of online activity. This information can be valuable in profiling suspects and identifying relevant digital evidence.
- Corroboration of Testimony: Browser artifacts can corroborate or refute testimony provided by suspects or witnesses regarding their online activities, providing objective evidence to support investigative findings.
- Attribution of Activities: Browser artifacts can aid in attributing specific activities or events to individual users, devices, or IP addresses, assisting in the identification and prosecution of perpetrators in criminal investigations.

METHODOLOGIES FOR EXTRACTION AND ANALYSIS

Web browsers leave behind a treasure trove of data, known as artifacts, which can be crucial for various purposes, including digital forensics, user behavior analysis, and website optimization. Extracting and analysing these artifacts requires a systematic approach. Extracting and analysing web browser artifacts involves a systematic approach that encompasses the following steps:

Step 1: Acquisition

The first step involves acquiring the relevant data from the user's device, including browser files, databases, and system logs. This can be accomplished using forensic imaging tools, acquisition scripts, or manual extraction techniques in a forensically sound manner, which ensures the data remains unaltered and can be used as evidence in legal proceedings.

- Windows: Tools like FTK Imager or EnCase can create a disk image of the drive containing the user profile directory. This directory typically holds browser data.
- macOS: Tools like DMG Extractor or Forensic Buddy can be used to acquire disk images or specific user folders.
- Linux: The dd command can be used to create an image of the desired partition or directory.

The data acquisition process using FTK Imager on Windows is presented in Fig. (**31**).

```
//Mount the target drive (e.g., D:)
FTK Imager -> Create Disk Image
// Select the drive to image (D:)
// Choose a destination for the image file (evidence.dd)
// Start the imaging process
```

Fig. (31). Acquisition Process: Using FTK Imager.

Step 2: Parsing

Once the data has been acquired, it must be parsed to extract relevant artifacts and metadata to identify the location of browser artifacts based on the specific browser used. This involves decoding proprietary file formats, parsing database entries, and interpreting timestamps and other metadata as shown below.

- Firefox: Profile directory: C:\Users\<username>\AppData\Roaming\Mozilla\Firefox\Profiles\<profile_name> on Windows).
- Chrome: User data directory: C:\Users\<username>\AppData\Local\Google\Chrome\User Data on Windows).
- Edge: User data directory: C:\Users\<username>\AppData\Local\Microsoft\Edge\User Data on Windows).

Step 3: Normalization

This involves organizing and standardizing the extracted data using specialised tools and scripts to facilitate analysis and comparison across different browsers and platforms. This may involve converting timestamps to a common format, resolving URLs to their canonical forms, and categorizing artifacts based on type and relevance.

- Forensics Software: Dedicated forensic software like FTK Imager or EnCase can parse browser data files and extract specific artifacts.
- Command-line Tools: Tools like grep or find (Linux/macOS) or findstr (Windows) can be used with regular expressions to locate specific files or data within the extracted data.
- Scripting: Languages like Python or PowerShell can be used to automate the extraction process based on specific needs.

Fig. (**32**) displays the use of 'grep' on Linux to find Chrome history.

```
# Find lines containing "
grep -r "url" /path/to/extracted/chrome/data/
```

Fig. (32). Using GREP to find Chrome History.

Step 4: Analysis

The extracted and normalized data is then analysed to identify patterns, trends, anomalies, and other actionable insights [17]. This may involve correlating artifacts across different sources, reconstructing user sessions, and visualizing the data using forensic analysis tools. The common artifacts and their analysis methods are:

- History Files: These files record visited URLs, timestamps, and potential titles. Scripts can parse these files to identify frequently visited sites, browsing patterns, and potential suspicious activity.
- Cache Files: Downloaded web page resources (images, scripts) are stored in the cache. Analyzing cached files can reveal previously visited websites, even if the history is cleared.
- Cookies: These files store website preferences and login information. Analyzing cookies can reveal browsing history, login details for accessed websites, and potential tracking mechanisms.
- Downloads: Downloaded files can be directly analysed based on their type and associated timestamps.

Python script to parse Firefox history is presented in Fig. (**33**).

```
import sqlite3

def parse_firefox_history(history_file):
  conn = sqlite3.connect(history_file)
  cursor = conn.cursor()

  cursor.execute("SELECT url, title, visit_time FROM moz_historyvisits")
  rows = cursor.fetchall()

  for row in rows:
    url, title, timestamp = row

# Analyze each entry (e.g., identify suspicious URLs, frequent visits)
  conn.close()

# Example usage
history_file = "/path/to/extracted/firefox/places.sqlite"
parse_firefox_history(history_file)
```

Fig. (33). Python script to parse Firefox History.

Step 5: Documentation

Finally, the findings of the analysis must be documented in a clear and concise manner, including detailed reports, timelines, and supporting evidence [18]. Proper documentation is essential for communicating findings to stakeholders, presenting evidence in legal proceedings, and ensuring the reproducibility of results. This report should include:

- Details about the acquisition process.
- Identification of the browser and versions used.
- Description of the extracted artifacts.
- Analysis findings and their significance (potential security risks, user behavior patterns).

DEMO – HINDSIGHT

This section presents a use case analysing web data using a tool called 'hindsight' [4]. This tool parses Download history, URLs, Caches, Autofill records, Bookmarks, Saved passwords, Browser extensions, Preferences, HTTP cookies, and local storage records (HTML5 cookies). Once extracted, this data can be correlated and placed in a timeline.

Step 1: On running the hindsight executable in the command line, the hindsight server is mentioned to be starting as shown in Fig. (**34**).

Fig. (34). Hindsight Executable.

Step 2: This starts with the Hindsight web browser which is packaged in this tool as http://localhost on port 8080, the web user interface is displayed in Fig. (**35**). This displays the input options for different browsers, profile path, and the cache path as well as available decryption.

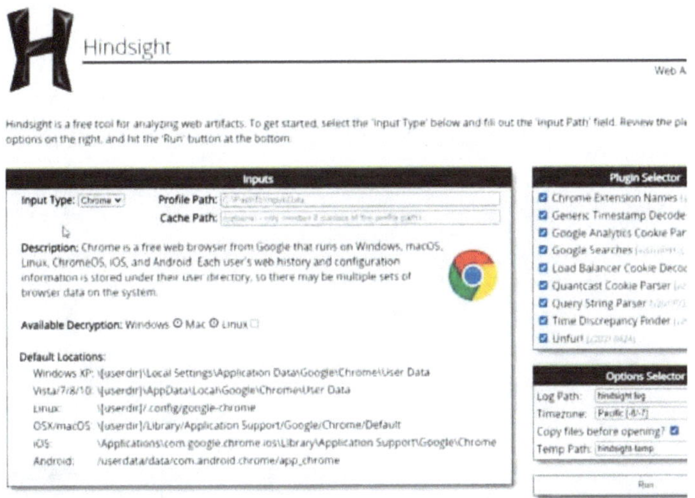

Fig. (35). Hindsight Web Server UI.

Step 3: Provide the Profile path as displayed in Fig. (**36**).

Inputs
Input Type: Chrome
Profile Path: C:\Documents and Settings\archoudh\AppData\Local\Google\Chrome\L
Cache Path:

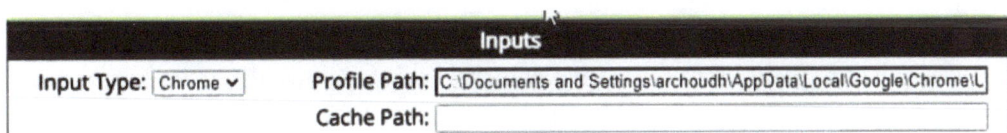

Fig. (36). Profile Path provided to Hindsight.

Step 4: In the backend (command line), the tool displays the web browser steps (GET method) and tries to gather the information and parse the data artifacts from the profile path and file as presented in Fig. (**37**).

```
################################################################################

Bottle v0.12.19 server starting up (using WSGIRefServer())...
Listening on http://localhost:8080/
Hit Ctrl-C to quit.

127.0.0.1 - - [18/Feb/2022 21:46:41] "GET / HTTP/1.1" 200 19433
127.0.0.1 - - [18/Feb/2022 21:46:43] "GET /static/styles.css HTTP/1.1" 200 5651
127.0.0.1 - - [18/Feb/2022 21:46:43] "GET /static/github.png HTTP/1.1" 200 1571
127.0.0.1 - - [18/Feb/2022 21:46:43] "GET /static/slack.png HTTP/1.1" 200 7645
127.0.0.1 - - [18/Feb/2022 21:46:43] "GET /static/twitter.png HTTP/1.1" 200 6650
127.0.0.1 - - [18/Feb/2022 21:46:43] "GET /static/chrome_logo.svg HTTP/1.1" 200 6245
127.0.0.1 - - [18/Feb/2022 21:46:43] "GET /static/h.png HTTP/1.1" 200 500313
127.0.0.1 - - [18/Feb/2022 21:46:43] "GET /static/fonts/OpenSans-Regular.woff2 HTTP/1.1" 200 47016
127.0.0.1 - - [18/Feb/2022 21:46:43] "GET /static/error.png HTTP/1.1" 200 322
127.0.0.1 - - [18/Feb/2022 21:46:44] "GET /static/fonts/OpenSans-Light.woff2 HTTP/1.1" 200 45900
127.0.0.1 - - [18/Feb/2022 21:46:44] "GET /static/brave_logo.png HTTP/1.1" 200 29951
127.0.0.1 - - [18/Feb/2022 21:46:44] "GET /static/icons/manifest.json HTTP/1.1" 200 720
```

Fig. (37). Hindsight Command line.

Step 5: The command line displays the input information after parsing as displayed in Fig. (**38**).

```
Profile: ...d Settings\archoudh\AppData\Local\Google\Chrome\User Data\Default
                   Detected Chrome version:     [  95-96 ]
                               URL records:     [  31005 ]
                          Download records:     [    375 ]
                     Media History records:     [   2441 ]
                             Cache records:     [      0 ]
                         GPU Cache records:     [      0 ]
                          Autofill records:     [    605 ]
                          Bookmark records:     [    250 ]
                     Local Storage records:     [  15885 ]
                   Session Storage records:     [    247 ]
                                Extensions:     [     16 ]
                  Extension Cookie records:     [      7 ]
                        Login Data records:     [    129 ]
                          Preference Items:     [   1221 ]
              Site Characteristics records:     [  21324 ]
                         File System Items:     [     26 ]
```

```
Profile: ...ings\archoudh\AppData\Local\Google\Chrome\User Data\Guest Profile
                   Detected Chrome version:     [  95-96 ]
                               URL records:     [      0 ]
                          Download records:     [      0 ]
                             Cache records:     [      0 ]
                          Autofill records:     [      0 ]
                     Local Storage records:     [      0 ]
                        Login Data records:     [      0 ]
                          Preference Items:     [     20 ]
              Site Characteristics records:     [      0 ]
```

Fig. (38). Command line parsed information.

Step 6: Web UI displays the parsed details as shown in Fig. (**39**) for the summary of the Chrome data, including parsed artifacts (Chrome version, URL records, download records, local storage records, autofill records, login data records, preference items, media history and site characteristics, which can be saved (say Excel format) and the plugin results.

Summary

Input Path: C:\Documents and Settings\archoudh\AppData\Local\Google\Chrome\User Data
Input Type: Chrome
Profile Paths:

- C:\Documents and Settings\archoudh\AppData\Local\Google\Chrome\User Data\Default
- C:\Documents and Settings\archoudh\AppData\Local\Google\Chrome\User Data\Guest Profile
- C:\Documents and Settings\archoudh\AppData\Local\Google\Chrome\User Data\Profile 1
- C:\Documents and Settings\archoudh\AppData\Local\Google\Chrome\User Data\System Profile

Parsed Artifacts	
Detected Chrome version:	95-96
URL records:	31082
Download records:	375
Cache records:	0
Local Storage records:	16897
Autofill records:	608
Login Data records:	130
Preference Items:	1313
Media History records:	2441
Site Characteristics records:	21346

Plugin Results	
Chrome Extension Names [v20210424]:	- 3 extension URLs parsed -
Generic Timestamp Decoder [v20160907]:	- 0 timestamps parsed -
Google Analytics Cookie Parser [v20170130]:	- 0 cookies parsed -
Google Searches [v20160912]:	- 1865 searches parsed -
Load Balancer Cookie Decoder [v20200213]:	- 0 cookies parsed -
Quantcast Cookie Parser [v20160907]:	- 0 cookies parsed -
Query String Parser [v20170225]:	- 11278 query strings parsed -
Time Discrepancy Finder [v20170129]:	- 0 differences parsed -
Unfurl [v20210424]:	- 415 values parsed -

Fig. (39). Summary of Chrome Data.

Step 7: Save this information as an XLSX report and it is automatically sorted and displayed in various tabs; Fig. (**40**) displays the timeline on when the URLs were accessed (browsed).

	A	B	C	D	
1	Hindsight Internet History Forensics (v2021.12)				
2	Type	Timestamp (US/Pacific	URL	Title / Name / Status	Data / Value / Path
641	bookmark	2017-07-21 03:10:36.000	https://www.virustotal.com/	VirusTotal - Free Online Virus,	Bookmarks bar > Tools and Techniques
642	bookmark	2017-07-21 03:11:37.000	http://www.ipvoid.com/	IP Address Tools, Network Toc	Bookmarks bar > Tools and Techniques
643	bookmark	2017-07-21 03:11:52.000	http://www.urlvoid.com/	Identify websites involved in	Bookmarks bar > Tools and Techniques
644	bookmark	2017-07-21 03:13:01.000	http://beta.senderbase.org/	SenderBase	Bookmarks bar > Tools and Techniques
645	bookmark	2017-07-21 03:13:30.000	https://www.mcafee.com/threat-intelligence/ip/spam-senders.aspx#n	Top Spam Senders - McAfee La	Bookmarks bar > Tools and Techniques
646	bookmark	2017-07-21 03:14:53.000	https://urlquery.net/	urlquery.net - URL Scanner	Bookmarks bar > Tools and Techniques
647	bookmark	2017-07-21 03:18:37.000	https://www.tcpiputils.com/	Online investigation tool - IP, I	Bookmarks bar > Tools and Techniques
648	bookmark	2017-08-01 07:18:18.000	https://www.abuseipdb.com/	AbuseIPDB - IP address abuse	Bookmarks bar > Tools and Techniques
649	bookmark	2017-08-01 07:18:55.000	https://cymon.io/	Open Threat Intelligence	Bookmarks bar > Tools and Techniques
650	bookmark	2017-08-01 07:54:50.000	https://www.tunnelsup.com/subnet-calculator/	Subnet Calculator - TunnelsUP	Bookmarks bar > Tools and Techniques
651	bookmark	2017-08-02 07:06:25.000	https://www.microsoft.com/en-in/software-download/windows7	Download Windows 7 Disc Ima	Bookmarks bar > Tools and Techniques
652	bookmark	2017-10-19 04:08:48.000	https://sitereview.zscaler.com/	Site Review - URL Category Lo	Bookmarks bar > Tools and Techniques
653	bookmark	2017-10-24 23:11:21.000	http://whatismyipaddress.com/ip-lookup	Instant IP Address Lookup	Bookmarks bar > Tools and Techniques
654	bookmark	2017-10-25 12:02:48.000	https://otx.alienvault.com/browse/pulses/?sort=-created	Browse Pulses - AlienVault OT	Bookmarks bar > Tools and Techniques
655	bookmark	2017-11-13 21:03:15.000	https://www.virustotal.com/graph/	VirusTotal Graph	Bookmarks bar > Tools and Techniques
656	bookmark	2017-12-10 05:56:17.000	https://www.abuseipdb.com/check/173.239.228.84	173.239.228.84 | Silicon Valley	Bookmarks bar > Tools and Techniques
657	bookmark	2017-12-17 17:46:50.000	https://securityriskadvisors.com/blog/post/strutting-your-stuff-identif	Blog » Post | Security Risk Adv	Bookmarks bar > Tools and Techniques

Fig. (40). Timeline Report by Hindsight.

Step 8: The second tab displays the stored data details inside the Chrome browser as shown in Fig. (**41**).

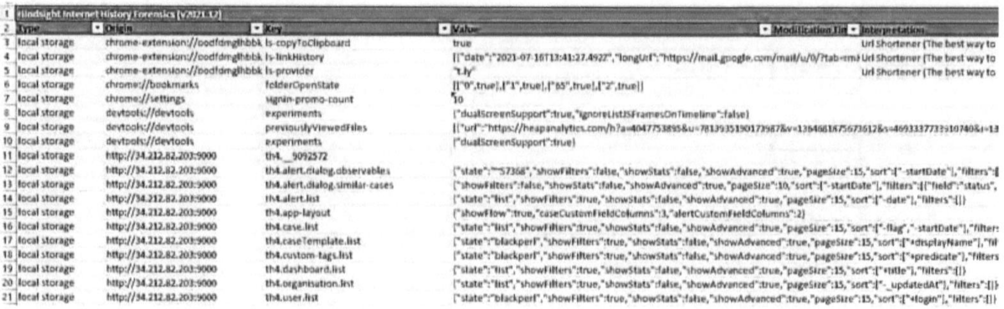

1	Hindsight Internet History Forensics (v2021.12)					
2	Type	Origin	Key	Value	Modification Tim	Interpretation
3	local storage	chrome-extension://oodfdmglhbbk	ls-copyToClipboard	true		Url Shortener (The best way to
4	local storage	chrome-extension://oodfdmglhbbk	ls-linkHistory	[{"date":"2021-07-16T13:41:27.492Z","longUrl":"https://mail.google.com/mail/u/0/?tab=rm		Url Shortener (The best way to
5	local storage	chrome-extension://oodfdmglhbbk	ls-provider	"t.ly"		Url Shortener (The best way to
6	local storage	chrome://bookmarks	folderOpenState	[["0",true],["1",true],["65",true],["2",true]]		
7	local storage	chrome://settings	signin-promo-count	10		
8	local storage	devtools://devtools	experiments	{"dualScreenSupport":true,"ignoreListJSFramesOnTimeline":false}		
9	local storage	devtools://devtools	previouslyViewedFiles	[{"url":"https://heapanalytics.com/h?a=4047753895&u=7813935190173987&v=1364661675673612&s=4693337733910740&i=13		
10	local storage	devtools://devtools	experiments	{"dualScreenSupport":true}		
11	local storage	http://34.212.82.203:9000	th4.__9092572			
12	local storage	http://34.212.82.203:9000	th4.alert.dialog.observables	{"state":"~57368","showFilters":false,"showStats":false,"showAdvanced":true,"pageSize":15,"sort":["-startDate"],"filters":[		
13	local storage	http://34.212.82.203:9000	th4.alert.dialog.similar-cases	{"showFilters":false,"showStats":false,"showAdvanced":true,"pageSize":10,"sort":["-startDate"],"filters":[{"field":"status",		
14	local storage	http://34.212.82.203:9000	th4.alert.list	{"state":"list","showFilters":true,"showStats":false,"showAdvanced":true,"pageSize":15,"sort":["-date"],"filters":[]}		
15	local storage	http://34.212.82.203:9000	th4.app-layout	{"showFlow":true,"caseCustomFieldColumns":3,"alertCustomFieldColumns":2}		
16	local storage	http://34.212.82.203:9000	th4.case.list	{"state":"list","showFilters":true,"showStats":false,"showAdvanced":true,"pageSize":15,"sort":["-flag","-startDate"],"filter:		
17	local storage	http://34.212.82.203:9000	th4.caseTemplate.list	{"state":"blackperl","showFilters":true,"showStats":false,"showAdvanced":true,"pageSize":15,"sort":["+displayName"],"fil		
18	local storage	http://34.212.82.203:9000	th4.custom-tags.list	{"state":"blackperl","showFilters":true,"showStats":false,"showAdvanced":true,"pageSize":15,"sort":["+predicate"],"filters		
19	local storage	http://34.212.82.203:9000	th4.dashboard.list	{"state":"list","showFilters":true,"showStats":false,"showAdvanced":true,"pageSize":15,"sort":["+title"],"filters":[]}		
20	local storage	http://34.212.82.203:9000	th4.organisation.list	{"state":"list","showFilters":true,"showStats":false,"showAdvanced":true,"pageSize":15,"sort":["-_updatedAt"],"filters":[]}		
21	local storage	http://34.212.82.203:9000	th4.user.list	{"state":"blackperl","showFilters":true,"showStats":false,"showAdvanced":true,"pageSize":15,"sort":["+login"],"filters":[]}		

Fig. (41). Stored data details inside the Chrome browser..

Step 9: Installed extensions on the Chrome browser are also displayed as shown in Fig. (**42**).

	A	B	C	D	
1	Installed Extensions				
2	Extension Name	Description	Version	App ID	Profile Folder
3	Slides	Create and edit presentations	0.10	aapocclcgogkmnckokdopfmhonfmgoek	Default
4	Docs	Create and edit documents	0.10	aohghmighlieiainnegkcijnfilokake	Default
5	Google Drive	Google Drive: create, share and keep all your stuff in one place.	14.5	apdfllckaahabafndbhieahigkjlhalf	Default
6	Hacker Anonymous Themes Ne	Replace your new tab with the Hacker Anonymous Custom page, with g	12.0.7	bimjehpklddkggeiifplmclnbcicdjpp	Default
7	YouTube		4.2.8	blpcfgokakmgnkcojhhkbfbldkacnbeo	Default
8	Adblock Plus - free ad blocker	Block YouTube™ ads, pop-ups & fight malware!	3.12	cfhdojbkjhnklbpkdaibdccddilifddb	Default
9	Galaxy-View	Galaxy-view	1.3	dcbeddldohkakodfncjnkkjfojggbahp	Default
10	Sheets	Create and edit spreadsheets	1.2	felcaaldnbdncclmgdcncolpebgiejap	Default
11	Google Docs Offline	Edit, create, and view your documents, spreadsheets, and presentation	1.39.0	ghbmnnjooekpmoecnnnilnnbdlolhkhi	Default
12	Youtube Video Downloader	YouTube to MP3/MP4 video converter for easy, free and extremely quic	1.3	gjndphdopaigpbbhdlgphjgfccacnbja	Default
13	APK Downloader	Download APK & OBB from Google Play Store (latest version)	1.2.0	idkigghdjmipnppaeahkpcoaiphjdccm	Default
14	Youtube downloader y2mate &	Youtube downloader & Converter for y2mate & keepvid.	1.1	lfldipeaaoaoaiipbdnijdfondjpdlmi	Default
15	TubeBuddy	The #1 Rated Extension for YouTube Creators	1.45.1132	mhkhmbddkmdggbhaaaodilponhnccicb	Default
16	Chrome Web Store Payments	Chrome Web Store Payments	1.0.0.6	nmmhkkegccagdldgiimedpiccmgmieda	Default
17	Url Shortener	The best way to create a short links using T.LY, JPEG.ly, Bitly, Rebrandly,	1.2.6	oodfdmglhbbkkcngodjjagblikmoegpa	Default
18	Gmail	Fast, searchable email with less spam.	8.3	pjkljhegncpnkpknbcohdijeoejaedia	Default
19	Slides	Create and edit presentations	0.10	aapocclcgogkmnckokdopfmhonfmgoek	Profile 1
20	Docs	Create and edit documents	0.10	aohghmighlieiainnegkcijnfilokake	Profile 1
21	Google Drive	Google Drive: create, share and keep all your stuff in one place.	14.5	apdfllckaahabafndbhieahigkjlhalf	Profile 1
22	YouTube		4.2.8	blpcfgokakmgnkcojhhkbfbldkacnbeo	Profile 1
23	Sheets	Create and edit spreadsheets	1.2	felcaaldnbdncclmgdcncolpebgiejap	Profile 1
24	Google Docs Offline	Edit, create, and view your documents, spreadsheets, and presentation	1.39.0	ghbmnnjooekpmoecnnnilnnbdlolhkhi	Profile 1
25	Chrome Web Store Payments	Chrome Web Store Payments	1.0.0.6	nmmhkkegccagdldgiimedpiccmgmieda	Profile 1
26	Gmail	Fast, searchable email with less spam.	8.3	pjkljhegncpnkpknbcohdijeoejaedia	Profile 1

Fig. (42). Installed Chrome Extensions.

Step 10: Any preferences done on the web browser are also displayed as shown in Fig. (**43**).

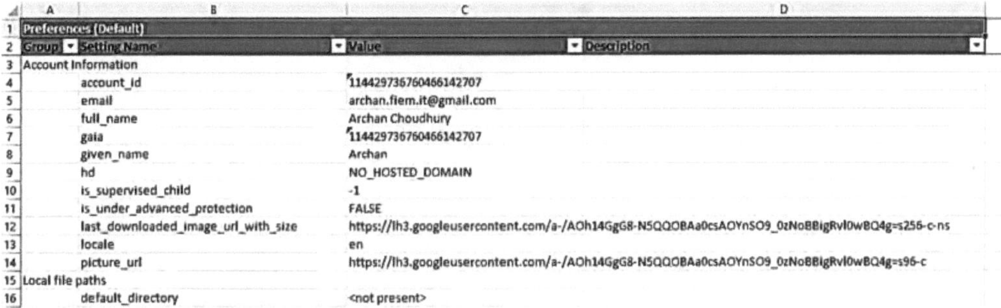

Group	Setting Name	Value	Description
Preferences (Default)			
Account Information			
	account_id	114429736760466142707	
	email	archan.fiem.it@gmail.com	
	full_name	Archan Choudhury	
	gaia	114429736760466142707	
	given_name	Archan	
	hd	NO_HOSTED_DOMAIN	
	is_supervised_child	-1	
	is_under_advanced_protection	FALSE	
	last_downloaded_image_url_with_size	https://lh3.googleusercontent.com/a-/AOh14GgG8-N5QQOBAa0csAOYnSO9_0zNoBBigRvl0wBQ4g=s256-c-ns	
	locale	en	
	picture_url	https://lh3.googleusercontent.com/a-/AOh14GgG8-N5QQOBAa0csAOYnSO9_0zNoBBigRvl0wBQ4g=s96-c	
Local file paths			
	default_directory	<not present>	

Fig. (43). Web browser preferences.

Step 11: The web browser data can also be displayed in SQLite database Figure 44.

installed_extensions

```
SELECT * FROM 'installed_extensions' LIMIT 0,30
```

Execute

name	description	version	app_id	profile
Slides	Create and edit presentations	0.10	aapocclcgogkmnckokdopfmhonfmgoek	Default
Docs	Create and edit documents	0.10	aohghmighlieiainnegkcijnfilokake	Default
Google Drive	Google Drive: create, share and keep all y...	14.5	apdfllckaahabafndbhieahigkjlhalf	Default
Hacker Anonymous Themes New Tab	Replace your new tab with the Hacker An...	12.0.7	bimjehpklddkggeiifpimclnbcicdjpp	Default
YouTube		4.2.8	blpcfgokakmgnkcojhhkbfbldkacnbeo	Default
Adblock Plus - free ad blocker	Block YouTube™ ads, pop-ups & fight mal...	3.12	cfhdojbkjhnklbpkdaibdccddilifddb	Default
Galaxy-View	Galaxy-view	1.3	dcbeddldohkakodfncjnkkjfojggbahp	Default
Sheets	Create and edit spreadsheets	1.2	felcaaldnbdncclmgdcncolpebgiejap	Default
Google Docs Offline	Edit, create, and view your documents, sp...	1.39.0	ghbmnnjooekpmoecnnnilnnbdlolhkhi	Default
Youtube Video Downloader	YouTube to MP3/MP4 video converter for ...	1.3	gjndphdopalgpbbhdlgphjgfccacnbja	Default
APK Downloader	Download APK & OBB from Google Play St...	1.2.0	idkigghdjmipnppaeahkpcoaiphjdccm	Default
Youtube downloader v2mate & keepvid	Youtube downloader & Converter for v2m...	1.1	ifldipeaaoaoaiipbdniidfondiodimi	Default

Fig. (44). Data in SQLite Database.

CHALLENGES AND CONSIDERATIONS

Despite the wealth of information provided by web browser artifacts, forensic examiners may encounter several challenges and considerations:

- Encryption and Compression: Modern browsers employ encryption and compression techniques to protect sensitive data, making it more challenging to extract and analyze browser artifacts. Forensic tools and techniques must adapt to these encryption mechanisms to recover encrypted data effectively.
- Anti-Forensic Techniques: Perpetrators may employ anti-forensic techniques to obfuscate or destroy browser artifacts, such as clearing browsing history, deleting cookies, or using privacy-enhancing tools. Forensic examiners must be vigilant in identifying and circumventing these anti-forensic measures to recover relevant evidence. This is discussed in detail in Chapter 9.

- Platform and Browser Variability: Web browser artifacts may vary significantly across different platforms (*e.g.*, Windows, macOS, Linux) and browser versions, necessitating a comprehensive understanding of platform-specific nuances and artifacts. Forensic tools and techniques must be adaptable to these variations to ensure comprehensive analysis and accurate interpretation of findings.
- Data Retention Policies: Some browsers and websites may implement data retention policies that limit the lifespan of browser artifacts, such as automatically deleting browsing history after a specified period. Forensic examiners must consider these policies when conducting investigations and prioritize timely acquisition of relevant data.
- Legal and Ethical Considerations: Forensic examiners must adhere to legal and ethical guidelines when extracting, analysing, and presenting browser artifacts as evidence. This includes obtaining appropriate authorization for data acquisition, ensuring data integrity and chain of custody, and protecting the privacy rights of individuals involved in the investigation.

FUTURE DIRECTIONS AND EMERGING TRENDS

As technology continues to evolve, web browser forensics faces several emerging trends and future directions:

- Mobile and IoT Devices: With the proliferation of mobile devices and Internet of Things (IoT) devices, forensic examiners must adapt their methodologies to address the unique challenges posed by these platforms. This includes extracting and analyzing browser artifacts from mobile browsers, apps, and IoT devices, as well as integrating mobile forensics with traditional desktop forensics.
- Cloud-Based Browsing: The shift towards cloud-based browsing platforms presents new challenges and opportunities for forensic examiners. Analyzing browser artifacts stored in the cloud requires novel techniques and tools for data acquisition, authentication, and privacy preservation.
- Machine Learning and Artificial Intelligence: Both these technologies hold promise for enhancing the efficiency and accuracy of web browser forensics. These technologies can be leveraged to automate artifact extraction, detect anomalies, and uncover hidden patterns in large datasets, thereby streamlining the investigative process.
- Blockchain and Cryptocurrency Forensics: The rise of blockchain technology and cryptocurrency transactions presents new challenges for forensic examiners in tracing and analysing digital transactions conducted through web browsers. Developing specialized tools and techniques for blockchain and cryptocurrency forensics will be essential in investigating cybercrimes and financial fraud.
- Privacy-Preserving Technologies: As concerns about privacy and data security continue to grow, browsers and websites are increasingly adopting privacy-

preserving technologies such as encryption, anonymization, and decentralized architectures. Forensic examiners must stay abreast of these developments and innovate their methodologies accordingly to adapt to the changing landscape of web browser forensics.

Web browser artifacts constitute a rich source of digital evidence that can provide valuable insights into an individual's online activities, preferences, and behavior. Analyzing these artifacts requires a systematic approach that encompasses data acquisition, parsing, normalization, analysis, and documentation. Despite the challenges posed by encryption, anti-forensic techniques, and platform variability, forensic examiners can leverage innovative tools and methodologies to extract actionable insights from browser artifacts, aiding in the investigation and prosecution of cybercrimes, unauthorized access, and other illicit activities. Looking ahead, the field of web browser forensics is poised for further advancements driven by emerging technologies, evolving threats, and shifting societal norms, necessitating ongoing research, collaboration, and adaptation among forensic professionals and researchers.

CONCLUSION

Web browser forensics is a multifaceted discipline that requires a deep understanding of both technical aspects and legal considerations. Despite the challenges posed by evolving technologies and encryption mechanisms, advancements in forensic tools and methodologies continue to enhance investigators' capabilities in extracting and analysing valuable evidence from web browsers. By staying abreast of emerging trends and adopting a proactive approach to digital investigations, forensic professionals can navigate the complexities of web browser forensics with greater efficiency and accuracy, ultimately aiding in the pursuit of justice.

REFERENCES

[1] Wisemonkeys, "Web Browser Forensics:Tools,Evidence Collection And Analysis," Medium, Jun. 28, 2023. Available from: https://medium.com/@wisemonkeysoffpage/web-browser-forensics-to-ls-evidence-collection-and-analysis-162a175fda87

[2] A. Bhardwaj, F. Al-Turjman, M. Kumar, T. Stephan, and L. Mostarda, "Capturing-the-Invisible (CTI): Behavior-Based Attacks Recognition in IoT-Oriented Industrial Control Systems", *IEEE Access,* vol. 8, pp. 104956-104966, 2020. [http://dx.doi.org/10.1109/ACCESS.2020.2998983]

[3] "Browser Artifacts - HackTricks," Hacktricks.xyz, 2022. Available from: https://book.hacktricks.xyz/generic-methodologies-and-resources/ba-ic-forensic-methodology/specific-software-file-type-tricks/browser-artifacts

[4] A. Bhardwaj, F. Al-Turjman, V. Sapra, M. Kumar, and T. Stephan, "Privacy-aware detection framework to mitigate new-age phishing attacks", *Comput. Electr. Eng.,* vol. 96, p. 107546, 2021. [http://dx.doi.org/10.1016/j.compeleceng.2021.107546]

[5] Kaspersky, "What are cookies?," Kaspersky, 2024. Available from: https://www.kaspersky.com/resource-center/definitions/cookies

[6] "What is Browser History? - Exploring Browser Privacy Risks," Reasonlabs.com, 2023. Available from: https://cyberpedia.reasonlabs.com/EN/browser%20history.html

[7] J. Holcombe, "What Is Cached Data? Explore 3 Easy Ways to Clear It," Kinsta®, Dec. 06, 2021. Available from: https://kinsta.com/blog/what-is-cached-data/

[8] S. Harris, "Understanding Your Browser History | Cookies & Caches," Allconnect, Aug. 01, 2020. Available from: https://www.allconnect.com/blog/understanding-your-browser-history

[9] "Bookmark in Google Chrome Browser," GeeksforGeeks, Sep. 28, 2023. Available from: https://www.geeksforgeeks.org/bookmark-in-google-chrome-browser/ (accessed Apr. 15, 2024).

[10] "HTML form method Attribute," www.w3schools.com. Available from: https://www.w3schools.com/tags/att_form_method.asp

[11] S. Datta, "What Are Sessions? How Do They Work? | Baeldung on Computer Science," www.baeldung.com, May 02, 2023. Available from: https://www.baeldung.com/cs/web-sessions

[12] "What is autofill? | Definition from TechTarget," WhatIs. Available from: https://www.techtarget.com/whatis/definition/autofill

[13] "Firefox browser features," Mozilla. Available from: https://www.mozilla.org/en-US/firefox/features (accessed Apr. 15, 2024).

[14] Wikipedia Contributors, "Web browser," Wikipedia, Feb. 04, 2019. Available from: https://en.wikipedia.org/wiki/Web_browser

[15] Wikipedia Contributors, "Google Chrome," Wikipedia, Feb. 04, 2019. Available from: https://en.wikipedia.org/wiki/Google_Chrome

[16] Google, "Chrome Browser system requirements - Google Chrome Enterprise Help," Google.com, 2012. Available from: https://support.google.com/chrome/a/answer/7100626?hl=en

[17] K. Kaushik, A. Bhardwaj, M. Kumar, S. K. Gupta, and A. Gupta, "A novel machine learning□based framework for detecting fake Instagram profiles", *Concurrency and Computation: Practice and Experience,* vol. 34, no. 28, p. e7349, 2022.
[http://dx.doi.org/10.1002/cpe.7349]

[18] A. Bhardwaj, S. Bharany, A. Almogren, A. Ur Rehman, and H. Hamam, "Proactive threat hunting to detect persistent behaviour-based advanced adversaries", *Egyptian Informatics Journal,* vol. 27, p. 100510, 2024.
[http://dx.doi.org/10.1016/j.eij.2024.100510]

CHAPTER 8

Anti-forensics Techniques

Abstract: Anti Forensics is a collection of methods and approaches to obstruct and avoid Digital Forensic investigations. For legal purposes, like criminal investigations or civil lawsuits, Digital Forensics includes gathering, preserving, analyzing, and presenting digital evidence. To make it more difficult for Forensic analysts to reconstruct events, assign acts to particular people, or prove guilt or innocence, people or organizations use Anti-Forensic strategies to obfuscate, distort, or delete digital evidence. The chapter presents techniques procedures and countermeasures for digital anti-forensics. The chapter also discusses anti-forensics ethical and legal ramifications.

Keywords: Anti-forensics, Cybercrime, Digital evidence, Digital forensics.

INTRODUCTION

Almost every human action in the modern world is connected in some way to one or more digital footprints. Because of this, Digital Forensics is now used in practically all cases, whether they are civil or criminal. A subfield of forensic science called "Digital Forensics" [1] is concerned with the recognition, storage, examination, and presentation of digital evidence in court. Finding information relevant to civil lawsuits, criminal investigations, or cybersecurity matters requires applying scientific methods and techniques to the gathering, analysis, and interpretation of data from digital devices and systems.

Digital forensics investigations follow a rigorous, consecutive process [2] as presented below:

i. Identification of digital devices and data sources relevant to an incidence.

ii. Maintaining the authenticity and custody chain of digital evidence to guarantee its acceptance in a court of law.

iii. Collection of digital evidence using forensically sound techniques to prevent alteration or contamination.

iv. Examination of the acquired data using specialized tools and techniques to extract relevant information and artifacts.

Akashdeep Bhardwaj, Pradeep Singh & Ajay Prasad

v. Analysis of the findings to reconstruct events, identify patterns, establish timelines, and attribute actions to specific individuals or entities.

vi. Presentation of the findings and conclusions in a clear, concise, and legally defensible manner, often through written reports or expert testimony in court.

Digital Forensics gathers, examines, and analyzes digital evidence using a range of methods and instruments. This includes network monitoring tools for recording and analyzing network traffic [3], Forensic analysis software [2] for parsing and interpreting data, Forensic imaging tools for making bit-by-bit copies of storage devices, and specialized hardware for removing data from embedded systems and mobile devices. Digital Forensics experts must follow all legal and ethical guidelines when conducting their investigation. This entails securing the required approval to carry out the investigation [4], guaranteeing the authenticity and admissibility of digital evidence, upholding people's right to privacy, and protecting the security and confidentiality of sensitive data. Since digital forensics offers insightful information about digital activity, it is essential to contemporary law enforcement [5], cybersecurity, and legal processes [6].

Contrary to the above statement, a digital investigator must be aware of such methods and be ready to overcome such situations where anti-forensics has been employed. Thus, Anti-Forensic Countermeasures [7] define certain tools and techniques designed specifically to detect and mitigate anti-forensic activities, employed by forensic investigators and security professionals. Anti-forensic tactics in cybercrime deal with examining how cybercriminals utilize anti-forensic techniques to cover their tracks and evade law enforcement [8].

Anti-forensics techniques can be viewed in the following three categories in terms of the approaches that are involved:

- Data Security tactics [9].
- Evidence Destruction tactics [10].
- Evidence Manipulation tactics [11].
- Obfuscation tactics [12].

Fig. (**1**) presents an outline of various means and methods of the above categories. The further sections of the chapter will discuss these in detail with various forensics countermeasures. The use of anti-forensic techniques raises important legal and ethical considerations [13]. While individuals may employ such tactics to protect their privacy or security, their use in criminal activities can have serious legal consequences. Additionally, the legality and admissibility of evidence obtained through anti-forensic methods [14] may be contested in court. Anti-

Countermeasures against cryptography aim to mitigate its effectiveness in concealing evidence and hindering investigations. Some of the main cryptographic countermeasures include:

- Cryptanalysis: Cryptanalysis involves the study of cryptographic techniques and algorithms to identify weaknesses or vulnerabilities that could be exploited to break encryption. By understanding the underlying principles of cryptography, forensic analysts can develop techniques to decrypt encrypted data or recover cryptographic keys.
- Brute Force Attacks: In a brute force attack, every key or password combination is methodically tried until the right one is discovered. This method can be laborious and resource-intensive, but it can also occasionally work, especially when used against insecure encryption methods or short keys.
- Side-Channel Attacks: As shown in Fig. (**2**), side-channel attacks [20] take advantage of unintentional information leakage from cryptographic devices, including timing data, power usage, or electromagnetic emissions. Forensic investigators might be able to obtain cryptographic keys or learn more about the encryption process by examining these side channels.
- Key Recovery: In some cases, Forensic analysts may attempt to recover cryptographic keys through various means, such as analysing memory dumps, examining network traffic, or exploiting vulnerabilities in the encryption implementation. Key recovery techniques can be effective in cases where cryptographic keys are inadvertently leaked or stored insecurely.
- Legal Measures: In certain jurisdictions, legal measures such as court orders or warrants may be used to compel individuals or organizations to provide access to encrypted data or cryptographic keys. Additionally, law enforcement agencies may collaborate with cryptographic experts or utilize specialized tools to assist in decryption efforts.
- Continuous Research and Development: Cryptography is a constantly evolving field, with researchers continuously developing new algorithms, protocols, and techniques to improve security and address emerging threats. Forensic analysts must stay abreast of the latest advancements in cryptography to effectively counter anti-forensic tactics.
- By employing these countermeasures, forensic analysts can enhance their ability to detect, analyse, and mitigate the use of cryptography in anti-forensic contexts, ultimately aiding in the investigation and prosecution of criminal activities.

STEGANOGRAPHY

The technique of discreetly hiding sensitive information within less-than-secret materials, such text, audio files, or pictures, is known as steganography. In the context of anti-forensics, steganography can be used to hide incriminating evidence or communication between perpetrators, making it difficult for forensic investigators to detect and analyse [21]. In 2001, investigators uncovered a case involving the use of steganography by terrorists to communicate covertly. Al-Qaeda operatives reportedly used steganography to embed messages within digital images shared on the internet [22], allowing them to communicate without raising suspicion or attracting the attention of authorities. Al-Qaeda operatives allegedly used software tools capable of embedding encrypted messages within digital images. These messages were then shared on publicly accessible websites or forums, appearing as ordinary images to the casual observer. However, hidden within the images were encrypted instructions or communications intended for other operatives.

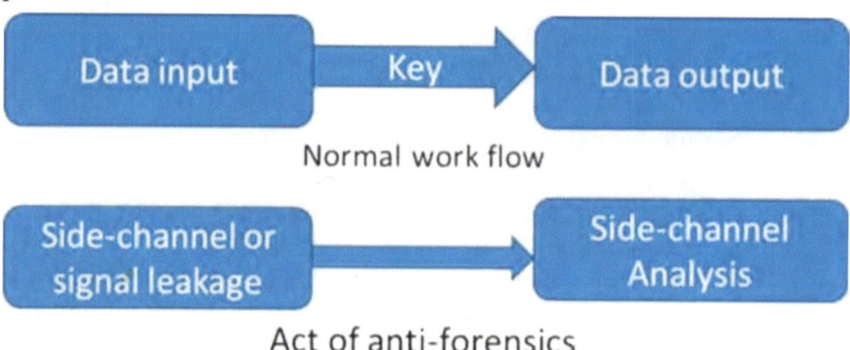

Fig. (2). Side channel analysis.

The use of steganography allowed terrorists to bypass traditional surveillance methods and evade detection by law enforcement agencies. Forensic investigators faced significant challenges in identifying and decrypting the hidden messages, as they appeared as innocuous image files. While specific details of these operations remain classified, the case highlighted the effectiveness of steganography in facilitating covert communications and the challenges it poses to forensic investigations. Steganography has also been used in cases of child exploitation to conceal illegal images or videos from law enforcement scrutiny [23]. Perpetrators may embed illicit content within seemingly innocuous images or videos, making it more difficult for forensic investigators to detect and prosecute offenders. In one notable case, investigators uncovered a network of individuals engaged in the distribution of child exploitation material. Perpetrators used steganography to conceal illegal images within legitimate-looking files, such as family photos or nature scenes. By embedding illicit content within innocuous files, perpetrators were able to evade detection by law enforcement agencies and conceal their criminal activities. Forensic analysts faced the daunting task of identifying and extracting hidden content from a vast amount of digital media, requiring specialized tools and techniques for steganalysis.

While law enforcement agencies have made significant strides in combating child exploitation and trafficking, cases involving steganography present unique challenges due to the covert nature of the communication and the difficulty of detecting hidden content. As steganography techniques continue to evolve, Forensic investigators must remain vigilant and adapt their methods to detect and analyse hidden information effectively.

Countermeasures against the use of Steganography involve techniques and strategies aimed at detecting, analysing, and mitigating the concealment of hidden information within Digital media.

Countermeasures incorporated to counter the use of steganography [24]:

- Steganalysis Tools and Techniques: Steganalysis involves the detection and analysis of hidden data within digital media. Specialized steganalysis tools and procedures are employed by Forensic investigators to detect suspicious patterns or anomalies that can point to the existence of hidden information. These tools may analyse file metadata, statistical properties, or visual artifacts to detect steganographic content.
- Statistical Analysis: Steganographic techniques often introduce subtle changes to the statistical properties of digital media, such as image or audio files. Statistical analysis methods can be employed to identify deviations from expected patterns, such as irregularities in pixel values or frequency distributions, which may indicate the presence of hidden data (Fig. **3**).
- Visual Inspection: Visual inspection of digital media can sometimes reveal artifacts or anomalies that suggest the presence of steganographic content. Forensic investigators may carefully examine images or videos for inconsistencies, unusual patterns, or suspicious alterations that may not be immediately apparent to the naked eye (Fig. **4**).
- Comparison with Known Cover Media: By comparing suspicious files with known cover media (*i.e.*, unaltered versions of the same content), Forensic analysts can identify discrepancies or differences introduced by steganographic embedding techniques. This approach can help detect subtle alterations or modifications made to conceal hidden information.
- Metadata Analysis: File sizes, compression settings, timestamps, and other information may contain traces or artifacts from steganographic processes. Through the analysis of metadata associated with Digital media files, investigators might unearth crucial details regarding the history and provenance of the content, as well as instances of steganography.
- Digital Watermarking Detection: For copyright protection or authentication, Digital watermarking is a related technology that embeds undetectable

identifiers or signatures within digital data. Digital watermarks can be identified and analyzed using steganography techniques; these techniques can be utilized either in addition to or instead of steganography.

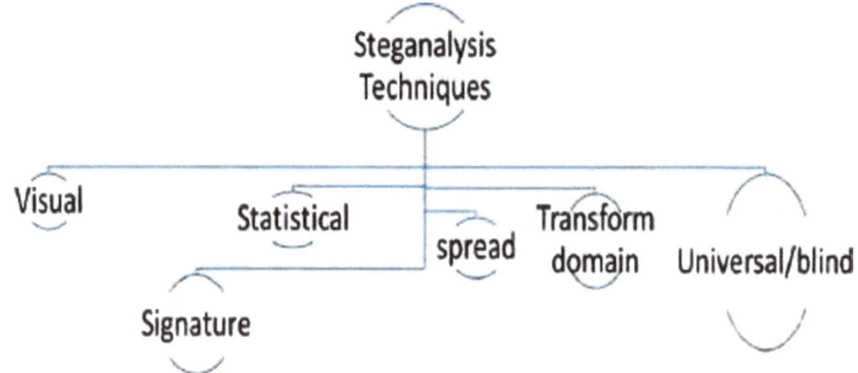

Fig. (3). Steganalysis techniques.

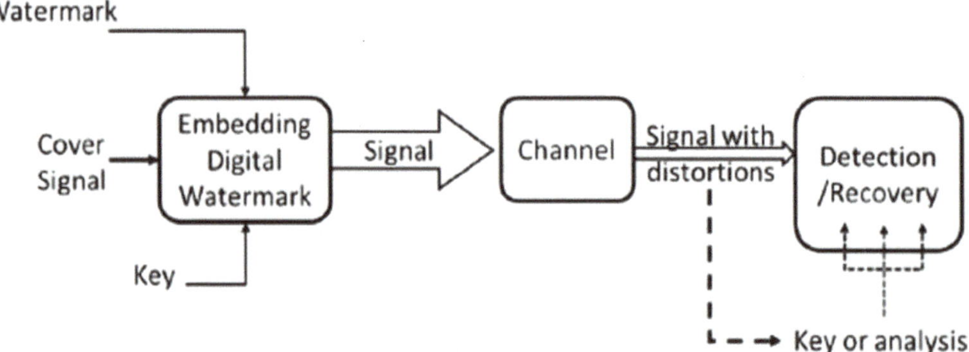

Fig. (4). Digital watermark detection.

DIGITAL LOCKS

Digital locks, also known as cryptographic locks, can be utilized in Anti-Forensic contexts to protect sensitive data or communications from unauthorized access or analysis. These locks typically rely on cryptographic techniques to secure information, making it difficult for Forensic investigators to decrypt or access without the appropriate keys or credentials.

Digital locks can be used for Anti-Forensics in the following ways:

- File Encryption: One common application of Digital locks in Anti-Forensics is file encryption. By encrypting files using strong encryption algorithms, individuals or groups can protect their data from unauthorized access or analysis. Forensic investigators may encounter encrypted files during Digital investigations, but without the encryption keys, they are unable to decipher the contents of these files.

- Communication Encryption: Encrypting communications, including voice conversations, emails, and instant messages, is another application for Digital locks. By limiting access to the contents of the communication to the sender and the intended recipient alone, end-to-end encryption techniques guard against third parties—including Forensic analysts—interception or eavesdropping. One can employ techniques, such as Secure S-Box Implementations of AES [25].
- Data Storage Encryption: Digital locks can be applied to encrypt entire storage devices, such as hard drives or USB drives, to protect the data stored on these devices from unauthorized access. Full-disk encryption ensures that all data stored on the device is encrypted, making it inaccessible without the decryption key, even if the device falls into the wrong hands.
- Cloud Storage Encryption: Individuals or organizations may employ Digital locks to encrypt data stored in cloud storage services. By encrypting data before uploading it to the cloud and retaining sole control over the encryption keys, users can prevent unauthorized access to their data, even if the cloud service provider is compromised or subjected to legal requests for data access.
- Mobile Device Encryption: Mobile devices, such as smartphones and tablets, often contain sensitive information that may be targeted by Forensic investigators during investigations. Digital locks can be used to encrypt data stored on mobile devices, including files, messages, and application data, to protect it from unauthorized access [26]. suggests an approach towards encrypted mobile Forensics as illustrated in Fig. (**5**).
- Database Encryption: Digital locks in database systems can be used to encrypt private data kept in databases, including financial records, user credentials, and personally identifiable information (PII). With encryption, you may be sure that even in the event of a database breach, the encrypted data will remain unreadable without the decryption key.

EVIDENCE DESTRUCTION TACTICS

Evidence destruction tactics in Anti-Forensics involve methods aimed at erasing, altering, or otherwise rendering Digital evidence unusable or unrecoverable by Forensic investigators. These tactics are employed by individuals or groups to evade detection, conceal illicit activities, or obstruct Forensic investigations.

During the investigation into the Enron scandal, which involved corporate fraud and accounting irregularities, employees at Enron Corporation engaged in extensive efforts to conceal evidence of their illicit activities. One of the tactics employed was the deliberate deletion of incriminating emails and electronic documents to obstruct the investigation. Enron employees, including executives and managers, were found to have systematically deleted emails and electronic files containing evidence of fraudulent accounting practices, insider trading, and other illegal activities. These deletions were intended to conceal the extent of the wrongdoing and hinder efforts by regulatory agencies and law enforcement to uncover evidence of the fraud. Forensic investigators faced significant challenges in reconstructing the deleted files and recovering evidence of the illicit activities. Despite the deliberate attempts at file deletion, Forensic experts were able to employ specialized data recovery techniques and Forensic analysis methods to reconstruct deleted files and uncover incriminating evidence, contributing to the successful prosecution of individuals involved in the Enron scandal.

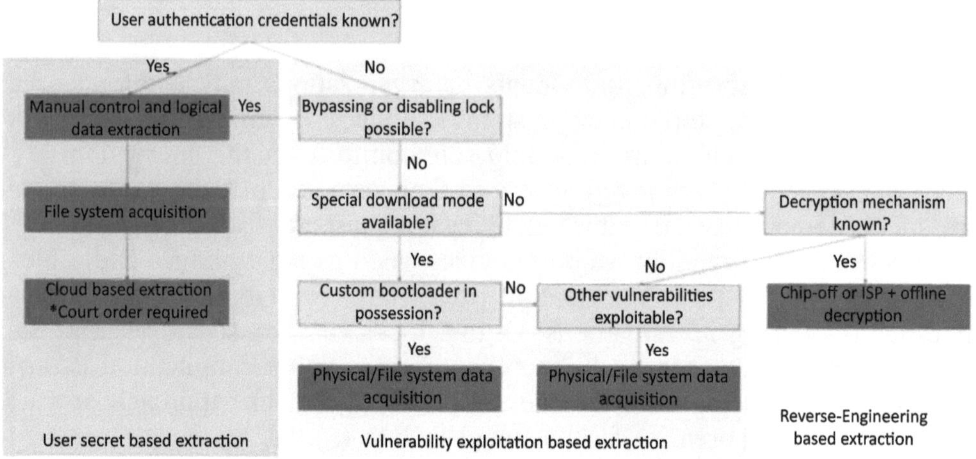

Fig. (5). Cracking an encrypted Mobile device.

- File Deletion: Simply deleting files from a storage device may not permanently erase the data, as it can often be recovered using Forensic tools. However, employing secure deletion techniques, such as overwriting the data multiple times or using file shredding utilities, can make it much more difficult for Forensic analysts to recover the deleted files.
- Data Wiping: Data wiping involves systematically erasing all data from a storage device, effectively rendering it empty or blank. This can be achieved using specialized data-wiping software or utilities that overwrite the entire storage medium with random data patterns multiple times, making it extremely challenging for Forensic tools to recover any remnants of the original data.
- Disk Formatting: Formatting a storage device can also be used as a crude form of evidence destruction. While formatting may erase the file system metadata and directory structure, it does not necessarily overwrite the underlying data, leaving it potentially recoverable by Forensic techniques. However, secure formatting methods that overwrite the entire disk with random data can be more

effective in rendering the data unrecoverable.

- Data Corruption: Deliberately corrupting data on a storage device can hinder Forensic investigations by making the data unusable or difficult to recover. Perpetrators may use various techniques, such as modifying file headers, altering data structures, or introducing random data corruption, to render the evidence unreadable or incoherent.
- Physical Destruction: In extreme cases, perpetrators may resort to physically destroying storage devices or other Digital media to prevent Forensic analysis. This can involve shredding, crushing, burning, or otherwise damaging the hardware beyond repair, effectively eliminating any possibility of recovering data from the destroyed devices.
- Remote Data Wiping: In situations where perpetrators have remote access to devices or systems, they may initiate remote data wiping commands to erase incriminating evidence remotely [27]. This tactic is often employed in cases involving stolen or compromised devices to prevent unauthorized access to sensitive information.
- Anti-Forensic Malware [28]: Some malware strains are specifically designed to employ Anti-Forensic tactics, including evidence destruction. These malware variants may overwrite data, delete files, or corrupt storage devices to thwart Forensic investigations and cover the tracks of malicious activities.

In numerous criminal investigations, perpetrators have attempted to evade detection and prosecution by deleting digital evidence relevant to their crimes. This tactic is often used in cases involving cybercrime [29], financial fraud, or other illicit activities where digital evidence plays a crucial role in establishing guilt or innocence. For example, in cases involving the distribution of illegal content, such as child exploitation material or pirated intellectual property, perpetrators may delete files or erase digital traces of their activities to avoid detection by law enforcement agencies. Similarly, individuals involved in cyberattacks, such as ransomware attacks or data breaches, may attempt to delete logs, erase incriminating files, or wipe data from compromised systems to cover their tracks and evade Forensic investigation.

Despite the efforts of perpetrators to delete digital evidence, Forensic investigators often employ specialized tools and techniques to recover deleted files, reconstruct digital artifacts, and piece together the evidence necessary for prosecution. Through careful forensic analysis and data recovery efforts, investigators can often overcome attempts at file deletion and uncover valuable evidence of criminal activity.

In 2007, TJX Companies, the parent company of retailers such as TJ Maxx and Marshalls, experienced one of the largest data breaches in history. Hackers gained unauthorized access to TJX's computer systems and stole sensitive customer information, including credit card numbers, over several years. As part of the data breach, the perpetrators tampered with logs and other Digital records to conceal their activities and evade detection by Forensic investigators. They altered timestamps, deleted or modified log entries, and manipulated other Digital artifacts to make it difficult for investigators to determine the scope and duration of the breach. The tampering with Digital records posed significant challenges for Forensic analysts tasked with reconstructing the timeline of the breach and identifying the methods used by the attackers. Despite the efforts to tamper with Digital evidence, Forensic experts were able to employ advanced analysis techniques and data recovery methods to uncover evidence of the breach and identify the perpetrators.

In 2011, allegations surfaced regarding the sexual abuse of minors by former Penn State an University assistant football coach [30]. The scandal involved accusations of a cover-up by university officials, who were accused of failing to report the abuse and tampering with evidence to protect the university's reputation. As part of the cover-up, university officials were accused of tampering with Digital evidence, including emails and other electronic records, to conceal their knowledge of the abuse and minimize the university's liability. They allegedly deleted or altered incriminating emails, modified timestamps, and manipulated other Digital artifacts to obstruct the investigation and protect themselves from legal repercussions. The tampering with Digital evidence complicated the Forensic investigation into the scandal, requiring Forensic experts to meticulously examine Digital records and reconstruct the timeline of events. Despite the attempts at data tampering, investigators were able to uncover evidence of the cover-up and hold those responsible accountable for their actions.

These cases illustrate how data tampering can be used as an Anti-Forensics tactic to obstruct investigations and conceal wrongdoing. Despite the challenges posed by tampered Digital evidence, Forensic analysts can often overcome these obstacles through careful analysis and reconstruction of Digital artifacts.

Countermeasures against data tampering in Anti-Forensics involve techniques and strategies aimed at detecting, preventing, and mitigating the manipulation of Digital evidence.

Countermeasures to combat data tampering are listed below.

- Digital Signature and Hashing: Implementing Digital signatures and cryptographic hashing mechanisms can help ensure the integrity of Digital data. Digital signatures offer a way to confirm the legitimacy and consistency of documents or communications, whereas cryptographic hash algorithms produce distinct IDs, or hash values, for Digital files. The hash value will change if the data is altered, alerting Forensic investigators to possible manipulation.

- Secure Logging and Auditing: Implementing secure logging and auditing mechanisms can help detect and deter data tampering by maintaining detailed records of system events and user activities. Secure logs can capture information such as file access, modification timestamps, and user actions, providing Forensic analysts with a reliable audit trail to track changes to Digital evidence.
- File Integrity Monitoring: Deploying file integrity monitoring helps detect unauthorized changes to critical system files, configuration files, and other Digital assets. FIM solutions continuously monitor file attributes and checksums, alerting administrators to any discrepancies or unauthorized modifications that may indicate data tampering.
- Access Controls and Permissions: Implementing robust access controls and permissions can help prevent unauthorized access to Digital evidence and minimize the risk of data tampering. Role-based access control (RBAC), least privilege principles, and strong authentication mechanisms can limit access to sensitive data and prevent unauthorized modifications by unauthorized users.
- Immutable Data Storage: Utilizing immutable data storage solutions can help safeguard Digital evidence from tampering by preventing any modifications or deletions once data is stored. Immutable storage solutions, such as write-onc--read-many (WORM) storage or blockchain-based systems, ensure the integrity and immutability of Digital evidence, making it resistant to tampering.
- Chain of Custody Procedures: Establishing and maintaining a robust chain of custody (CoC) [31] is essential for preserving the integrity and admissibility of Digital evidence in legal proceedings. CoC procedures document the handling and transfer of evidence from collection to analysis, ensuring accountability and traceability throughout the Forensic investigation process. Use of secure processes of capturing and protecting Digital devices need to be incorporated. One such way is to use faradays bags/cages (Fig. **6**) or similar approach to avoid remote data wiping.
- Regular Data Backups: Regularly backing up Digital data can help mitigate the impact of data tampering by providing a means of restoring unaltered copies of files or systems. Backup solutions should employ secure encryption and authentication mechanisms to prevent unauthorized access or manipulation of backup data. By implementing these countermeasures, organizations and Forensic investigators can enhance their ability to detect, prevent, and mitigate data tampering in Anti-Forensic contexts, ensuring the integrity and reliability of Digital evidence in Forensic investigations.

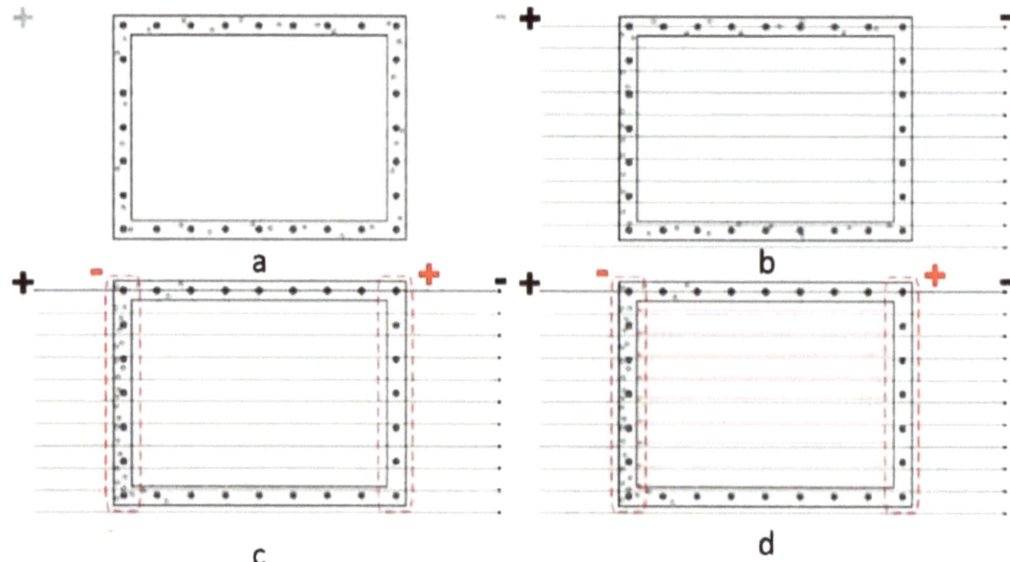

Fig. (6). Faraday Cage - a) Passing Signals, b) Charged Electrons, c) Formation of Charged walls, d) Neutralization of Charges.

EVIDENCE MANIPULATION TACTICS

Evidence manipulation tactics in Anti-Forensics involve techniques aimed at altering, falsifying, or otherwise manipulating Digital evidence to mislead Forensic investigators or obstruct investigations. These tactics are employed by individuals or groups to undermine the integrity and reliability of Digital evidence, making it more challenging for investigators to uncover the truth.

Major evidence manipulation tactics are mentioned below.

- File Forgery: File forgery involves creating counterfeit Digital files or documents that appear genuine but have been intentionally altered or fabricated. Perpetrators may forge documents, spreadsheets, images, or other Digital artifacts to falsify evidence or create false narratives that support their agenda.
- Metadata Manipulation: Metadata manipulation involves altering or falsifying metadata associated with Digital files to misrepresent the origin, creation date, authorship, or other attributes of the files. Perpetrators may modify timestamps, file properties, or other metadata fields to create misleading impressions or conceal incriminating information.
- Digital Image Manipulation: Digital image manipulation encompasses techniques for altering or editing Digital photographs or images to distort reality or create false impressions. Perpetrators may use image editing software to retouch photographs, remove or add elements, or manipulate visual content to mislead Forensic analysts or distort the truth.

- Document Tampering: Document tampering involves altering or modifying electronic documents, such as PDFs, Word documents, or email messages, to falsify information or create false records. Perpetrators may edit text, insert or delete content, or manipulate formatting to fabricate evidence or mislead investigators.
- Database Manipulation: Database manipulation entails altering or falsifying data stored in databases to conceal incriminating information or create false records. Perpetrators may modify database entries, delete or insert records, or manipulate queries to distort the data or mislead Forensic investigators.
- Communication Fabrication: Communication fabrication involves creating counterfeit messages, emails, chat logs, or other Digital communications to falsify evidence or create false narratives. Perpetrators may forge messages, alter timestamps, or fabricate entire conversations to mislead investigators or cast doubt on the authenticity of Digital evidence.
- Tampering with Digital Signatures: Tampering with Digital signatures involves altering or falsifying cryptographic signatures associated with Digital files or messages to undermine their authenticity or integrity. Perpetrators may tamper with Digital signatures to falsify evidence, create false certifications, or manipulate the verification process.
- Manipulation of Memory and Artifacts: Memory Forensics, which involves analysing the volatile memory (RAM) of a computer system, is an important aspect of Digital investigations. Anti-Forensic techniques may seek to manipulate or evade detection in memory by altering the contents of volatile memory, injecting code into running processes, or employing rootkits to hide malicious activities.

Operation Ore was a high-profile international law enforcement operation targeting individuals involved in accessing and distributing child pornography online. In one instance related to Operation Ore, evidence manipulation was used to discredit the validity of Digital evidence and challenge the integrity of the investigation. During the investigation, defense attorneys representing some of the accused individuals alleged that evidence, particularly Digital images depicting child pornography, had been tampered with or planted on their clients' computers. They claimed that malware or other malicious software could have been used to remotely download and store illegal images without the users' knowledge or consent. The defense argued that the presence of illegal images on their clients' computers was not proof of guilt, as the evidence could have been manipulated or fabricated. This raised significant challenges for Forensic investigators, who had to demonstrate the integrity and authenticity of the Digital evidence despite claims of tampering. While the Operation Ore investigation ultimately resulted in numerous convictions, the case highlighted the complexities and challenges associated with Digital evidence manipulation in Anti-Forensic contexts, particularly in cases involving sensitive and contentious issues such as child exploitation.

The Enron email investigation involved the examination of thousands of emails and electronic documents related to the Enron scandal, which exposed corporate fraud and accounting irregularities at the energy company. Evidence manipulation tactics were used by perpetrators to conceal incriminating information and obstruct the investigation. During the investigation, it was discovered that certain individuals at Enron had engaged in evidence manipulation by deleting or altering emails and electronic documents to conceal their involvement in fraudulent activities. Perpetrators sought to undermine the integrity of the investigation and create false narratives by tampering with Digital evidence.

Forensic investigators faced significant challenges in reconstructing the email trail and uncovering evidence of fraud amidst attempts at evidence manipulation. They had to employ advanced Forensic techniques and data recovery methods to recover deleted emails, analyse metadata, and reconstruct the timeline of events. Despite the efforts to manipulate Digital evidence, Forensic experts were able to uncover incriminating information and contribute to the successful prosecution of individuals involved in the Enron scandal. The case underscored the importance of robust Forensic methodologies and countermeasures to combat evidence manipulation in complex investigations.

These cases illustrate how evidence manipulation can be used as an Anti-Forensic tactic to challenge the integrity of Digital evidence and obstruct Forensic investigations. Despite the challenges posed by evidence manipulation, Forensic investigators can often overcome these obstacles through meticulous analysis, advanced Forensic techniques, and adherence to best practices in Digital Forensic investigations.

Countermeasures against evidence tampering in Anti-Forensics involve techniques and strategies aimed at detecting, preventing, and mitigating the manipulation of Digital evidence to undermine Forensic investigations.

Countermeasures to combat evidence tampering are:

- Digital Signatures and Hashing: Implementing Digital signatures and cryptographic hashing mechanisms can help ensure the integrity of Digital evidence. Digital signatures provide a means of verifying the authenticity and integrity of files or messages, while cryptographic hash functions generate unique identifiers (hash values) for Digital content. Any tampering with the data will result in a change in the hash value, alerting Forensic investigators to potential manipulation.

- Secure Logging and Auditing: Implementing secure logging and auditing mechanisms can help detect and deter evidence tampering by maintaining detailed records of system events and user activities. Secure logs can capture information such as file access, modification timestamps, and user actions, providing Forensic analysts with a reliable audit trail to track changes to Digital evidence.
- Chain of Custody Procedures: Establishing and maintaining a robust chain of custody (CoC) is essential for preserving the integrity and admissibility of Digital evidence in legal proceedings. CoC procedures document the handling and transfer of evidence from collection to analysis, ensuring accountability and traceability throughout the Forensic investigation process.
- Data Encryption: Encrypting sensitive Digital evidence can help protect it from unauthorized access and tampering. Strong encryption algorithms and secure key management practices can prevent unauthorized parties from modifying or tampering with encrypted data, ensuring its integrity and confidentiality.
- Digital Watermarking: Digital watermarking involves embedding imperceptible identifiers or signatures within Digital media to deter tampering and ensure authenticity. Watermarking techniques can be applied to images, documents, videos, and other Digital assets to provide a means of verifying their origin and integrity.
- File Integrity Monitoring: Deploying file integrity monitoring (FIM) systems can help detect unauthorized changes to critical system files, configuration files, and other Digital assets. FIM solutions continuously monitor file attributes and checksums, alerting administrators to any discrepancies or unauthorized modifications that may indicate evidence tampering (Fig. 7).
- Access Controls and Permissions: Implementing robust access controls and permissions can help prevent unauthorized access to Digital evidence and minimize the risk of tampering. Role-based access control (RBAC), least privilege principles, and strong authentication mechanisms can limit access to sensitive data and prevent unauthorized modifications by unauthorized users.
- Regular Data Backups: Regularly backing up Digital evidence can help mitigate the impact of evidence tampering by providing a means of restoring unaltered copies of files or systems. Backup solutions should employ secure encryption and authentication mechanisms to prevent unauthorized access or manipulation of backup data.

Evidence manipulation tactics demonstrate the diverse range of techniques employed by individuals or groups in Anti-Forensic contexts to manipulate Digital evidence and undermine the integrity of Forensic investigations. Forensic analysts must remain vigilant and employ robust methodologies and techniques to detect and counteract evidence manipulation in Digital investigations.

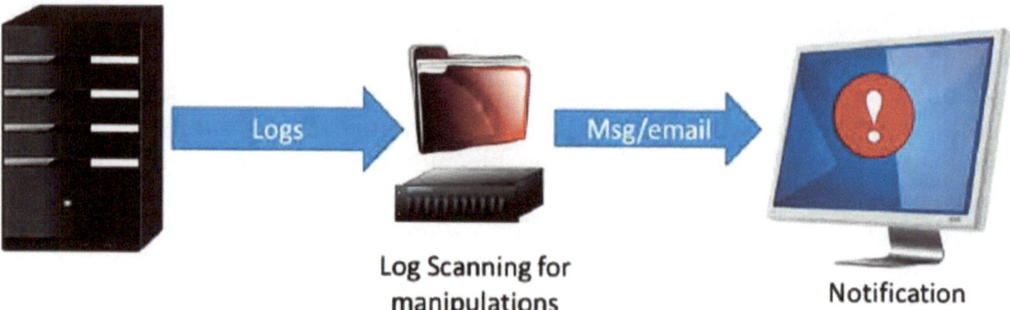

Fig. (7). File Integrity Monitoring.

OBFUSCATION TACTICS

Obfuscation tactics in Anti-Forensics involve techniques aimed at concealing, disguising, or obfuscating Digital evidence to hinder Forensic analysis and investigation. These tactics are employed by individuals or groups to make it more challenging for Forensic investigators to interpret and extract meaningful information from Digital artifacts. Here are several obfuscation tactics used in Anti-Forensics:

- File and Data Compression: Compressing files or data can obfuscate their contents and reduce their size, making it more challenging for Forensic tools to analyse or reconstruct the original information. Compression techniques, such as ZIP or RAR archives, can conceal files within compressed containers, complicating Forensic analysis and data recovery efforts.
- File and Data Fragmentation: Fragmenting files or data into smaller pieces and scattering them across different locations or sectors of a storage device can obfuscate their structure and make them more difficult to reconstruct. Fragmentation techniques can hinder Forensic investigators' efforts to recover and analyse Digital evidence by dispersing it across multiple fragments or clusters.
- Data Encoding: Encoding data using encoding schemes, such as Base64 or hexadecimal encoding, can obfuscate its original format and structure. By converting data into alternative representations, perpetrators can conceal sensitive information and evade detection by Forensic tools that rely on pattern recognition or signature-based analysis.
- Code Obfuscation: Obfuscating code or scripts using techniques such as renaming variables, adding redundant instructions, or employing code obfuscation tools can obscure the functionality and purpose of the code, making it more difficult for Forensic analysts to understand and reverse-engineer [32]. Code obfuscation is commonly used in malware to evade detection by Antivirus software and Forensic analysis tools.

- Network Traffic Obfuscation: Obfuscating network traffic using encryption, tunnelling, or traffic shaping techniques can conceal communication patterns, protocols, or payload contents [33], making it more challenging for Forensic analysts to monitor and analyse network activities. Perpetrators may employ encryption protocols, such as VPNs or Tor, to anonymize their online activities and evade detection.
- Rootkit installation: in Anti-Forensics Rootkit installation refers to the clandestine deployment of rootkits on targeted systems to conceal malicious activities and evade detection by Forensic investigators [34]. Rootkits are stealthy malware programs designed to gain privileged access to a computer system while hiding their presence and activities from users and security software. They operate at the lowest levels of the operating system, known as the kernel, allowing them to exert control over system functions and hide their presence effectively.
- Memory Forensics evasion: This refers to techniques used by attackers to prevent or hinder the detection and analysis of malicious activities and artifacts in a system's volatile memory (RAM) by Forensic investigators. Memory Forensics involves the examination and analysis of data stored in a computer's RAM to uncover evidence of malicious activities, such as malware infections, unauthorized access, or data theft (Fig. **8**). However, attackers may employ various evasion techniques to make it more difficult for Forensic analysts to identify and attribute malicious behaviour in memory. Some common memory Forensics evasion techniques include Rootkit-based Evasion, Memory Injection, Memory Encryption, Process Hollowing and Process Doppelgänging, Memory Scanning Evasion, Fileless Malware, Memory Compression, *etc*.

Fig. (8). Memory Forensic analysis.

These obfuscation tactics demonstrate the diverse range of techniques employed by individuals or groups in Anti-Forensic contexts to obscure Digital evidence and hinder Forensic investigations. Forensic analysts must remain vigilant and employ advanced techniques and tools to overcome obfuscation challenges and uncover meaningful information from Digital artifacts.

The Zeus banking Trojan [35], also known as Zbot, was a notorious piece of malware designed to steal sensitive financial information, such as online banking credentials and credit card details, from infected systems. In one instance, the Zeus malware employed obfuscation techniques to evade detection by Antivirus software and Forensic analysis tools. The Zeus malware used various obfuscation techniques, including code encryption, packing, and polymorphism, to conceal its malicious functionality and evade detection. The malware employed encryption algorithms to encrypt its code and configuration files, making it difficult for traditional Antivirus programs to detect and analyse. Additionally, the malware used polymorphic techniques to generate unique variants with different code signatures, further complicating detection and analysis efforts.

The obfuscation tactics employed by the Zeus banking Trojan enabled it to evade detection by traditional security solutions and carry out successful attacks against numerous individuals and organizations worldwide. The sophisticated evasion techniques posed significant challenges for Forensic investigators attempting to analyse and mitigate the threats.

Another example of obfuscation is the TeslaCrypt which was a notorious ransomware strain that targeted Windows systems, encrypting users' files and demanding ransom payments for decryption keys. In one instance, TeslaCrypt employed obfuscation tactics to conceal its malicious activities and evade detection by Antivirus software and Forensic analysis tools. TeslaCrypt used obfuscation techniques to conceal its ransomware payload and evade detection by security solutions. The malware employed code obfuscation and encryption to make analysis and detection more challenging for security researchers and Forensic analysts. Additionally, TeslaCrypt utilized packing techniques to compress and obfuscate its executable files, making it more difficult for Antivirus programs to detect and analyse.

The obfuscation tactics employed by TeslaCrypt ransomware enabled it to evade detection by traditional security solutions and carry out successful attacks against numerous victims, encrypting their files and demanding ransom payments for decryption. The use of obfuscation techniques posed significant challenges for Forensic investigators attempting to analyse and mitigate ransomware threats.

These use cases prove how obfuscation tactics are commonly used by malware authors and cybercriminals as Anti-Forensics techniques to evade detection and hinder Forensic analysis efforts. The sophistication of these obfuscation techniques underscores the importance of employing advanced analysis methods and countermeasures to detect and mitigate cyber threats effectively.

Countermeasures against obfuscation tactics in Anti-Forensics involve techniques and strategies aimed at detecting, mitigating, and overcoming the obfuscation of Digital evidence to facilitate Forensic analysis and investigation.

There are several countermeasures to combat obfuscation tactics as listed below.

- Memory Forensics Analysis: Conducting comprehensive memory Forensics analysis can help uncover hidden or obfuscated artifacts in volatile memory (RAM). Memory Forensics tools and techniques can identify and extract malicious code, payloads, or artifacts hidden in memory, enabling Forensic analysts to reconstruct the timeline of events and identify the scope of malicious activities.
- Employing code de-obfuscation techniques can help unravel obfuscated or encrypted code used by attackers to conceal malicious activities. Reverse engineering tools and static analysis techniques can be used to de-obfuscate and analyse obscured code, revealing its functionality and purpose.
- Signature-based Detection: Utilizing signature-based detection methods can help identify known obfuscation patterns or indicators of compromise (IOCs) associated with malicious activities. Signature-based detection engines can scan Digital artifacts, such as files, memory dumps, or network traffic, for signatures or patterns indicative of obfuscated code, malware, or suspicious behaviour.
- Heuristic Analysis: Implementing heuristic analysis techniques [36] can help identify anomalies, deviations, or suspicious behaviours indicative of obfuscation or tampering attempts. Heuristic analysis algorithms can analyse system behaviour, file attributes, or network traffic patterns to detect and flag potentially obfuscated or manipulated data for further investigation.
- Behavioural Analysis: Conducting behavioural analysis of Digital artifacts and systems can help identify abnormal or suspicious behaviour indicative of obfuscation or evasion attempts. Behavioural analysis tools and techniques can monitor system activities, process behaviour, or network communications to detect anomalies or deviations from normal operation.
- Data Decryption: Employing decryption techniques and cryptographic analysis can help recover encrypted or obfuscated data used by attackers to conceal malicious activities. Cryptanalysis tools and cryptographic experts can analyse encryption algorithms, keys, or cipher texts to decrypt encrypted data and uncover its original content.

ADVANCED FORENSICS

Forensic investigators can use advanced tools and techniques specifically designed to overcome obfuscation challenges in Digital investigations. These tools may include memory Forensics frameworks, code de-obfuscation tools, and data recovery utilities capable of handling encrypted or compressed data. There are various advanced Forensic tools designed to handle Anti-Forensic challenges and aid Forensic investigators in detecting, analysing, and mitigating the effects of Anti-Forensic tactics as listed below.

- Volatility Framework: Volatility [37] is an advanced open-source memory Forensics framework that enables Forensic analysts to extract and analyse Digital artifacts from volatile memory (RAM). It provides a wide range of plugins for analysing memory dumps, including processes, network connections, registry keys, and file system structures. Volatility is effective in detecting and analysing Anti-Forensic techniques such as rootkit installation, process injection, and memory-based malware.
- IDA Pro: IDA Pro [38] is a widely used interactive disassembler and debugger that allows Forensic analysts to analyse and reverse-engineer binary executables. It provides advanced features for code analysis, graphing, and debugging, making it suitable for de-obfuscating and analysing obscured or encrypted code. IDA Pro is instrumental in handling Anti-Forensic tactics involving code obfuscation, packing, and encryption.
- Wireshark: Wireshark [39] is a powerful open-source network protocol analyser that enables Forensic analysts to capture, dissect, and analyse network traffic. It provides comprehensive features for inspecting packet contents, filtering traffic, and reconstructing network conversations, making it effective in identifying and attributing malicious activities. Wireshark is useful for detecting network obfuscation techniques and uncovering hidden communication channels used by attackers.
- Sleuth Kit and Autopsy: The Sleuth Kit (TSK) [40] is an open-source Forensic toolkit that provides command-line tools for analysing disk images and file systems. Autopsy is a graphical interface built on top of TSK, offering advanced features for disk imaging, file analysis, and keyword searching. Sleuth Kit and Autopsy are effective in handling Anti-Forensic tactics involving file deletion, hiding, and data carving.
- Cuckoo Sandbox: Cuckoo Sandbox [41] is an open-source automated malware analysis platform that enables Forensic analysts to execute and analyse suspicious files in isolated environments. It provides features for dynamic analysis, behaviour monitoring, and threat intelligence integration, allowing analysts to uncover malware capabilities and evasion techniques. Cuckoo Sandbox is useful for analysing Anti-Forensic tactics employed by malware, such as code obfuscation, sandbox evasion, and network communication encryption.
- OSSEC: OSSEC (Open Source Security) [42] is an open-source host-based intrusion detection system (HIDS) that provides file integrity monitoring (FIM),

log analysis, and real-time alerting capabilities. It monitors system files, registry keys, and configuration settings for unauthorized changes, helping Forensic analysts detect Anti-Forensic activities such as file manipulation and tampering. OSSEC is effective in handling Anti-Forensic tactics aimed at modifying system configurations, compromising system integrity, and evading detection.

- Ghidra: Ghidra is a free and open-source software reverse engineering (SRE) suite developed by the National Security Agency (NSA) [43]. It provides features for disassembling, decompiling, and analysing binary executables, making it suitable for code analysis and reverse engineering tasks. Ghidra is useful for analysing Anti-Forensic techniques involving code obfuscation, packing, and encryption.

These advanced Forensic tools provide Forensic analysts with the capabilities to overcome Anti-Forensic challenges and effectively investigate Digital incidents, ensuring the integrity and reliability of Digital evidence in Forensic investigations.

LEGAL AND ETHICAL ASPECTS

Tackling Anti-Forensics presents various legal and ethical considerations that Forensic investigators must navigate to ensure their actions comply with laws, regulations, and ethical standards.

Here are some of the key legal and ethical aspects involved:

- Legal Compliance: It is crucial to abide by the laws and rules controlling computer crime, data protection, and Digital investigations. Investigators must guarantee that their actions, encompassing the utilization of Forensic tools and techniques, conform to relevant legal frameworks such as the Information Technology (IT) Act, 2000 in India, the General Data Protection Regulation (GDPR) in the European Union, and the Computer Fraud and Abuse Act (CFAA) in the United States.
- Search and Seizure Laws: Investigators must adhere to search and seizure laws when collecting Digital evidence. This includes obtaining proper authorization, such as search warrants or subpoenas, before seizing or accessing electronic devices or data. Violations of search and seizure laws can lead to the exclusion of evidence or legal repercussions.
- Data Privacy and Confidentiality: Respecting the privacy rights of individuals and organizations is essential. Investigators must handle Digital evidence in a manner that protects sensitive information and ensures confidentiality. This includes implementing appropriate security measures to safeguard evidence and complying with data protection laws and regulations.

- Informed Consent: Obtaining informed consent from relevant parties before conducting Forensic investigations is crucial, particularly when accessing personal devices or sensitive data. Investigators must inform individuals about the purpose, scope, and potential impact of the investigation, as well as any risks or consequences associated with the collection and analysis of Digital evidence.
- Ethical Conduct: Upholding ethical principles and professional standards is paramount in Forensic investigations. Investigators must demonstrate integrity, objectivity, and impartiality throughout the investigation process, avoiding conflicts of interest, biases, or unethical behaviour that could compromise the integrity of the investigation or the rights of individuals involved.
- Transparency and Accountability: Maintaining transparency and accountability in Forensic investigations is essential for building trust and credibility. Investigators should document their actions, methodologies, and findings accurately and comprehensively, ensuring transparency in the investigative process and facilitating peer review and oversight.
- Expert Testimony: When presenting Digital evidence in legal proceedings, Forensic experts must provide accurate, reliable, and unbiased testimony based on sound Forensic methodologies and practices. Expert witnesses should adhere to professional standards of competence and ethics, ensuring that their testimony is credible and admissible in court.
- Continuous Education and Training: Forensic investigators should engage in continuous education and training to stay abreast of evolving legal, technological, and ethical challenges in Digital investigations. This includes keeping up-to-date with changes in laws, regulations, and industry best practices to ensure compliance and proficiency in Anti-Forensics mitigation.

By considering these legal and ethical aspects, Forensic investigators can conduct Digital investigations with integrity, professionalism, and adherence to legal and ethical standards, ensuring the reliability and admissibility of Digital evidence in legal proceedings.

CONCLUSION

The term 'Anti Forensics' describes tactics intended to obstruct or evade Digital Forensic investigations, which entail gathering, preserving, analyzing, and presenting digital evidence for court cases. These tactics can be employed by individuals or groups to obscure, manipulate, or destroy digital evidence, making it difficult for forensic analysts to reconstruct events, attribute actions to specific individuals, or establish guilt or innocence. Digital Forensics investigations typically follow a structured process, including identifying digital devices and data sources, preserving the integrity of digital evidence, collecting data using forensically sound techniques, examining data using specialized tools, analyzing findings, and presenting findings in a clear, concise, and legally defensible manner. Digital Forensics practitioners must adhere to legal and ethical standards throughout the investigation process, including obtaining proper authorization, ensuring the integrity and admissibility of Digital evidence, respecting privacy rights, and maintaining confidentiality and security of sensitive information. Anti-Forensic countermeasures are tools and techniques designed specifically to detect and mitigate Anti-Forensic activities, particularly in cybercrime, where cybercriminals use Anti-Forensic techniques to cover their tracks and evade law enforcement.

REFERENCES

[1] J. Pande and A. Prasad, "Digital Forensics," *Uttarakhand Open Univ* ., 2016, Accessed: Apr. 01, 2024. [Online]. Available from: https://uou.ac.in/sites/default/files/slm/MIT(CS)-202.pdf

[2] F.E. Salamh, M.M. Mirza, and U. Karabiyik, "UAV Forensic Analysis and Software Tools Assessment: DJI Phantom 4 and Matrice 210 as Case Studies", *Electronics (Basel),* vol. 10, no. 6, p. 733, 2021.
[http://dx.doi.org/10.3390/electronics10060733]

[3] A. Prasad, S.S. Verma, P. Dahiya, and A. Kumar, "A Case Study on the Monitor Mode Passive Capturing of WLAN Packets in an On-the-Move Setup", *IEEE Access,* vol. 9, pp. 152408-152420, 2021.
[http://dx.doi.org/10.1109/ACCESS.2021.3127079]

[4] A. A. Mughal, "A COMPREHENSIVE STUDY OF PRACTICAL TECHNIQUES AND METHODOLOGIES IN INCIDENT-BASED APPROACHES FOR CYBER FORENSICS,", *Tensorgate J. Sustain. Technol. Infrastruct. Dev. Ctries.,* vol. 2, no. 1, p. 1, 2019.

[5] V. Patel, R. Mohandas, and A.R. Pais, *"Attacks on Web Services and mitigation schemes," in 2010 International Conference on Security and Cryptography.* SECRYPT, 2010, pp. 1-6.https://ieeexplore.ieee.org/abstract/document/5741656 [Online]

[6] G. Kessler, "Anti-Forensics and the Digital Investigator", *Aust. Digit. Forensics Conf.,* 2007.
[http://dx.doi.org/10.4225/75/57ad39ee7ff25]

[7] A. Hawari, "Anti-Forensics Techniques, Detection and Countermeasures", Accessed: Apr. 01, 2024. [Online]. Available from: https://www.academia.edu/15441665/Anti_Forensics_Techniques_Detection_and_Countermeasures

[8] L. Schmitt, and G. Kul, Anti Forensic Measures and Their Impact on Forensic Investigations.*Adversarial Multimedia Forensics.,* E. Nowroozi, K. Kallas, A. Jolfaei, Eds., Springer Nature Switzerland: Cham, 2024, pp. 237-261.
[http://dx.doi.org/10.1007/978-3-031-49803-9_10]

[9] A.M. Balogun, and S.Y. Zhu, "Privacy Impacts of Data Encryption on the Efficiency of Digital Forensics Technology", *(IJACSA) International Journal of Advanced Computer Science and Applications,* vol. 4, no. 5, pp. 36-40, 2013.

[10] L. B. Solum, and S. J. Marzen, "Destruction of Evidence", *Litigation,* vol. 16, no. 11, p. 1990, 1989.

[11] T.Z. Zarsky, "Privacy and Manipulation in the Digital Age", *Theor. Inq. Law,* vol. 20, no. 1, pp. 157-188, 2019.
[http://dx.doi.org/10.1515/til-2019-0006]

[12] S. Hosseinzadeh, S. Rauti, S. Laurén, J-M. Mäkelä, J. Holvitie, S. Hyrynsalmi, and V. Leppänen, "Diversification and obfuscation techniques for software security: A systematic literature review", *Inf. Softw. Technol.,* vol. 104, pp. 72-93, 2018.

[http://dx.doi.org/10.1016/j.infsof.2018.07.007]

[13] B. Roux, and M. Falgoust, "Ethical Issues Raised by Data Acquisition Methods in Digital Forensics Research", *J. Infor. Ethics,* vol. 21, no. 1, pp. 40-60, 2012. [http://dx.doi.org/10.3172/JIE.21.1.40]

[14] J.P. Van Belle, "Anti-Forensics: A Practitioner Perspective", *International Journal of Cyber-Security and Digital Forensics,* vol. 4, no. 2, pp. 390-403, 2015. [http://dx.doi.org/10.17781/P001593]

[15] B. Sartin, "ANTI-Forensics – distorting the evidence", *Comput. Fraud Secur.,* vol. 2006, no. 5, pp. 4-6, 2006. [http://dx.doi.org/10.1016/S1361-3723(06)70354-2]

[16] "What Was the Silk Road Online? History and Closure by FBI," Investopedia. Accessed: Apr. 01, 2024. [Online]. Available from: https://www.investopedia.com/terms/s/silk-road.asp

[17] "Hstoday Computer Forensics Critical in the Trial of Silk Road's Ross Ulbricht - HS Today." Accessed: Apr. 01, 2024. [Online]. Available from: https://www.hstoday.us/best-practices/compute--Forensics-critical-in-the-trial-of-silk-road-s-ross-ulbricht/

[18] "Ransomware Attacks and Types | How do Locky, Petya and other ransomware differ?" Accessed: Apr. 01, 2024. [Online]. Available from: https://www.kaspersky.com/resource-center/threats/ransomware-attacks-and-types

[19] "What was the WannaCry ransomware attack?" Accessed: Apr. 01, 2024. [Online]. Available from: https://www.cloudflare.com/learning/security/ransomware/wannacry-ransomware/

[20] F-X. Standaert, *Introduction to Side-Channel Attacks.* In: Verbauwhede, I. (eds) Secure Integrated Circuits and Systems. Integrated Circuits and Systems. Springer, Boston, MA, 2010, pp. 27-42. [http://dx.doi.org/10.1007/978-0-387-71829-3_2]

[21] A. Jain, and G.S. Chhabra, "Anti-Forensics techniques: An analytical review", *2014 Seventh International Conference on Contemporary Computing (IC3),* pp. 412-418, 2014. [http://dx.doi.org/10.1109/IC3.2014.6897209]

[22] C. B. S. Investigates, "Jihadis Learn To Hide Data In Digital Images - CBS News." Accessed: Apr. 01, 2024. [Online]. Available from: https://www.cbsnews.com/news/jihadis-learn-to-hide-data-in-D-gital-images/

[23] Email, "Dutch Forensic Institute Working to Uncover Criminals' Hidden Messages." Accessed: Apr. 01, 2024. [Online]. Available from: https://www.Forensicmag.com/588533-Dutch-Forensic-Instit-te-Working-to-Uncover-Criminals-Hidden-Messages/

[24] Z. Katamara, "Taxonomy for Anti-Forensics Techniques & Countermeasures," *Culminating Proj. Inf. Assur.*, Apr. 2020, [Online]. Available from: https://repository.stcloudstate.edu/msia_etds/109

[25] A. Singh, A. Prasad, and Y. Talwar, Compact and Secure S-Box Implementations of AES—A Review.*Smart Systems and IoT: Innovations in Computing.,* A.K. Somani, R.S. Shekhawat, A. Mundra, S. Srivastava, V.K. Verma, Eds., Springer: Singapore, 2020, pp. 857-871. [http://dx.doi.org/10.1007/978-981-13-8406-6_80]

[26] A. Fukami, R. Stoykova, and Z. Geradts, "A new model for forensic data extraction from encrypted mobile devices", *Forensic Science International: Digital Investigation,* vol. 38, p. 301169, 2021. [http://dx.doi.org/10.1016/j.fsidi.2021.301169]

[27] "Remote Wiping and Secure Deletion on Mobile Devices: A Review - Leom - 2016 - Journal of Forensic Sciences - Wiley Online Library." Accessed: Apr. 01, 2024. [Online]. Available from: https://onlinelibrary.wiley.com/doi/abs/10.1111/1556-4029.13203

[28] M. Guri, G. Kedma, T. Sela, B. Carmeli, A. Rosner, and Y. Elovici, "Noninvasive detection of Anti-Forensic malware", In: *2013 8th International Conference on Malicious and Unwanted Software: "The Americas" (MALWARE)*, 2013, pp. 1-10.

[http://dx.doi.org/10.1109/MALWARE.2013.6703679]

[29] "Crime patrolling assistance using passive monitoring: A Proof of Concept of a proactive Wi-Fi Surveillance system | IEEE Conference Publication | IEEE Xplore." Accessed: Apr. 02, 2024. [Online]. Available from: https://ieeexplore.ieee.org/abstract/document/9579805

[30] "Penn State Scandal," Ethics Unwrapped. Accessed: Apr. 01, 2024. [Online]. Available from: https://ethicsunwrapped.utexas.edu/video/penn-state-scandal

[31] Y. Prayudi, and A. Sn, "Digital Chain of Custody: State of The Art", *Int. J. Comput. Appl.,* vol. 114, no. 5, pp. 1-9, 2015.
[http://dx.doi.org/10.5120/19971-1856]

[32] A. Balakrishnan, and C. Schulze, "Code Obfuscation Literature Survey", 2012.

[33] L. Chaddad, A. Chehab, I.H. Elhajj, and A. Kayssi, "Network Obfuscation for Net Worth Security", In: *2020 Seventh International Conference on Software Defined Systems (SDS)*, 2020, pp. 83-88.
[http://dx.doi.org/10.1109/SDS49854.2020.9143919]

[34] L.E. Beegle, "Rootkits and Their Effects on Information Security", *Information Systems Security,* vol. 16, no. 3, pp. 164-176, 2007.
[http://dx.doi.org/10.1080/10658980701402049]

[35] "Zeus Virus," www.kaspersky.com. Accessed: Apr. 01, 2024. [Online]. Available from: www.kaspersky.comhttps://www.kaspersky.com/resource-center/threats/zeus-virus

[36] S. Shafiee Hasanabadi, A. Habibi Lashkari, and A.A. Ghorbani, "A survey and research challenges of anti-forensics: Evaluation of game-theoretic models in simulation of forensic agents' behaviour", *Forensic Science International: Digital Investigation,* vol. 35, p. 301024, 2020.
[http://dx.doi.org/10.1016/j.fsidi.2020.301024]

[37] "The Volatility Foundation - Promoting Accessible Memory Analysis Tools Within the Memory Forensics Community," The Volatility Foundation - Promoting Accessible Memory Analysis Tools Within the Memory Forensics Community. Accessed: Apr. 01, 2024. [Online]. Available from: https://volatilityfoundation.org/

[38] "Hex Rays - State-of-the-art binary code analysis solutions." Accessed: Apr. 01, 2024. [Online]. Available from: https://hex-rays.com/ida-pro/

[39] "Wireshark · Go Deep," Wireshark. Accessed: Apr. 01, 2024. [Online]. Available from: http://localhost:3000/

[40] "The Sleuth Kit (TSK) & Autopsy: Open Source Digital Forensics Tools." Accessed: Apr. 01, 2024. [Online]. Available from: https://www.sleuthkit.org/

[41] "What is Cuckoo? — Cuckoo Sandbox v2.0.7 Book." Accessed: Apr. 01, 2024. [Online]. Available from: https://cuckoo.readthedocs.io/en/latest/introduction/what/

[42] "OSSEC - World's Most Widely Used Host Intrusion Detection System - HIDS." Accessed: Apr. 01, 2024. [Online]. Available from: https://www.ossec.net/

[43] "Ghidra." Accessed: Apr. 01, 2024. [Online]. Available from: https://ghidra-sre.org/

CHAPTER 9

Forensics Investigation Reporting

Abstract: Digital forensic investigation reports are integral components of forensic examinations, providing comprehensive documentation of the investigation process, methodologies employed, and findings unearthed. In a landscape inundated with digital complexities and evolving cyber threats, these reports serve as vital tools for legal proceedings, regulatory compliance, and organizational security measures. The chapter presents a set of abstract templates that may assist investigators to plan and document their proceedings. The sections will guide the investigators towards proper and foolproof case records and evidence collection. By documenting lessons learned and best practices, one can foster continuous improvement in digital forensic techniques. Ultimately, digital forensic investigation reports uphold the credibility and reliability of investigative outcomes.

Keywords: Chain of custody, Digital forensics, Digital evidence, Investigations, Investigation report.

INTRODUCTION

Digital investigations [1] employ methodical methodology to guarantee a comprehensive analysis of digital evidence while preserving data integrity. The steps in a digital forensic inquiry are as follows:

Step 1: Case Assessment and Planning [2]:

• Recognize the circumstances surrounding the case, such as the alleged offense, incident specifics, and the investigation's goals.

• Establish the investigation's parameters, the resources required, and any applicable legal issues.

• Create an investigation strategy that outlines the necessary actions, such as gathering, analysing, and reporting evidence.

Step 2: Evidence Identification [3]:

• Determine which digital evidence sources to look for, such as servers, mobile devices, PCs, network logs, and cloud storage.

Akashdeep Bhardwaj, Pradeep Singh & Ajay Prasad

• Keep track of the location, kind, and significance of every possible piece of evidence.

Step 3: Acquisition and Preservation of Evidence [4]:

• Make sure there is no illegal access to the crime scene by keeping it secure.

• To gather digital evidence while preserving its integrity, use the right methods and equipment. This includes taking forensic pictures of storage devices.

• To guarantee that any piece of evidence is admissible in court, record the chain of custody for each item.

Step 4: Analysis and Evaluation of the Evidence [5]:

• Examine the gathered evidence in-depth utilizing forensic instruments and methods.

• Examine digital artifacts, files, logs, and metadata to piece together what happened, find pertinent details, and find hints that might lead to it.

• To retrieve information, use forensic methods such as chronology analysis, data carving, and keyword searches.

Step 5: Data Reconstruction and Recovery [6]:

• Recover information that has been buried or erased that might be important to the inquiry.

• Reconstruct digital events and activities to comprehend the order in which persons engaged took their respective actions.

• Reconstruct files, emails, chat discussions, and other digital artifacts using specialist tools and techniques.

Step 6: Documentation and Reporting of Evidence [7]:

• Keep thorough records of all observations, findings, and analysis outcomes.

• Write reports that are easy to read and understand, summarizing the methods utilized, the findings, and the investigative process.

a. Provide pertinent logs, timestamps, screenshots, and other proof in the reports.

b. Make sure the reports meet all legal criteria and are appropriate for presenting in court.

Step 7: Reporting of Results [7]:

• Report the investigation's conclusions to the appropriate parties, including management, legal counsel, and law enforcement.

• If called upon in court, give expert testimony on the procedures and findings of the forensic analysis.

Step 8: Closure and Follow-Up [8]:

• Once all goals have been achieved and the matter has been settled, end the investigation.

• Make sure that case closure is properly documented, including final reports, how evidence is handled, and any necessary follow-up activities.

• To find opportunities for improvement in subsequent investigations and lessons learned, conduct a review of the investigation process.

To guarantee a successful digital forensic investigation, it is essential to follow legal and ethical norms [9] and [10], protect the integrity of the evidence, and maintain confidentiality throughout these procedures.

Proper reporting [11] plays a crucial role in digital forensics investigations for several reasons:

• Documentation: Reports provide comprehensive documentation of the investigation process, including the steps taken, methodologies used, and findings obtained. This documentation ensures transparency and accountability in the investigation process.

• Legal Admissibility: Well-documented reports increase the credibility and admissibility of digital evidence in legal proceedings. Courts and regulatory bodies require clear documentation of the investigation process to ensure the integrity and reliability of the evidence presented.

• Communication: Reports serve as a means of communication between forensic examiners, investigative teams, law enforcement agencies, legal counsel, and other stakeholders involved in the investigation. They convey important information, findings, and recommendations in a clear and organized manner.

• Analysis and Review: Reports provide a structured format for analyzing and reviewing the findings of the investigation. They enable examiners and stakeholders to review the evidence, identify patterns or trends, and draw conclusions based on the analysis.

• Decision Making: Reports aid decision-making processes by providing relevant information and insights to investigators, decision-makers, and stakeholders. They help in determining the appropriate course of action, such as further investigation, legal action, or remediation efforts.

• Quality Assurance: Properly documented reports support quality assurance efforts by ensuring that investigations are conducted in accordance with established standards, procedures, and best practices. They enable supervisors and management to review the quality and integrity of the investigation process.

• Knowledge Transfer: Reports facilitate knowledge transfer by documenting lessons learned, best practices, and recommendations for future investigations. They serve as a valuable resource for training new forensic examiners and improving investigative techniques.

Proper reports (Figs. **1** and **2**) are essential for maintaining the integrity, credibility, and effectiveness of digital forensics investigations. They ensure that investigations are conducted in a systematic, transparent, and legally defensible manner, ultimately leading to reliable and actionable outcomes.

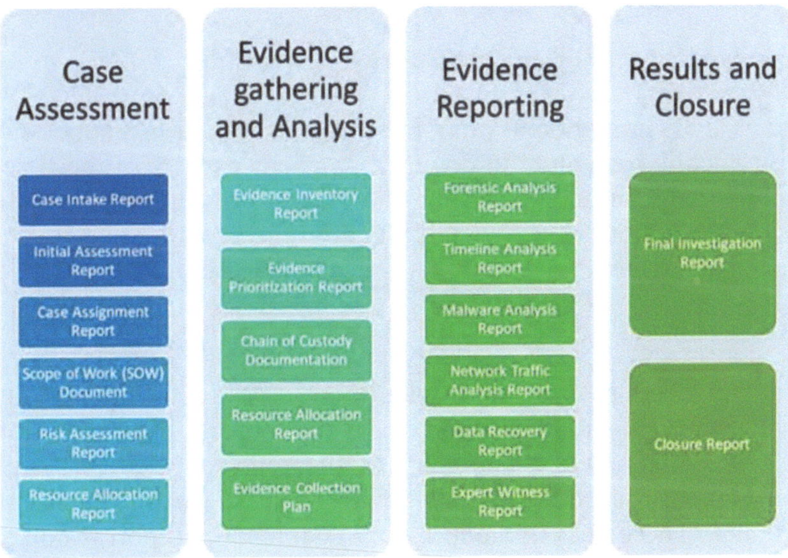

Fig. (1). Digital Forensics Phases and aligned reports.

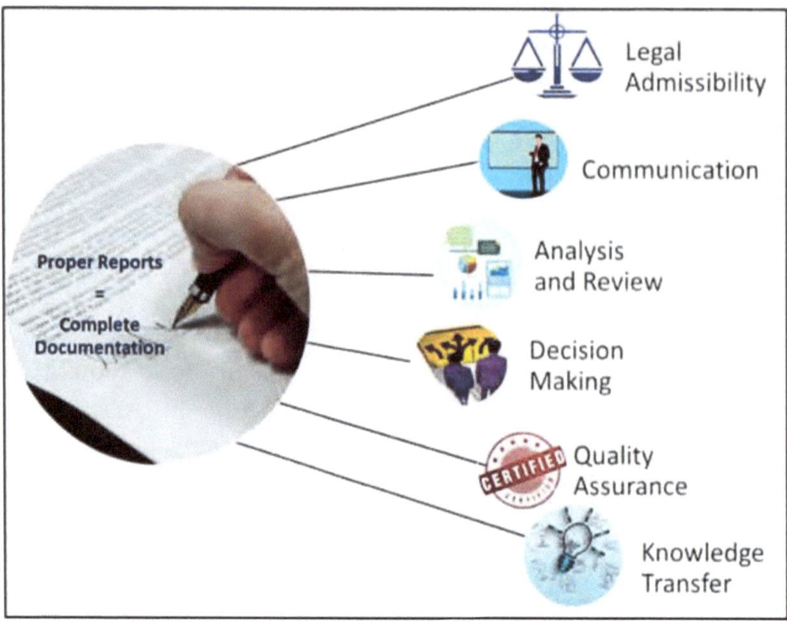

Fig. (2). Proper reporting.

The chapter presents various types of reports that need to be prepared for the agencies at several phases of case investigations. Templates of these reports are also presented as figures. However, the templates are just abstracts and can be structured, added, and subtracted according to needs and requirements from time to time.

REPORTS FOR CASE ASSESSMENT & PLANNING

During the case assessment and planning phase of digital investigations, several reports are typically generated to document various aspects of the investigation. These reports help in understanding the nature of the case, outlining the objectives, determining the scope, and planning the investigative steps. Here are the various reports generated during this phase:

Case Intake Report [12]:

This report documents initial contact with the client or reporting party. It includes details such as the date and time of the initial communication, contact information of the reporting party, and a summary of the reported incident or allegation. Separate documents can be built along with the case intake report for specific record keeping. These may include Case Assignment Report, Scope of Work (SOW) Document, Risk Assessment Report, Resource Allocation Report, *etc.*

The resource allocation report provides an overview of the case based on the information gathered during the initial assessment phase. It outlines the objectives, goals, and scope of the investigation. The report may include preliminary findings, potential areas of focus, and initial recommendations for further action.

In organizational settings or law enforcement agencies, a case assignment report may be generated to formally assign the investigation to a specific forensic examiner or team. It includes details such as the case name or identifier, assigned investigator(s), and any specific instructions or requirements for the investigation. Scope of Work (SOW) document [13] defines the scope of the investigation in detail, including the specific tasks to be performed, resources required, and timelines. It outlines the methodologies, techniques, and tools that will be used during the investigation. The SOW document serves as a reference for the investigative team and helps ensure that all relevant aspects of the case are addressed.

A risk assessment report [14] may be generated to evaluate potential risks and challenges associated with the investigation. It identifies threats to the integrity of the evidence, legal or regulatory considerations, resource constraints, and other factors that could impact the investigation. The report may include risk mitigation strategies and recommendations to address identified risks. The Resource Allocation Report documents the allocation of resources, such as personnel, equipment, and budget, for the investigation. It ensures that sufficient resources are available to conduct the investigation effectively and efficiently. The report may be updated as needed throughout the investigation to reflect changes in resource requirements.

By generating these reports during the case assessment and planning phase, forensic examiners can establish a solid foundation for the investigation, clarify objectives, define the scope, allocate resources effectively, and mitigate potential risks. These reports also serve as reference documents for the investigative team and stakeholders throughout the investigation process. In general, the Case Intake report and its elaborated or detailed documents comprise the initial phase of any digital forensic investigation. The format of a Case Intake Report (Fig. **3**) may vary depending on the organization's policies, the nature of the investigation, and specific requirements. However, a typical case intake report generally includes several vital information.

"Case Intake Report" or similar title indicating the purpose of the document. A unique identifier is assigned to the case for tracking and reference purposes. The date and time when the initial communication or report regarding the case was received; Name, contact details, and any relevant affiliations or roles of the individual or organization reporting the incident; Summary of the reported incident or allegation, including relevant details such as the type of offense, affected systems or devices, and any known circumstances; The date and time when the incident occurred or was discovered if known; Categorization of the case based on the nature of the incident (*e.g*., cybercrime, data breach, intellectual property theft); The urgency or priority assigned to the case based on factors such as severity, impact, and deadlines; Preliminary observations or findings based on the information provided during the intake process; Any initial leads, suspects, or relevant information identified during the intake process; The forensic examiner or investigative team member assigned to the case; Contact details (phone number, email) for the assigned investigator.

Case Intake Report

1. Title or Heading:

2. Case Information:

3. Case Number/Identifier:
    1. Date and Time of Intake:
    2. Reporting Party Information

4. Incident Details:

5. Description of Incident:
6. Date and Time of Incident:

7. Case Classification:
8. Priority Level:
9. Initial Assessment:

10. Initial Findings:

11. Potential Leads or Suspects:

12. Assigned Investigator:
    1. Name of the Investigator:
    2. Contact Information:
13. Action Plan:

14. Follow-up Actions:

Approval/Authorization:

Signature/Approval:

Remarks:
References/Attachments:

Fig. (3). Sample template - case intake report.

Next steps also need to be captured here in this report like, proposed steps or actions to be taken next in the investigation, such as evidence collection, analysis, or further inquiries. Any additional tasks or follow-up actions required, including coordination with other stakeholders or agencies, are recorded. Space for signatures or initials of individuals authorizing the initiation of the investigation or approving the intake report are recorded. Any additional information, comments, or notes relevant to the intake process or initial assessment of the case are saved. Any supporting documents, emails, or attachments related to the intake process or initial incident report are recorded.

The Case Intake Report serves as a foundational document that captures essential details about the case at the outset of the investigation, providing a reference point for subsequent actions and documentation.

Evidence Identification Report

During the Evidence Identification [15] phase of a digital forensics investigation, various reports may be generated to document the identification of potential sources of digital evidence (Fig. 4). These reports help in organizing and prioritizing evidence for further examination.

Evidence Identification Report

Case Information:
Case Number/Identifier:
Date of Report:
Investigating Agency/Department:
Introduction:

Summary of Findings:

Details of Identified Evidence Sources:
Source #1:

1. **Description:**
2. **Relevance:**
3. **Initial Observations:**
4. **Potential Importance:**

[Repeat the above section for each identified evidence source]

Evidence Prioritization:

Chain of Custody form Number:
Recommendations:

Conclusion:

Appendices:

Signature/Approval:

Fig. (4). Evidence identification report.

Fig. 4 presents the basic template where a few very vital information is maintained like the details of Identified Evidence Sources, Evidence Prioritizations, Chain of Custody (CoC) forms and numbers, recommendations, *etc*. Other reports in this phase can be Evidence Inventory Report [16], Evidence Prioritization Report, Resource Allocation Report [16], *etc*. The Evidence Inventory Report lists all potential sources of digital evidence identified during the initial phase of the investigation. It includes details such as the type of device or system, location, ownership, and relevance to the investigation. The inventory may be organized by category (*e.g*., computers, mobile devices, servers) for clarity.

Evidence Prioritization Report identifies high-priority evidence sources or areas that are likely to yield critical information for the investigation. Prioritization may be based on factors such as relevance to the alleged offense, likelihood of finding evidence, and potential impact on the case. The Resource Allocation Report documents the allocation of resources (*e.g*., personnel, equipment, budget) for evidence identification and collection. It ensures that sufficient resources are allocated to prioritize and collect evidence effectively. The report may include information on resource availability, timelines, and any constraints that may impact the evidence identification process.

By generating these reports during the Evidence Identification phase, forensic examiners can systematically document and prioritize potential sources of digital evidence, ensuring a structured approach to evidence collection and analysis in subsequent phases of the investigation. This template provides a structured format for documenting the findings of the Evidence Identification phase, including details of identified evidence sources, prioritization, recommendations, and conclusions. Adjustments can be made to customize the template based on specific case requirements and organizational preferences.

Chain of Custody Form

The Chain of Custody format ([17] and [18]) provides a structured framework for documenting key details related to the chain of custody of digital evidence, including receipt, transfer, and release. It helps ensure the integrity and admissibility of the evidence in legal proceedings by documenting each custodial change and maintaining accountability throughout the investigative process. Adjustments can be made to customize the form based on specific organizational requirements or case particulars. While CoC is not necessarily a report, a chain of custody documentation is crucial during evidence identification. It records the custody, control, transfer, and access to digital evidence from the initial identification through the entire investigation process. Chain of custody documentation ensures the integrity and admissibility of the evidence in legal proceedings (Fig. **5**).

Property Record Number: ____________________

Anywhere Police Department

EVIDENCE CHAIN OF CUSTODY TRACKING FORM

Case Number: ____________________ Offense: ____________________
Submitting Officer: (Name/ID#) ____________________
Victim: ____________________
Suspect: ____________________
Date/Time Seized: ____________________ Location of Seizure: ____________________

Description of Evidence		
Item #	**Quantity**	**Description of Item** (Model, Serial #, Condition, Marks, Scratches)

Chain of Custody				
Item #	**Date/Time**	**Released by** (Signature & ID#)	**Received by** (Signature & ID#)	**Comments/Location**

Final Disposal Authority

Authorization for Disposal

Item(s) #: __________ on this document pertaining to (suspect): ____________________
is(are) no longer needed as evidence and is/are authorized for disposal by (check appropriate disposal method)
☐ Return to Owner ☐ Auction/Destroy/Divert
Name & ID# of Authorizing Officer: ____________________ Signature: ____________________ Date: ____________

Witness to Destruction of Evidence

Item(s) #: __________ on this document were destroyed by Evidence Custodian ____________________ ID#: ______
in my presence on (date) ____________________.
Name & ID# of Witness to destruction: ____________________ Signature: ____________________ Date: ____________

Release to Lawful Owner

Item(s) #: __________ on this document was/were released by Evidence Custodian ____________________ ID#: ________ to
Name ____________________
Address: ____________________ City: ____________________ State: ______ Zip Code: ________
Telephone Number: (____) ____________________
Under penalty of law, I certify that I am the lawful owner of the above item(s).

Signature: ____________________ Date: ____________________

Copy of Government-issued photo identification is attached. ☐ Yes ☐ No

This Evidence Chain-of-Custody form is to be retained as a permanent record by the Anywhere Police Department.

Fig. (5). Chain of custody form.

Forensic Analysis Report

This report provides a detailed analysis of the digital evidence collected during the investigation [19]. It includes findings related to file artifacts, deleted data recovery, internet history, email communications, *etc*. The report may also include information about the tools and techniques used for analysis. Forensic Analysis Report in digital forensics serves as a comprehensive document that presents the findings of the investigation, including the analysis of digital evidence. Fig. (**6**) gives the template for the Forensic Analysis Report.

Forensic Analysis Report

Case Information:

Case Number/Identifier:
Date of Report
Lead Investigator:
Investigating Agency/Department:

Executive Summary:

Introduction:

Analysis Methodologies:

Analysis Findings:

CoC forms #:

Internet History Analysis:

Email Communications:

Deleted Data Recovery:

Timeline Analysis:

Conclusions:

Recommendations:

References/Appendices:

Date: Signature of Lead Investigator:_______________

Fig. (6). Forensic analysis report.

Other reports in this phase could be the timeline analysis report, malware analysis report, network traffic analysis report, data recovery report, expert witness report, final investigation report and closure report. A timeline analysis report presents a chronological sequence of events based on the digital evidence collected. It helps reconstruct the sequence of actions taken by involved parties and provides insights into the timeline of the incident. If malware is discovered during the investigation, a malware analysis report may be generated. It describes the characteristics of the malware, its behavior, and its potential impact on the system or network. In cases involving network-based evidence, such as cyberattacks or data breaches, a network traffic analysis report may be prepared. It includes information about network traffic patterns, suspicious activities, and communication between devices [20].

If data recovery efforts were conducted to retrieve deleted or damaged data, a data recovery report may be generated. It documents the data recovery process, including the methods used and the data successfully recovered. In legal proceedings, an expert witness report may be prepared to present findings and opinions in court. The report summarizes the investigation process, methodologies, and conclusions in a format suitable for legal purposes. A comprehensive final investigation report summarizes the entire investigation, including background information, objectives, methodologies, findings, conclusions, and recommendations. It provides a detailed account of the investigation process and its outcomes. After completing the investigation, a closure report [21] may be prepared to formally close the case. It includes details about the resolution of the case, any actions taken, and recommendations for future prevention.

Final Investigation Report

The Final Investigation Report [22] provides a comprehensive overview of the entire investigation process, including background information, objectives, methodologies, findings, conclusions, and recommendations. Fig. (7) presents the template for this report. The Final Investigation report includes sections like an introduction, where the purpose and scope of the investigation are briefly introduced. It also provides background information on the case, including the nature of the incident, the stakeholders involved, and the objectives of the investigation. The next section of this report has the investigator [23] describing the methodologies, techniques, and tools used during the investigation and explains the approach to evidence collection, preservation, analysis, and reporting. The findings section is the most important in this report. Here the investigators present the findings of the investigation, organized by relevant categories such as:

• Incident Overview: Summary of the incident, including date, time, location, and nature of the offense. Description of the systems, devices, and networks involved in the incident.

• Evidence Collection: Summary of the evidence collected, including types of evidence, sources, and chain of custody documentation. Details of the evidence acquisition process, including methods used and challenges encountered.

• Forensic Analysis: Summary of the forensic analysis findings, including examination of digital artifacts, internet history, email communications, *etc.* Overview of key observations, recovered data, deleted data recovery, and timeline analysis.

• Findings Summary: Consolidated summary of the key findings and observations of the investigation. Identification of significant evidence, patterns, trends, and anomalies discovered during the investigation.

Final Investigation Report

Case Information:

Case Number/Identifier:
Date of Report:
Lead Investigator:
Investigating Agency/Department:

Executive Summary:

Table of Contents:

Introduction:
[can be several pages]
Methodologies:
[can be several pages]

Findings:
[can be several pages]

Incident Overview:
[can be several pages]

Evidence Collection:
[can be several pages]

Forensic Analysis:
Description of the FAR
[can be several pages]

Findings Summary:
[can be several pages]

Conclusions:
[can be several pages]

Recommendations:
[can be several pages]

Lessons Learned:
[can be several pages]

Appendices:
[can be several pages]

Signature/Approval:

Signature of Lead Investigator: ____________

Date:

Fig. (7). Final investigation report.

Finally, the report presents the conclusions and recommendations along with the lessons learned. In these sections, the investigators [24] summarize the conclusions drawn from the investigation findings. Also, this provides insights into the significance and implications of the findings for the case. They also offer recommendations for further action based on the investigation conclusions and provide suggestions for improving digital security, mitigating risks, or preventing future incidents. The investigators also present their reflections on lessons learned from the investigation process, including successes, challenges, and areas for improvement.

Fig. (**7**) template provides a structured format for documenting the findings, conclusions, and recommendations of the investigation in a clear and organized manner. Adjustments can be made to customize the template based on specific case requirements, investigation methodologies, and organizational preferences.

Closure Report

Closure Report [25] serves to formally close the case and document the resolution of the investigation. Fig. (**8**) gives the template for a Closure Report. In the Executive Summary of the closure report, the investigator should provide a concise summary of the investigation's resolution, including key outcomes and actions taken. This template as illustrated in Fig. (**8**) provides a structured format for documenting the closure of a digital forensic investigation, ensuring that all relevant information is captured and communicated effectively. Adjustments can be made to customize the template based on specific case requirements, investigation outcomes, and organizational preferences.

The introduction produces a brief purpose and scope of the closure report along with a recap of the background of the case and the objectives of the investigation. The Case Resolution section summarizes the resolution of the case, including any findings, conclusions, or outcomes reached during the investigation. It also describes any legal actions taken, disciplinary measures implemented, or other resolutions achieved. The actions taken are jot down next keep details of any actions taken because of the investigation, such as:

- Legal actions (*e.g.*, arrests, prosecutions)
- Disciplinary measures (*e.g.*, employee sanctions)
- Remediation efforts (*e.g.*, security improvements, policy changes)
- Recovery of assets or damages
- Lessons Learned:

• Reflect on lessons learned from the investigation process, including successes, challenges, and areas for improvement.

• Identify any best practices or recommendations for future investigations.

Closure Report
Case Information: Case Number/Identifier: Date of Report: Lead Investigator: Investigating Agency/Department:
Executive Summary:
Introduction:
Case Resolution:
Actions Taken:
Lessons Learned:
Closure Documentation:
Acknowledgments:
Conclusion:
Appendices:
Signature/Approval:
Signature of Lead Investigator: ____________________ Date:

Fig. (8). Closure report.

The action taken part is followed by a Closure Documentation which provides details on the documentation and record-keeping procedures followed to formally close the case. It confirms that all evidence has been properly documented, stored, and disposed of according to legal and organizational requirements. Acknowledgments and conclusions follow thereafter. It is important here to acknowledge the contributions of individuals or teams involved in the investigation, including forensic examiners, law enforcement, legal counsel, and other stakeholders. Finally, we summarize the key findings, actions taken, and outcomes achieved in resolving the case. We reiterate the closure of the investigation and the finality of the case. Appendices include any supporting documentation, reports, evidence artifacts, or references used during the investigation.

Cases of Mishandled or Inappropriate Reports

While specific cases of digital forensic investigations gone wrong due to improper reports may not always be publicly disclosed, there have been instances where deficiencies in reporting have led to challenges in legal proceedings or questioned the reliability of the investigation's findings.

Here are two hypothetical scenarios illustrating the potential consequences of improper reports in digital forensic investigations.

Case 1: Chain of Custody Errors

In a criminal case involving digital evidence obtained from a suspect's computer, the forensic examiner failed to properly document the chain of custody. The evidence was collected without clear records of who handled it when it was transferred, and how it was stored. During the trial, the defense raised concerns about the integrity of the evidence due to these chain of custody errors. As a result, the court questioned the admissibility of the digital evidence, leading to a mistrial or acquittal of the defendant.

Case 2: Inaccurate Analysis Findings

In a corporate investigation into employee misconduct involving digital communications, the forensic examiner conducted an analysis of email exchanges but failed to accurately document the analysis findings in the report. Subsequently, during legal proceedings, discrepancies were identified between the examiner's testimony and the written report. The defence exploited these inconsistencies to challenge the credibility of the investigation's findings, casting doubt on the reliability of the digital evidence presented.

These reports serve to document the findings and conclusions of digital forensic investigations accurately and comprehensively, ensuring that the results are properly documented and can be used effectively for legal, regulatory, or organizational purposes and provide a structured format for documenting the findings of the forensic analysis, ensuring clarity, organization, and completeness in presenting the evidence and conclusions. Adjustments can be made to customize the template based on specific case requirements, analysis methodologies, and organizational preferences.

Other Scenarios

Discussing real cases, especially those involving criminal activities, can be sensitive. However, certain hypothetical scenarios (Fig. **9**) to illustrate how improper reports in digital forensic investigations could lead to challenges or complications are given below.

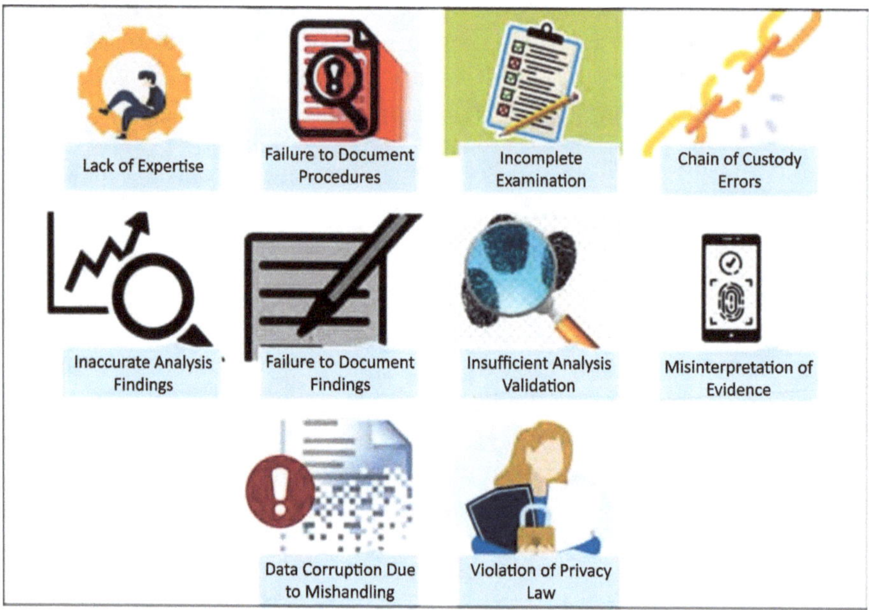

Fig. (9). Failures due to mishandled reports.

• Failure to Document Procedures: Digital forensic investigation lacks proper documentation of procedures followed, including evidence acquisition, analysis methodologies, and conclusions. This absence of documentation results in confusion and challenges during legal proceedings regarding the credibility of the investigation.

• Incomplete Examination: In a criminal case involving digital evidence from a mobile device, the forensic examiner fails to conduct a thorough examination of all relevant data. As a result, crucial evidence is overlooked, leading to incomplete findings, and potentially impacting the outcome of the case.

• Lack of Expertise: A digital forensic investigation is conducted by an examiner lacking expertise in a specific area, such as network forensics or malware analysis. The report fails to accurately analyse complex digital artifacts, raising questions about the competency of the examiner [26] and the validity of the findings.

• Data Corruption Due to Mishandling: During the collection and preservation of digital evidence, mishandling occurs, resulting in data corruption or loss. The improper handling of evidence compromises its integrity, making it inadmissible in court and undermining the investigation's credibility.

• Violation of Privacy Laws: In an investigation involving the retrieval of digital evidence from personal devices, the forensic examiner violates privacy laws or regulations. Improperly obtained evidence is deemed inadmissible in court, leading to legal repercussions and challenges in prosecuting the case.

• Failure to Document Findings: A digital forensic examination uncovers significant findings, but the examiner fails to adequately document these findings in the report. This oversight leads to confusion and disputes during legal proceedings, hindering the prosecution's ability to present a convincing case.

• Insufficient Analysis Validation: The analysis methods used in a digital forensic investigation are not adequately validated or tested for accuracy. As a result, the findings presented in the report lack reliability, and defence attorneys successfully challenge their validity in court.

• Misinterpretation of Evidence: A digital forensic examiner misinterprets key evidence during the analysis process, leading to erroneous conclusions in the report. The misinterpretation is discovered during cross-examination, casting doubt on the credibility of the investigation's findings.

In the above scenarios, the lack of proper documentation or inaccuracies in reporting compromised the integrity and admissibility of the digital evidence, leading to legal challenges and potentially impacting the outcome of the cases. Properly documented and accurate reports are essential in ensuring the credibility and reliability of digital forensic investigations.

In conclusion, digital forensics reports are indispensable components of forensic investigations, providing comprehensive documentation of the investigation process, methodologies employed, and findings uncovered. These reports serve a multitude of purposes, including supporting legal proceedings, ensuring regulatory compliance, and enhancing organizational security measures. By offering transparency, accountability, and admissibility in court, they uphold the integrity and reliability of digital evidence. Moreover, these reports facilitate effective communication among forensic examiners, investigative teams, and stakeholders, conveying critical insights and recommendations. By documenting lessons learned and best practices, they contribute to continuous improvement in digital forensic techniques. In essence, digital forensics reports play a pivotal role in safeguarding the credibility and efficacy of investigative outcomes in the ever-evolving digital landscape.

REFERENCES

[1] S. Raghavan, "Digital forensic research: current state of the art", *CSI Transactions on ICT,* vol. 1, no. 1, pp. 91-114, 2013. [http://dx.doi.org/10.1007/s40012-012-0008-7]

[2] R. Montasari, "A comprehensive digital forensic investigation process model", *International Journal of Electronic Security and Digital Forensics,* vol. 8, no. 4, pp. 285-302, 2016. [http://dx.doi.org/10.1504/IJESDF.2016.079430]

[3] R. Lutui, "A multidisciplinary digital forensic investigation process model", *Bus. Horiz.,* vol. 59, no. 6, pp. 593-604, 2016. [http://dx.doi.org/10.1016/j.bushor.2016.08.001]

[4] J. Jones, and L. Etzkorn, "Analysis of digital forensics live system acquisition methods to achieve optimal evidence preservation", In: *in SoutheastCon*, 2016-6. [http://dx.doi.org/10.1109/SECON.2016.7506709]

[5] H. Arshad, A.B. Jantan, and O.I. Abiodun, "Digital Forensics: Review of Issues in Scientific Validation of Digital Evidence", *J. Inf. Process. Syst.,* vol. 14, no. 2, pp. 346-376, 2018. [http://dx.doi.org/10.3745/JIPS.03.0095]

[6] C. Hargreaves, and J. Patterson, "An automated timeline reconstruction approach for digital forensic investigations", *Digit. Invest.,* vol. 9, pp. S69-S79, 2012. [http://dx.doi.org/10.1016/j.diin.2012.05.006]

[7] G. Horsman, "Formalising investigative decision making in digital forensics: Proposing the Digital Evidence Reporting and Decision Support (DERDS) framework", *Digit. Invest.,* vol. 28, pp. 146-151, 2019. [http://dx.doi.org/10.1016/j.diin.2019.01.007]

[8] L. Luciano, I. Baggili, M. Topor, P. Casey, and F. Breitinger, "Digital Forensics in the Next Five Years", [http://dx.doi.org/10.1145/3230833.3232813]

[9] R.I. Ferguson, K. Renaud, S. Wilford, and A. Irons, "PRECEPT: a framework for ethical digital forensics investigations", *J. Intellect. Cap.,* vol. 21, no. 2, pp. 257-290, 2020. [http://dx.doi.org/10.1108/JIC-05-2019-0097]

[10] A.M. Balogun, and T. Zuva, "“OPEN ETHICAL ISSUES IN DIGITAL FORENSIC SYSTEMS,” Int", *J. EBusiness EGovernment Stud.,* vol. 9, no. 1, p. 1, 2017.

[11] F. Sharevski, "Rules of professional responsibility in digital forensics: A comparative analysis", *Journal of Digital Forensics, Security and Law,* vol. 10, no. 2, 2015. [http://dx.doi.org/10.15394/jdfsl.2015.1201]

[12] D.S. Dolliver, C. Collins, and B. Sams, "Hybrid approaches to digital forensic investigations: A comparative analysis in an institutional context", *Digit. Invest.,* vol. 23, pp. 124-137, 2017. [http://dx.doi.org/10.1016/j.diin.2017.10.005]

[13] A.K.S. Alshebel, “Standardization Requirements for Digital Forensic Laboratories: A Document Analysis and Guideline,” Auckland University of Technology, 2020. Accessed: Apr. 12, 2024. [Online]. Available from: https://hdl.handle.net/10292/13541

[14] “METRICS-BASED Risk Assessment and Management of DIGITAL FORENSICS - ProQuest.” Accessed: Apr. 12, 2024. [Online]. Available from: https://www.proquest.com/openview/4d49785fe340b472aad3cb795706d957/1?pq-origsite=gscholar&cbl=29577

[15] F. Bouchaud, G. Grimaud, and T. Vantroys, “IoT Forensic: identification and classification of evidence in criminal investigations,” in Proceedings of the 13th International Conference on Availability, Reliability and Security, in ARES ’18. New York, NY, USA: Association for Computing Machinery, Aug. 2018, pp. 1–9. [http://dx.doi.org/10.1145/3230833.3233257]

[16] T. F. Efendi, "The Management of Physical Evidence and Chain of Custody (CoC) in Digital Forensic Laboratory Storage", In: *Int. J. Seocology*, 2019, pp. 1-10. [http://dx.doi.org/10.29040/seocology.v1i01.3]

[17] Y. Prayudi, and A. Sn, "Digital Chain of Custody: State of The Art", *Int. J. Comput. Appl.,* vol. 114, no. 5, pp. 1-9, 2015. [http://dx.doi.org/10.5120/19971-1856]

[18] S. Ballou, M. Stolorow, M. Taylor, P.S. Bamberger, L. Brown, R. Brown, Y. Burney, D. Davenport, L. DePalma, S. Williams, C. Jones, R. Keaton, W. Kiley, J. Latta, M. Kline, K. Lanning, G. LaPorte, L.E. Ledray, R. Nagy, B.E. Ostrom, L. Schwind, and S. Stoiloff, "The biological evidence preservation handbook : best practices for evidence handlers; technical working group on biological evidence preservation", *National Institute of Standards and Technology, NIST IR,* vol. 7928, 2013. [http://dx.doi.org/10.6028/NIST.IR.7928]

[19] O.L. Carroll, S.K. Brannon, and T. Song, "Computer Forensics: Digital Forensic Analysis Methodology", *U. S. Atty. Bull.,* vol. 56, p. 1, 2008.

[20] E.S. Pilli, R.C. Joshi, and R. Niyogi, "Network forensic frameworks: Survey and research challenges", *Digit. Invest.,* vol. 7, no. 1-2, pp. 14-27, 2010. [http://dx.doi.org/10.1016/j.diin.2010.02.003]

[21] R. Montasari, R. Hill, V. Carpenter, and A. Hosseinian-Far, "The Standardised Digital Forensic Investigation Process Model (SDFIPM)", In: *in Blockchain and Clinical Trial: Securing Patient Data.,* H. Jahankhani, S. Kendzierskyj, A. Jamal, G. Epiphaniou, H. Al-Khateeb, Eds., Springer International Publishing: Cham, 2019, pp. 169-209. [http://dx.doi.org/10.1007/978-3-030-11289-9_8]

[22] G. Horsman, "The different types of reports produced in digital forensic investigations", *Sci. Justice,* vol. 61, no. 5, pp. 627-634, 2021. [http://dx.doi.org/10.1016/j.scijus.2021.06.009] [PMID: 34482943]

[23] A. Bhardwaj, F. Al-Turjman, M. Kumar, T. Stephan, and L. Mostarda, "Capturing-the-Invisible (CTI): Behavior-Based Attacks Recognition in IoT-Oriented Industrial Control Systems", *IEEE Access,* vol. 8, pp. 104956-104966, 2020. [http://dx.doi.org/10.1109/ACCESS.2020.2998983]

[24] L.R. Leibrock, "Duties, Support Functions, and Competencies: Digital Forensics Investigators,", In: *in Handbook of Digital and Multimedia Forensic Evidence.,* J.J. Barbara, Ed., Humana Press: Totowa, NJ, 2008, pp. 91-102. [http://dx.doi.org/10.1007/978-1-59745-577-0_7]

[25] A. Bhardwaj, F. Al-Turjman, V. Sapra, M. Kumar, and T. Stephan, "Privacy-aware detection framework to mitigate new-age phishing attacks", *Comput. Electr. Eng.,* vol. 96, p. 107546, 2021. [http://dx.doi.org/10.1016/j.compeleceng.2021.107546]

[26] K. Kaushik, A. Bhardwaj, M. Kumar, S. K. Gupta, and A. Gupta, "A novel machine learning□based framework for detecting fake Instagram profiles", *Concurrency and Computation: Practice and Experience,* vol. 34, no. 28, p. e7349, 2022. [http://dx.doi.org/10.1002/cpe.7349]

SUBJECT INDEX

A

B

C

Akashdeep Bhardwaj, Pradeep Singh & Ajay Prasad

D

S

T

U

V

W

www.ingramcontent.com/pod-product-compliance
Lightning Source LLC
Chambersburg PA
CBHW050821220326
41598CB00006B/279